W9-COH-246

Jerusalem Delivered

TORQUATO TASSO

Jerusalem Delivered

Gerusalemme liberata

Edited and Translated by

Anthony M. Esolen

The Johns Hopkins University Press

Baltimore and London

Printed in the United States of America on acid-free paper
9 8 7 6 5 4 3 2 1

The Johns Hopkins University Press
2715 North Charles Street
Baltimore, Maryland 21218-4363
www.press.jhu.edu

Library of Congress Cataloging-in-Publication Data
will be found at the end of this book.
A catalog record for this book is available from the
British Library.

ISBN 0-8018-6322-8
ISBN 0-8018-6323-6 (pbk.)

Contents

Acknowledgments

I OWE A DEBT of gratitude to those who have gone before me into the breach: Ralph Nash, Joseph Tusiani, and the redoubtable Elizabethan Edward Fairfax. Nash's prose translation helped remove many a thorn from my path, and Fairfax's reminded me ever and again that a translation of an epic like Tasso's had better be grand, if it is anything at all.

Finally, words of thanks to my wife, Debra, who suggested this project and has always encouraged me in it; to my colleagues in the Development of Western Civilization Program at Providence College, whose commitment to historically based criticism and to the great works of the Renaissance has never flagged and from whom I have learned more than I care to confess; to the administration of Providence College for their financial support; to the fine librarians at the Biblioteca Angelo Mai in Bergamo, who cherish the world's greatest collection of Tassiana (including a little known but worthy 1596 translation of Tasso's first five cantos into English by one Richard Carew, from whom I culled scattered pearls); and, finally, to Professor Thomas P. Roche Jr. of Princeton University, *sine quo non.* He it was whose courses in Renaissance literature first stirred in me the love for Shakespeare and Spenser, Ariosto and Tasso, and whose deeds even more than his words show that Tasso was right, that true faith and intellect are the closest friends. *Tu, pater, es rerum inuentor.*

Note on the Translation

ALL TRANSLATION is treacherous, but translation of poetry is so obviously absurd that the treason loses its threat. Some will admit the impossibility of delivering the ineffable of one language over to the very different ineffable of another and make themselves heavenly comforts of despair. "Since I cannot make this delivery, I might as well indulge my own creativity and give the reader what I can: the original author filtered through me, what I would have been if I were he. My reader cannot expect otherwise."

Alas, the translator's job is more humbling than that. He must try his best to do what he knows no one can do, and yet capture enough of the power or the charm of the original, not to mention its thought, its language, so as to spur the curious reader on. "What is the Italian like?" That is the question I wish to provoke. Thus my philosophy of translation is rather conservative. I attempt to preserve all of Tasso's metaphors, including even those encapsulated etymologically in single words. When Tasso uses a word as a leitmotif, I try to translate consistently—except for when doing so will make no sense in English. The untranslatable "pio," applied to Godfrey, is "reverent" in my translation, but sometimes also "pious" or "dutiful," as the context unfortunately demands. (Actually the word means all three things and more.) I am particularly sensitive to rhetoric and rhythm. English will not allow, with rhymes, as many end-stopped lines as Tasso employs, but when Tasso builds to a rhetorical climax, I try to do so, too, allowing the syntactical unit to begin and end in a single regular, full-rhymed line: "Fair enough," she returned. "I am content,/ Alone in honor and in punishment" (2.23.7–8).

What cannot be done with any regularity in English: the reproduction of Tasso's ottava rima in iambic pentameter English stanzas employing no flagrant archaisms and no syntactic gyrations. These last may have once been tolerated by the reading public; their day, I think, is long past. It must be English such as one might really read nowadays; therefore the archaisms and inversions must go; therefore a strict adherence to ottava rima must go, for English words may end in practically innumerable combinations of vowels and consonants, and without syntactic license to place at the end of a line virtually any word in the sentence, the ABABABCC scheme of the Italian original cannot be sustained in English. At which point one may well wonder whether verse itself must go, too.

I think not, and I hope the reader will agree with me. It seemed to me crucial that the eight-line stanza be preserved, for on it the very structure of Tasso's imagery and rhetoric and narrative depends. Most especially the concluding couplet, so often used for terse summary or sudden reversal or aphoristic climax, must be preserved, and in full rhyme as often as possible. There remains the question of what to do with the previous six lines. My expedient is simple. Since a pattern of unrhymed odd lines is traditional in English (as, for example, in the ballad scheme ABCB), I thought it best to preserve the sestet by rhyming on the even lines at least. These rhymes would pull the stanza together and lead more naturally to the couplet than would, say, lines of blank verse. Thus my rhyme scheme is XAXAXABB. Yet I have attempted, as often as I could without jarring the sense, to rhyme on the odd lines, too, often with slant or consonantal rhymes—to which I have occasionally resorted for the even lines—but often with full rhymes. The result is that anywhere from five to all eight lines will rhyme, and the rhymes will vary from close assonance to (the more frequent) full bell ringers. In my rhyming I have availed myself of all the dodges that English rhymers have always employed, as, for instance, rhyming the vowel in "lie" with the vowel that concludes "impurity." Such feints, I trust, add more to the music of English verse than does a faithful recapitulation of final vowels. In any case, about 90 percent of the rhymes on couplets and on the even lines of the sestets are full, as they ought to be. I hope that will satisfy both the iconoclast and the purist. My meter is accentual pentameter, five strong beats per line, no more than two short beats between each long. The normative rhythm, however, is iambic, with all the sonic modulations to be found in that supple instrument, English iambic pentameter.

As for the text itself, I have chosen the 1585 edition of Bonna (referred to in the notes as Bon. 3), as the best in a series of versions before the poem was transmuted into *Gerusalemme conquistata.* But I have adopted the occasional reading from the earlier edition of Osanna if that reading was reinstated by Tasso for *Gerusalemme conquistata* and if it seems superior to Bon. 3. In general I reserve the right to use any of the readings if that of my preferred text is clearly inferior or corrupt. All deviations from Bon. 3 which affect the translation have been flagged in the notes, along with the occasional unadopted but interesting variant. In general, for both the text and the notes, I am indebted to the fine 1929 edition of Pietro Papini (Florence: G. C. Sansoni), whose leads helped me navigate through the shoals of the primary texts.

Jerusalem Delivered

☙ Introduction

Tasso's Life

Torquato Tasso is one of those late Renaissance prodigies whose lives are marked by fitful periods of splendor and darkness. A kind of Caravaggio of poetry, Tasso could do nothing without firing it in the crucible of his ambitious, self-tormented soul. His greatest work, *Gerusalemme liberata,* revives the ancient pagan epic, constructed according to the recently rediscovered prescriptions for tragedy set out in Aristotle's *Poetics* and combined as harmoniously as possible with the fanciful subject matter and the dazzle of the *poesia cavalleresca.* In other words, it was an attempt—made by several predecessors, who had failed—to revive epic by rules not established for epic, using a great deal of material alien to epic, while hewing to a strict historical basis that was thought to underlie epic. It should have been a fool's errand, to fuse the amours of knights-errant with so forbidding a subject as the storming of Jerusalem by the Crusaders in 1099. Yet Tasso inserted into that history all manner of youthful tales of love which temper epic severity with the delights of romance.

It is a tribute to Tasso's talent that a poem so contradictorily conceived can live at all, as a unified whole, and not as a bizarre amalgam of disparate parts. It may be a tribute, too, to the strenuous efforts he had to make to hold together the parts of his own soul. Perilous though it is to read poetry in the light of the author's psychological wars, with Tasso some attention to these is inevitable. His heart was never at rest. He was a post-Tridentine Catholic and a classical humanist. He wrote of passionate sexual love, but for all we can tell he never enjoyed such love. His literary instincts turned to the strict architectonics of Aristotle; his readers, and dare one say he himself, at least in youth, preferred the sprawling romances of Pulci, Boiardo, and Ariosto. His poetry scorned court life; he was an avid seeker of advancement at court. His scruples about the doctrinal purity of *Gerusalemme liberata* drove him to madness, yet he deplored the severity of the age. Contradiction lay at the heart of his poetic genius, as of his life.

Let us then take a quick look at that life. Torquato Tasso was born in Sorrento in 1544, the son of the romance poet and courtier Bernardo Tasso. When he was ten, the boy accompanied his father to the court of Guidobaldo II at Pesaro. In 1560 his father sent him to Padua to study law. Tasso did not take that career seriously; his ambitions lay elsewhere. At Padua he received his first taste of poetic fame when he published his

Rinaldo (1561–62), a poem of cavalier adventures after the manner of Ariosto's *Orlando furioso* and his own father's *Amadigi*. In 1562 he resumed his studies at Bologna but was shortly thrown out of the university for, supposedly, composing satires against the students and the professors. The year 1565 finds him at Ferrara, the city where our errant poet will spend the most stable years of his life, first as attendant to the cardinal Luigi d'Este of the ruling Ferrarese family, then as attendant to the duke Alfonso d'Este. For some time the young man was a delight at court. His literary labors were intense. In a few years he published the *Discorsi dell'arte poetica* (1567), a work in which he delineated the task he had set for himself, that of writing the first true epic since antiquity; the *Osservazioni sullo state di Francia* (1570–71), a political treatise commissioned by his patrons; the great pastoral drama *Aminta* (1573); the first act of the tragedy *Galeolto re di Norvegia* (1573); and several cantos of *Gerusalemme liberata* (1573), some of which he had written when he was but a boy in his teens. It is important to note this touch of precocity, for the epic he had conceived before he had reached manhood would grow into the ruling obsession of his life. By 1575 the *Gerusalemme* was nearly finished, and Tasso sent copies to various literati.

At this point Tasso's life began to fray. He had expected acclaim for *Gerusalemme liberata* but was greeted with sharp criticism, much of it directed at the "digressive" love stories that modern readers consider the heart of the poem. His obsessions are revealed in his innumerable letters, by turns defiant and humble, farsighted and engrossed in controversy over trivia. The modern wit may be apt to diagnose paranoid schizophrenia brought on by taking Aristotle too seriously. For Tasso put himself under the pressure of another contradiction: that of employing Aristotle as a vanguard against his critics, all the while using the philosopher to justify a special subject matter and manner for epic which the philosopher himself explicitly denies. Nor was the Holy Office of the Inquisition of any great help. Tasso submitted his work to its purview, worried that his tales would strike the censors as too amorous, too dangerously delightful. They did not—but Tasso's obsessions remained. The duke Alfonso finally had to put him in an asylum when he attacked a servant with a knife.

Sick and destitute, Tasso returned to his sister Cornelia in Sorrento. But the attraction of court life proved too strong. He returned to Ferrara in 1578; he left the next year; Alfonso then imprisoned him for seven years in the hospital of St. Ann. A hospital for the mad was, in those days, something of a dungeon. Nevertheless, Tasso's treatment was fairly mild. He was granted furloughs, under supervision, and he had all the books and materials he needed to write love poetry, religious lyrics, encomia for his patrons, and feverish revisions of his epic. In 1580 an unauthorized version of the epic *Goffredo* appeared in twelve cantos. Tasso repudiated it and, though he then cooperated with several editors of his work, would never acknowledge the finality of any publication of *Gerusalemme liberata* as long as he lived.

Tasso spent the last years of his life, 1586 to 1595, as a literary vagabond, wandering from Ferrara to Mantua, Bergamo, Naples, Mantua again, Naples again, and other places along the way, until he finally died, prematurely old, in the cloisters of Sant' Onofrio in Rome. During this time he continued to write prolifically: *Il re Torrismondo* (1587), *Genealogia di casa Gonzaga* (1591), *Rime* (1591, first part; 1593, second part), *Il Mondo Creato* (1592), *Discorsi del poema eroico* (1594), and, what he hoped would be the crowning effort of his career, *Gerusalemme conquistata* (1593), his heroic poem drastically revised, eviscerated of its amorous play, of its traces of Ariostan romance, and rendered in the grave, stern beauty, if it may be called that, of the words of a Hebrew prophet or the bust of a Roman senator. One wonders how disappointed he would be to learn that we remember him for what he came to believe were his artistic mistakes.

Ariosto and Tasso

Most English readers will encounter Tasso, the great Italian poet of the latter half of the sixteenth century and arguably the greatest Italian poet after Dante, alongside the work of his Ferrarese predecessor, Ludovico Ariosto. (In Tasso's own day the inevitable comparisons spurred a great deal of controversy; Galileo, for one, cherished Ariosto so much that he sentenced Tasso to his own private Dunciad.) But Ariosto is a hard act to follow. A reader may come to Tasso expecting the same vivacity and panache of Angelica's falling in love with the gravely wounded, lovely young Medoro, or the same wild imagination that places Saint John the Evangelist on the moon with Enoch and Elijah and, for a most practical means of locomotion, Elijah's chariot of fire. If mildly affectionate, cerebral irony appeals to you, Ariosto is your poet. Tasso will then strike you as a throwback to a darker era of half-mad saints dying for the faith.

Yet after a few readings that embarrassment must fade. For unlike *Orlando furioso, Gerusalemme liberata* really is an epic, an attempt to see the cosmos, natural and human and superhuman, in the light of a few enduring truths. The grandness of the attempt commands respect. By contrast, Ariosto's very strengths appear as limitations of vision. Ariosto shows us the brilliance and insouciance of one for whom the old has become the antique. He loves the silly old stories of knights and ladies, loves them for their innocence and charm, and it is to his credit that he can see their potential to charm even the jaded philosophes of his Ferrarese court—or the jaded philosophes of ours. His great war between the Christians and the Saracens, with Rodomont clearing a thirty-foot trench at a leap, or six knights skewered on Orlando's lance like hunks of meat on a spit, is not to be taken terribly seriously. He believed in the classical virtues of magnanimity, courage, prudence, and patience, seasoned by Christian chivalry and selflessness. His was a wise and kindly humanism, neither agnostic nor dogmatic in matters theological. Ariosto's verse has the studied effortlessness of the easy man of the world, the diplomat, the conversationalist, the bon vivant. Ariosto knows one side of us, our folly, as well as it can be known; yet his good-natured awareness of his own folly prevents the humor from coarsening into invective. His harmonies are true, his imagination fertile, his taste impeccable, his skill in telling interwoven stories exceeded only by the thorny complexities of Shakespeare and the madcap Dickens. Yet unlike those two he has not the power to move to action, to penetrate the soul. A man will not die for the sake of good taste.

Tasso's poetry is another thing altogether. Like Ariosto, Tasso was a lover of the old romances; he was a great proponent of Ariosto's favorite virtue, magnanimity ("Magnanima menzogna!" he exclaims, in praise of Sophronia's virtuous lie [2.22.3]); he has been unsettled by the various and incompatible claims for truth made by the proliferating Christian sects in the sixteenth century. Yet he writes after the Council of Trent, for a church eager to reassert its moral authority. No doubt he would have agreed with Ariosto, that it is a difficult thing to find the truth. But one Truth there is, and if man cannot find it, well then, that Truth will come and find him. He, like Ariosto, shows how often men can be absolutely certain about what turns out to have been wrong. Unlike Ariosto, he is moved by the multiplicity of human opinion to an ever more energetic pursuit of the truth. There is nothing of the sophist in Tasso. And if the truth cannot be found by means of reason and the evidence of the senses (for Tasso, like Aquinas and Aristotle, believed very much, more than did the urbane Ariosto, in the ability of reason to discover at least some truth), then Tasso's imperative is clear. Man must obey. For Tasso, that means obedience to the self-revelation of God in Holy Scripture and in the Holy Church. It is folly to believe that one mind, even were it wedded to the greatest genius who ever lived, could discover of its own the truths slowly and laboredly revealed for more than two thousand years by God to the faithful. Reason rebels against such an exaltation of reason. In this twilight battle it is best, urges Tasso, not to trust one's small capital of insight. Submit to authority, submit to the church. It is, ironically enough, a Mohammedan sort of self-discipline which Tasso enjoins.

Truth and Obedience

That is why, in Tasso, as in Plato, the epistemological problem of the divergence of opinion is at the heart of the political problem, the divergence of wills. Contrary to our democratic presupposition that, since the truth is possessed by no one in its entirety, it is best that every man follow where conscience and reason lead him, Tasso insists that that is all the more cause for submission to authority. In *Gerusalemme* authority is neither inherited nor virilely wrested from other men. It is, following the pastoral wisdom of Saint Paul (cf. Rom. 13:1–7), given by God for the common weal. That authority is not given without some measure of the gift that Solomon prayed for: wisdom. Note well, it is wisdom, not knowledge. The wise ruler in Tasso is the prudent ruler, who literally "sees ahead," providing for all vicissitudes. He is an image of the Providence that steers the sun and all the stars. To disobey him merely because one disagrees with his interpretation of events is folly.

Thus it is that Tasso gives us only rulers whom it is never embarrassment to obey. Godfrey, of course, is the wisest, but he is not alone. The hardhearted Aladine, tyrant of Jerusalem, commands our grudging respect. He is not motivated by virtue, nor does he play by the cleanest rules; but his poisoning the wells before the Christians arrive at Jerusalem, his preparations of woollen bales to soften the blows of the Christian rams, his restraint of the hothead Argante, his wise delegation of authority to Soliman and Clorinda are deeds of a man who knows how to govern. When he is confronted with Argante, whose lack of self-government makes his leading any excursion a disaster, he maintains his composure and somehow manages to refrain from laughing at his robust young fool:

> But you! temper a little that hot courage
> which seethes in you, by God, and tops the crest!
> And wait until the time is ripe to claim
> my vengeance, and the glory of your name. (6.11.5–8)

The king of Egypt is a glorious Sardanapallus, sinfully opulent. But he knows how to rule, says Tasso: "He was prince by blood, but more/By merit in the royal art of war" (17.6.7–8). And he, like Godfrey and Aladine, knows how to choose his subordinates well. No Argante leads his troops to war, but Emiren, a kind of Julian the Apostate, noble of heart although, *sub specie aeternitatis,* in the wrong camp. No one, not the brave and prudent Soliman, not the virginal Sven, not the silver-haired Dudon, is misplaced as a leader of men.

Perhaps there are two exceptions: Hydrotes, the conniving lord of Syria, and the unnamed and ever vilified Greek emperor. But both men reject true rulership. Hydrotes is a milksop, a charlatan who uses a slick slogan, "For faith and fatherland all things are just" (4.26.8), prostituting his niece to corrupt the Christian camp. His "wisdom" is a delusion arrived at by consulting demons. That sets him apart even from Aladine, who allows the sorcerer Ismen to aid him but who never makes that aid the heart of his military plans—see Clorinda's wise demolition of the magician's pretenses (2.51). Hydrotes is too cowardly to fight the Christians directly. As for the Greek emperor—whose people are but scantily and temporarily represented in the Christian army—it can hardly be called "rule" when one sits "like some grand patron in a theater" (1.51.6). The emperor does not command obedience because, to put it simply, he does not command. All he does, Godfrey says, is dally and cause others to delay; he lies; his circumlocutions and broken promises bespeak a waste of precious, providentially given time. He does not possess even the prudence of Aladine, who at least knows to protect his city vigorously when it is being besieged. Yet Godfrey treats even him with a deference he does not deserve.

Indeed, Tasso is at pains to show the reader the unreliability of opinion, particularly when it arises from the vox populi, or, as Tasso might put it, the *vox vulgi.* At first the reader might find Tasso's reports of popular opinion superfluous. Why do we care what the common people thought of something, particularly when those same commoners play no further role in the plot? Thus we are told that when Armida left Damascus, "Of her departure there were given out/Many causes for the crowd to noise about" (4.27.7–8). And rumor gets the better of Aladine, who is driven by it into a bloodthirsty frenzy that leads nowhere (at 1.82 ff.). And thus we encounter the far more serious mistake of the headless trunk, and the generally false suppositions of Rinaldo's whereabouts, and the foiled attempt by the Saracens to infiltrate the Christian army in disguise and kill Godfrey, and the rumor—which would be comical did it not probe so painfully our propensity to believe selfish delusions—that while the Christian armies are dying of thirst, Godfrey is in the captain's tent mixing water with Cretan wines!

Tasso was no democrat. We now are so attached to our talisman, decision by vote, that we refuse to see where it is bound to fail. An army cannot decide strategy by plebiscite. Nor can it even decide strategy by cooperation of its various leaders—by representative government, if you will. Peter the Hermit puts the case succinctly:

> When rule is not united in one man
> whose verdicts deal rewards and punishment,
> who delegates responsibilities,
> you have a fickle and wandering government.
> O make one body of members in accord!
> One head, to give direction and restraint.
> The power and scepter, then, to one man bring—
> and let him be acknowledged as a king. (1.31)

What keeps this from being a mere elevation of monarchy, however, is the theological and philosophical pressure brought to bear upon the role of monarch. Tasso's monarch is not a tyrant: he is the head of a body. The role of the common people is to acclaim, not to elect, their leader. After Godfrey is chosen by his peers to be no longer their peer, he is presented to the common soldiers, who greet the selection with cheers of joy. The people ratify his kingship—and it is clear from the sedition stirred up by the false rumors of Rinaldo's death that against his soldiers' will Godfrey cannot rule.

Here it is instructive to mention two metaphors for government: the charioteer from Plato's *Phaedrus,* and the Body of Christ from Paul's letters to the Corinthians. According to Plato's well-known flight of fancy, the soul is like a charioteer driving a pair of horses, one high mettled and obedient, the other unruly and tending to pull the chariot out of the right track. The evil horse represents the appetites; we need them, they are part of our humanity; without them we go nowhere, since this is a chariot built for two horses, after all. But woe betide us if they prevail. The good horse is what Plato calls "spirit," or what we might call "aggressiveness," "energy," "ambition." Although it can be corrupted, and although it, too, can run away with the chariot, it generally obeys and keeps the evil horse in line. The charioteer is, of course, the rational faculty. He knows where to go; he directs the horses toward their goal. Now this metaphor of body-mind tension, of opposition between will and intellect, even when it comes to self-government, is for Tasso, as it was for Plato, instructive when it comes to government of a nation or a church or an army, too. No one wins a war without soldiers, just as no one goes quickly from Athens to Sparta without a chariot and horses. But neither the soldiers nor the horses are capable of rule, and it is in their own best interests that they should not try.

Furthermore, hierarchy and equality—though not equivalence of role or status—can be reconciled in Christ, whose kingdom embraces all manner of Greeks and Jews, freemen and slaves, women and men, yet in whom there is "neither Greek nor Jew, neither slave nor free, neither male nor female" (Gal. 3:28). That is a paradox captured by the structure of Dante's *Paradiso,* wherein the souls participate unequally in the beatific vision yet receive all as much of the vision as they can receive, and are all equally saved, equally a part of the Divine symphony. Male and female they notably remain, though in Christ that distinction implies no necessary hierarchical superiority for the male. They are parts of the Body of Christ. Now Paul, attempting to still the bickerings of the Corinthians jockeying for status as proponents of the true faith, reminds them that all are members of Christ's mystical body: some members are created for one purpose, others for another. The head must perform its role, the hands must perform theirs. The head is greater than the hand in its role, but no more a part of Christ than is the hand: "For just as the body is one and has many members, and all the members of the body, though many, are one body, so it is with Christ" (1 Cor. 12:12). The key is a unity and equality expressed by means of diversity and hierarchy. Humility—or, to put it differently, a willing acceptance of the role God has called you to play—is the virtue that keeps the church, the earthly manifestation of this body, together.

With the foregoing in mind, the reader may appreciate how subtly Tasso has drawn his hero, Godfrey. Critics are wont to dismiss Godfrey as pallid, wooden, too much the *pio capitano,* just as Tasso's model, Virgil's Aeneas, was too much the *pius Aeneas.* A man fulfilling his duty just does not stir excitement. But we should be clear about what Godfrey's duty entails, for it will show the difference between him and Aeneas. He must coordinate an army full of headstrong, sinful, wayward men and lead them to the recovery of the Holy Land, which is but a symbol for the attainment of the Heavenly Jerusalem itself. The men are, in other words, also in his spiritual charge, and their spiritual warfare is never far from his mind. Thus, unlike Aeneas, he must play the preacher even as he plays the motivating captain. He must be—just as Armida is in her amorous way—a reader of hearts. He is "all things to all men," to cite Paul (1 Cor. 9:22); he uses the power of words to bring each soul into line so as to begin the final march to Jerusalem:

> With every man his art is forcible:
> he finds the words to please them, and compel. (1.19.7–8)

And Tasso shows in Godfrey's speeches (for speech is the ruler's most significant action) just such versatility. Godfrey always has about him something of the august, something that defies easy approach. Yet he can condescend to his rank-conscious lieutenant Guelph, with just the right touch of affability and manly reproof:

> Dismissing all the others, by himself
> he spoke to him in grave tones, and began,
> "When anger spurs your nephew's heart, O Guelph,
> he runs ahead too far indeed . . ." (5.54.1–4)

Or deliver to the obsequious Alete a polite refusal of the truce his pagan master offers, while returning veiled threat for the threats Alete has made:

> The friendship of your master pleases us,
> joining with him would be no grave affair—
> but you yourself know if Judea lies
> under his rule, and so why should he care?
> We wish that kingdom. Let him not deny it,
> and let him rule his own in peace and quiet. (2.87.3–8)

He can make his listeners' wills one with his own, through words of passionate religious conviction:

> Princes, I swear to you—and what I swear
> cries to the present and the future, cries
> to all the blessed in heaven above—the hour
> is ripe already for the enterprise. (1.28.1–4)

Most moving of all are those moments when he and his men are one, fighting together for the great goal. It is then that Godfrey's religious vision and his political leadership merge, as the "chief of all the chiefs" reminds the soldiers how well he and they know each other, how much they have endured together, and how their comradeship is bound together by the aim they all long for, to free the holy walls of Sion:

> But I am captain of a chosen band;
> we fought together, and together won;
> and then you placed yourselves at my command.
> Your fatherlands, your kinfolks—is there one
> I do not know? Which of your swords to me
> is new? Why, from what bow the arrow's flown
> whistling above me I can tell, I know
> whether it's Irish or French, and often who
>
> it was who shot it! All I ask you now,
> be as I've seen you be: that has sufficed.
> Recall your usual zeal, and keep in mind
> my honor, your honor, and the honor of Christ. (20.18, 19.1–4)

To such words the men themselves time and again will give the fit response, "Invincible leader, give the sign to go!" (20.3.8)

The Vicar of Christ

Why did Tasso choose to write about the Crusades, and what did the choice have to do with the issues of his day? Tasso himself answers the first question at length in his *Discourses on the Heroic Poem.* If what poets say about their own poetry is to be trusted, his choice of the Crusades was due mainly to considerations of epic form. The event described must be rooted in history. It must not be so long ago that men have forgotten it, or so recent that it cannot admit of the marvelous. Tasso, it seems, found an event, the taking of Jerusalem, which happened at about the right time and was grand enough and coherent enough for epic treatment. He admits that the subject had preoccupied him even in his youth, at the same time, we may note, when he was also preoccupied with overcoming the reputation of Ariosto; but nowhere does Tasso mention that Ariosto's magical tour de force about Christians and Saracens had anything to do with Tasso's decision to write about Christians and Saracens.

It is one of those cases in which accidents of history orchestrate themselves into design. For Ariosto's choice was already determined for him by Matteo Boiardo's romp *Orlando innamorato,* which poem Ariosto "finished," and Boiardo himself was the urbane inheritor of a long tradition of popular romances centering around the deeds of Charlemagne, Roland, Oliver, Rinaldo, and the rest. Neither Boiardo nor Ariosto really had any thought of stirring up patriotic fervor against the Saracens. There were the Saracens of folklore and the all-too-real Turks harassing the shores of Italy, and they had precious little to do with each other. It was a fortunate stroke for Tasso that his poetic predecessors fairly pitched him into the one subject matter most fitting for his sensibility and his faith. And, we might add, for the upheavals of his day: that is, the Reformation, the colonization of the New World, and the threat, which we descendants of the victors are apt to ignore, of the Turks. In other words, Tasso wrote to change the men's minds and hearts and spur them to action on behalf of the embattled faith.

The reader cannot expect any thoroughgoing discussion of these matters here. I can, however, suggest that for Tasso's contemporaries the splintering of Christianity, the battle against the Turks, and the exploration of the world were all moments in the general battle to spread the gospel and unite the world under the authority of the successor of Peter. I can also suggest that a model for Godfrey was readily available to Tasso in the formidable person of the Dominican Michele Ghislieri, Pope Saint Pius V, whose task it was to implement the reforms established by the Council of Trent and to reinvigorate the Catholic Church in its struggle against schismatics in the north and Turks in the south.

In a hagiography published shortly after Pius's death, we read of the pope's tireless labor to reconcile the feuding kings of Spain and France, uniting them against the common enemy the Turk. He himself wanted personally to go to war, adding, "What a shameful thing it would be for the young men staying at home, to see an old man go" (Girolamo Catena, *Vita del Gloriosissimo Papa Pio V* [1580; Rome, 1697], 200.) He sent embassies to persuade the Russian Orthodox to resist the Turks in the East, and to invite them back under the jurisdiction of Rome "to whom it was granted by Jesus Christ never to go astray" (203). He entered into a league, bound together despite their mutual mistrust, with Spain and Venice, resulting in the glorious naval victory of Lepanto in 1571. Before that battle he sent Capuchins and Jesuits to the ships to keep the men from vice and to turn their hearts toward God, enjoining upon them a three days' fast and the receiving of the sacraments of penance and the Eucharist, and promising to all a plenary indulgence for their willingness to fight. The Christians were outnumbered, and the generals were against engagement, until one old sea dog rose in the assembly and said that "Our holy father Pius has commanded it, whom we should obey." And that was that. With divine intervention—the Turks were becalmed at sea—the proud and ferocious were defeated by the dutiful and holy. Thirty thousand Turks were slain and fifteen thousand Christian galley slaves set free. A great commemorative column was erected in Rome to honor the heroes. Pius attempted to follow up the victory by inviting other Catholics, Protestants, and even Muslims to join him in league against the Turk (sending, among other missives, a letter to one Menna, Christian king of Ethiopia, popularly known as "Prester John," urging him to attack the Muslims from the south while the Europeans attacked from the north). For, says the biographer, the pope attempted "to dispose all such kings to his will, as the realm of the Pope knows no boundaries or limits, all Christians being subject to his rule and his monarchy" (126).

Naturally the pope had more on his mind than protecting the European coasts and the eastern Danube, though that was quite a lot. There was the matter of the "heretics," the Lutherans and Zwinglians of the north. Two things emerge when one examines the many speeches in the decades-long Council of Trent which mention the Turk: first, that the Turks can only grow in strength if Europe is disunited; second, that the present dangers are sent as castigations by God, whose church has too long winked at corruption. The latter is the message of a remarkably blunt oration by Cardinal Pole to the council on January 7, 1546: "For at once one shall discover that it was our ambition, our greed, our lusts which first infected the people of God with all these troubles, and by their might we drove the true shepherds from the church and deprived them of the food of the Word, taking the goods of the Church, which are the goods of the poor, from them, and handing them to men unworthy of the priesthood. . . . Which of us can deny that for years we have done so? Therefore if the Turk, if the heretics rise against us, what else is it but our own crimes and the just punishment of God, though a punishment full of mercy? For if he were to punish us as our sins merit, we would long ago have become like Sodom and Gomorrah!" (*Concilium Tridentinum Acta I* [Fribourg: Herder, 1904], vol. 4, item no. 372). But it is not the business of the laity to reform the church. True reform must make the church more, not less, monarchical. Thus, at tremendous political risk, Paul III rebukes his staunchest ally, Emperor Charles V, for *assuming a role not properly his* when he tried to remove Protestants from the convent at Speyer. In his letter of August 24, 1544, the pope compares the church to a well-run house in which various servants have various duties: "Nor is it allowed to anyone to act according to his own judgment; and even if the particular thing he does is done well, and with good will, nonetheless he is justly rebuked by the master of the household, for by his untimely zeal he will have taken away that which is most lovely in a house, the order without which it cannot stand for long. . . . So too in the Church of Christ" (*Concilium Tridentinum Acta I,* vol. 4, item no. 276).

The results of such ordered reform would be a fairly strong front against the Turk in the Mediterranean and a vigorous attempt to spread the faith worldwide. Those had already occupied the minds of many a soldier and missionary: the year 1492 was commemorated not only for Columbus's voyage but for the expulsion of the Moors from Granada. Now they became of paramount importance. "Against the Pope," said a Venetian ambassador in 1592, "the Great Sultan has an immortal hate, not only because he is the head of our religion which is contrary to his own, but because he is the one and fitting instrument for uniting all of Christendom against him" (P. I. Rinieri, *Clemente VIII e Sinan Bassa' Cicala* [Rome: Civilta' Cattolica, 1898], 1). The soldierly Society of Jesus is formed—as a boy Tasso was taught by Jesuit tutors—to fight and die for the faith in China, Japan, and the Americas. These are two prongs of one war. Thus the historian Michele Zappullo, writing his 1603 *Historia di quattro principali città del mondo, Gerusalemme, Roma, Napoli, e Venetia* (History of the four principal cities of the world, Jerusalem, Rome, Naples, and Venice [Vicenza: Greco]), a book devoted to recording the triumph of Christianity against its foes (especially the Saracens), concludes with a chapter on the Indians of the New World. As he writes, "The means that the Divine Majesty used for [the spread of the gospel] was Christopher Columbus of Genoa, truly a most remarkable man." The first Indians he encountered "to please him adored the Cross, kneeling for the Hail Mary and performing all the gestures of Christians" (380).

The relevance of the cursory discussion above should be clear. Tasso aimed to remind us of certain truths about our nature, so that we then might serve as decent instruments in the ongoing battle. The poem is not "about" Protestantism but about that need of ours for leadership, which will undo all attempts to establish a society or a church upon the sands of public opinion and desire. It is not "about" war but about our longing for something beyond us to which we might joyfully surrender our pride, our lust, our earthly possessions, our very bodies and souls. Tasso was mistaken; his poem is first romance, then epic. To sail the uncharted seas, to fight, to love, to lay one's bones at the foot of the Cross: that is the romance of Christianity; that is what the *Gerusalemme* celebrates.

Desire and Death

When Tasso revised *Gerusalemme liberata* and turned it into, pessimistically enough, *Gerusalemme conquistata,* he removed much of what did not fit neatly into his epic tale, and thus he removed much of his best poetry. He had reason. His passages on love, he believed, would distract the reader from his more important doctrinal purposes. The tales of Erminia and Tancred, Clorinda and Tancred, and Rinaldo and Armida threaten to run away with the poem. Of this Tasso was well aware, for even in *Gerusalemme liberata* he must apologize for delighting his readers a little too much:

> You know the world delights in lovely things,
> for men have hearts sweet poetry will win. (1.3.1–2)

We are apt, these days, to shake our heads with benign condescension. "My dear fellow," we might say, "there's no need to worry. When truth does not exist, there can be no urgency; no urgency, no distraction. You may veer a bit from your aesthetic norm now and then with those love stories, but in the end they still fit rather nicely, and you can't have too many battles in a row without losing our interest. There's more to the world than maces and splintered lances." But to ignore Tasso's marked anxiety over the love stories is to fail to take seriously either warfare or sex. For from this anxiety the poem acquires much of its power. In Tasso, as it never is in Homer, *war is intensely sexual, as sex is hostile.* The Greek could see the glamour of battle, rather as presexual boys might see it, as the most dangerous, exhilarating, brightly bannered joy. Even if the motive behind the Trojan War is the rape of a woman, and even if the occasional Penthesilea fights alongside the men, there is in the conduct of the war a virginal innocence, brilliantly broken here and there by Andromache with her baby son, or a flashback to the days when the Trojan women washed their laundry in the rock pools beside the Scamander, or an Achilles weeping with Priam over the mortality of man, that revelation that has ever stricken the male of our species as an affront. By contrast, Tasso's warriors themselves embody the confusion of love and warfare. Mars and Eros are companion gods, incomprehensible without the other, driving the warriors on to their ravishing agonies.

A few examples will suffice. When Tancred first sees his beloved Clorinda at Jerusalem, he lures her away from the battlefield with the prospect of a duel, to test each other's mettle, as it were. When she fails to understand him and fetches him a good blow, he kneels before her, strips his breastplate, and topples, as I think, over the verge into comic relief:

> See, I let drop my arms, I lay my chest
> open—now's your chance to kill me. Take it!
> You want it easier still? I'll strip the rest—
> take off this mail, and you can kill me naked. (3.28.1–4)

There is, however, nothing at all comic about the climax of this love affair, the twilight moment of Clorinda's death. She and Tancred have been laboring all the night. He does not know who she is, and she, as I read it, will not tell Tancred, for she *does* recognize him and thus knows full well that it is her lover she is trying to kill. To tell him would be to end the fight and to save herself ignominiously—and after all, she has long been trying, with modest success, to flee her very womanhood. Far be it from Clorinda to invoke Love. Thus as they pause, midbattle, just before dawn, and look at each other, he in cocksure ignorance, she in a torrent of self-conscious foreboding, it is with the respect of enemies whose fury will soon pass into tenderness:

> Upon the pommels of their swords they leaned,
> blood-drained; looked at each other wearily. (12.58.1–2)

When the death stroke comes, Clorinda is transformed instantaneously from the warrior *virgo intacta* to a lovely, gentle woman, and all reference to her armor is henceforth forgotten, while the brutality of Tancred's joy is thrown into high relief by his complete ignorance of what is going on. For Clorinda is also being transformed from pagan to Christian:

> He rails against the virgin on his sword,
> pressing against her in his victory.
> But as she falls she speaks her life's last word,
> in a voice broken with extremity,
> and a new spirit in her proclaims that word,
> spirit of faith, and hope, and charity.
> Rebel in life, on her such grace is poured
> that she may die the handmaid of the Lord. (12.65)

What keeps Tasso's poetry from being *merely* a stunning proto-Freudian analysis of human drives is his Christianity, which always urges him on to higher truths. If God created the lust for sex and the lust for honor, they must be good in themselves, provided they are properly ordered. That proper ordering implies direction more than it implies dampening. For God uses the wild passion of Tancred as the very instrument of Clorinda's salvation and then, in an astonishing reversal, uses that same passion, now rendered sublime by Clorinda ensainted, as the instrument of Tancred's own salvation. So Clorinda, now supremely feminine, appears in a dream to her desperate lover:

> "Live, and know that I love you—what I feel
> I will not hide from you—as tenderly
> as a creature may be loved." With that, such zeal
> flamed in her eyes past mortal powers, that she
> closed herself in her rays profoundly bright,
> and so instilled new comfort in the knight. (12.93.3–8)

And it is the same head-tossing thirst for honor which leads Rinaldo to turn upon the slandering Gernando with all the fury of a thunderbolt and which later leads him, against unthinkable odds, to be the first to scale the wall of Jerusalem:

He fends them off,
he presses on, he but redoubles his force—
as a bent palm-tree springs the harder and higher,
his strength when he's resisted gains in force—
and beats the enemy back at last, bears spears
and obstacles against him, blunts their force,
and scales the wall, and masters it, and clears
a safe way for the rest of his climbing peers. (18.78)

The true faith, like love and war, is not for the faint of heart.

Nor is it for the hard of heart. What I have said above makes Tasso's poem a profoundly probing work. It is also profoundly human. Tasso had not the Dantean mind to see theology as poetry. He always returns from doctrinal Truth to a sensitive appreciation of the actions, great and small, which distinguish us as human beings. Men are all in desperate need of salvation; but some measure of Grace may shine forth to render believer and unbeliever alike worthy of admiration or compassion. Such is Clorinda's surprised and feminine reaction to the plight of the self-sacrificing lovers Sophronia and Olindo:

Clorinda's heart grew tender at this sight,
grieved with them, and a tear welled in her eye. (2.42.1–2)

Or the heroic death of Soliman:

He put up little fight, but as he died
did not forget he was a noble man;
he gave no groans, but met the blows, uncowed.
To the last all he did was great and proud. (20.107.5–8)

Or, most poignantly, the moment when Tancred, near death, regains consciousness to see the woman who has saved his life; Erminia does not say who she is but, in a moment of mingled boldness and longing and tenderness, hints broadly that her love, too, must be fulfilled:

"Vafrine," he asks, "how did you get here? When?
My merciful physician, who are you?"
She sighed for doubt and happiness at once,
shading her lovely face with a rosy hue.
"As your physician I'm prescribing rest,
so you be still. You'll know, when the time's due.
You will be cured—get ready for the fee."
And she held his head to her bosom tenderly. (19.114)

For, as Michael the Archangel might say, what is Heaven itself if not the realm of friends, where those mere human beings who went before us still care for us, still fight beside us as we play our small part in the symphonic battle of the Lord?

Torquato Tasso

Jerusalem Delivered

Gerusalemme liberata

Canto One

1
I sing the reverent armies, and that Chief
who set the great tomb of our Savior free;
much he performed with might and judgment, much
he suffered in the glorious victory;
in vain hell rose athwart his path, in vain
two continents combined in mutiny.
Heaven graced him with its favor, and restored
his straying men to the banner of the Lord.

2
O Muse, who do not string a garland of
the fading laurel fronds of Helicon,
but far in heaven among the blessed choirs
wreathe deathless stars into a golden crown,
breathe into my heart the fire of heavenly love,
illuminate my song, and if I have sewn
embroideries of the truth in any place,
I ask forgiveness for their lesser grace.

3
You know the world delights in lovely things,
for men have hearts sweet poetry will win,
and when the truth is seasoned in soft rhyme
it lures and leads the most reluctant in,
as we brush with honey the brim of a cup, to fool
a feverish child to take his medicine:
he drinks the bitter juice and cannot tell—
but it is a mistake that makes him well.

4
Alfonso great of heart, who from the rage
of fortune guide me into port, and save
this wanderer gone astray, tossed between reef
and the near-drowning fury of the wave,
welcome these pages, take them up with joy,
which as a sacred gift to you I have
devoted; and soon my pen may dare to write
what now it dimly hopes shall come to light,

5
for it were just, if ever that day dawns
when the good Christian people are at peace,
and with their ships and horses seek to cleanse
Palestine of those pillagers from Thrace,
that you be given the scepter over land,
or, if you wish, admiralty of the seas.
Now strive with Godfrey as your exemplar,
heed my song well, and gird yourself for war.

6
Six years had passed already in the east
for the Christian host and their high enterprise;
Nicaea they had conquered by main force,
and taken fortressed Antioch by surprise,
which they defended afterwards against
innumerable Persian enemies,
then stormed Tortosa, finally yielding to
the close of the old year, waiting for the new.

7
The end of that rainy winter would soon come
that forced the interruption in the war,
when the eternal Father from his throne
high in the realm of heaven that is most pure
(and as far as from the stars to the depths of hell,
so far is He above the starry sphere)
looked down, and in one instant, in one glance,
surveyed the world in His omnipotence.

8
He viewed all creatures, and in Syria
upon the Christian princes fixed His eye,
and with His sight which spies into the heart
of human loves in deepest secrecy,
saw Godfrey ardent for one aim, to rout
the heathen from the land of the Most High;
faithful, zealous, he holds all earthly gain
of power and glory and riches in disdain.

9
But God saw Baldwin restless and intent
on all the grandeur to which men aspire;
saw Tancred, careless of his life or death,
crushed in the grip of amorous desire;
in Antioch saw Bohemond who lent
his land a new foundation, setting higher
principles, customs for the common good,
laws, arts, the worship of the one true God,

10
cares which so concentrate his busy thought
he has forgotten every other goal.
In Rinaldo God sees a warrior's heart,
a spirit that cannot suffer to be still—
for gold, for power he has no appetite,
but his thirst for honor is unquenchable;
he hangs on the lips of Guelph to learn the ways
of brilliant heroes of the olden days.

11
Now that the Ruler of the world had seen
what these and others held for heart's desire,
He summoned from the foremost ranks that shine
Gabriel, second in the angel choir,
who between God and the souls of righteous men
is herald of gladness, faithful messenger.
He bears the decrees of heaven to earth, and bears
with him to heaven our fervor and our prayers.

12
The Lord said to His herald, "Go and find
Godfrey: in My name ask, 'Why do you rest?
Why do you not renew the war assigned
to liberate Jerusalem oppressed?'
Let him call his chiefs and urge each sluggish mind
to the high task, for he must lead the rest.
In heaven I choose him, so on earth will they,
once peers, now his lieutenants in the fray."

13
This said, the angel Gabriel girt himself
with all speed to fulfill the high commission,
clothing his invisible form with air
and so submitting it to mortal vision,
assuming human limbs and a human face
but heaven's majesty in composition,
of age between a boy and man outright—
and tressed his golden hair with rays of light.

14
Clad in white wings, with feather fringe of gold,
nimble and never wearying and swift,
above the earth and sea the angel soared
and left the clouds behind him cut adrift,
parting the winds; then to this lower world
veered the celestial messenger, aloft
over the peak of Lebanon where he stood
and paused, his pennons balanced and spread wide;

15
then straight on to Tortosa's coast he bore,
hurling his flight headlong from the mountaintop.
Dawn was arising over the eastern shore,
the sun half hid below the wave, half up,
when Godfrey rose to offer morning prayer,
as was his habit, to the Lord of hope,
and brighter than the sun in which he shone
the angel appeared to him out of the dawn

16
and said, "Godfrey, behold! This is the day,
the time for waging war is opportune—
why should you tolerate the least delay
to liberate Jerusalem cast down?
Summon a council of the chiefs today,
hurry the listless to the end and crown
of all your work. God chooses you to be
their head—they shall yield to you willingly.

17
"God sends me as His herald: I reveal
His plans to you, in His name. O what great
hope should be yours for triumph, O what zeal
for the hosts now entrusted you by fate!"
This said, he vanished, and flew back to heaven,
his place the utmost realms of peace and light.
The speech and splendor left the captain blind—
dazzled, no less astonished in the mind,

18
but once he had recovered and considered
who came, Who sent him, what commands were given,
if once he had but hungered, now he burned
to end that war for which he had been chosen
leader—not that to see himself preferred
above the others puffed him with ambition,
but now his will in the Lord's will flamed the higher,
as a spark enveloped in the flame of fire.

19
And so he calls his champions scattered round
and the great peers, to gather in assembly,
plying letter on letter, one envoy after another,
good counsel ever seconding his plea;
what would entice or pierce the generous soul
or waken manhood from its lethargy.
With every man his art is forcible:
he finds the words to please them, and compel.

20
The leaders came with their troops following,
and Bohemond alone remained behind.
Some camped outside the city, some within
Tortosa took what lodgings they could find.
A glorious senate on a solemn day,
the army's great men gathered with one mind
to hear the reverent Godfrey, who now spoke
with a resounding voice and august look:

21
"Warriors of God, whom the King of heaven chose
to fight for Truth, and see His faith restored,
Who led you through the snares of land and sea,
upheld you in the clash, your shield, your sword,
so that of many rebels, in six years,
we have made nations subject to the Lord,
and among their people, broken with war, subdued,
spread the victorious standards of our God:

22
"Unless I am wrong we did not leave the sweet
nest of our birth and all whom we hold dear,
baring our very lives to the faithless seas
and all the dangers of a distant war,
to gain a barbarous country and the noise
of the brief fame the crowds can offer here.
That would have been a pitiful reward,
imperiling our souls for spilling blood.

23
"Rather it was the target of our hopes
to storm the noble walls of Sion, seize
our fellow Christians from their shameful yoke,
the bitter slavery and indignities,
to establish a new realm in Palestine
where piety should hold perpetual lease,
where no one would prevent the pilgrim from
fulfilling his vow to adore the Savior's tomb.

24
"For what we've risked what we have done is great,
our labor has been less, our honor poor,
our real achievement nothing—if we wait
or turn the thrust of the army here or there.
We muster all of Europe, and for what?
What gain, to set this continent afire,
if of our grand attempt the culmination
is no new kingdom raised, but ruination?

25
"Not upon the foundations of this world
should a man build if he designs to rule—
where his faith is alien, countrymen few, among
limitless numbers of the infidel,
where succor from the west is so far off
and hopes of Greece are unreliable.
He can destroy, but when the walls come down
he will have built a sepulcher of his own.

26
"We took the Turks, the Persians, Antioch—
glorious in name, magnificent and bold—
not by our works but by the gift of God,
and the triumphs were a wonder to behold.
But God shall take these gifts away if we
turn them against the aims which He has willed;
our fame now trumpeted will then become
an idle tale throughout all pagandom.

27
"For the love of God, let not so free a gift
be squandered or recalled for our misuse!
Let our work's thread and finish correspond
with the noble design which set our course.
Now that the way is clear of obstacles,
now that the season is favorable to us,
what shall prevent our racing to the aim
of all our triumphs—to Jerusalem!

28
"Princes, I swear to you—and what I swear
cries to the present and the future, cries
to all the blessed in heaven above—the hour
is ripe already for the enterprise:
else we will place in doubt what now is sure,
losing advantage as we temporize.
For I predict, if we are slow to work,
Egypt will come to reinforce the Turk."

29
He spoke; a tremor passed among the chiefs
until the solitary Peter stood,
a private man who sat with princes at
council, the author of the great crusade,
"What Godfrey urges you, I too advise;
there is no room to doubt what has been said;
it is self-evident, as he has shown.
You should approve it. I add this alone:

30
"From what I gather of all your rivalry,
the taunts you hurl and suffer, purposes crossed,
your mulish holding back and sluggish help
and botching operations in mid-course,
the rise of every conflict and delay
I trace to one originating source:
authority balanced out among so many
that no one properly possesses any.

31
"When rule is not united in one man
whose verdicts deal reward and punishment,
who delegates responsibilities,
you have a fickle and wandering government:
Oh, make one body of members in accord,
one head, to give direction and restraint;
the power and scepter, then, to one man bring—
and let him be acknowledged as a king."

32
The old man spoke no more. What minds and hearts
are shut to you, blest Breath and holy Fire?
You breathe in the hermit's words, You press and burn
them deep in the heart of every cavalier,
clear the ingrafted or the inborn lust
for pride of place and willfulness and power—
so Guelph and William, in rank the highest of all,
are first to proclaim Godfrey general.

33
They all approved: let it be his by right
to weigh all options, and command the rest,
to take the fight to whom he wished and when,
and give their subjects laws as he thought best;
his former peers will be his officers,
obedient to each signal and behest.
This done, the news takes wing, the word is out,
and it is all the soldiers talk about.

34
He showed himself before them, and they thought
him well deserving of that honored station,
and with his features poised and calm he took
their military cheers of jubilation.
For this their humble show of love and duty
he spoke a little in appreciation,
then ordered the whole camp the following day
to march before him in their battle array.

35
The sun returned into the eastern sky
exceptionally brilliant and serene,
when with their martial pennons flaring high
the warriors came forth armed in the rising sun,
circling the field in all their finery,
parading for the reverent Bouillon.
He stood attentive and with careful sight
observed each passing footman and each knight.

36
Foe to the years and to oblivion,
O Memory, the steward of all I sing,
lend me your strength, that I may tell again
who were the chiefs and troops; let their names ring
through centuries, let their ancient glory shine,
now dull and silent from time's ravaging.
May your treasures adorn my song, to tell
what every age shall hear, and never quell.

37
The French were first in the parade: led once
by the king's brother Hugh before he died.
The men were picked from the rich Ile de France,
between four streams, a lovely countryside.
After the death of Hugh, the fearless bands
followed their golden lilies of old pride
under their captain, the excellent Clothar—
his blood as lordly as his character.

38
Heavily armed are they, one thousand strong.
There follow another thousand cavaliers;
in arms, insignia, discipline, and skill
they are the first band's counterparts and peers,
under the care of Robert, Normans all,
and he a Norman born and prince of theirs.
Two bishops shepherd the next bands to war—
the troops of William and of Ademar.

39
These men had sung the holy office once,
had spent their days as pious ministers,
now bound their long locks under a steel helm
and learned the bitter practice of the wars.
From Orange and the neighboring lands the first
recruited his four hundred warriors;
Ademar led as many from Le Puy,
men who were no less skilled in soldiery.

40
See Baldwin following in the march; his brother's
troops are combined with squadrons of his own,
for now the worthy Godfrey is chief of chiefs
he grants him all the soldiers from Bouillon.
The count of Chartres succeeds him in parade,
in strategy and strength a paragon;
four hundred go with him; armed in the saddle,
Baldwin leads thrice that number into battle.

41
Guelph occupied the field nearby, a man
as meritorious as fortunate,
who by his Latin father could derive
a lineage through the Estes old and great,
but, as his name and lands are German, is
a scion of the Guelphian estate:
his rule stretched from the Danube to the Rhine,
old Swabia, Rhaetia, and the Carinthine.

42
To this his mother's heritage he joined
conquests of other great and famous lands,
whence he drew men who snap the finger at
marching to challenge death when he commands.
They allay the winter before a roaring fire,
eating and making merry with their friends.
They were five thousand leaving; now remain
hardly a third from the Persian campaign.

43
Then followed a race of men fair skinned and blond,
from the tidewater between France and Germany
where wash the Rhine and the Meuse, a fertile land
good for the harvest of grain and husbandry;
with them the levee-building island men
who fight the ravenous hunger of the sea,
for floods which prey on cargoed ships there roll
and swallow towns and even kingdoms whole.

44
The Dutch and Flemish were a thousand each;
another Robert had their governing.
Slightly more were the men from England, led
by William, the young son of their great king.
And some whose homes lie closest to the pole
compose the troops the English bowmen bring:
Ireland the Farthest, cut off from the rest of the earth,
from deep woods sends her burly warriors forth.

45
Then Tancred: of all these men—except Rinaldo—
none in the swordplay takes a greater part,
or is more handsome in his looks and manners,
or is more fearless and sublime of heart.
Only the folly of love can dull the luster
which all his vaunted victories impart—
a war-born love, of but a moment's sight,
that feeds on hardship and grows great in might.

46
The rumor was that on that glorious day
when the French put the Persian host to rout,
Tancred, exhausted by the victory,
pursuing the retreaters all about,
searched for a place to rest his heaving sides,
a cool brook to refresh his parching throat,
and fell at last where a fresh spring in the glade
invited him to enjoy its summery shade,

47
when out of nowhere a young girl appeared
all clad in armor—all except her face;
she was a pagan, and had likewise come
seeking refreshment at that very place.
He saw her pleasing form and stared, amazed,
enkindled by such loveliness and grace:
O wondrous love! now born, now on the wing,
now grown a Titan armed and triumphing.

48
On goes her helm; had no one else come near
she would have struck at him immediately,
but the proud maiden left her conquest there,
retreating only for necessity;
yet the image of the lovely warrior
he so treasures in his heart and memory
that there she dwells alive, both how and where
he saw her: constant fuel for the fire.

49
Reading his looks the wisest in love's ways
remarked, "He's burning—it's a hopeless case."
So he went sighing along with drooping brow
and every sign of sorrow in his face.
He was the leader of eight hundred knights
from fair Campania, that idyllic place
of Nature's pride—lush hills and greenery
kissed by the waves of the Tyrrhenian sea.

50
Then came two hundred soldiers born in Greece,
virtually free of steel from top to toe;
at each man's side hung the bent scimitar,
on the back rattled the quiver and the bow.
They rode lean, strapping horses, bred to race,
sparing of food, but tireless even so.
They are quick to charge or to retreat, and fight
even while in the disarray of flight.

51
The band was led by Tatin, the sole Greek
to fight beside the Latins in the war.
Shame on you, Greece, shame for your base neglect,
for weren't, Greece, those battles near your shore?
And yet you sat awaiting the last act
like some grand patron in a theater.
Now you have no complaint if you must serve—
your slavery is just what you deserve.

52
See the last squadron in the order, last,
but first in honor, discipline, and worth—
the brave Adventurers, never defeated heroes,
terror of Asia and lightning over the earth.
Silence, you Argonauts, silence, you wandering knights
of Arthur's table—whose tales contain no dearth
of empty dreams! Beside the glory of these
let every memory of old champions cease.

53
Who is fit to lead them? Dudon of Contz; and as
prowess and bloodlines both are a common boast,
the others agreed as one to follow him
who had accomplished most and witnessed most.
He shows a touch of gray in his still-fresh strength,
of a grave and seasoned manliness composed,
and as a handsome badge of honor shows
the deep-cut signs of battle with his foes.

54
Eustace is near the front: his own deeds ring
with glory, as the brother of Bouillon;
Gernando too, the son of the Norse king,
bragging continually of title and crown;
and with the best the old traditions sing
of Roger Balnaville and Engerlon,
and celebrates among the stoutest hearts
one Genton and Rambald, and two Gerhardts.

55
Ubaldo earned his praises too, and Rosmond,
heir to the great duchy of Lancaster;
nor will the name of Tuscan Obizzo plummet
into the maw of time the predator,
nor will time steal from us three Lombard brothers
Achilles, Sforza, and Palamedes, or
great Otto and his shield: its heraldry
a snake whose mouth gave birth to a naked boy.

56
Nor will I leave behind Rudolph, Gascon,
or the illustrious pair of men named Guy,
or overlook Gernier and Everard
hid in ungrateful silence and passed by.
But you, Edward, Gildippe, spouses and lovers,
who share as one the trials of battle—I
am weary of naming, but you seize me with wonder!
Not death itself shall put your love asunder.

57
What is not mastered in the school of Love?
For she, who cleaved unto her man's dear side,
the ardent lady, learned to fight there too.
Their lives are one, and so together ride
their fates: there never falls a blow that hurts
but one of them, nor can the pain divide—
wound him, and on his wife it takes its toll,
and if her blood is spilled, he spills his soul.

58
But there you see Rinaldo the brave lad,
taller than these in all their fighting trim;
with a sweet fierceness he lifts his princely head,
in wonder all the others look to him.
The promise of his youth has raced ahead;
with the first bloom the fruit is on the limb.
He is Mars in armor lightning the skies above;
but when he doffs his helm, the God of Love.

59
On the banks of the Adige he was born
to Berthold and Sophia, a mother fair,
a father great and bold; and yet as soon
as he was weaned from mother's milk his care
was given to Matilda, who nurtured him
and taught him courtly arts. One home they share
till his young heart is wooed by the trumpet blast
which he can hear resounding from the east.

60
Then—not even fifteen years under his belt—
he fled alone, along roads as good as lost,
crossed the Aegean and passed the shores of Greece
and in a distant country joined the host.
A noble flight it was! Perhaps some great-
souled grandson of his house can make that boast!
Three years he'd fought, and early on his chin
the first soft down of manhood had come in.

61
So passed the knights, and marching after these
came the infantry, with Raymond at their head.
He ruled Toulouse; his men from the Pyrenees,
between the river Garonne and the ocean bed.
Four thousand men, made stalwart, not by ease
but toil and hardship, well armed, battle-bred,
in short, good soldiers. As for the squad's leader,
in prowess and experience no man better.

62
But Stephen of Ambois came afterwards
leading five thousand men from Blois and Tours.
Brilliant in iron they shine as they march along
yet not so hardy, not trained to endure.
The lands are gentle, lush, full of delight,
as soft as the inhabitants they bear:
for these are first to charge to the attack,
but all too easily tire, and fall back.

63
Alcasto was third in line—like Capaneus
at the gates of Thebes—with menace in his bearing.
From the castles of the Alps he rounded up
six thousand Swiss, a folk both fierce and daring,
whose steel was used for the harrow and breaking sod,
now turned to a more noble sort of shearing:
with hands that drove bedraggled flocks they hurled
defiance to the emperors of the world.

64
See where the lofty banner is streaming free
blazoning the keys of Peter and his crown;
here good Camillus leads his company.
Seven thousand mail-bright foot troops march as one.
Heaven chose him for the task, and glad was he
thus to revive his nation's old renown
and show our Latin manhood lacking in
nothing—or lacking only discipline.

65
Now all the troops had passed in smart array
and military pomp, with this the last,
when Godfrey called his generals away
and to them made his thinking manifest.
"Soon as the east shows signs of the new day
I want the army to decamp, and fast,
so that we may, as far as in us lies,
come to the holy city by surprise.

66
"Make your men ready then for our advance
and for the battle and victory once more."
Such fiery words from a man so calm and wise
stirred every man with valor to the core.
The force was eager for the rays of dawn
and in impatience spent the night before,
but for all that the far-seeing Bouillon
worried—though in his heart he kept it down.

67
For he had been delivered certain news
that Egypt's ruler was now on his way
to Gaza, a fine fortress he could use
to front against the dukes in Syria;
nor could he think that a man of such bold use
would now ease back and trifle time away,
but expecting him to be bitter foe,
he spoke to Henry, his trusty courier, so:

68
"With a light sail I want you to cross the sea
swift as an arrow shot to the land of Greece.
There has arrived—as my informant writes,
and I know I can rely on what he sees—
a royal youth, invincible of soul,
who wants to join us with his troops. He is
Prince of the Danes; the men in his command
dwell where the pole is zenith to the land.

69
"But maybe that liar the Greek emperor
will ply him with his usual subtle arts
to turn him back or swerve his bold career
far from our army, into distant parts.
You, my herald, my faithful counselor,
dispose him in my name to the best course
for him and us—urge him to come away!
His honor should not tolerate delay.

70
"Do not return with him, though. Stay in Greece
to procure reinforcements from the king,
which he has promised to us more than once,
by treaty an obligatory thing."
Instructed thus, as soon as he received
the letters and the greetings he must bring,
making all possible haste he took his leave
and Godfrey gave his worries a reprieve.

71
Next morning, as the gleaming gates were thrown
open unto the sun in the orient,
was heard the sound of trumpets and of drums
urging the men to march with bold intent.
Thunder is not more welcome in summer heat,
bringing men hope of showers heaven-sent,
than to the fierce high-mettled men was dear
the proud roll of the instruments of war.

72
At once each warrior, pierced with great desire,
clothes all his limbs in their accustomed armor,
and at once reporting to his squadron's head
presents in perfect military manner.
And the full host now gathered in formation
sets streaming to the wind each army's banner,
and in the grand imperial flag lets fly
the Cross unfurled triumphant to the sky.

73
Straightaway the sun, which from the fields of heaven
was ever advancing higher in the skies,
struck flames and flashes from their armor, so
glittering and brilliant as to blind the eyes.
The air about them seemed to kindle and spark,
dazzling as if in one terrific blaze;
fierce neighings made a concord with the sound
of clashing steel, deafening the lands around.

74
Godfrey, who wished to keep his army safe
from enemies in ambush, sent to scout
many light-armored knights riding ahead
to reconnoiter all the land about.
He also sent the demolition squad,
the pioneers, to smooth the journey out:
to plane the rougher ground and fill the rut,
and open all the passages choked shut.

75
No army mustered by the pagan foe,
no fortress wall engirt with deepest trench,
no racing river or mountain capped with snow,
no woods can halt their ever advancing march.
So too at times the king of rivers, Po,
beyond all moderation swells so large
he sweeps his banks and in destruction flows—
a flood so great that nothing dare oppose.

76
Only the king of Tripoli with his riches,
weapons and troops and well-watched gates shut tight,
might have been able to slow the marshaled French,
but he dared not provoke them to a fight.
Rather appeased them with his greetings, presents,
and welcomed them into his realm outright,
accepting as the terms of a cease-fire
whatever the good Godfrey should desire.

77
Here from the lofty mountain of Sehir,
which from the east juts high above the town,
a crowd of men and women, young and old
and faithful all, into the plain came down,
carrying gifts to the Christian conqueror,
talking with him, or glad to gaze upon
his brightly armored troops from far and wide.
In them would Godfrey find a trusted guide.

78
By a straight route the captain leads his host,
always advancing by the ocean waves,
for well he understands that near the coast
the armada of the Christian allies shaves,
to make sure their munitions are well stocked
and they have all the food an army craves:
for him the Grecian isles have cut the wheat,
Schios has crushed the grape, and so has Crete.

79
The nearby ocean sighs under the freight
of the tall galleys and the lighter pines,
so thick with ships it opens no safe route
through the Mediterranean for the Saracens,
for with the fleets Saints George and Mark sent out
from Genoa and Venice in defense,
Holland and England and France have put to sea
along with ships from fertile Sicily.

80
This various navy, which is all made one,
hawsered together by one strong desire,
is laden with provisions from all ports
of everything that ground troops would require.
The army, finding the path before them free
of enemy soldiers, and all passes clear,
march onward with the greatest speed to be
where Christ endured his mortal agony.

81
Ahead of them runs fame, the post express
of rumors that may tell the truth or lie,
saying, the conqueror's army is amassed
in one great thrust, no hosts to slow their way;
telling the squads they mustered, and their status,
the names of the boldest, and their bravery,
their haughty boasts—and with a fearful front
threatens the pirates of the holy mount.

82
Ill expectation is perhaps much worse
than present ills appear. At every chance
shift in the winds of rumor, all men's ears
prick, and their very thoughts hang in suspense.
So through the sorrowing city and the fields
there runs a whispered fear, confused in sense;
but the old king, with danger near, designed
accursed measures in his wavering mind.

83
His name is Aladine, and since his reign
is new, his worries are continual;
a cruel man, but his ferocious vein
with mellowing age had grown less terrible.
When he heard of the Latin army's plan
to lay his towers low and scale the wall,
he joined new doubts to his old trepidation,
of both his foes and his own population.

84
For there were dwelling in one town a mingled
people of faiths irreconcilable:
the lesser and weaker part believed in Christ,
in Mohammed, the greater and more formidable.
But when the king had annexed Sion and
searched for a way to make his seat more stable,
the public debt of his pagans he relaxes
while burdening the poor Christians under taxes.

85
Those thoughts revived in him the innate beast
which lay for years in dull suspense, and drowsed,
so stinging, pricking, goading it that now
more than ever before his thirst for blood is roused.
In summer the serpent is fierce again who slept
so harmless when the winter held him housed;
so the tamed and captive lion, vexed, harassed,
resumes the native fury in his breast.

86
"I notice in this mob of infidels,"
he said, "the certain signs of some new glee.
They alone trust to gain by all our ills;
they smile upon the common misery.
And now they're hatching plots among themselves
on how to kill their king, or, it may be,
how to betray the gates, which they intend
to open to my enemy and their friend.

87
"But no—I shall prevent their wicked plans,
venting my anger to the full instead.
Kill them, for a harsh lesson! Sluice the child
even at the mother's breast where it has fed,
then burn their homes and temples all together
and let these be the pyres they owe their dead!
And of their priests I'll make—amid such prayers—
a sacrifice above that tomb of theirs."

88
So the king thought to himself, iniquitous,
but never put in force the plans he drew;
yet if those guiltless folk have gained a truce
give cowardice, not clemency, its due.
For if one worry whips him to let loose
his cruelty, another checks him too:
fear to cut off all compromise, and spur
too hard the army of the conqueror.

89
So the sly traitor tempers his insane
wrath—yet must seek release for it somewhere.
He levels the farmers' hovels to the plain
and gives their harvest to the prey of fire,
so that no wholesome country would remain
for the Frank to feed his troops, no house entire,
and he spoils the pure waves of stream and spring,
that all who drink may die of poisoning.

Provident in his evil, he meanwhile
does not forget to make his city sure:
already on three sides impregnable,
only the north was somewhat insecure.
But with high ramparts he shored up that wall
soon as he heard the whispering news of war,
and gathered a great host—nor did he tarry—
composed of citizen and mercenary.

ꙮ Canto Two

1
As tyrant Aladine began to arm,
one day, alone, Ismen the mage came forth,
Ismen, who could draw out of the sealed tomb
the corpse beneath, and give it sense and breath,
Ismen, whose muttering incantations make
old Pluto tremble in his realm of death,
employing demons in his wicked rites,
binding and loosing them, as acolytes.

2
He adores Mohammed, as once he adored Christ,
but cannot now abandon the first way,
so often to profane and evil use
confounds the two religions ignorantly.
Now from his cave far from the common herd,
his den for exercise of magic, he
comes to his lord in time of public care,
to a perfidious king, worse counselor.

3
"My lord," he said, "the host is on the move,
the conquerors are hastening along.
But let us do what we are called to do;
both earth and heaven will assist the strong.
You have provided for the far-off threat,
fulfilled the roles which to a king belong.
If others too discharge their duties so,
this land will prove a graveyard for your foe.

4
"For me, I come to join the fight you wage,
to share the risk and toil, assisting you:
I vow to give all of my long years' sage
counsel, with all that magic arts can do.
The angels banished by the Almighty's rage
shall do our errands—my obedient crew.
But when I would begin my chants, and how,
let me discover to your lordship now.

5
"Within the Christian temple lies a shrine
hidden beneath the earth, and there that crowd
adore the face of Her they call divine,
the mother of their born and buried God.
Torches before the icon ever shine;
she is enveloped in a slender shroud.
There in a long row hang the offered prayers
brought by her all-believing worshipers.

6
"Out of the church I want this effigy
stolen, and then conveyed by your own arm
and set within the confines of your mosque.
I meanwhile will devise so strong a charm
that so long as she is guarded here, by fate
she will be forced to guard these gates from harm.
Within sure walls, by this mysterious spell,
your power will be unassailable."

7
So the king was persuaded—impatiently
flew in his fury to the house of God,
compelled the deacons and irreverently
stole the chaste icon from its just abode,
bringing it to that church of heresy
where heaven is provoked by foolish fraud.
In so profane a place Her icon lies—
and the mage begins to mutter his blasphemies.

8
But when the heavens gleamed with the new dawn,
the watchman in that house of the unclean
suddenly noticed that the image was gone;
he searched, but it was nowhere to be seen.
At once he informed the king, who turned upon
him and his news with anger quick and keen.
"This is a theft some Christian would commit,"
the king supposes, "and is hiding it."

9
It was the stealthy work of a faithful hand,
or heaven interposed its potent will,
disdaining that the image of its queen
be smuggled somewhere so contemptible.
The legend cannot show if it was due
to human art, or to a miracle.
Let human piety and zeal give way
to faith in heaven—for that is piety.

10

The king then turned the city inside out
with a rash search of every church and house,
laying a bounty on the thief and goods
but promising harsh punishment for those
who keep them hidden. Ismen, to spy the truth,
without success plies all the art he knows;
for heaven—if it was heaven, or someone else—
hides it from him in spite of all his spells.

11

But when the cruel king could not find out
the hidden Christian thief (as he was styled),
he burned in wrath, he hated the whole rout,
and gave free rein to a fury vast and wild.
Come what may, vengeance is all he cares about,
forgotten are all thoughts of being mild!
"The thief shall die—for my rage shall not fall—
die unknown in the slaughter of them all.

12

"If but the culprit does not slip my hands
what matter if the just and innocent die?
But what am I saying, 'just'? In all their bands
there never yet was one man friend to me!
Clean of this new crime? Still the old crime stands!
Let that suffice for this new penalty!
At them, my faithful, at them with a will!
Take up your swords and torches! Burn and kill!"

13

So he whipped up the mob. News of this spread
throughout the Christian quarter instantly,
but they sat stunned; none had the heart to take
arms in defense, or to attempt to flee;
so ambushed by the fear of a present death
none of them even tried excuse or plea.
But for these people, frightened, undirected,
salvation came from whence they least expected.

14

A virgin dwelt among them, of an age
now ripe for marrying; sublime and noble were
her thoughts, sublime her beauty, honor's stage—
for beauty otherwise she did not care.
She hides her worth within the narrow cage
of a small house, so far the worthier,
and from the praise and amorous looks of men
she steals away, unadorned and alone.

15
And yet no guard could ever quite conceal it,
that loveliness so worthy to admire,
nor, Love, do you consent—for you reveal it
to a young man of passionate desire.
Love, now you are blind, now an Argus of hundred eyes,
now hooded, and now your glance turns everywhere.
Although a thousand sentinels are placed
you lead his glances into haunts most chaste.

16
Sophronia she was called, Olindo he,
both of one city and one faith in God.
As is her beauty, so his modesty:
he yearns much, hopes little, asks nothing. He cannot
reveal his longing, or cease to love; and she
scorns him, or does not see, or takes no note.
Thus the poor lover's service, unregarded,
has long been overlooked and unrewarded.

17
Now all have heard the news—carnage is near,
the grief to which the Christians are resigned.
But the girl is as noble as she is chaste:
a plan to save her people comes to mind.
Bravery spurs it; maiden decency
and shame rebel—it is not of their kind;
bravery wins—or agrees to terms, and thus
strength is made modest; modesty, valorous.

18
The maiden, all alone, passed through the crowd.
Her beauty she did not cover or expose.
Keeping her eyes to herself, and straitly veiled,
with grace and shy gentility she goes.
If chance or art has touched her lovely face,
if she neglects or adorns herself, who knows—
of nature, of Love, and of all the heavens impart,
her artlessness is but the noblest art.

19
Unlooking but looked on by everyone,
the brave girl came in presence of the king
who stared at her in anger; nonetheless
she stood her ground, fearless, unfaltering.
"My lord, I come—and I beg, suspend your wrath,
rein in your men at once," she said; "I bring
what you would know—I bring as prisoner
the great offender you are searching for."

20
Stunned by her honest courage, by the flash
of her high loveliness and sanctity,
the king—as if confounded, at a loss—
bridled his scorn and softened his fierce eye.
He would have grown her lover on the spot
had he been less severe of soul, or she
of look; but stubborn beauty never warms
the stubborn heart: Love must be lured by charms.

21
It was amazement, fancy, or desire,
not love, which stirred in the king's low-born soul.
"Tell the whole truth," he said, "for see, I swear
your Christians are no longer liable."
She answered, "By this hand the work was done;
here in your sight now stands the criminal.
I stole the sacred image, I am she
you wish to find. Sir, you must punish me."

22
She gave her proud head for her people's sake,
gathering in herself the fate of all.
Greathearted lie! What truth could ever make
a finer claim to be so beautiful!
The tyrant had to pause, was not so quick
to hurtle into rage as usual,
and said, "I want you then to tell me who
advised you in it, and assisted you."

23
"I did not wish to share the slightest part
of my glory," she replied, "with anyone.
I was the only one who knew of it,
one counselor, one executor alone."
"Therefore on you alone," the king shot back,
"the brunt of my avengement shall come down."
"Fair enough," she returned. "I am content,
alone in honor and in punishment."

24
The tyrant's scorn began to surge once more.
"Where," he demanded, "is its hiding place?"
"I did not hide," she said, "I burned it, for
burning it seemed to me a work of praise.
The hands of misbelievers should no more
use it for profanation and disgrace.
Sir, you want the robbed and the robber: this you see,
that, you will not find in eternity.

25
"And yet that was no theft, I did not steal—
to take back what was stolen is but right."
When he heard this the king quivered with rage,
hissed, and let slip the bridle of his spite.
Gentle looks, lofty spirit, and pure heart,
hope no more to find pardon, for too slight
a shield is womanly grace for Love to fling
against the crude resentment of the king.

26
The lovely girl is seized. For cruelty
he condemns her to burning at the stake.
They tear away her veil and her modest cloak,
bind hard her tender hands behind the back.
She says nothing, is not frightened; but her brave
heart is yet troubled, she cannot help but shake—
and the lovely rose of her face is lost in white
which is not pallor, but a glowing light.

27
Word of the great event is spread; already
the crowds have gathered to watch. Olindo came
running, afraid that it might be his lady—
only the fact was certain, not her name.
But when he sees the gentle prisoner now
not merely accused but sentenced to the flame,
with the officers intent and pitiless
headlong he pushed his way through the thick press

28
and cried, "She's not, she's not the thief, O king!
She's boasting of it out of foolishness!
She couldn't have thought, or dared, or done the thing,
a girl alone and inexperienced!
How could she trick the guards? How could she bring
the goddess's holy image from its place?
Let's hear! I was the thief, sir, you shall learn—"
So much he loved, yet unloved in return!

29
Continued he, "On that side there, at night,
where your towering mosque takes in the light of day,
I scaled the wall, I scrambled through a tight
window—where no man goes, I felt my way.
The honor is mine, the death is mine by right—
she shall not take my punishment away!
Mine are those chains, for me the flames mount higher,
for me the execution and the pyre."

30
Sophronia raised her eyes and looked upon
her lover, full of human sympathy.
"What did you hope to do, poor innocent man?
What plan impelled you? what insanity?
Do you think I am not brave enough alone
to bear what one man's wrath can do to me?
I too have a heart, confident it can die
but once. It does not ask for company."

31
So she spoke to the one who loved her, but
from his firm words and thoughts he would not part—
what a stupendous spectacle, to see
Love dueling with Virtue great of heart!
A fight for which the champion seizes death
as his reward, and life's the loser's part!
But the more persistent their self-accusation
the more the king is stung with irritation.

32
He felt that he was left of small account—
scorning the punishment, they scorned him too.
Said he, "Let both be taken at their word.
Both win! Give both the laurels they are due!"
Ready and waiting to clap the lad in irons,
the executioners take their tyrant's cue
and back to back they bind both to one post.
To each the sight of the other's face is lost.

33
The kindling is stacked about them for the fire,
and the bellows already are fanning the flame high,
when the lad spoke to her now one with him
and broke his sorrows to her in this cry:
"Are these the bonds I hoped for, then, to couple
our lives together with a lasting tie?
Is this the fire I trusted would inflame
the hearts of two whose love might burn the same?

34
"Love promised other bonds, a different fire;
it is an evil fate we bow beneath.
Too far apart she held us once before,
too far!—and now she marries us in death.
And yet though it seems strange, I ask no more
than that, if you must die, I share this hearth,
though not your bed. Your fate I rue, my bride,
not mine, so long as I die at your side.

35
"How sweet and fortunate all my torments now!
How I would feel myself perfectly blest
if I could only turn, and let my soul
breathe its last on your lips; then breast to breast
together with me you might, that moment, send
into me your last sighs before we rest."
So he says, weeping, and the girl replies
tenderly, with these words of good advice:

36
"My friend, the time requires far different thoughts,
there is a far more urgent cause to moan.
It is time to think of your sins and call to mind
the great reward God promises His own.
Suffer in His Name, and the pains will be sweet;
aspire with gladness to the heavenly crown.
Look at the sky, how lovely! See the sun,
how it seems to console and call us on."

37
Here even the crowd of pagans raised a cry,
but quietly and low the Christians wept.
A something, who can say what, unusual, soft,
into the hard heart of their ruler crept—
he felt it coming, spurned it, would not bend,
averted his eyes and drew back. All except
you, Sophronia, share in the common pain.
They weep for you, but you do not complain.

38
Their lives hang in the balance—but there, see,
a proud and noble-countenanced warrior,
for so he seems; his dress and weaponry
show he has come a pilgrim from afar.
A tigress is his helmet's heraldry,
drawing the gaze of all, for so at war
Clorinda is known to sport that famous sight.
So they believe it is she, and they are right.

39
She from her greenest years had scorned the ways
of women, and the skills which these demand.
To the work of Arachne, the spindle and the loom,
she never deigned to apply her proud hand;
she fled the silken dress and the shut-up room
for in the field too chastity can stand.
Pride is her armor. She sets her face to learn
sternness—and yet it is attractive, stern.

40
A little girl of tender arm, she hurled
the sword and spear and bridled the swift horse;
hardened her muscles in the wrestler's ring
and raced to lend them stamina and force;
then in the mountains or through the rugged woods
she followed bears and lions in their course,
then followed the wars. In both, all are beguiled:
wild beasts think her a man, men think her wild.

41
She had come from the land of Persia, for
she would resist Christ's hosts as best she could,
though she had often scattered their limbs before,
leaving the shores and waters steeped in blood.
And now at her arrival she saw where
the place prepared for execution stood.
Curious to watch and craving to know the crime,
she spurs on to the scene in little time;

42
the crowds yield; there are the two, bound together.
She halts to look upon them from close by,
wonders, that one of them moans while the other is silent,
and the weaker sex shows more tenacity;
sees the one weep as a man weighed down with sorrow,
not pain—or if pain, not his, while silently
the woman looks to heaven with such fixed eyes
she seems to leave this world before she dies.

43
Clorinda's heart grew tender at this sight,
grieved with them, and a tear welled in her eye,
yet felt more pain for the woman who felt none,
moved by her silence more than by his cry.
Without more hesitation then she turned
and asked a gray-haired gentleman standing by,
"Oh tell me, who are these people? Have they come
by chance or judgment to this martyrdom?"

44
Thus she; and in a brief reply he gave
a full recounting of the incident.
Hearing it in astonishment at once
she saw that both were fully innocent.
As far as her requests—or arms—were able,
already she has determined to prevent
their death, runs to the flames and puts them out,
and cries to all the officers about,

45
"None of you be so bold to take one step
farther along this task of cruelty
until I speak to the king; and he will not
blame you for tardiness—I guarantee."
The sergeants, struck by her countenance, obeyed—
struck by her greatness and nobility.
Toward the palace she rides without delay
but finds the king approaching on the way.

46
"I am Clorinda; you have heard my name
mentioned, perhaps," she says. "Sire, I have run
to join my strength with yours at the defense
of your reign and the faith we share as one.
I am ready—try me—for any task; the humble
I do not scorn, the lofty I do not shun.
Assign me the open field, put me to use
behind closed walls. No work shall I refuse."

47
At that the king replied, "What land so far
cut off from Asia, O maiden of renown,
or so untouched by the sun's bright career
that there your fame and honor have not flown?
I gain assurance and allay my fear
now that your sword is wedded with my own.
Though a whole host should come to rescue me,
I would not hope with greater certainty.

48
"I think, yes I do think Godfrey has dallied
too long! As for the duties you demand,
I say that nothing else is worthy of you
but enterprises difficult and grand.
Over our soldiers I grant you the rule,
they shall observe as law what you command."
So the king; Clorinda thanks him for his praise
with perfect courtesy, and then she says,

49
"It surely must appear a novelty
to ask for a reward so out of turn,
but I shall trust your liberality:
give me those two, for what my deeds will earn.
Yet if their guilt admits uncertainty,
a ruthless doom has sentenced them to burn.
But that aside, and the clear evidence
whereby I might conclude their innocence,

50
"I'll only say, it's common wisdom here
that he who stole the image must be Christian.
I disagree—and am not satisfied
without some strong support for my conviction.
It was irreverence against our laws
to do what was advised by the magician;
within our mosques no idols are allowed,
much less the idols of another god.

51
"I prefer that the wonder be imputed
to Mohammed above, and for this cause,
to show his temples must not be polluted
by any strange religion and its laws.
Let Ismen do his worst with all his chanting,
whose spells and hexes are the sword he draws.
With mere steel let us cavaliers fight on;
that is our magic. Trust in it alone."

52
This said, she was silent. Though it was hard for mercy
to make the wrath of the king's heart subside,
still, he wanted to please; her reasons were persuasive,
and prayers, from her, commanding. He replied,
"Let them have life and liberty—to such
an intercessor nothing is denied.
They are yours, be it justice or clemency.
Guilty or innoçent, I set them free."

53
And so they were unbound. For young Olindo
things fell out surely for the happiest,
as he was able to show his love in action
and waken love within her generous breast.
He left the stake, not merely to be loved,
but to enjoy sweet marriage ever blessed.
He would share her death, and now that they have life
she will not scorn to spend it as his wife.

54
But the king, wary of dangers that might grow
if such joint virtue should too clearly shine,
gave orders that the two be forced to go
settle beyond the bounds of Palestine.
He carries out his cruel counsel, to
banish some of the faithful, or confine;
they leave their children with a heavy heart
and from their fathers and sweet wives depart.

55
A harsh divorce! He drives off only those
whose bodies are robust and spirits bold,
keeping with him in pledge, as hostages,
the gentler sex, the children, and the old.
Many men wandered aimless; others, in whom
scorn could do more than fear could do, rebelled,
and joined their forces with the Christian host
the day Emmaus' city gates were crossed.

56
Emmaus is a little town which lies
near royal Jerusalem, along the way;
a man who starts at dawn and takes his ease
arrives there by the middle of the day.
O how sweet is this news to the French ears!
O how it spurs their yearning not to stay!
But as the sun was now in its descent,
here the captain ordered the army to pitch tent,

57
so the tents were pitched; and the mild light of the sun
was setting just above the western sea
when two great noblemen were seen approaching
in strange attire and foreign company.
Each aspect of their bearing showed they came
to speak to the Christian captain peaceably.
Messages from the Egyptian king they bear,
and squires and grooms attend them everywhere.

58
The one, Alete: who rose from mean estate
among the foulest commoners apt for vice,
scaling the highest honors of the state
by an easy tongue well filed for flatteries,
by his fickle spirit prompt to fabricate,
by his soft compliance and his cunning lies.
Poet of slanders dressed in such strange ways,
he most accuses when he seems to praise.

59
The other was Argante the Circassian,
who came a stranger to the royal court,
was made an imperial satrap, enrolled among
the highest of the military sort:
impatient and inexorable and fierce,
tireless in fighting, invincible—in short,
despiser of every God, he puts his trust
in might—his sword determines what is just.

60
These asked for audience, and they were admitted
to come before the famous Godfrey; there
they found him sitting among his fellow chieftains
in a plain coat and on a humble chair,
and yet true valor is its own decoration,
shines of itself, and needs no special care.
Argante makes him a slight bow, as one
who is too great to notice anyone,

61
but Alete lays his right hand on his breast,
bends head and eyes to the ground in prostration,
lavishing honor fully manifest,
demanded by the customs of his nation.
Then he began, and from his lips expressed
sweeter-than-honey rivers of oration,
in a tongue which the French had often heard
in Syria, so they understood each word:

62
"You alone of such dignity that these
most famous heroes deign to follow you—
who know that for the lands and palms they seize
to your sure counsel is the credit due—
not resting beside the pillars of Hercules,
your great name now resounds among us too;
and every region of our nation reads
brilliant reports of all your valorous deeds.

63
"There is no man who will not hear these news
as one hears tell of wonders beyond measure,
but by the king my master they are heard
not only with astonishment, but pleasure,
and he loves to tell them over again sometimes—
what others fear and envy, is his treasure—
if not in faith, in love my king desires
union with you, whose valor he admires.

64
"Spurred on therefore by such a handsome cause,
friendship with you and peace is his request,
and if religion cannot grant the means
let virtue be the bond in which you rest.
But as he's heard that to dethrone his friend
is now the task to which you are addressed,
he wishes, before more harm should ensue,
that we should open all his thoughts to you.

65

"Those are as follows. If you rest content
with what you have done already in your campaign,
and do not harass Judea or any parts
protected by the favor of his reign,
he vows in turn to guarantee your state
not firmly founded. If you two remain
as one, the Turk will never dare attack
nor Persia hope to win her kingdoms back.

66

"My lord, you've done great things in a short time,
even for the ages unforgettable,
armies defeated, cities sacked and razed,
obstacles overcome on foreign soil,
so that lands far and near are stunned and dazed,
bewildered by the greatness of it all.
Thus, even could you add another reign,
your hopes to get new glory would be vain.

67

"You are now at the peak of your ascent.
Henceforth you should shy away from the chance of war,
for if you win, your state gains in extent,
true, but your glory can advance no more,
while if you lose, you lose that government
and all the honor that was yours before.
Only a fool would risk the great and sure
to win the little and the insecure.

68

"But maybe one who hates to see you hold
what you have conquered counsels you awry,
or your always having triumphed in the field,
or that natural desire which boils most high
in the enkindled passions of the bold,
to press whole nations into slavery,
these things, perhaps, cause you to flee peace more
than other men would shun the risk of war.

69

"They urge you on to follow still the road
opened to you so broad and free by fate,
and never to lay down that famous sword
whose strength makes every triumph past debate,
until Mohammed's faith must fall and fade
and you have left all Asia desolate—
things sweet to listen to, but pleasant lies
which can produce the worst calamities.

70
"But if high spirits do not hoodman-blind
your eyes, or leave your light of reason blurry,
wherever you take your battle you will find
less cause for hope and confidence, than worry:
fortune on earth has no sure place assigned
but by turns makes us satisfied or sorry,
and for impetuous flights that soar too high
a fall as fast and headlong waits nearby.

71
"If Egypt moves against you with her stock
of gold, and arms, and generals versed in war,
if the Persians, the Turks, and the prince of Antioch
should all engage hostilities once more,
say, where would you flee, what could you use to check
the furious forces they would have in store?
Relying on holy treaties, would you seek
assistance from your friend the scoundrel Greek?

72
"Who does not understand Greek promises?
One instance shows you how they will betray,
rather a thousand—for a thousand snares
that grasping, faithless folk set in your way.
The one who has begrudged each step of yours
will suddenly risk his life for you today?
He blocked your sailing on the common flood
but now will make a gift of his own blood?

73
"Perhaps you rest all of your hope on these
strong squadrons who surround you where you sit,
trusting again to overcome with ease
in one, those hosts you vanquished separate,
although your troops have dwindled from disease
and loss in battle (you must notice it),
and although a new hostile army lurks,
Egypt's, to join the Persians and the Turks.

74
"But if you think it is ordained by fate
that you cannot be conquered by the sword,
fine, grant it, and, as for the will of heaven,
let its decrees be taken at your word.
Hunger will do instead—against this ill,
by God, what refuge can there be? What ward?
Brandish the steel against *her!* Shake the spear!
Dream for yourself another triumph there!

75
"For the inhabitants nearby have showed
great foresight, burning every field about,
and many days before your coming stowed
within their walls and granaries all their fruit.
You whose bold march till now has not been slowed
would feed your men and horses—but with what?
You say, 'Our laden fleet will soon arrive.'
On the winds lean your chances to survive?

76
"Perhaps your fortune can command the wind,
to hold it bound or loose, at your desire?
The sea hears you alone, bows to your will,
though deaf to cries and prayers as men expire?
And cannot Egypt, leagued with the Turks and Persians,
marshaling all the forces we require,
muster up an armada just as great
to unite in attack against your fleet?

77
"My lord, you need a double triumph to
carry the honor of this enterprise.
One loss alone can bring deep shame to you,
and cause you even greater injuries:
For if we rout your fleet, what must ensue
but mass starvation—all your army dies,
while if to war and hunger here you fall
a naval triumph cannot help at all.

78
"Since this is so, then, if you still refuse
the king of Egypt's bid of truce and peace—
let the truth be spoken plainly—all your virtues
will be outmatched by lack of common sense.
Let it be heaven's will, if your thought pursues
war, that your counsels make an about-face;
give war-weary Asia a chance to breathe free
while you enjoy the fruits of victory.

79
"And you who share with him the risk, the labor,
you partners in the glory he has won,
do not be fooled; to instigate new wars
do not let fortune's favor urge you on.
But as a pilot at the wished-for port
turns from the sea's deceit and brings her in,
so should you furl your spread sails and remain
at harbor. Do not trust the sea again."

80
Alete spoke no more. His speech was met
by a low grumbling among the valiant men,
who showed quite clearly what they thought of it
with gestures of annoyance and disdain.
Three or four times the captain looked about
to read the faces of his warriors, then
fixed his eyes on the eyes of him who stayed
for his response. "Ambassador," he said,

81
"you have proposed to us with the sweetest grace
now a friendly invitation, now a threat.
If our deeds move your king to love and praise,
that is his kindness, and I welcome it.
But to those portions of your speech which place
all pagandom at war against our host,
I shall respond just as I always do—
frank sentiments in simple words and few.

82
"Know, then, we have endured so much till now
at sea, on land, in weather fair and foul,
only that we might open up the way
that leads us to this venerable wall,
winning God's favor and grace, to set it free
from a subjection so intolerable.
It is no burden, for such a worthy gain,
to risk our worldly honor and life and reign,

83
"for what drove us on to the task and led our way
was never some high-reaching ravenous
lust (let the Father of heaven clear from our souls
that plague, if it should nest in any of us,
and keep that sweetness from infecting him
which pleases when it is most venomous);
God's hand, which penetrates the hardest men
and gently takes away their hearts of stone,

84
"God's hand it was that led us to this place,
snatched us from each entanglement and danger,
laid mountains low and made the rivers dry,
relieved the heat of summer, the ice of winter;
that soothed the stormy billows of the sea
and held a careful rein upon the weather;
and thus we burnt the walls and breached the towers
and slew and scattered all our enemies' powers.

85

"Thence is our fire, and thence our hope is born,
and not from our own force so weary and weak,
not from the navy, not from the French arms,
not from the hosts provided by the Greek.
So long as He does not abandon us
there can be nothing we will want or seek.
The man who knows how God's hand guards and strikes
enjoys already all the aid he likes.

86

"But if our sins or His own hidden plan
deprive us of it, we will not complain.
Which one of us would be reluctant to
lie buried where the limbs of God have lain?
We will die, envying no living man;
we will die, but we shall not die in vain:
God shall avenge. At our lot, Asia shall
not smile, nor shall we need to mourn our fall.

87

"Yet you should not believe we fly from peace,
seeking out death and battles everywhere.
The friendship of your master pleases us,
joining with him would be no grave affair—
but you yourself know if Judea lies
under his rule, and so why should he care?
We wish that kingdom. Let him not deny it,
and let him rule his own in peace and quiet."

88

Such his reply, and with a stinging fury
it ran Argante's heart upon the stake.
Nor did he hide it, but with lip puffed out
he stationed himself before the chief, and spoke:
"Whoever does not want peace, let him have war!
There are many opportunities to take
when one wants strife! Reject our terms and prove
how lightly you esteem our offered love!"

89

Argante took his mantle by the edge,
tucking it round to make a sort of purse,
holding it out in front, resuming speech,
in sheer offense and disrespect far worse:
"You who think the doubtfulest tasks are nothing much,
I bring you peace or war, a truce, a curse—
the choice is yours. Make up your mind, be quick.
Whichever one best suits your wishes, pick."

90
His savage words and gesture roused them all
to cry for war, for war in unison,
not waiting to hear what answer would be given
by their magnanimous leader from Bouillon.
The brute unfurled his pouch, shook off his mantle.
"In mortal combat I shall take you on,"
he roared—with such impiety and hate
be seemed to batter open Janus' gate.

91
Argante seemed, in opening his cloak,
to draw out bestial Discord and mad Furor,
and in his horrifying eyes awoke
the great torch of Alecto and Megaera;
such was that giant once who would provoke
heaven when he built the battlement of error,
and in such posture watched his Babel raise
its menacing facade against the stars.

92
Godfrey retorted then, "Go back and tell
your king to come to battle, and make haste,
for we accept your challenge. If not, well!
let him stay by his Nile and wait for us."
Honoring them with presents that excel
the finest, Godfrey plays the gracious host:
a splendid helmet to Alete he
offers, from his Nicaean victory;

93
and a sword to Argante, hilt and knob
superbly studded with gold and precious stone,
whose handiwork, so skillful, seemed to rob
the praise that such rich stuff should claim alone.
When he had studied as a connoisseur
its carvings and embellishments and tone,
Argante said to Godfrey, "Soon you'll see
to what use I shall put your courtesy."

94
They took their leave, and the fiercer of the two
turned to his fellow, "Now we go our ways,
I to Jerusalem, back to Egypt you,
I with the moon and stars, you with the rays
of dawn. I am not needed where you go,
so long as you report what Godfrey says
to the king. I shall not write or make delay,
but wish to be at hand where weapons play."

95
And so Argante comes a messenger
and leaves a foe, by overhasty speeches
or by design, nor does he think or care
about the ancient rules of war he breaches.
Under the friendly silence of the stars,
without reply, he rides until he reaches
the lofty walls, not suffering any stay.
The Christians too were eager for the day.

96
The night seemed to envelop the whole world,
and all the winds and the waves were deep in rest;
the weary creatures who dwell in the wave-swept sea
or those who find the dark lake bottoms best,
those who lie hidden in the den or fold,
and the dappled birds, plunged in forgetfulness
under the awful silence of the night,
gave respite to their troubles, soothed the heart,

97
but neither loosening sleep nor rest so sweet
eased Godfrey or his army in the least,
so hungry were the faithful hosts to greet
the long-awaited morning in the east,
the morning like a lamp unto their feet
to lead them to their journey's goal at last.
Time after time into the dark they gaze
for any sign of the dawn's brightening rays.

☙ Canto Three

1

By now the news that Dawn is on her way
is borne a-stirring on the gentle air;
with roses culled from the garden of heaven she
has decked herself, wreathing her golden hair,
when the Christian camp, called early to take arms,
hums with a grave, deep harmony. The blare
of trumpets seconds their anticipation,
pealing out hope and joy in preparation.

2

The captain, like a prudent rider, both
heartens and guides their passions, gingerly,
for to shave Charybdis would be easier, swerving
close to that whirl of changeability,
or to rein the north wind ruffing the mountains' backs
and drowning ships in the bottom of the sea.
He sets the martial tempo they maintain:
they march fast, but they march with discipline.

3

Each man has wings to his feet, wings to his heart,
yet no one marks how quickly the miles fly.
But when the sunlight strikes the stubble fields
with rays now bright and rising in the sky,
behold, they see Jerusalem appear!
Behold, Jerusalem is drawing nigh!
And behold, a thousand voices now acclaim
as one the promised land—Jerusalem!

4

So the brave crew of an adventurer
sailing to search for some uncharted strand,
in dubious seas and under unknown stars,
attempts the lying waves and the treacherous wind;
if at long last they spy the far-off shores
they burst into cheers, they hail their mates, "There, land!"
Long was the voyage; now in one moment, done;
forgotten all the hardships undergone.

5
After that first glimpse and the joy it breathed
sweetly into the hearts of all who saw,
a profound sadness fell upon the men,
a sorrow tinged with reverent love and awe.
Upon the city where Christ chose to dwell
they hardly dared to look with lifted eye—
where He was laid to rest after His strife,
where He arose, and clothed His limbs with life.

6
Their voices low and solemn, their hushed words,
their broken sobs, and the lamenting sighs
of men who felt both joy and grief at once
made a low murmur through the air arise
and stir like troubled leaves in the deep woods
when through the tangle of branches the wind cries,
or like the moaning sea and its hoarse roar
as it batters the reef or pounds the rocky shore.

7
Bare are the feet of every soldier as
following their chiefs in penitence they tread
the highway to the city; gold-trimmed helms,
plumes, gaudy vizors, they take from the head
and with them let the habits of pride fall
that cloak the heart. Warm, reverent tears they shed,
yet as if tears could not fight their way clear,
each man rebukes himself for all to hear:

8
"Now, O Lord, on the earth which You left
dyed in a thousand rivers of Your blood,
I cannot make two living fountains spill,
recalling how You suffered for my good?
My heart of ice! Why do you not at last
melt into streams of tears? My heart so hard,
will you not yield your stoniness and break?
When will you weep, if not now for His sake?"

9
A sentinel who looked out over the fields
and all the hills from the city's lofty spire,
glanced down and saw the beaten dust arise
as if a mighty cloud marched through the air—
and the cloud burned and glinted as if full
to bursting into newborn streaks of fire;
he discerns at last the shine of steel, and then
distinguishes the horses and the men.

10
This man cries out, "How vast a cloud of dust
I see approaching—dust, that shines so bright!
Up, up, citizens, arm yourselves at once,
ascend the walls and be prepared to fight—
the enemy is here!" Then, louder yet,
"Every man hurry—the enemy is in sight,
take up your weapons, now! Look up and see
how dark a pall is spreading through the sky!"

11
The innocent children and the unarmed old
and the crowd of women quivering with fear,
who cannot thrust the sword or parry a blow,
flock to the pagan mosques in grief and prayer.
The rest, of sturdier limbs and hearts more bold,
have snatched whatever weapons they can bear
and some race to the gates, some to the wall,
while the king makes the rounds and sees to all.

12
He deals out his instructions, then withdraws
to a tower that rises high between two gates,
looking out over the hills and plains below,
close by, as duty now necessitates.
He orders that Erminia come with him,
the beautiful Erminia who waits
at Aladine's court, her Antioch forsaken,
the king her father slain, and the town taken.

13
Clorinda meanwhile turns against the French.
Many go with her, she at the head of all,
but Argante ready to support her move
waits in a secret exit in the wall.
She free of heart incites her followers with
her fearless countenance and brave speech: "We shall
begin this day aspiring, and build up
the firm foundation of all Asia's hope!"

14
While she addressed her troops, not far away
she caught sight of a French scavenging crew,
as usual sent ahead to gather prey
from farm and sheepfold, now returning to
camp with their stolen flocks. She leads the way
at them—the captain of that retinue
charges in turn, Gardo, a mighty man—
who cannot battle as Clorinda can.

15
At that fierce clash Gardo is pitched to the earth
before the eyes of the French and pagan troops—
the pagans break into shouts and take that first
fall as presaging triumph; but their hopes
proved vain. She closes hard upon the rest,
one right arm worth a hundred where she crops;
her fellow fighters follow along the road
planed by her blows and opened by her sword.

16
Soon she has seized the prey from the predators.
The French retreat, little by little, till
they reach a vantage to support their force,
regrouping on the brow of a steep hill.
Then as a whirlwind bursts its prison house
and sends its flame and lightning down to kill,
so the good Tancred, at Godfrey's sign, "Advance!"
deploys his troops and couches his great lance,

17
so great a lance and so unflinchingly handled,
so fierce and handsomely agile the young man,
it makes the king from up above conclude
the best can do no more than this lad can,
and he turned to the girl there at his side
just as the flutterings in her heart began,
"After so long you must know without fail
who the Christians are, under the arms and mail.

18
"Then who is he, who sits so well in the saddle,
ready to joust, whose look stirs up such fear?"
Instead of a response there came unto
her lips a sigh, unto her eyes a tear;
she stifled the tears, choked back her breath, yet not
so well but that some passion must appear,
for a tender purple tinged her brimming eyes,
and hoarse and partly broken were her sighs,

19
as she concealed under the cloak of hate
another passion. "That one from a band
of thousands I could single out; of late
he gave me cause. Too well I know his hand,
know how it left the fields and trenches filled
with the blood of the people of my land.
His wounds are cruel, striking to the heart—
herbs cannot cure them, nor can magic art.

20
"He is Prince Tancred. Oh, that I might have
that man my captive, and alive, not dead—
alive I want him for a sweet revenge
so my desires may yet be comforted!"
So she said, and the king who heard her rave
turned the truth wrong side out, and was misled.
But with her last words uttered, nonetheless
there came a sigh she could not quite suppress.

21
Clorinda goes at once to meet the assault
from Tancred, and she too couches her spear.
They slash each other's vizors, and the shafts
splinter and fly far, in part leaving her
naked—for, her helmet's laces sliced,
off it flies at one wondrous blow! And there
a maiden in the battlefield she stands,
her golden tresses scattered to the winds.

22
Her eyes glared—she flashed lightnings at her foe.
In anger, sweet—what would her laughter be!
What are you thinking, Tancred, staring so?
The face of the proud woman—don't you see?
That is the lovely face—your heart should know,
for there is her image graven—this is she
you burn for, she whom one day you saw cool
her brow beside the solitary pool.

23
He had not seen her crest or painted shield,
but now he stood as stone, stood thunderstruck;
she covered her bare head as best she could
and charged at him again—but he turned back.
He assails the others and flails his bloody sword
yet does not gain a truce from her attack,
for she pursues him threatening, "Turn!" and with
one sword's point challenges a double death.

24
He does not try to guard against her sword;
if stricken, he will not return the blow;
her beautiful eyes and cheeks are his sole regard,
whence Love draws taut his inescapable bow.
"The blows her right arm deals, though iron-clad,
may fall in vain," he thinks, "but never so
those of her beautiful uncovered face—
they pierce my heart, they never miss their place."

25
Resolves—past hope for pity—if he must die
he will no longer hide his love from her,
but show his weakness, kneeling tremblingly,
and have her know she strikes a prisoner.
So he cries out, "O you who show that I
am your sole foe among so many here,
let's turn aside a little from the battle
where you and I can test each other's mettle.

26
"So we shall see whether your valor is
equal to mine." She heard him, and accepted,
as if her shattered helmet were small loss
she strode on, while he followed, lost, dejected.
The amazon assumed her battle stance,
one of her blows already had connected,
when "Hold," he cried, "let's start our contest right
and settle on the terms by which we fight."

27
She stayed her hand, and in a moment he
lost all his fear, made bold by desperate love.
"Since you don't wish to make your peace with me,
the terms," he said, "are these. You must remove
my heart, my heart no more. It will agree
to die, if it displeases you alive.
Come, tear my heart out—it has long been yours.
Now is the time and I shall not refuse.

28
"See, I let drop my arms, I lay my chest
open—now take your chance to kill me, take it!
You want it easier still? I'll strip the rest—
tear off this mail, and you can kill me naked."
And bitterer complaints might yet have pressed
from his sad heart, but had no chance to break it,
for an untimely crowd got in the way,
pagans and his own men in a melee.

29
Now Palestinian gave way to Christian,
retreating whether by design or fear.
One of the men pursuing them, inhuman,
sees streaming in the wind the maiden's hair,
and from behind aims at her naked head
raising his hand to strike in mid-career,
when Tancred—who caught sight—gave a loud cry
and parried such a piece of villainy.

30
Yet the blow was not wholly thrust aside—
struck near the white neck of that lovely head,
a glancing wound; her golden hair was dyed
rose color, from the gentle drops she shed,
as gold beaded with rubies by the hand
of an illustrious jeweler blushes red.
The prince in rage now draws his saber back
and presses hard upon that wretch's track,

31
who darts away, with Tancred, his wrath blazing,
after him like an arrow through the air.
She pauses, wondering; looks at both of them
now far out of the field, nor does she care
to follow. But with her squadron she retreats,
and now they attack the French, and now repair,
now turn, and turn again; they flee, pursue,
and no one can quite tell what they will do.

32
As a bull in the amphitheater,
when at the harrying dogs he butts his horn,
they scamper free, but when he tries to veer
back to the eager chase the hounds return.
Clorinda holds her shield in back of her
to guard her head while fleeing—so the Moors learn
to do when they play "skirmishes," and shield
themselves from the ball hurlers in the field.

33
Now the walls of the city are close by
for those retreating and those giving chase,
when the pagans hurl out a hair-raising cry
and execute a sudden about-face,
wheeling in a wide turn, their strategy
to strike the rear, while from their hiding place
Argante sends his band down from the mount
to counterpunch the Christians at the front.

34
The fierce Circassian leaves his troops behind,
longing to be the first to land a blow,
and flattens his first victim to the ground,
the horse heaped belly-up and head below;
and before his lance flies shattered in the air
many will fall and with their fellow go;
then draws his sword, and where he joins the fight
he wounds, or batters down, or slays outright.

35
Clorinda, as Argante's rival, took
the life of strong Ardelio, one mature
but of unbowed old age, and buttressed with
two tall young sons. Still he was not secure;
Alcandro could not play the stalwart son—
of that a bitter injury made sure—
and Polyphernes who remained beside
fought all he could, or he too would have died.

36
But the prince Tancred, failing to catch that churl
who luckily rode the speedier horse for war,
looked back and saw that his all-daring men
had struck too boldly, and advanced too far,
saw them surrounded, and at once he flew,
tugging the reins and digging with the spur.
He is not alone to help: here come those squads
who race to fight against the strongest odds,

37
the men of Dudon, the Adventurers,
flower of heroes, the host's vigor and might.
Rinaldo, bravest and most dashing, rides
first—and no swifter is the lightning's flight.
His bearing, and his sign of the eagle in
the fields of heaven, Erminia knew by sight
and said to the marveling Aladine, "Behold!
This is the man who breaks and tames the bold.

38
"Though he is still a lad, the glory of
his sword enjoys few peers, or rather none;
if there were seven of him among our foes
all Syria would be captive, overrun—
subdued would be the lands of the farthest south
and the realms closest to the rising sun,
and even the Nile's far undiscovered springs
might bend the head under the yoke he brings.

39
"His name, Rinaldo. And the walls should fear
his right arm more than any siege machine.
Now turn your glance and let me show you here
the man whose blazonry is gold and green,
his name is Dudon, and he guides this band,
a band of fortune's soldiers. He has been
a princely warrior, tested in the field;
his age commands, his valor does not yield.

40
"See Gernando there, the king of Norway's brother,
the tall man who goes covered in dark brown;
for sheer pride the whole earth can boast no other;
his glory is bedimmed by that alone.
Those two who always stand by one another,
trimmed all in white on white, who fight as one,
are Edward and Gildippe—valorous of
arms, and renowned for their devoted love."

41
So she—but now they looked below and saw
slaughter already swelling worse and worse.
Rinaldo and Tancred have now broken through
the packed-thick circle of armed warriors,
and then the band conducted by Dudon
join them and hit the foe with bitter force:
Rinaldo decks Argante to the plain—
Argante himself can hardly rise again!

42
Perhaps he never would have risen at all
had not Rinaldo's horse just then been struck,
pinning his foot beneath it in the fall,
making him pause to get himself unstuck.
Meanwhile the pagans toward the city wall
flee, put to rout; their only bank and dike
Clorinda and Argante against the wrack
of inundating fury at their back.

43
They guard the rear, and the surge of hosts pursuing
is partly checked, or forced to surge again,
so that less danger meets the pagans fleeing
than met the first of their retreating men.
But Dudon, heart afire for triumph, pressing
hard on those pagans, hunts the proud Tigran,
jarring him with his horse, and with his blade
tumbling him to the earth without a head.

44
No help, that tempered mail of Algazzar,
nor that tough helmet of robust Corban;
Dudon's blows pierced the back and neck so far
they pierced the chest and face as those two ran.
And the souls of Amurat and Almansar
and Mamet were evicted by his hand
from the sweet body. Even the great Circassian,
in danger, gnashed his teeth for indignation.

45
And cannot take one step safe from his sword,
but halts, and sometimes turns, and yet gives ground,
till at last he wheels so suddenly upon him,
catching his side with such an end-around
that the steel plunges deep within. The blow
robs the French duke of life. Without a sound
he falls; his eyes, which he must fight to keep
open, are pressed by silence, iron sleep.

46
He opens them three times, seeking the sweet
sunlight, and bracing one arm tries to rise,
but falls three times, until a shadow cloaks
his vision, and he shuts his weary eyes.
His limbs relax and melt, drenched in cold sweat,
till finally they stiffen in death's vise.
Savage Argante does not mind the dead—
does not stand over him, but runs ahead,

47
and as he runs he turns to the French troops
and, without stopping, hurls this boast away:
"O cavaliers! This bloody sword's the same
your chief presented me just yesterday.
Let him know—he would gladly hear the news—
what fine use I have put it to today.
Why, it should warm his heart to hear you tell
how his fair present stood the test so well.

48
"Tell him that now a surer proof awaits,
for his own guts will feel this sword's effects!
And if he's in no hurry to attack
I'll come and find him when he least expects."
Infuriated by his brutal taunts
the Christians charge, but now the town protects
both him and his retreating soldiers, all
shut safe within the shelter of the wall.

49
Then the defenders from that wall began
to let so great a storm of stones hail down,
with quiverfuls of arrows for each man,
a limitless stock, no matter how many had flown,
that the French troops perforce had to hold back
while the Mohammedans all entered town.
By now Rinaldo had gotten his foot freed
that had been pinned under the fallen steed,

50
and hastened to exact a harsh revenge
for the barbaric murder of Dudon.
"What are you waiting for? What delay is this?"
he shouted in fierce pride among his own.
"Now that the lord is dead who guided us
shall we not race to vengeance? This poor stone
so easily breached will make us halt and wait
now, when our cause for anger is so great?

51
"Not if these bulwarks were of double steel,
or of impenetrable diamond rock,
could the gloating Argante hide within
from your great prowess, and withstand the shock—
then let us take these walls by storm!" He charged
before the others even as he spoke,
for rain of stones and arrows could not daunt
that man whose confidence was adamant.

52
He, tossing his great head, lifted his eyes
full flaming with so terrible a fire
that the defenders even within the walls
felt their hearts freeze with unaccustomed fear.
But while he heartens these and threatens those,
one intervenes to check his wild desire,
for Godfrey sends them orders by Siger,
for those grave counsels a curt messenger,

53
who in his name condemns such fiery haste,
imposing an immediate retreat.
"Turn back!" he said to them. "Contain your wrath.
Neither the moment nor the place is meet.
It is Godfrey who commands you." At these words
Rinaldo, who spurred others, pulled up short—
although he fumed and champed the bit inside
and clearly showed the scorn he could not hide.

54
The Christian band turned back, and in returning
were left in peace by all their enemies.
Nor was the body of Dudon deprived
its due last rites and full solemnities.
His true friends bore him on their pious arms,
cherished and honored burden, borne with ease.
Meanwhile Bouillon, from a high point, surveyed
defenses which both art and nature made.

55
Upon two mountains of unequal height
the town Jerusalem was situate;
a valley split the center of the site
and held the facing mountains separate.
On three sides the approach was difficult;
on the fourth side the way was clear and flat.
But this, the smooth way on the northern side,
a tower had more firmly fortified.

56
Within, the town has running springs and pools
and many places to conserve the rain;
without, no streams or fountains interrupt
the sterile stretches of the bare terrain,
nor even tall broad trees to shield against
the summer's arrows beating on the plain,
except six miles away, where dark woods loom
with dread and terror lurking in the gloom.

57
On the side of the city toward the dawn
the glad and noble river Jordan pours,
and to the west the Mediterranean
washes its waves upon the sandy shores.
To north, the land of the Samaritan
and Bethel's golden-calf idolaters,
but to the rainy south lay Bethlehem
that cradled the great Savior in her womb.

58
While Godfrey studied the lie of the land about,
the countryside, the walls, the city's site,
designing where to camp, and where their clout
might shatter the ramparts fastest in the fight,
Erminia saw and pointed the captain out
as she spoke to the tyrant from the height,
"That man is Godfrey, whose purple mantle is
but a sign of his native kingliness.

59
"For truly he was born to rule; he knows
the art of how to govern and command,
yet is no less a knight than general.
His is a double valor. In all that grand
army before your eyes I cannot show
a greater warrior or a wiser man.
In counsel only Raymond is his peer,
only Tancred and Rinaldo with the spear."

60
The pagan king replies, "I know him well,
for once I saw him at the court of France,
when I was an Egyptian diplomat;
in tournaments I saw him tilt the lance
and though his cheek was still smooth as a boy's
his youth endowed his every word and glance
and deed with promise that in future days
he would prove worthy of the highest praise—

61
"a promise, ah too true." And here he lowered
his troubled eyes; then raising them once more,
"Tell me," he asked, "who is that other man
standing in crimson by the conqueror?
How closely he resembles him—although
for stature Godfrey has the better score."
"Baldwin; that he is Godfrey's brother shows
clear by his looks, but more by what he does.

62
"Now look at him on Godfrey's other side
who stands as does a man giving advice.
Raymond's his name, whose hair is silvered now;
I praise him for his mind of keen device.
No French or Latin leader is so subtle
a weaver of military artifice.
He with the golden helmet further on
is the good William, the king of England's son.

63
"Guelph is with him, his rival in handsome deeds,
in his high rank and bloodlines of the best.
I recognize him well by those squared shoulders
and by that prominent and full-built chest.
And yet I cannot find among the troops—
though I am looking—him I most detest,
murderous Bohemond my enemy,
destroyer of my royal family."

64
By now the captain had surveyed the site
and came down to his troops. Useless to send
forces, he thought, to scale the city's height
on those three sides where the steep banks ascend;
so in the plain before the northern gate
he chose to raise his tents; then, to extend
his front beneath the so-called Angle Tower,
ordered the other chiefs to set their power

65
there. But a third of Jerusalem at most
within the compass of that field is bounded;
so broad the city stretches that he had
not men enough to keep the whole surrounded;
but all the ways by which their help might come
Godfrey attempts at least to keep confounded,
and stations troops at every crucial route
for entering the town or coming out.

66
He orders that the camp be ringed about
with ditches and deep trenches everywhere
to front against the citizens charging out
and guard against attackers from the rear.
But, these works all accomplished, Godfrey went
to look upon the body of his peer,
and came where, lifeless, the good Dudon lay,
girt by a crowd of tearful men to pay

67
their final debt of love, to dress with pomp
the height where their brave leader was to lie.
When Godfrey entered, the crowd lifted up
their voices in a more pathetic cry,
but with a countenance neither clear nor darkened
Bouillon restrained his grief, and silently
upon his comrade for some moments cast
his eyes and his sad thoughts, then said at last,

68
"We have no cause to weep for you. Although
you died on earth, you are reborn above,
and leave for us the traces of your glory
etched on this mortal robe you have removed.
In life you were a soldier, Christian, holy;
so too in death. Now feast your eyes full of
the God you hungered for, O happy soul;
your good works seize the crown, and win the goal.

69
"Live now in joy. It is not your mischance
which moves us to this sorrow, but our own.
For you took your courageous leave of us,
and now a worthy part of us is gone.
But if what common folk call death deprives us
of your help here on earth, you are the one
to intercede to bring us help from heaven,
for you are numbered there among the chosen.

70
"And as we watched you fighting for our good
with mortal arms, yourself of mortal state,
so now we hope, spirit divine, to see you
wielding those heavenly arms whose stroke is fate:
learn now to marshal all the prayers we send!
Assist us in our trials! We dedicate
ourselves to you, and shall fulfill our vows—
so I pronounce—triumphant at God's house."

71
Thus Godfrey; and already the dark night
had quenched the light of day, and lent redress
or truce, at least, to care and pain and weeping,
all trouble silent in forgetfulness.
But the chief knows, without good engineering
those walls will never be taken, and so, sleepless,
he plans, he thinks, where can the timber be—
and how to build the works most cunningly.

72
With the first sun he rose, desiring to
follow the funeral march himself. A tomb
for Dudon they had fashioned of sweet cypress;
at the foot of a hill his little room
close to their palisades. Above it waved
the lofty branches of a lone, high palm.
They placed him here; priests sang the last request,
that his soul might enjoy eternal rest.

73
Here and there in the branches they had hung
a captive's arms, a foe's insignia,
wrested by him in happier battle days
from conquered hosts of Persia and Syria.
They covered his great torso with his cuirass
and all the rest of a fighting man's regalia,
then had these words inscribed: "Here lies Dudon.
Honor the most exalted champion."

74
But when the chief had shed tears with the rest
upon this sacred work, again he thought
of duty; and a Syrian he could trust
to lead the way, and an armed escort, brought
his carpenters into the only woods,
tucked in a valley, a secluded spot.
They came for joists to build machines against
whose might the city would have no defense.

75
They urge each other to bring those trees to earth,
an outrage never done that place before.
From their keen axes fell the woody ash
and the palm sacred to the conqueror,
cherry and pine, and the funeral cypress tree,
the branching holm, and the tall beech and fir,
and the husband elm, to whom the vine is given:
she cleaves to him and rings her way toward heaven.

76
These men chop down the yews, those men the oaks
that had renewed their crowns a thousand years,
a thousand years stood fast against all shocks
and broke the winds and mastered their stiff force;
while others load the aromatic trunks
of elm and cedar on their groaning cars.
At the clash of steel and garbled shouts of men
abandoned is each lair and nest and den.

℘ Canto Four

1
While on their good work these are all intent
(they must soon use the engines they devise),
man's enemy, on man's destruction bent,
against the Christians turns his livid eyes.
Discovering that the soldiers are content,
our adversary for sheer fury gnaws
his lips, and vents his sufferings to the full,
bellowing and groaning like a wounded bull.

2
To bring Christ's flock to everlasting pain—
that is his cause. He ponders the design,
then (ghastly Senate) at the royal throne
commands that his subordinates convene,
as if it were light undertaking—fool!—
to battle against Providence divine,
to match himself in his oblivious pride
with the thundering wrath of the right arm of God.

3
The raucous temples of the underworld,
reverberating through the caves of hell,
causing the dark to quiver at the cry,
summon to the assembly all who dwell
in that eternal night. With such harsh roar
no thunderbolt from heaven ever fell,
nor have the winds that swell the womb of earth
with such terrific fury broken forth.

4
At once to the high gates come hastening all
the variegated gods of the abyss.
Ah, how bizarre and horrible their forms!
What terror and what death lurk in their eyes!
Some print the soil of hell with a beast's tracks,
marring the human face with locks that hiss,
coiling behind them an enormous tail
which they can reel out snapping like a flail.

5
Here you would see thousands of squalid harpies,
thousands of sphinx and centaurs and pale gorgons,
of all-devouring Scyllas groined with wolves,
thousands of snorting hydras, hissing pythons,
of chimaerae vomiting out their bitter flames,
of Polyphemuses and Geryons,
and all strange monsters never seen or known,
a rabble of discordances in one.

6
These prodigies proceed to left and right
to take their seats before their cruel king.
He, Pluto, lifts his gnarled and weighty staff
as he sits in the center of the ring;
from the sea juts no pinnacle so high;
to him, not Atlas nor the towering
Rock of Gibraltar is more than a small slope.
Such is the great horned front he raises up.

7
In his fierce glance a horrid majesty
made him more arrogant and terrible.
His eyes flared with a bleary poisonous light
like comets heralding disaster; all
his chin was thicketed with a great beard,
barbed and curled to the haired chest where it fell,
and like a chasm or all-engulfing void
his mouth hung open, filthy with black blood.

8
As the noxious smell and the thunder when Mount Aetna
belches its sulfurous and fiery flumes,
such are the black blasts from his tigerish maw,
such are the flames he breathes, such are the fumes.
The roar struck dumb the seven-headed hydra
and Cerberus held his howling; Cocytus' glooms
lay still. A tremor shuddered through the abyss
reechoing as the tyrant uttered this:

9
"Gods of the underworld, worthier of those thrones
where once you sat in glory above the sun,
whom great mischance has hurled from our glad realms
to fall with me into this loathsome pen,
you know too well our high attempt, you know
the hate and envy of the other One:
the turning stars are now in His control,
while each of us is judged a rebel soul.

10
"And in place of the starry wheels of heaven
and golden sunlight in tranquility,
He has imprisoned us in this deep gloom,
forbidden to strive for our first dignity.
And then—ah, the mere memory is pain,
this above all my suffering tortures me—
man, man the vile, born of vile mud, He invites
to rise instead to those celestial heights.

11
"But that would not suffice. Merely to spell
our greater harm, He gives His Son as prey
to Death. The Son bursts free the gates of hell,
robbing us of the souls that fell our way,
daring to set His foot where devils rule,
to heaven spiriting those rich spoils away,
conquering Hero; and to mock us well,
flinging out broad the signs of conquered hell.

12
"But why speak, and renew the grief? Who has
not heard and understood our injuries?
And where or when has He ever been known
to let His constant battle with us cease?
No use to dwell on old offenses now;
the present wrongs require new strategies.
Do you not see how He attempts to claim
as His all nations, to adore His Name?

13
"And shall we fritter away our hours and days,
careless of what should set our wrath afire?
Shall we then suffer that His people raise
a greater force in Asia every hour?
That they subdue Judea? That His praise,
His worship, be extended ever more?
That His Name be uttered now in other tongues,
graven in marble and bronze, and penned in songs?

14
"That our idols should lie shattered in the dust?
Our altars be made His throughout the world?
That to Him alone the smoke of incense rise,
to Him, the votive gifts of myrrh and gold?
That now no way lies open to our art
against which, once, no temple door would hold?
That the usual tax of souls should come up short
and Pluto govern in an empty court?

15
"Let it not be! They have not guttered out,
valorous souls of my rebellious band,
when girt with steel and armed with towering fire
we fought that day against heaven's high command.
We lost that battle—I will not deny it—
yet there was virtue in what we had planned.
Something, whatever it was, made Him victorious;
courage is ours, unconquerable and glorious.

16
"But why waste time with words? Go forth, my true
consorts, O you my faithful force, my might,
go quickly, and these mutineers subdue
before their power attains a greater height;
before the blaze sweeps all the land of the Jew
its surging must be cooled, or put out quite.
Enter among them. To their final misery
use force sometimes, and sometimes trickery.

17
"May what I will be fate. Let some lie slain,
let others scatter, straying willfully;
let others, bathed in the wanton cares of love,
make a sweet smile into idolatry;
let the blade be turned against the head that guides,
their camp fraught with dissent and mutiny.
Perish and fall to ruin all their host—
with every trace of their rebellion lost!"

18
The traitors of the Most High did not wait
until the words of Satan ceased to sound,
but taking flight to see the stars again
they have already surged from the profound
darkness of hell—as roaring, frothing waves
break from their sea-birth grottoes underground
to blot the light of heaven, and carry war
to the great kingdoms of the sea and shore.

19
At once, spreading their sails to every part,
over the face of the wide world they scatter
and immediately begin to ply their art,
to fashion lies of strange and various matter.
But tell, Muse, how the Christian troubles start,
tell what the devils send, and from what quarter.
Fame's breeze is weak to whisper what you know
of such a great event so long ago.

20
Damascus and her neighboring cities were
ruled by Hydrotes, noble and famed magician,
who from his boyhood and then ever more
gave his love to the arts of precognition.
And yet the end of that uncertain war
did not, for all their help, enter his vision:
neither the fixed nor wandering stars could tell
the truth, nor the replies he drew from hell.

21
Their verdict? Ah, how blind the heart of man,
how all our empty judgments go awry!
For the unvanquished armies of the west,
heaven had prepared that they should fall and die.
So he, trusting that Egypt in the end
should carry off the palm of victory,
wanted his people too to realize
some gain and glory of the enterprise.

22
But he fears the victory's great cost in blood—
for with French valor he is much impressed—
so broods on how his art and cunning could
anticipate the Christians and divest
some of their force—then he and Egypt would
all the more easily repulse the rest.
Goading him, pricking him on in this bad plan,
came the crooked angel, enemy of man,

23
showing him how to clear the task of trouble,
administering tactical advice.
There was a woman—the magician's niece—
to whom the Orient granted beauty's prize.
Whatever a woman or a witch employs,
what art or sleight or secretest device,
she knew. He shares the strategy with her,
to sign her on as his conspirator.

24
"O my delight—who under gentle looks
and golden hair have hidden a man's heart
and a mind worthy of the silver of age,
O you who have surpassed me in my art,
I am designing a great plan, which shall
effect all that we hope, if you take part.
Weave the web I begin. Wary and old
am I; let my executress be bold.

25
"Go to the enemy camp. Win them for love,
ply every art of feminine allure;
let all you say be broken and confused
by sighs, bathe with your tears each honeyed prayer;
let beauty in its pitiable grief
bend the most stubborn hearts to your desire;
enveil your mastering fire with modesty
and clothe truth in the mantle of a lie.

26
"Of these sweet looks and lovely painted words
let Godfrey, if you can, swallow the bait,
so that the duties of a war begun
will rankle in the newly infatuate.
If not, then hook the rest of the great chiefs;
lead them to an inexorable fate."
He laid out the details, then said in trust,
"For faith and fatherland all things are just."

27
Lovely Armida, proud of her peerless form,
of the charms of her youth and womanhood,
takes up the challenge, leaves that very night,
traveling ever along the hidden road
and in her woman's habit nursing hope
to rout armed legions never yet subdued.
Of her departure there was given out
many causes for the crowd to noise about.

28
Now where the tents of the French battalions are,
the young girl has arrived in a few days.
Beauty like hers was never seen before—
the soldiers whisper—toward her each turns his gaze
as if she were a comet or new star
filling the daylit heavens with her blaze.
All the men run immediately to see
who the beautiful traveler may be.

29
Troy never beheld her shapeliness and poise;
Diana and Venus never were so dear.
Here the white veil enfolds a subtle glow,
but here, revealed, her locks of gold appear
as when the heavens are calmed after a storm:
now the sun gleams through the white cloud, now clear
it breaks forth from the haze and spills its light,
radiance making daytime doubly bright.

30
The breeze that played on her disheveled tresses
curled them in ringlets, already curled by nature;
but for herself she hoarded up her glances,
hiding away the secrets of love's treasure.
In her lovely face the sweet color of roses
blended into the ivory in fine mixture,
but on her lips, where the breath of love blows,
ruddy of blush and single blooms the rose.

31
Her shapely breasts showed the uncovered snow
that stirs and nourishes the fire of love.
They looked, in part, like fruit not fully ripe,
part sheltered by her gown that lay above,
envious—yet if it shuts the pass for sight,
imagination, you have room to rove,
for not content with outward beauty, deep
among the hidden secrets would you keep.

32
As when through water or a crystal stone
the rays of sunshine do not separate,
so now, through the drawn mantle, into lands
forbidden, the mind dares to penetrate,
and there it walks at ease, and one by one
scouts out those wondrous sights to contemplate,
then relays their description to Desire,
fanning the flames within him all the higher.

33
Thus through the amorous crowd Armida passed
admired and praised by all—as she could see.
Unaware she seemed, but in her heart she smiled,
designing glorious spoils and victory.
She asks meanwhile for a man to guide her to
the captain—asks a little hesitantly,
but Eustace, younger brother of the chief
of all the squadrons, runs to her relief.

34
And as the lamp attracts the butterfly,
he turned to face her divine radiance,
wishing to gaze upon those eyes close by
(which now she cast down in sweet diffidence),
and from them kindled into flame, as dry
tinder beside a fire has no defense.
To her he spoke, made gallant now and bold
by both the heat of love and his young blood,

35
"Lady—if it is just to call you so,
for you resemble nothing earthly, nor,
of all of Adam's daughters graced with light,
I think that heaven has never showered more—
where have you come from? What chance of yours or ours
has led you here? What are you searching for?
Say who you are, and show me what is due.
I will bow to the earth to honor you."

36
"Your praises," she replied, "soar far above—
our merits do not reach so great a height.
What you see, sir, is mortal, is alive
for sorrow alone, and dead to all delight.
My evil fortune drives me to this place,
a young girl wandering in a lonely flight.
I shall trust Godfrey now to shelter me—
so famous is his liberality.

37
"Arrange that I may see him, if indeed
your soul is moved by pity for another."
"It's only right that I should intercede
for you," said he, "and lead you to my brother.
Beautiful lady, you have had good speed,
my favor with the chief is great. Whatever
it pleases you to spend you may afford:
all the worth of his scepter, or my sword."

38
He led her where, retreating from the crowd,
among his heroes sat the good Bouillon.
Toward him in reverence Armida bowed,
then lost her voice, bashful and all alone.
But the soldier consoled and reassured
her blushes and her fear, till at last, grown
confident, she unfolded her deceit,
binding their senses by a sound so sweet:

39
"Never-defeated prince," she said, "whose name,
adorned with brightest praise, has taken wing,
that to be won by you and rendered tame
is cause of glory now for land and king,
everyone greets your valor with acclaim,
its praises even your enemies will sing,
and all may place their trust there, unafraid
to seek you out and to entreat your aid.

40
"And I, born to a different faith, which you
have humbled and attempt to batter down,
nevertheless hope by your aid to gain
my parents' royal scepter and their throne.
To fight the fury of an invading tribe
another might beg help among her own—
but they have no more place for pity, so
against my kinsmen I invoke my foe.

41
"I call on you, my only hope, to raise
me to those heights whence I was shoved aside.
To lift someone, no less than to abase,
is work to which your arm is well applied—
as good as leading conquered enemies,
piety is a worthy cause for pride.
You who have snatched from many a king his reign,
may glory as well to give me mine again.

42
"But if the difference in our faiths should move you
to set the value of my prayers as slight,
let my faith in your piety assist me—
to disappoint that faith would not be right.
I call to witness God who is good to all,
your aid will never have been more in the right!
But listen to the treasons which comprise
my own misfortunes and another's lies.

43
"I am the daughter of Arbilan, who ruled
lovely Damascus; born of low estate,
he won the hand of queen Cariclia,
who made him the successor of her state.
But she anticipated me in dying
before I came out of the womb. One fate
gave death to her, and birth to me: she lay
lifeless, when I first saw the light of day.

44
"And yet five years had hardly come and gone
since the day she had slipped this mortal robe,
when, surrendering to fate, my father died,
perhaps rejoining her in heaven above.
And so he left me, with the kingdom, in
his brother's care, to whom he'd shown such love
if piety ever dwelt in mortal breast
his brother's faith and truth should need no test.

45
"This uncle, in his role as guardian,
appearing so desirous of my good,
drew praise for his unbreached fidelity,
his loving piety and fatherhood.
Either under a different cloak already
he let his secret malice hatch and brood,
or his desires were still sincere, as he
had planned a marriage for his son and me.

46
"I grew and the son grew, but he could learn
no art or manners of a gentle knight.
He delighted in nothing rare or nobly done,
for his soul never understood such height;
an ill-formed face to match a coward's spirit,
his heart a furnace for his appetite,
uncouth in manner, and in habits such
that no man ever courted vice so much.

47
"So my good guardian had designed that this
most worthy man should share my bed and throne,
uniting me with him in wedlock, as
on many occasions he made clearly known.
All his shrewd arts and speech he put to use
to compass what he set his sights upon;
he pressed, but with no promise I supplied him—
I still held back, fell silent, or denied him.

48
"At last he left me with a darkened face
wherein the evil of his heart showed clear,
and the story of my future woes, now traced
openly on his brow, began to appear.
And then my night's repose was haunted by
strange dreams and phantoms, and a fatal fear
impressed upon my spirit prophesied
of all the sufferings I must abide.

49
"Often my mother's shade appeared to me,
a pallid image, grieving and dismayed—
alas, how very changed and different she,
from how I'd often seen her face portrayed!
'Daughter,' she cried, 'make haste to leave, and flee
the murder hanging over you, betrayed!
I see the sword and poison lie in wait
for the faithless tyrant to prepare your fate.'

50
"But oh, what did it profit, that my heart
could now divine the danger drawing near,
if my tender youth in reaching a decision
was rendered so irresolute by fear?
To flee, naked, in self-banishment
and wander from my fatherland so dear,
saddened me so that it must seem less grim
to shut my eyes where I first opened them.

51
"Death frightened me, and yet away from death—
who would have thought?—I did not long to fly,
but still I feared to let my fear be known,
lest that should hasten the hour when I must die.
And so my life was torment without end,
drawn restless out in one long troubled sigh,
as a man whose naked neck expects to feel
at any moment the executioner's steel.

52
"In such a state—whether in friendly sort
or saving me for worse—my fortune smiled.
One of the ministers of the royal court
raised by the king my father from a child,
let me know that the time was growing short
when the tyrant would have me dead; revealed
how he had pledged that fiend to make me away,
slipping me poison on that very day.

53
"And added then, that as for my life's course,
only by fleeing could I lengthen it,
and since I could turn nowhere for recourse
himself he offered for my immediate
assistance. He lent desire such strength and force—
fear could no more restrain me with its bit—
that I escaped with him in the blind night,
leaving my uncle and fatherland by flight.

54
"Night fell, a night unusually dark,
mantled with friendly shadows, when with two
maidens I stole, secure, outside the walls—
those I could trust in bad times to be true
companions. Yet I could not help but cast
my tearful eyes upon the city, to
look again and again upon the walls, the earth—
to bid farewell to the land of my birth.

55
"My eyes and thoughts traveled the road back home,
and yet in spite of them the feet strode on,
as a ship torn from its beloved cove
by a sudden and impetuous hurricane.
That night we went and all the following day
where there appeared no sign of anyone,
until we found ourselves under the arch
of a fortress on my kingdom's furthest march,

56
"Arontes' castle (he it was who had
drawn me from danger, and accompanied us).
But when the traitor learned that I had fled
his deadly and insidious device,
he blazed with wrath against us both, and turned
upon us his own sin and wickedness,
pronounced us guilty of that crime which he
himself would have committed against me,

57
"claiming that I had bribed his man Arontes
to adulterate his drink with lethal bane,
so that no one, as soon as he was dead,
should set me laws or hold me under rein,
and I—pursuing my natural wanton ways—
with a whole troop of lovers I'd have lain!
Ah, let the flames of heaven come down on me
when I break your holy laws, O chastity!

58
"Bad enough that he hungered after gold,
and that he thirsted for my innocent blood!
More did the cruel one oppress my heart,
trying to smudge my whitest maidenhood.
And since he feared a popular revolt,
the wicked man adorned the bad with good
and wove so well, that the city in suspense,
doubting, took up no arms for my defense.

59
"Nor did it satisfy that now he sat
enthroned, and wore the splendor of a crown.
There was no limit to his bestial hate;
desire to see me suffer spurred him on.
Arontes must surrender in chains; if not,
he vowed to burn him and his castle down.
But war is not sufficient. He intends
torture and death for me with all my friends.

60

“He said that he would do so, to wash clean
the shame of my pollutions from his face,
and to restore what I had so demeaned,
the throne, the honor of our royal race.
The people would have seized his scepter and given it
to its true heir; fear kept them in their place.
Only if I should fall can he sustain—
upon my ruined fortunes—his own reign.

61

“And it will surely come to pass, the end
to which the despot’s mind is wholly bent,
and his wrath will be extinguished in my blood
that in my sorrow never could be spent,
unless you forbid it. You are my refuge, sir,
I a poor maiden, orphaned, innocent.
My tears have bathed your feet. May it do me good,
so that I need not also spill my blood.

62

“By these your feet that tread upon the proud
and wicked, by that arm that aids the right,
by your great triumphs, by those holy temples
for whose relief you fought and seek to fight,
oh, let your pity save my life and reign,
fulfill my longing! You alone have the might!
But pity will be worthless unless you
are also moved to uphold the just and true.

63

“You, to whom heaven has given the power of fate,
to will the just and compass your desire,
O you can save my life and save my state—
and all that I regain, you will acquire.
Let me lead ten of your bravest, strongest heroes,
ten of so many—all that I require!
I’ve well-placed friends, the people’s loyalty too—
to restore me to my nest, those ten will do.

64

“Indeed, the one entrusted to keep watch
over our secret gates, one of the best,
has vowed to open them and let us reach
the palace itself at night—his lone request
that I seek your assistance, for in such
relief, however modest, he will rest
happier than if his own battalions came.
Such he esteems your banners and your name.”

65
That said, Armida silently attended,
but in her silence a still voice was pleading.
Godfrey weighed all this in his heart, suspended
by many thoughts, unsure where they were leading.
He feared the pagan tricks, and understood
man finds no faith where God meets unbelieving;
but there stirred in him, from another part,
pity which never sleeps in the gentle heart.

66
But not alone his usual, innate pity
wanted to hold her worthy of his grace,
but usefulness besides, for it would be
a boon to have in her imperial place
a tributary, who would clear the way
for his designs, facilitate the race,
her men and arms and gold as ministrations
against the Egyptians and their allied nations.

67
And while, considering both sides, he fixed
his glance upon the earth and quietly pondered,
the woman stared at him, intent to learn
what he might say. At all his acts she wondered,
the more since he delayed beyond belief;
she feared and sighed, her self-assurance foundered.
At last he spoke, and denied her petition,
but softly, with knightly honor—and on condition:

68
"If our swords here had not their work assigned
to be wielded in the cause of the Most High,
you might build up your hopes on them, and find
in us your rescue—more than piety.
But till we have returned God's faithful flock
and set these oppressed walls at liberty,
it were unjust to let my ranks diminish
and slow our race to the victorious finish.

69
"I promise you—and you can live assured
it is a noble pledge I now submit—
that once these walls beloved of heaven are freed
and all their shameful subjugation quit,
our duty and our piety shall be
to win your realm and bring you back to it.
Piety now would make me impious
if I failed to render to God, first, what is His."

70
At that the woman bowed her head and stared
upon the earth a moment, stood quite still,
then raised her brimming eyes, and played her words
with gestures properly lamentable:
"Wretch that I am! To whom has heaven decreed
a life so heavy and immutable
that before her luck should alter from the worst
it alters another's mind and nature first?

71
"There is no hope for me. I weep for nothing.
Prayers have no power in men's hearts anymore.
My grief which cannot move you will perhaps
move the king—is that what you are hoping for?
I don't accuse you of hardheartedness,
denying me the small help I implore.
No, I blame heaven, the source of all my ill,
that makes your piety inexorable.

72
"Oh sir, it is not you, it is not your goodness
which denies me assistance, but my fate.
You cruel and malevolent destiny,
put a prompt finish to this life I hate!
To have snatched away my parents in their prime
was but an evil at a modest rate,
unless you see my kingdom also lost
and me a victim led to holocaust.

73
"For now that faith and the law of honest pride
forbid that I should any longer stay,
to whom should I turn at last? Where shall I hide?
What shelter have I from the tyrant's sway?
There is no place so secret under heaven
which money cannot open. Why delay?
For if I cannot shun the death I see,
my own hand still can bring it home to me!"

74
Here she fell silent, and, one might perceive,
regal disdain was kindled in her look.
Turning her foot, she made as if to leave,
sadness and scorn in all she did, and took
no hold upon her tears, but freely wept
and with a kind of angry sorrow shook.
Her tears glinted like pearl as they were born
or perfect crystals in the brilliant morn.

75
Armida's cheeks, dashed with those living waters
that trickled to the margin of her gown,
were as a field of white and crimson flowers
after the dew has settled on the down,
opening their bosoms to the gentle airs
that greet the first appearance of the dawn,
and the morning cannot help but wonder and stare,
longing to have them to adorn her hair.

76
But that adornment to her lovely cheek
and breast, the glistening of her gathered tears,
works like a warmth of secretest mystique—
a thousand hearts are kindled with desires.
O miracle of love! O flame unique,
distilled from tears, sprinkling the heart with fires!
Love over Nature lords it from above,
but she augments what he is master of.

77
This show of grief lured many a genuine tear,
melting the sternest-hearted of the men.
Everyone quietly said, grieving with her,
"If even now she gains no mercy, then
a savage tiger gave our captain suck
and he was born in a rugged alpine den
or from the wave that breaks and foams at sea.
To hurt such loveliness is cruelty!"

78
But the young Eustace, in whose heart the brand
of pity and love more violently flared,
while all the others whispered underhand,
stepped forward challenging and thus declared:
"My brother and chief, your thoughts are fixed too fast
to what you have initially prepared,
if even in the least you will not bow
to what the common wisdom begs for now.

79
"I do not say that chiefs who stand in charge
of soldiers in their care should all deflect
their steps from this walled city under siege,
for they have duties they should not neglect.
But what of us Adventurers, fortune's soldiers?
From us you can quite lawfully select
ten defenders of the just, for the laws bind
our men less strictly; we have no charge assigned.

80
"And a man who fights to help an innocent virgin
has not abjured the service of the Lord,
and for the spoils of a slain tyrant, heaven
will grace the slayer with a rich reward.
But even if the sure gain to be given
to those who undertake this were ignored,
duty would move me. To help all ladies is
the firmest of our knightly promises.

81
"Ah, let them never, by God, say back in France,
or wherever else men prize courtesy's laws,
that we here ran away from trouble or chance,
and in so pious and so just a cause.
Why, I shall toss aside my shield and lance,
unbelt my sword at once, and no more use
my weapons and war stallion shamefully,
usurping the great name of chivalry."

82
Such was the gallant's speech. His comrades' voices
rang out that they were all of the same mind,
calling the counsel good and useful, circling
the chief, pressing with prayers, until, resigned,
he finally spoke, "I give in, I am beaten
by the wishes of so many men combined.
If you think it proper, give her what she seeks.
In this not mine but your own counsel speaks.

83
"But if you still find Godfrey worth your trust,
listen to me, and temper your desire."
This much he says, and since the men accept
what he concedes, no more do they require.
What can the sweet words of a lovely lady,
what can the tears of beauty not inspire?
From her delightful lips a golden chain
puts their souls under her will's spur and rein.

84
"Sweet lady," Eustace says, calling her back,
"let be your grief, shed not another tear,
for you will soon enjoy such help from us
as I believe shall soothe your greatest fear."
Armida then allayed her stormy look
and on the surface smiled so fair and clear
her beauty could infatuate the skies—
wiping her lovely veil across her eyes.

85
In sweet and precious notes she gracefully
thanked them for the high grace they would impart,
for oh, its fame should last eternally,
and it should be engraven in her heart.
And what the tongue could not express, her gestures
spoke eloquently in their silent art.
Her thoughts were hid so well by the fictitious
that not one soldier ever grew suspicious.

86
As a result, seeing that luck had smiled
upon the great beginning of her fraud,
before the plot could be cut short, she aimed
to draw out to its end this work so good,
and do with a sweet face and pretty ways
what neither Circe nor Medea could,
and with a siren's melody to keep
the most vigilant minds lulled fast asleep.

87
To catch every new lover in her net
the lady uses all the craft she can,
not keeping always the same face for each;
she fits her looks and actions to the man.
Now she reddens for shame and lowers her eyes,
but now she lets them rove and lovingly scan—
she pulls his reins, she whips him on to go,
just as she sees their lusts are fast or slow.

88
If she finds a man whose soul retires from love,
whose lack of confidence restrains his mind,
in sweet serenity she turns her eye
upon him, and her smile is free and kind.
Thus she spurs on the sluggish and the shy,
and reassures with hope the disinclined,
and touches off their amorous wills afire
so that fear's frost is melted in desire.

89
But in the hot-blood lover overleaping
the mark, led by the blind and willful Boy,
she instills fear and veneration, keeping
her rare words and her lovely glances coy.
Yet he might see a ray of pity peeping
out of her furrowed forehead anyway,
so that he fears, but still hopes, as he ought.
The prouder she, the surer is he caught.

90
Sometimes the lady stands a bit aloof,
lending her looks and actions the facade
of sorrow, yet at last drawing the tears
into her eyes, and squelching them inside.
And thus a thousand simple little souls
weep with her, led along by artful fraud.
She tempers her arrows of love in pity's fires;
against such potent arms the heart expires.

91
Then as if stealing away from her sad thoughts,
as if a new hope saw the light of day,
toward her lovers she would turn and speak,
her countenance adorned with sudden joy,
and her sweet heavenly smile and shining face
flashed like a double sun clearing the sky
of all the clouds of sorrow overcast
which she had suffered gathering in the breast.

92
But while she sweetly speaks and sweetly smiles,
doubly intoxicating to the sense,
out of the heart she seems to cut their souls,
unaccustomed to delights so immense.
O bitter Love, equally deadly with
the honey and the gall which you dispense;
for poisons come continually from you,
but with the antidotes that kill us too!

93
Between such stark extremes, in fire and ice,
in grief and joy, caught between hope and fear,
the lovers waver, played for all they're worth
by this most beautiful deceptioneer;
and if, with tremulous and broken voice,
anyone dares to make his sorrows clear,
she pretends, as a novice raw in love,
to miss his soul in what he's speaking of.

94
Or, keeping her bashful glances meek and close,
paints with the pretty blush of modesty,
mantling the fresh snow under the blooming rose
that makes her lovely countenance like May,
as in the earliest and freshest hours
we look upon the dawn's nativity—
the blushing of her scorn flowers the same,
and is blended with the blushing of her shame.

95

But if by what he does she should discover
one who attempts to show his blazing lust,
now she avoids him, stealing from her lover,
now calls a parley, and takes him back at once.
It is an aimless track she leads him over,
wandering, weary, deluded, till at last
he loses hope, as, having lost the trace,
the hunter at fall of night gives up his chase.

96

These were the arts whereby she could surprise
their spirits by the thousands, stealthily,
or rather the arms that took them prisoner
and forced them into loving slavery.
But if fierce Achilles, Theseus, Hercules
fell prey to love, what wonder should there be
if those who sheathe the sword of Jesus find
themselves caught in the impious Cupid's bind?

Canto Five

1

While thus the sly Armida lures the men
into the insidious meshes of her love,
trusting not only to lead the promised ten
but to steal others over and above,
Godfrey is wondering whom he should assign
the dubious attack she leads; for of
the many worthy Adventurers at hand
each one is willing to go at his command.

2

At last, with foresight, he decreed that they
should freely choose some soldier of their own
(with whom the choosing of the champions lay)
to succeed the magnanimous Dudon.
He would avert hard feelings in this way—
complaints that he had favored anyone—
and at the same time have them understand
how much he justly prized the excellent band.

3

And so he summoned them before him, saying,
"My sentiments in this matter you all know—
not to deny the woman help, but wait
until the time is opportune to go.
I propose this once more. You may well yet
follow it as your own opinion: so
fickle and changing is this world, we find
that to be constant we must change our mind.

4

"But if you still believe that to shun danger
is inconsistent with your rank and name,
and if your generous and ardent souls
reject a cautious counsel as too tame,
I shall not hold you here against your wills,
nor what I gave you do I now reclaim.
No; you should feel my power, as is right,
to be a rein whose pull is loose and light.

5
"Therefore going or staying all depends
on your free pleasure, as I have agreed.
But first choose someone to assume the role
of the slain duke, a new captain to lead
your troops. Let him choose ten as he thinks best,
but only ten—the number may not exceed
what I have set by my authority.
In all the rest his judgment will be free."

6
That said, his younger brother rose to speak,
to answer for himself and all his peers:
"As caution is, O captain, fit for you,
and seeing long before the threat appears,
so the brave heart and vigorous hand for us;
to lend them is our charge as cavaliers.
One man proceeds with seasoned, slow advice;
in us such prudence would be cowardice.

7
"And since what we are risking is so light,
weighed in the balance with the benefit,
let ten engage this honorable fight,
accompanying the lady, as you permit."
He finishes, and with a lie so bright
tries to veneer and hide intentions lit
by another passion. Under the fiction of
yearning for honor, they all yearn for love.

8
Now the youngest Bouillon, who can't behold
Sophia's son without a jealous eye,
envious of his beauty and great strength,
a paragon of rare virility,
wished he would stay behind. His heart conceived
a cunning plan inspired by jealousy,
and drawing his competitor apart
he argued with astute and flattering art:

9
"O you the greater son of a great sire,
whose praises won in battle are most grand
although you are still a youngster—who will be
chosen as leader of our valorous band?
Only in deference to seniority
could I live under Dudon's famed command!
I, Godfrey's brother, ask myself then who
is fit to be my leader, if not you?

10
"In rank you are the equal of any other,
in glory and merit my superior,
nor would it gall even my greater brother
to grant himself a lesser man in war.
I want you for our head. You need not bother
to be this Syrian lady's rescuer,
nor do you care for honor that proceeds
from the coverts of night and nightly deeds.

11
"Your valor here has a fine situation;
with all the brighter fame you may employ it.
Let all the rest yield you the highest station—
agree, and I shall see that you enjoy it.
But since my heart is in some hesitation—
shall I pass up this enterprise, or try it—
I ask that I may choose whatever I do,
to follow Armida, or stay here with you."

12
Here Eustace halted. Those last words broke out
with a slight flush, a redness in the face.
Rinaldo almost smiled, for he could scout
the ardent thoughts in their poor hiding place.
But since the shot of love had grazed his flesh
and beyond that had hardly left a trace,
he wasn't worried by a rival wooer,
nor did he care so greatly to pursue her.

13
Instead, chiseled more deeply in his thought
was Dudon's death in all its bitterness
(dishonorable, that bold Argante ought
survive the duke for any length of days),
and those words pleased him also which besought
him to accept the honors which were his
(the young man's heart enjoyed the sweet delight
of hearing all his praises sung aright).

14
So he replied, "To merit the first rank,
more than to seize it, is what I desire.
So long as my own virtue lifts me up,
what matter whose authority is higher?
But if you call me to an honor which
you think is mine by right, I will not tire;
and I appreciate how handsomely
you show that you esteem my bravery.

15
"So I won't seek the station or refuse it.
If I'm the leader, you will be selected."
Eustace takes leave and goes about to try
his comrades' wills, to make sure they reflected
his own. But Prince Gernando wants the place,
for though Armida's arrows have infected
him too, his eager pride sets him apart—
for honor is the mistress of his heart.

16
Gernando was descended of the grand
Norse king, commander over many a nation.
So many ancestral crowns and so much land
were, to his mind, good cause for exaltation.
Rinaldo took pride in the works of his own hand,
not those performed by some long-dead relation—
though his race had for centuries and more
been bright in peace, illustrious in war.

17
But the barbaric lord, who measured worth
according to one's reach of wealth and might,
and counted every virtue of itself
dim, if a king's name did not make it bright,
could not endure that what he craved, should be
challenged—for *"merit's"* sake—by a mere knight!
And so, self-tortured, with scorn and anger harried,
beyond all bounds of reason he was carried,

18
whence the malevolent spirit of hell, perceiving
how in him there had opened a broad way,
silently snaked into his breast, deceiving,
swaying his thoughts with lies and flattery.
And now the wrath and hate he was conceiving
grew ever bitterer, as she would flay
and goad his heart with one continuous
whispering in the soul, which reasoned thus:

19
"Rinaldo spars with you . . . as if his petty
number of family heroes were so great . . .
your equal! Let him say how many peoples
pay tribute to him as their potentate!
Let him show the scepters and compare his dead
with yours yet living in their regal state,
he, a lord born in slavish Italy,
a lord lowborn for such effrontery!

20
"Whether he wins or loses—and he won
till the day he became your rival—what
will the world say? Be that his highest honor:
'The great Gernando and this man once fought.'
The noble rank which Dudon held before
can bring you glory and luster, true, but not
less than the glory you yourself confer.
But *his* claim only leaves it commoner.

21
"If men who can no longer speak or breathe,
if good Dudon takes care how we are faring,
then from the heavens, incensed with noble wrath,
how angrily he must behold his bearing
whenever he turns his eyes on the proud youth,
whenever he thinks about his heedless daring,
who, holding age and merit but a toy,
would match Dudon—an inexperienced boy!

22
"And yet he dares . . . he actually tries it . . .
gains for it no rebuke, but honor and laud.
For there are some who urge it, who advise it,
and (shame on the whole army!) who applaud.
So what if Godfrey sees and won't chastise it!
You yourself need not let the boy defraud
you of your rights. He shall not go so far.
You will show what you can, and what you are."

23
Such whisperings were the spark to indignation
that blazed within him like a whirling torch—
too great for his swollen heart, the conflagration
leapt from his glances and his violent speech.
All hateful things, all worthy of detestation
which he thought of Rinaldo, he would preach,
painting him vain and proud; his valorous soul
the mad and reckless fury of a fool.

24
And all he had of the magnanimous,
all the sublime, the gloriously bright,
Gernando reprehended as mere vice,
artfully shading truth in an ill light,
speaking so flagrantly in public that
news of his slanders reached the rival knight.
Still he could not exhaust his wrath at all
or break the blind drive hurtling to his fall,

25
for the wicked demon seized his spirit's power,
moved the man's tongue and fashioned all he said,
made him renew his outrage hour by hour,
whereby the blazes in his breast were fed.
Now often there would congregate the flower
of the French army in an open field
for jousting games and tilts, wherein at length
their limbs would toughen in discipline and strength,

26
and here, and when the crowd was thickest, he
accused Rinaldo, as it was his fate,
shooting his speech at him like a sharp arrow
steeped in the venom of infernal hate.
Nearby, Rinaldo overhears the words
and can no longer hold his wrath in wait,
but leaping to him at once, he cries out, "Liar!"
and with a voice like thunder, a flash like fire

27
announcing the imminent fall of the lightning bolt,
he shakes in his right arm the naked steel.
Gernando shudders—sees no hope, no flight
from death impending and irreparable.
Yet since the whole host stands to witness it,
he puts on a most strong and fearless will
and draws his sword (his enemy attending)
and staunchly sets his stance as one defending.

28
Immediately a thousand brandished swords
were seen to flash together in the air,
for a great crowd of reckless men had pressed
into the thick of the fight from everywhere.
Of garbled accents and uncertain shouts
a noise whirled round, as on the beach you hear
the muttering of the shoreward wind confounding
with the roar of the ocean breakers pounding,

29
but no mere shouts and threatenings could restrain
the wrath of the insulted warrior.
He cared not for the cries of men in vain
who tried to shield his rival, but longed for
vengeance—and swept his swift-as-lightning blade
in a wide swath behind him and before,
despite their armed defense, to clear a place
to meet Gernando alone and face to face.

30
And with his arm, masterful tool of ire,
he scatters deft blows at his enemy,
now striking at the chest, now at the head,
now to the right, now to the left—thus he
deceives the eyes and the art of the sword, his blade
darting so swiftly and impetuously
that he draws blood, sudden and unexpected,
from spots apparently safe and best protected,

31
and does not pause until at last his sword
plunges once, and again, into the breast.
Spilling his breath and soul through the twin road
Gernando tumbles to his final rest.
The victor lay his arms down splashed with blood
and paid him no more care, but, undistressed,
turning away, at once he set apart
his infuriated will and his fierce heart.

32
But reverent Godfrey, led to the fray at once,
sees this wild spectacle: Gernando lies
spread on the earth, his hair and mantle wet
and matted with blood; and death is in his eyes.
The crowd stood over the slain man. Godfrey heard
their accusations, their laments and sighs.
Amazed, he asked, "Who has abused this place?
Who has dared to commit such a disgrace?"

33
Arnaldo, a close friend of the dead prince,
says—and he aggravates the matter—says
Rinaldo killed him, driven to the deed
by foolish fury in a petty cause,
turning his sword against Christ's champions,
he who had buckled it on for Christ; that laws
which Godfrey had laid down by express word
Rinaldo had belittled and ignored;

34
that by the law he was condemned to die,
that he must take the prescribed punishment,
both for the crime's inherent gravity
and for the circumstance of the event;
that if his sin were pardoned and put by,
all brawlers would be given a precedent,
and that from now on those who held a grudge
would don the avenging office of the judge,

35
which would provide rich soil to sprout unrest
or sow dissension and disharmony.
He called to mind the merits of the deceased,
and said all that would waken sympathy
and indignation. But Tancred speaks against him,
portraying the youth as led to battle by
honor. Godfrey, unflinching, hears the case,
less leniency than sternness in his face.

36
Then Tancred added, "My wise lord, recall
both who and what the young Rinaldo is:
how honor both befits him for himself
and for that bright and princely race of his,
and for his uncle Guelph. A ruler must
not deal to all men the same penalties.
One crime is not the same for low and high.
Only peers may demand equality."

37
"From those in higher station," said the chief,
"let those beneath them learn how to obey.
Your counsel is as wrong as your belief,
Tancred, that I should leave the nobles free—
for my authority would be small and brief
if only the common crowd fought under me.
An impotent scepter for a shameful position:
I shall not take it under that condition.

38
"But it was given freely, with respect,
which no one shall diminish. Well I know
how and when one who rules should now select
diverse rewards and punishments, and now,
the tenor of equality intact,
make no distinction between high and low."
So he; and Tancred offered no defense
to words which conquered him with reverence.

39
Then Raymond praised his speech, for he was one
whom the sternness of the ancient world directed.
"This is the art," he said, "a ruler needs
to make it certain he will be respected,
for discipline can never be complete
when men look to be pardoned, not corrected.
Rule falls, and mercy aids the ruination,
when reverent fear is not its firm foundation."

40
So he declared, and, having heard these things,
among them Tancred would no longer stay,
mounting a horse who sped as if on wings,
galloping for Rinaldo straightaway,
who had returned to quarters, having snatched
his fierce enemy's pride and soul away.
And here he found Rinaldo and related
a full account of what had been debated.

41
"Although I seldom trust the outward show,"
he added, "as reliable evidence
of what is in men's hearts, for all too low
lie all our secrets and our dark intents,
yet from my reading of the captain, who
has spoken, I can say with confidence
that you will bear the common penalty
and wait your trial in Godfrey's custody."

42
Rinaldo smiled at that, and in his smile
there flashed the slightest traces of disdain.
"Let slaves or other peasants just as vile
defend their rights while under block and chain.
Fetters? I'd sooner die than yield to that!
I have lived free, and free I will remain.
This arm is used to the triumphant sword—
not to a ruffian's manacle and cord.

43
"If this is the reward Godfrey would give
for my deservings—if he'd shackle me
and cart me off to the common brig, as if
I were a member of the rabble—he
can come himself—I'll plant my foot here—and
let arms and fortune be our referee!
The two of us would stage a tragic show,
a play of merrymaking for the foe!"

44
That said, "Give me my arms!" Rinaldo called,
adorned his trunk and head with bronze well tried,
and trussed his arm with the weight of his great shield,
and slung his fatal saber at his side,
shining like lightning in his weaponry,
a man greathearted and of regal pride.
Mars, he resembles you, when from the skies
you come girt with the steel that terrifies.

45
Immediately Prince Tancred tries to soothe
his fierce soul and his too-proud heart. "For your
valor, as I know well, invincible youth,
no task is hard, no enterprise unsure.
Battles and terrors do not shake this truth
for then your virtue is the more secure.
But God forbid you raise your noble arm
so cruelly to bring our people harm.

46
"Tell me, what you are doing? Would you foul
your hands by steeping them in civil blood?
And through these members of Christ's body, pierce
Christ Himself, as no worthy Christian would?
Are faith and zeal in you of lesser force
than the vain seeking after that slight good
'honor,' which, like the tide, is transitory
and cannot bring you to eternal glory?

47
"Ah, for God's sake don't overthrow yourself!
Put off this fierce and arrogant mind. Give way!
Not fear but a correct and holy will
will save for you a victory someday.
And if my age, for I'm a young man still,
can teach you a good lesson, let me say
I too was once provoked, but held my wrath
and did not fight my comrades in the faith.

48
"When I had seized the kingdom of Cilicia
and had unfurled the bannerets of Christ,
Baldwin arrived and shamelessly took over
and made a pretty profit from the heist—
for he'd led me to trust that we were friends,
yet friendship in his mind was cheaply priced.
Even so, I did not try to take it back,
though he might well have bowed to my attack.

49
"But if you still refuse to go to prison,
to bear the lowly iron and the block,
following worldly custom and opinion
which in the code of honor puts its stock,
then leave—I will excuse you to the captain—
and go to Bohemond in Antioch.
I do not think you will be safe from harm
bearing his judgments in this first alarm.

50
"If we should come to face the Egyptian host
or other pagan armies, we'll soon see
how your extraordinary valor must
shine from a distance far more splendidly.
Our camp will be a body that has lost
an arm or hand, when you are gone." So he;
and his advice soon meets with Guelph's approval,
who recommends Rinaldo's quick removal.

51
Their good advice so sways the daring lad
that finally his haughty spirit bends
and he agrees to leave the host at once,
and trust his welfare to his faithful friends.
Meanwhile a crowd of well-wishers come running,
begging that they might go too. He extends
his thanks to all, whose love he must renounce,
chooses two squires to ride with him, and mounts.

52
He leaves, in hunger for eternal glory
by which his noble heart is fed and spurred,
intent to undertake magnanimous
labors, whereof the world had never heard—
to die a Christian champion among foes,
or seize the palm of triumph for the Word,
to cut through Egypt and race many a mile
unto the unknown sources of the Nile.

53
But when the boy so spirited and proud
had taken leave (he was in haste to go),
Guelph did not stay behind, but went with speed
where he expected to find Godfrey, who,
when he caught sight of him called out aloud,
"Guelph, I was looking for you only now,
and sent our messengers to search around
in all the places where you might be found."

54
Dismissing all the others, by himself
he spoke to him in grave tones, and began,
"When anger spurs your nephew's heart, O Guelph,
he runs ahead too far indeed. Nor can
he be accredited, to my belief,
with a just reason to have killed that man.
I'd love to hear of such excuse, but I
Godfrey am leader of all equally

55
"and must serve as the guardian and defender
in every case of what is just and right,
and never allow my judgment to surrender
unto the passions' tyrannizing might.
Some say Rinaldo was a forced offender,
breaking the sacred discipline of a knight,
breaking my law. Then let him make that clear,
and let him bow before our judgment here.

56
"Let him come of his own volition, free.
So much to his deservings I can yield.
But if he will persist in obstinacy
(I know his untamed boldness in the field),
I want you to devise some way to see
that he does not compel a chief so mild
to be the stern avenger, for just cause,
of his authority and of the laws."

57
So he, and Guelph responded thus. "A soul
who cannot bear the smear of infamies,
whenever he hears the slandering words of scorn,
must fight back and return the injuries.
What if he put the slanderer to death?
Just anger can discern no boundaries!
Who counts the blows? Who measures and weighs what
is the offense due, when the fight is hot?

58
"But as for your request, that the boy come
and submit to your sovereign arbitration,
I am sorry to say it can't be done.
He has left this army without hesitation.
Yet by this hand I'll prove to that foul one
who tried to tear him with false accusation,
or to any man so eager to backbite,
that it was just to punish unjust spite.

59
"I say that he was right to chop the horn
of the swell-head Gernando's haughty pride!
He did forget your ban—that gives me pain,
the only thing that can't be justified."
Silence. "Well let him go and wander then
and take his squabbles elsewhere," Godfrey replied.
"Nor shall you sow new seeds of trouble! These
quarrels of pride, by God, at last might cease."

60
Meanwhile Armida the deceiver never
let up in her attempt to beg his aid,
by day entreating, putting to use whatever
cunning or beauty or artifice she had,
but when the night had closed that day forever
within its western mantle overspread,
along with two of her ladies and two knights
she went to Godfrey's tent to plead her rights.

61
But though she was the mistress of deception
with her suave manners and her gracious air,
and lovely, so that heaven never before
and never since formed anyone so fair,
and though the army's most illustrious heroes
were captured by her pleasure's iron snare,
she could not flatter Godfrey into taking
the pleasing bait she set for his unmaking.

62
Vain her attempts to lure the captain with
fading delights into a life of love.
As a bird fed full cannot be lured with seed,
the fowler's call he takes no notice of,
so Godfrey, sated with the world, ignored
its frail delights, set his lone flight above,
and as he soared toward heaven kept far away
from the snares faithless love set in his way.

63
No obstacle could turn his holy thoughts
from the sure path which God had marked out for him;
she tried a thousand shapes, a thousand arts,
appearing like a Proteus before him,
and his cold sleeping love would have been roused
by the sweet acts and the sweet looks she bore him,
but heavenly grace made all her ventures vain,
nor would it profit her to try again.

64
The lovely girl, who with one raised brow tried
to set the purest hearts in palpitation,
oh, how she lost the labor of her pride!
What wonder did she feel, and indignation!
At last, on the defense's weaker side,
she resolved to aim her forces' concentration,
as a frustrated, weary general
gives up, and leaves for lands more conquerable.

65
But Tancred's heart, no more than Godfrey's, her
weapons of passion could harass or bother;
his heart was pressed already by desire,
a love that left no room for any other.
This passion thus wards off that passion, as
one poison will protect against another.
These two she did not conquer. More or less,
the others all burned for her loveliness.

66
Although it irked her that she didn't see
the full success of her design and art,
to have seized so many heroes as her prey
consoled her for the loss of that small part.
Before someone should see her treachery
she had resolved to lead her men apart
to where she could more safely entertain them—
to where a different sort of chain would chain them!

67
And since it had already passed the day
established by the captain for her aid,
she went to him in reverence, to say,
"The day you chose has come and gone, my lord,
and if the tyrant hears news that I may
be moving with what help you can afford,
he would prepare his forces in defense,
making it harder to achieve our ends.

68
"And so before the shifting wind of rumor
—or some reliable spy—brings him this news,
let me go with a few of your strongest knights,
only a few—let your compassion choose!
If heaven does not forget the innocent
or look askance at what a mortal does,
I'll be restored, and you will gain a land
whose duty in peace and war you may command."

69
So she said, and the captain heard her out,
and granted all that couldn't be denied,
although he saw that her departing haste
meant that the help was his now to decide.
But everyone insisted that he be
one of the ten selected for her side,
and the rivalry awakened in their breasts
made all the more demanding their requests.

70

Seeing this, she who read their open hearts
derived new hope for strategy, and so
applied the whip of jealousy to their flanks,
torturing them with fear to make them go,
well knowing that without such tricks, desire
eventually grows old and fat and slow,
as a stallion is less speedy on the run
when he is not pursuing anyone.

71

So carefully she parceled out her words,
flattered them with her glance, and sweetly smiled,
that each was envious of his comrade's luck;
in hope and fear at once they were beguiled.
So, pricked on by the art of a lying face,
her foolish herd of men in love ran wild—
and shame itself could not apply the rein,
for their chief had reproached them all in vain.

72

He, who wanted that all be satisfied,
who wished to show no partiality
(though he was often enraged, or mortified
by his knights' undirected vanity),
when he observed them stiff-necked in their love,
chose a new plan to bring them to agree.
"Let all your names be entered in this urn.
The ten will go, to whom the chances turn."

73

Everyone wrote his name down right away
and placed it in the urn, where they were shaken
and drawn at random; and the count of Pembroke
Artemidorus was the first name taken;
then they heard call the name Gerard, and then
the aged Wenceslaus, who had forsaken
the dignity he had been master of
to babble like a gray-haired boy in love.

74

How glad the face, how brightly the eye shines
with a delight that wells up from the heart—
in those first three, whose amorous designs
fortune now smiles upon, to take their part!
The rest, whose names the urn conceals, show signs
of jealousy and an uncertain heart,
and hang upon the lips of him who spreads
the folded slips of paper drawn, and reads.

75
Guasco came fourth, with Rudolph hard upon,
then Olderic completed the next three;
then they read out William of Roncillon,
Bavarian Eberard, and French Henri.
Rambaldo was the last name to be drawn,
who, changing faith, became Christ's enemy—
is Love so potent then? And thus concluded
the choosing of the ten, the rest excluded.

76
Burning with envy, wrath, and jealousy,
the others blamed the wickedness of chance,
and blamed you too, Love—you who would agree
to give it judgeship in your governance.
Forbid a man to taste a thing, and he
craves it with all the greater vehemence:
wherefore many decide, in fortune's spite,
to follow the lady in the dark of night.

77
They longed to follow her always, in sun and shade,
and risk their lives by fighting in her cause.
Inviting them to do just that, she played
with sweet sighs, broken words, and the forced pause,
and now with that one, now with this one, made
as if she grieved to say goodbye—and draws
his spirit on. Meanwhile the chosen ten
arm, and take leave of Godfrey, who again

78
admonishes them wisely, one by one,
how pagan faith is dubious and light,
a fickle pledge; and how a man must shun
mischance and treachery by prudent flight;
but his words are all scattered to the wind.
Love will not heed a man who counsels right.
At last he let them go. The conquering lady
does not delay till morning, but already

79
has left the camp, before her the ten rivals
led on like captives in a long parade.
They left the mob of suitors far behind,
left them with countless reasons to be dismayed,
but in the darkest hours, when sleep and silence
and wandering dreams are hovering in the shade,
many such lovers, with desire their spy,
followed Armida's traces on the sly.

80

Eustace was first, and he could hardly wait
for the advancing shadows, but took flight
all in a flutter where Love beckoned him,
blind leader through the blindness of the night.
He wandered all that cool and quiet evening,
but with the sweet arrival of dawn's light
appeared Armida and her band, where they
took lodgings in a village until day.

81

He galloped toward her, but as he drew near
Rambaldo knew him by his shield, and cried,
"What do you want from us? Why are you here?"
"I've come to follow Armida," he replied.
"My help will be as prompt, my service true
as any man's, if I am not denied."
The other shot back, "For the honor of
this service, who chose you?" He answered, "Love."

82

"I was chosen by Love, and you, by chance.
Which do you think had greater right to choose?"
"Your false title is worthless," said Rambaldo,
"and just as worthless are the tricks you use.
You can't intrude among the champions
of the virgin princess, chosen by the laws.
You—you're a bastard slave!" "And who would try
to stop me?" snarled the boy, his temper high.

83

"I'll stop you well enough!" the other cried,
and in so saying rushed to the attack,
and with a will no less thrust on by pride
and passion, Eustace moved to beat him back.
But here the tyrant of their passion spied
the fight, and stepped between and held them back,
saying to the one, "Ah, do not be displeased
if the number of my champions is increased.

84

"You love my safety? Then why should you deprive me
of new assistance in my great distress?"
To Eustace then, "Defender of my fame
and of my life, it would be reasonless
if I renounced your kind and timely help,
and a companion of such graciousness."
With such words she picked up along the way
a couple of new champions before day,

85
some here, some there; none aware of any others;
each looking at the next sour-eyed and grim.
Yet she was glad to have each in her fold—
with feigned relief and joy she welcomed him.
But Godfrey was aware of their defection
soon as the dawn had cleared the twilight dim,
and seemed to suffer for them in his mind,
on account of the troubles he divined.

86
But meanwhile there appeared an envoy, breathless,
dusty, affliction in his look; somehow
he seemed a man who has to bring bad news;
worry and pain were written on his brow.
He spoke, "My lord, the great armada of
Egypt is sailing on the ocean now,
and he who sends you this announcement is
William, the admiral of the Genovese."

87
He added that a convoy of supplies
was en route to the army from the ship,
but the caravan had found its way cut off
and ambushed in the middle of the trip;
that their escorts were all hewn down in battle
or seized as slaves; that not a soul could slip
out of the valley, trapped both front and rear
by the thieving villains of Arabia.

88
And that the wanton madness and the rage
of those barbarian nomads was so great,
which like a swollen river with no check
was spilling everywhere to inundate,
that a detachment must be sent there quick
to put some fear into them, and create
safe conduct for the convoys from the shore
to bring the host supplies to fight the war.

89
In a flash, from one speaker to another,
the news was passed along for all to hear,
and it aroused within the common soldier
great worry for the hunger waiting near.
But the wise chief, who saw their usual valor
conceding to an unaccustomed fear,
tried to console his troops and reassure them,
and with a cheerful face he spoke before them:

90
"You who have suffered through a thousand troubles
and endured perils everywhere with me,
you champions of God, you who were born
to restore His Christian faith from injury,
you who survived Greek lies and the arms of Persia,
and storms and winters and mountains and the sea,
who bore the pains of thirst and hunger too—
what is there that should stir such fear in you?

91
"And will the Lord, Who moves you and is your guide,
as we have seen in dangers far more grave,
not bear you up—as if He turned aside
His merciful eye and right hand strong to save?
Your vows someday will all be satisfied,
and you will gladly think of all you have
endured. Persist, be bold of heart, I pray!
Preserve yourselves for the more prosperous day."

92
With these words he consoled their straying thoughts,
and with a happy and untroubled eye,
but deep within the center of his breast
a thousand cares pressed at him painfully;
he worries how to feed so great a host,
about the defections, about their poverty,
how to oppose the armada at sea, and worse,
how to subdue the Arab predators.

Canto Six

1
But there was surer hope and comfort for
the besieged people on the other side.
Besides their gathered food, in the dead of night
other provisions had been brought inside,
and the city ramparts facing to the north
with arms and war machines were fortified,
so that the heightened, solid, thick-laid wall
seemed to stand fearless and unshakeable.

2
And still the king gave orders roundabout
to buttress up those walls, or raise those towers,
in the golden rays of the sun, or the pale gleam
of the dark sky lighted by moon and stars;
and in the weary forging of new arms
his sweating blacksmiths slogged for hours and hours.
In the midst of this a warrior approached him,
the intolerant Argante, and reproached him:

3
"How long shall we be jailed behind this wall,
trapped by a siege that seems interminable!
Oh, I can hear the clashing hammer fall
on anvil, beating shields and helmets—still
I never see them put to use at all!
Yet those thieves run through town and field at will,
and we don't halt their passage, or raise slight
alarms at least to break their sleep at night.

4
"Their noonday meals are never broken short,
they eat their happy suppers unmolested;
rather they draw out the long day and night
in perfect safety, reassured, well rested.
But you—hunger and hardship will compel you
to give the city over uncontested,
or you must die here, die a coward's fate,
if the Egyptian troops should come too late.

5

"For my part, I refuse to end my days
under the dim pall of oblivion,
with a vile death. The next life-giving rays
of dawn shall not discover me shut in.
What of this life of mine? A settled case—
fixed by the fates above, decided on—
but not my fall! I shall not die without
the thrust of sword, and leave my fame in doubt!

6

"If in you there is still some spark, some seed
of the valor you once showed in days gone by,
not only an honorable battle death indeed,
but you can hope for life and victory!
Then let us go together with all speed
to meet our fate and fight the enemy!
When with the gravest dangers we are pressed
the boldest counsel often is the best.

7

"But if you put small hope in overdaring
and will not charge with every regiment,
at least propose that two picked fighters may
decide the outcome of your argument.
And, that the Frankish captain may be more
eager to take the challenge we present,
let the arms and the rules be his decision,
whatever he thinks will bolster his position.

8

"For if the foe has two hands and one soul—
whatever fiery boldness may commend it—
you need not fear misfortune for your cause;
right will not lose when I'm there to defend it.
Instead of fate and fortune, my right arm
can grant you triumph in this war, and end it!
I give it as a pledge now, safe and sure.
Trust in it, sire. Your reign will be secure."

9

He finished. "Brave young man," the king replies,
"although you see me now weighed down and old,
this soul is not so base and listless, this
sword-wielding hand is not so slow and cold,
that I prefer to live in cowardice
than die a death magnanimous and bold—
if I had any fear or any doubt
of the hunger and hard times you warn about.

10
"Perish the thought. But now I wish to tell you
what I have hidden from the art of spies.
Soliman of Nicaea, who, in part,
craves vengeance for inflicted injuries,
has gathered up the wandering Arab clans
from here to where the shore of Libya lies.
To bring us aid and sustenance, they propose
launching a night attack upon our foes.

11
"He will arrive soon. Meanwhile, if our towns
are overrun and captured and oppressed,
no matter, for I yet preserve my throne,
and the royal mantle that enfolds my breast.
But you! temper a little that hot courage
which seethes in you, by God, and tops the crest!
And wait until the time is ripe to claim
my vengeance, and the glory of your name."

12
The bold Saracen chafed at such a thing
(for he was an old rival of Soliman),
so bitterly it stung him that the king
expected such deliverance from this man.
"Sire," he replied, "it's up to you to bring
both war and peace. I say no more. You can
dally here until Soliman has shown.
Let him defend your reign, who lost his own.

13
"Let him come like some angel post from heaven,
sent down to set the pagan people free.
But I, I am sufficient for myself;
this hand alone secures my liberty.
Then while the others rest here, let me go
down to the plain for battle. I shall be
a private knight, and not your champion,
and fight among the Frenchmen, one on one."

14
Answered the king, "Although you should reserve
your sword and anger for a better use,
yet if it pleases you to challenge some
enemy warrior, I will not refuse."
At that, Argante waited not a moment,
but "Go," he said to a herald, "bring this news
to the French chief. Make sure the whole host knows,
for it is no small matter I propose:

15
"There is a knight who hates having to rest
behind this strongly buttressed shield of stone,
and is hungry to put his fighting to the test
in the plain between his forces and your own,
to make his prowess widely manifest.
He comes prepared to prove his valor: one
who puts more faith in the strength of his own hand
than in the manhood of the Christian band.

16
"Add that he straps his weapons not to dare
one or two fighters from the enemy,
but after those a third, and then two more,
anyone, commons or nobility!
Free passage guaranteed, and as in war
the loser is the victor's slave." So he
gave his instructions, and the other dressed
his armor in the envoy's purple vest,

17
and when he had found Godfrey and his peers,
the regal prince and all his baronry,
he asked, "My lord, do you give messengers
full leave to speak to you at liberty?"
"We do," answered the captain. "Have no fears.
Tell us whatever you wish to say. Be free."
"Now," said the herald, "it shall be come to light
whether my news brings terror or delight."

18
He went on, and described Argante's challenge
in words high-soaring and magnificent.
That proud band muttered as the envoy spoke,
their fierce resentment all too evident,
and Godfrey answered without delay, "Your knight
will find it hard to realize his intent.
This enterprise will pain him, have no doubt—
our fifth man will not need to try him out!

19
"Even so, I will offer him a field
free and secure, for him to prove his sword.
Then let him come and battle without odds
one of my champions. I give my word."
And that was all he said. The herald then
retraced his steps, and made his way back toward
the city, with not a moment's hesitation,
till he reported to the proud Circassian.

20
"Arm, my great lord! What are you waiting for?
The Christians fling the challenge back at you,
and not only the chiefest warriors are
eager to fight, but the less valiant too.
A thousand threatening faces I saw there,
a thousand hands ready to cut and hew.
The chief grants you a place secure from harm."
So he, and Argante at once began to arm,

21
girding himself, calling for weapons, impatient
to race down to the field and start the fight.
But the king said to Clorinda, who was present,
"That he should go while you stay is not right.
Escort him with a thousand-strong detachment
and thus ensure safe passage for our knight.
But you, retire a little with your band
and let him fight alone, as the rules demand."

22
So the king finished, and the pagan force,
armed, left the shut gates for the open air,
led by Argante mounted on his horse
decked in the trappings he was used to wear.
Between the Christian palings and the towers
there was a broad, capacious area
where the level land seemed fashioned by design
to be a Field of Mars in Palestine.

23
And there the proud Argante went alone,
and there he stopped, by all his enemies seen,
with his great heart, his great bulk, and great strength,
of haughty and intimidating mien,
like an Enceladus in Phlegra, or
the valley-shadowing giant Philistine.
Many were unafraid of him because
they didn't fully know how strong he was.

24
Among so many, though, the pious Godfrey
had singled out no fighter as the best.
But all eyes turned to Tancred . . . He could see
the wishes and affection they expressed,
and the ideal of the nobility
was in their faces fully manifest.
Then the youth's name was whispered, and not low,
and the captain approved him with his brow.

25
Everyone else gave way to him. And now
the good chief made no secret of his desire.
"Go," he said, "I do not forbid you, go!
And put out that mad villain's raging fire."
Then with a face of confidence and joy
for such high honor, the proud lad called his squire
to fetch his horse and helmet. Many stayed
beside him, riding out from the stockade,

26
but he was still far from the field where stood
Argante, when a vision struck his eye,
a rare and lovely sight: for he beheld
the lofty maiden warrior nearby.
Her mantle was far whiter than the snow
on Alpine hills; she wore her visor high,
showing her face, and stood on rising ground,
discovering her splendor all around.

27
No more he watches the Circassian raise
his terrifying forehead to the skies,
but moves his steed along at a slow pace,
and toward the hill and lady turns his eyes.
Then he stops, as a stone fixed in its place;
he boils within; without, as cold as ice.
His pleasure gazing on his love is such
that the fight no longer matters to him much.

28
Argante saw no sign on the French side
of anyone preparing for the match.
"Who's coming forward for our joust?" he cried.
"I'm here to fight a contest, not to watch!"
The other, as if stunned or stupefied,
stood riveted, and no sound seemed to catch
his ears. Then Otto spurs his war horse on,
first to enter the empty arena—one

29
who had been burning with a high desire
to go against the pagan champion,
yet had conceded the first place to Tancred,
following after as the youth set on,
but now, seeing him stand, unwilling to fight
(there's something else his mind is fixed upon),
the youth, bold and impatient, eagerly
seized the offered opportunity

30

and quicker than a panther in the woods
or supple tiger with his loping stride,
he raced to strike the arrogant Saracen
who couched his huge lance on the other side.
Tancred now shook himself, at last awaking
from the sloth of his dreamy thoughts, and cried,
"Stay put! This fight belongs to me!" Instead
Otto had already run too far ahead,

31

so Tancred stopped, and flushed a fiery red,
seething inside for rage and sheer vexation—
that someone else should be the first afield
was a grave insult to his reputation.
But meanwhile in mid-gallop the bold lad
struck a blow on the helm of the Circassian,
but he for his part met him ready steeled,
cleaving the breastplate under his slashed shield.

32

The Christian falls. It is a bitter stroke
that yanks him by the crupper off his horse,
but the pagan, far from falling, never flinched—
possessed of stronger stamina and force.
Over the fallen knight he stood and spoke,
with his demeanor arrogant and coarse:
"Give up, and let your greatest glory be
that you can say you battled once with me."

33

"We never lay our weapons down so soon!
No, no, that's not our way!" came the reply.
"Someone can find excuses for my fall,
But I'll avenge my honor here, or die."
Argante's breathing seemed to seethe in flame,
Medusa and Alecto in his eye.
"Then you will know my strength by proof," said he,
"since you're so pleased to spurn my courtesy."

34

With that he gave his horse the spur, forgetting
all things required by the chivalric code.
The Frank gave ground, eluded the rough meeting,
but pierced the pagan's right side as he rode.
So serious and so cruel was this beating
that the blade was retracted streaked with blood.
Yet what's the use, if a blow can't dispel
the victor's power, but wakes his rage as well?

35
Argante reins his thoroughbred mid-run
and wheels him roundabout so fast, his foe
(who hardly had a moment to see it come)
was pummeled by an unexpected blow.
The knocking set his legs atremble, shook
his heart with terror, made his breathing grow
faint, his face white. Exhausted, sapped of strength,
on the hard earth he bruised his feeble length.

36
A felon in his wrath, Argante rides
trampling the fighter's breast like a bare street,
shouting, "Let every one who loves his pride
end up like him who lies beneath my feet!"
But now, disgusted by this cruel deed,
Tancred who never yet had known defeat
charged—hoping his once-bright courage would yet make
illustrious amends for his mistake—

37
charged, and called to the pagan, "Soul of a coward!
Scandalous even in your victory!
You expect noble praise for a reward
when your ways are so full of villainy?
You were brought up in a thieving Arab horde
or some such other barbarous crew. Go flee
the light, go to the woods to find your lair
and with the other beasts be cruel there!"

38
The pagan bit his lip, consumed with fury—
he was not used to suffer such talk before—
and wanted to say—but the sound came out confused
and garbled in an animal growl or roar—
or as the impetuous bolt of lightning bursts
the cloud that pent it up within its core,
so it seemed, from the pressure they were under,
his words burst from his fiery breast like thunder.

39
Now that fierce threats had made the two agree—
they chafed each other's wrath and arrogance—
both swung their horses round immediately
to give good room for the career with lance.
Now Muse, lend power to the voice in me,
inspire a fury as great as theirs, enhance
my verse, to make it fit the deeds I sing.
Echo the sounds that from great battles ring!

40
Now the two ready warriors set their thick
and knotty lances, aiming them well high,
nor was there ever a leap or a race so quick,
swifter than even the feathered birds can fly,
nor ever rage as mad as Tancred's rage
assaulting, and Argante's in reply.
The lances strike the steel of helms and shatter,
and fiery sparks and shards and splinters scatter.

41
The thunder alone of that collision moved
the immovable earth, and made the hills resound,
but their proud heads were still not forced to bend
under the shock of the furious blows dealt round;
both one and the other horse staggered so badly
they were not quick to get up from the ground.
The grand masters of war then left the saddle,
planted their feet firm, drew their swords for battle.

42
Each moves his watchful right hand well prepared
to parry the blow—each shifts his eyes, his feet
to answer stance for stance, to keep on guard;
now they circle, or lunge forward, or retreat,
now feint as if to strike here, and now there,
looking to wound where they have made no threat;
now leave themselves defenseless in some part,
art trying to make mockery of art.

43
His right flank to the pagan Tancred shows,
poorly protected by his shield and sword.
The pagan runs to strike, but must expose,
without hope of defense, his left side's ward.
With one thrust Tancred slashes back his foe's
raw steel, and fetches him a blow off-guard;
that done, he is not slow then to step back
and gather himself to ward the counterattack.

44
The wild Argante, who beholds his armor
bespattered now and soaked with his own blood,
shudders and gasps with unaccustomed horror,
with pain and agitation half gone mad,
and swept by the momentum of his anger
raises his voice together with his sword
and turns to strike, but instead takes a blow
just where the shoulder joins the arm below.

45
As a bear in the mountain woods, whose rage
mounts as he feels the spear stuck in his side,
who hurls himself against the hunter and
takes death and danger on unterrified,
so the indomitable pagan as
blow follows blow and insults cut his pride,
longs for revenge with such inflamed devotion
risk and defense are a forgotten notion;

46
and joining to his hot and reckless passion
extraordinary strength and tireless vigor,
so smartly swept the blade of the Circassian,
he made the heavens rumble, the earth quiver.
The other had no time for his own slashing,
to strike, to catch his breath, to gain some cover,
and no shield could have left him the securer
against Argante's unremitting furor.

47
Tancred, drawn in and huddled, waits in vain
for the tempest of those blows to pass him by,
now puts up a defense, now turns aside
quick-stepping to evade the enemy.
But since the pagan's rage did not subside,
he had to let himself be swept away,
and, anger and fury overwhelming sense,
whirled his sword with his utmost violence.

48
Reason and art are conquered now by wrath.
Ministering fury makes their forces grow.
Wherever the blade falls, it cuts a path
through mail or breastplate, landing every blow.
Iron shards stained with blood litter the earth,
shards stained with blood, blood mingled with sweat. For now
their flashing and resounding swords are like
deafening bolts of lightning when they strike.

49
The Christians and the pagans hang in doubt,
looking upon this strange and savage sight,
in fear and hope awaiting the end of the bout,
watching the wavering fortunes of the fight,
and no one hears or sees in all that rout
a whisper or a sign however slight,
but everyone stands silent, without motion,
except the tremor of the heart's commotion.

50
By now both men were weary, and who can tell,
both might have fought to an untimely end,
but on a sudden such a darkness fell
that it hid even objects near at hand.
So heralds from both camps raced to compel
their parting (and they did so in the end):
Arideus of the Christian alliance
and Pindor, who'd delivered the defiance.

51
Between the swords of the combatants they
made bold to interpose their rods of peace,
with the assurance granted to them by
the law of nations from the ancient days.
"You are, O warriors," Pindor began to say,
"of equal prowess, merit equal praise.
Therefore observe, by ceasing now to fight,
the repose and prerogatives of night.

52
"The time for work is while the sun is high,
but in the night all living creatures rest,
nor is a deed that's hid and silenced by
night what the noble heart can cherish best."
"Shade or no shade," Argante made reply,
"it does not please me to give up my test.
I'd love to have the witness of the day,
but will *he* promise to resume our play?"

53
"You promise too," the other counterchecked,
"and bring your prisoner with you. My condition.
For if you don't, you never need expect
another day to end our competition."
They swear. The heralds (chosen to select
a better time for fighting), in submission
to wounds that justified a good delay,
decided on the dawn of the sixth day.

54
Within the Saracen and Christian hearts
the horrible battle left a deep impression
which did not vanish for the longest time,
a kind of frightening awe and admiration.
The ardor and the bravery they both showed
was the continual topic of discussion,
but as for which of the two should be preferred,
the many-opinioned crowd never concurred,

55
but hung in expectation and suspense,
wondering how the savage fight would end:
would fury defeat virtue? would patient strength
compel the neck of arrogance to bend?
But more than all the rest, lovely Erminia
is in a torment—for she sees depend
half of her very life and soul, or more,
from the nod of the fickle god of war.

56
King Cassan used to be the emperor of
Antioch, and Erminia was his daughter.
But when that reign was taken by the Christian,
along with other spoils the triumph brought her
into Prince Tancred's power, who was so kind
while he was lord, no further harm distraught her,
and though her noble fatherland had been
defeated, she was honored as a queen.

57
The knight par excellence paid her due honor,
preserved her life, and gave her liberty,
and all her riches he bestowed upon her,
leaving untouched her gold and jewelry.
She—recognizing in his looks and manner
and his green years the soul of royalty—
was bound and taken Cupid's prisoner.
He'd never bound so hard as he bound her.

58
So if her body had liberty again,
servitude kept her spirit shackled tight.
Although to leave her dear lord caused her pain—
for now her prison was her chief delight—
her regal honor, which a great-souled woman
must not neglect, no matter what the plight,
forced her to leave her land with her aged mother
and seek out better fortunes in some other.

59
To Jerusalem she came, and was received
by the tyrant ruler of the Hebrew state.
But soon, enshrouded in the black of mourning,
Erminia wept her mother's bitter fate.
But neither the sorrow of death nor her unhappy
exile could in the least eradicate
from her true heart her amorous desire,
nor could it douse one spark of such a fire.

60

Poor girl, she loves, and burns in love. So little
presents itself to soothe her misery,
that in her heart she tends the hidden fire
much less with hoping than with memory,
and the more this fire is shut in a secret place
the more it blazes uncontrollably.
But Tancred wakened all her hopes again
when he came to Jerusalem with his men.

61

At the appearance of so many proud
triumphant peoples, others shook with fright,
but her once troubled countenance grew calm.
She gazed at their great squadrons with delight,
and searching over among their weaponed bands
avidly tried to catch him in her sight,
her dearly beloved. Often her searches miss
but often she sees him clearly—"There he is!"

62

Within the royal palace there arose
an ancient tower near the city wall,
from whose high vantage all the Christian foes,
the mountains, and the plain were visible.
Here from the time the lamp of dawn first shows
until the world is darkened with night's fall
she sits; upon the camp she turns her eyes,
and with her secret thoughts she talks and sighs.

63

From there she saw the combat, and she felt
the tremors in her beating heart so rife
they seemed to speak to her, "There is your love,
there he is, and in peril of his life."
So full of anguish, full of fear, she watched
blow after blow of that uncertain strife;
when the pagan raised his sword, her soul would feel
the shock and penetration of the steel.

64

But when she heard the truth, and learned that she
would have to suffer through the battle twice,
a new fear gripped her heart so thoroughly
she felt the blood within her turn to ice.
Sometimes she wept in secret, sometimes she
had to conceal her scattered groans and sighs.
In her face fear and sorrow were portrayed—
pallid and bloodless, trembling and dismayed.

65
Her thoughts are thick with images, atrocious,
troubling and torturing her constantly,
and, worse than death itself, sleep is ferocious,
presenting nightmares of strange fantasy,
for she dreams that her beloved cavalier
lies mangled, bleeding—and she hears him cry
"Erminia, help me!" Wakened by her fears
she finds her eyes and breast are wet with tears.

66
The fear of future loss was not alone
what shook her troubled heart with loving care,
but the strokes he had already undergone
made a quiet soul impossible for her,
and cares of things far distant and unknown
grow all the worse from rumors people hear—
so that she sees the mighty warrior lying
oppressed and languishing and close to dying.

67
And since her mother had once taught her all
the secret healing powers that herbs retain,
and with what magic incantations one
can make hurt members whole, and ease the pain
(an art it seems passed down throughout the years
by all the princesses in that domain),
by her own hands his wounds must be restored,
returning health to her beloved lord.

68
So she desired to be her loved one's nurse
but had to cure his enemy instead.
Sometimes she even thought she should asperse
poisonous juices where Argante bled,
but the hand of the pious maiden was averse
to the black arts—she would not do the deed.
Rather she wished that all the powers were void
in the charms and the aloes she employed.

69
She would have had no fear to go among
the foe—for she had come a fugitive;
she had seen much of war and slaughtering;
she had a weary and dangerous life to live,
so that her womanly temper had, by long
custom, grown bold and hardy far above
its nature, and was undisturbed by things
less fearful than the gravest sufferings.

70
But more than anything else, audacious Love
unburdened all the fear from her soft breast,
and among the ripping claws and venom of
African beasts she'd have gone undistressed,
but though she wasn't frightened for her life,
attending to her good name still seemed best.
Two potent foes began to duel within her—
Honor and Love—and doubtful which the winner.

71
One reasoned with her thus, "O virgin lady,
with you my laws have always been regarded.
When you were handmaid to the enemy
I kept your mind and members chastely guarded;
and now you're out of prison, now you're free,
will that most precious virtue be discarded?
What are you thinking? What can your hopes impart?
Ah, who can arouse such thoughts in your soft heart?

72
"Do you esteem the praise of honesty
so lightly, and the fame of being chaste,
that you'll go skulking to the enemy,
nocturnal lover, and seek to be dispraised?
Then he will say, proud in his victory,
'Your kingdom's lost, your royal soul's defaced.
You are not worthy of me.' And send you out
among the mob as spoils to pass about."

73
On the other side the lying counselor
uses his pleasing flatteries to entice:
"You were not born of a voracious bear,
my girl, nor from some rock as hard as ice,
that you should always flee what pleases you
and hold Love's torch and arrows at small price!
Your breast's not made of adamant or steel
that you should be ashamed of the love you feel.

74
"Oh, follow where desire is tempting you!
What 'cruel victor' are you dreaming of?
Don't you remember how your pain became
his own, and how your tears and sorrow clove
his heart? No, *you're* the cruel one, so slow
to bring recovery to your faithful love.
The worthy Tancred languishes, while you—
proud and ungrateful—sit to cure his foe!

75
"Go then and cure Argante, that you may
thrust to his death the man who set you free!
All of your obligations, toss away—
and prettily rewarded he would be.
Yet is it possible that you can stay
ministering your office of impiety,
and not feel such revulsion and disgrace
that they alone would make you flee this place?

76
"Ah, it would be a kind and human duty,
and with what joy and pleasure you'd be blessed,
if you could lay your healing, pitying hand
near to the Christian hero's valorous breast;
and your lord's color, lost, would blush again,
for you would make him whole. And this gift's best
reward for you: to gaze in wonderment
upon his manly beauty, now all spent.

77
"Then you would share a part of all his praises,
and all the deeds that give him high renown,
and then he'd gladden you with pure embraces
and a happy wedding day. You would be known
by all the mothers of the Latin races
and all the wives, and honor would be shown
wherever you went in lovely Italy,
the land of courage and fidelity."

78
Lured by such hopes—ah, foolish girl—she dreamed
she'd find the highest happiness of all,
yet found herself enmeshed in many doubts,
whether to leave were safe or feasible,
for the sentinels were watchful in their rounds
outside the palace and upon the wall.
Nor would they ever, under martial laws,
unbar a gate without the gravest cause.

79
Erminia used to while the hours away
in the company of the lady warrior.
The sunlight dropping in the western bay,
the dawn arising saw Clorinda with her,
and at the dousing of the light of day
in the same bed they sometimes slept together.
None of their thoughts the girls kept under cover,
unless Erminia's thoughts about her lover.

80
That is the only thing Erminia keeps
secret from her, although she must pretend
(Clorinda often hears how much she weeps)
that her misfortunes make her heart descend
into unhappiness. Their love is such
that she may come and go and not offend.
No room to her is under lock or bar,
whether Clorinda's in, or at the war.

81
There came, in fact, a day when she was out,
and, deep in thought, Erminia stopped by,
revolving how to shrewdly bring about
her much-desired departure, secretly.
While her uncertain soul wavered from thought
to various thought without a rest, nearby
she looked and saw the mail and weapons of
Clorinda hanging, and she sighed for love,

82
and to herself complained amid her sighs,
"How blest by fortune is this warlike lady!
How much I envy her! and what I prize
is not a woman's fame or boast of beauty.
Petticoats never slow her where she flies,
her valor's not pent in some jealous study,
she straps her weapons when she wants, and goes!
Fear and shame never hinder what she does.

83
"Ah, why did heaven and nature make me frail!
Why not so powerful of chest and limb? It
would have permitted me to change my veil
and bodice for a breastplate and a helmet!
Then my fierce love would fear no rain or hail,
no fire or ice would check or overwhelm it.
Accompanied or alone, by night or day,
I would go armed to battle anyway.

84
"And you, O pitiless Argante, you
would never have met my lord first in the fight.
I would have run to meet him long ago.
Maybe by now imprisoned by my might,
suffering enslavement to his loving foe,
he'd find his yoke was sweet, and burden light . . .
And my own bonds, because of his, would please,
weighing upon me lightly and with ease.

85
"Or maybe his right arm would pierce my side
and open up my wounded heart again,
and in this way my heart would be made whole;
the pain of the entering sword would ease Love's pain,
and then my weary body and my mind
would rest in peace. Perhaps then he would deign—
the victor—to let my bones and ashes have
the honor of a few tears, and a grave.

86
"Alas, I want what is impossible!
I'm carried away by an empty, silly thought!
Here I will stay, timid and sorrowful,
one of the ordinary female rout.
But why can't I put armor on for once?
I won't stay, no! Be confident, my heart!
For a short time can't I sustain the weight,
although I am weak and soft and delicate?

87
"Yes, yes, I can! The tyrant Love will make
me powerful enough to bear it! For
even the gentle deer, love-stricken, take
the arms of strong desire, and go to war.
I only want to pull a cunning trick—
fighting's not what I want these weapons for.
I'll dress up as Clorinda! Her appearance
will grant to me an automatic clearance.

88
"None of the sentries at the gate would dare
put up resistance to her passing through it.
I puzzle, but no other means appear—
this seems the only obvious way to do it.
Now on my innocent fraud, Fortune, look fair;
and Love, for you inspire me to pursue it!
The hour is perfect now to try the thing:
Clorinda is in council with the king."

89
So she resolves, goaded on by the spurs
of the furies of Love—and no delay.
From that adjoining chamber into hers
she runs to bring the stolen arms away
(and she could do so since, when she appears,
the others leave her by herself, give way,
and also her theft is sheltered under cover
of night, the friend of every thief and lover).

90
Seeing the darkness dropping in the sky—
already sown with a few stars' scattered fire—
without allowing hesitation she
secretly summons her most faithful squire
and a loyal maid she loved devotedly,
and reveals to them a part of her desire,
her plan to flee; but makes them both believe
another cause is forcing her to leave.

91
The trusty squire immediately sets out
to put all they would need in readiness.
Erminia meanwhile slips out of her clothes;
unto her feet falls the luxurious dress,
and in a slender garment she exceeds
belief, such is her simple loveliness.
Except the ones she chose to help her flee
she had no other aid or company.

92
She buckled tight and hurt with hardest steel
her neck so delicate, her golden hair.
Her tender hand took hold of the great shield,
a burden still too great for her to bear.
So all decked out in iron she shone still,
and conquered her sweet self, a soldier fair;
Love, who was present, laughed until he hurt,
as when he made Alcides wear a skirt!

93
Oh, what a trouble it was for her slow steps
to move beneath that disproportionate load,
and she leaned on her loyal handmaid's arm
who kindly walked before her on the road.
Love and hope lent her girlish limbs new strength
and vigor for her spirits, that never slowed
till they reached where the trusty squire was placed
to wait their coming; mounted then in haste.

94
Disguised they go, and take the secretest
and most roundabout way they can, by art,
yet they encounter many, and see the night
lit up with glints of steel in every part,
but no one dares to interrupt their journey;
they give them a wide berth and walk apart,
for even in the dark they recognize
the white cloak and its terrible device.

95
Although she had in part settled her doubts,
Erminia's confidence had a slender hold.
She frets she'll be discovered in the end
and starts to fear that she's been overbold.
But when she reached the gates she squelched her fear
and fooled the guard. Now with her doubts controlled,
"I am Clorinda, open the gate!" says she,
"on serious business the king commissions me."

96
The feminine voice was like Clorinda's own,
and that made the deception easier—
for who would think to see, mounted and armed,
one of those who knew nothing about war?
So the porter readily obeyed, and quickly
she passed through, and the two who went with her.
And that they might be safe and hard to find,
they enter glens by paths that err and wind.

97
Seeing the solitary lands about,
Erminia allowed her pace to slow.
The first dangers were past, without a doubt;
she had no fear of being taken now.
But then she thinks what she had not thought out
so well before—for in her haste to go
desire had not shown clearly her position,
how hard it would be for her to gain admission.

98
She sees that riding among fierce enemies,
dressed like a soldier, is not very wise;
on the other hand, until she finds her lord,
she'd not reveal herself to any eyes;
desires to meet him, honesty secured,
a lover come in secret and surprise;
so, made more careful by her better thought,
she paused, and spoke thus to her squire. "You ought,

99
"my loyal friend, to run ahead of me,
announce my coming, but be shrewd and quick.
Go to the camp, have someone lead you to
the tent where Tancred now is lying sick;
then tell him that a lady is on her way
to bring him healing, and that all I seek
is peace—a peace to give him health once more,
and me, a respite from the heat of war

100

"Love wages . . . Say her faith in him is so
sure and alive, she fears no spite or scorn.
Say only that. If he asks more, you know
nothing. Come back as quickly as you can.
Here in the meantime I'll be lying low,
waiting in this place till you return."
Such were the lady's words. The loyal one
took off as speedily as if he'd flown.

101

He knew just how to work it, that they might
take him behind the palings, amicably.
And so they led him to the resting knight,
whose looks were brightened by his embassy.
Leaving the prince to ponder all these things,
stirring a crowd of restless questions, he
hurried back with a sweet response to tell:
She may enter, as secretly as possible.

102

But meanwhile she, impatient, chafed and trembled
under the heavy burden of delay,
counted her courier's steps and thought to herself,
"Now he's arrived—now there—now on his way."
And it seems to her—and the thought brings her pain—
that he is not so fleet of foot today.
At last she pushes on, and uphill, whence
she can begin to glimpse the Christian tents.

103

The night had fallen. Without cloud or haze
its clear and starry veil began to unfurl,
and the moon arising scattered its soft rays
all mingled with a frost of living pearl;
the flames of her own love rose one by one,
as with the heavens went the enamored girl,
and in the friendly silence she revealed
the secrets of her love to the quiet field

104

where the Christian host was stationed. And she said,
"How sweet the Latin tents are to my eyes!
I draw near you and I am comforted,
refreshed and heartened by the airs that rise . . .
in you alone I look for rest. O heaven,
grant me some honest moments of repose,
and let the pain and warring in me cease.
Only in the midst of arms can I find peace.

105
"Accept me then, you tents; in you I find
that pity which Love promised I should see,
which I have seen, in my sweet lord so kind
and gentle, when I was in his custody.
Not for my rank of princess have I pined;
winning it back does not mean much to me.
It does not matter to my joy. But grant
that I may serve you—that is all I want."

106
So she said to herself, but could not see
how sorrowful a misfortune was preparing.
She was standing in a spot where the lovely ray
of heaven struck the armor she was wearing,
so that its polished gleam flashed far away,
with the pure white of her circling cloak appearing,
and her tigress emblem flashed so splendidly
that anyone would say, "That must be she."

107
Just as her luck would have it, very near
a whole platoon of soldiers lay in wait,
whose chiefs were Polyphernes and Alcander,
two Latin brothers sent there to frustrate
anyone bringing herds of sheep or cattle
in to the Saracens behind the gate.
(Her servant managed to get by them fast
because his turn was somewhat further past.)

108
Young Polyphernes, whose father had been slain
by Clorinda before his eyes, caught sight
of the noble warrior lady, having seen
her graceful clothing gleaming in the night,
and charged against her with his hidden men,
not holding the reins of his heart's motions tight
(his mad rage was too sudden to resist).
Crying, "You're dead!" he flung his spear—and missed.

109
As a deer, dying of thirst, with patient hoof
searches for water, vital, glistening,
where a stream is hid by the banks thick in leaf,
or out of the rock comes trickling a sweet spring,
if she meets the hounds just where she sought relief
in the summer shade and the wave's sweet comforting,
she turns and flees and in her great distress
forgets the parching heat and weariness,

110
so she who thought to quench the thirst of love
(whereof her infirm heart is ever afire)
in an honest and a joyous welcoming,
and give her weary thoughts chance to retire,
now that one comes against her to forbid it
and she hears the noise of swords and threats nearby her,
abandons herself and her desires perforce
and fearfully puts the spurs to her swift horse.

111
Unhappy Erminia fled, and eager to gallop
over the earth the hooves of her war horse pounded;
her maid fled too, and after the women followed
the troops and their chief, whose furious wrath abounded;
when from the tents, bringing his tardy news,
the loyal squire has just arrived; confounded,
with an anxious mind he joins them in the rout,
fear scattering them through all the hills about.

112
But the wiser brother, who had also seen
what surely appeared to be Clorinda, did
not wish to follow, as he was too far off,
but kept to where the waylayers were hid,
and sent a courier to bring the camp this news,
that his brother was pursuing no goat kid
or woolly flock or any similar prey
but Clorinda stricken with fear and running away;

113
that it was not reasonable to think that she
would choose to leave the town at such an hour
for any flimsy opportunity—
a chief, and not a common warrior.
Let the pious Godfrey judge and order; he
would do whatever his chief required him for.
The army soon hears news of the events,
the rumors reaching first the Latin tents.

114
Tancred, whose heart had hung precariously
from the first word he caught, now hearing this,
thinks, "Maybe the courteous lady came to me,
and now the danger's all my fault," and is
unwilling to rest; takes some of his weighty gear,
mounts, and departs the camp in stealthiness,
following the fresh traces, spurring his steed
to gallop after the lady at full speed.

Canto Seven

1

Meanwhile into the wooded, dark terrain
Erminia is swept away on her thoroughbred.
Her trembling hand no longer holds the rein;
she seems halfway between alive and dead.
She takes so many paths out of the main
(for by her horse's instincts she is led)
that none of the Christians can pursue her flight—
she and her horse have slipped too far from sight.

2

As after a prolonged and grueling chase
the hounds return, droopheaded, short of breath,
once they have lost for good their quarry's trace,
hid in the woods and out of the open heath,
so, tired and flushed with anger and disgrace,
the cavaliers give up. Still, scared to death,
she keeps on fleeing—as for those pursuing,
she dare not turn to see what they are doing!

3

She fled all the night long and all the day,
wandering without a plan, without a guide.
Her tears were all that she could ever see;
the only sound she heard was when she cried.
But when the sun had nestled in the sea,
his team unharnessed from their glorious ride,
she reached the Jordan River clear and deep,
and on its banks laid herself down to sleep.

4

She took no food, but fed on sorrow alone,
and thirsted for laments that did not cease,
when sleep, that gives to miserable men
quiet oblivion and its sweet release,
lulled both her senses and her grief, and fanned
its wings above her in a silent peace.
Yet still Love's various phantoms ever kept
troubling her peace and quiet while she slept.

5
She did not waken till she heard the birds
greeting the dawn with their glad chattering,
and the breeze playing with the waves and flowers,
and the bushes and the river murmuring.
Raising her languid eyes, she looks upon
a solitary haunt for shepherding,
and amid the rustling leaves and waters hears
sounds that recall her to her sighs and tears.

6
But while she wept, her sighs were broken by
clear notes which seemed to her (and were indeed)
singing of shepherds to accompany
their rough-hewn music of the woodland reed.
She rises, and in slow steps makes her way
where an old graybeard in the pleasant shade
sees his flocks graze and weaves a wicker tray,
listening to three lads who sing and play.

7
At the sight of her armor suddenly
they start—for arms were not so common there.
She sweetly reassured them to allay
their fears, and showed her eyes and golden hair.
"Fortunate folk, favored of heaven on high,
continue your good work and have no care,"
said she; "these arms bring war where war belongs,
not to your labors, not to your sweet songs."

8
Adding, "Good father, now when battle shocks
all the lands round in war's tremendous blaze,
how without fear of soldiers and attacks
can you stay here, enjoying peaceful days?"
"Child," he replied, "my family and my flocks
have always lived here safe from the disgrace
and the offense of war. Mars' raucous call
never disturbs these distant parts at all.

9
"Whether by heaven's grace the humble lives
of harmless shepherds are spared, and lifted up,
or as a bolt of lightning never rives
the lowly plains, but strikes the mountaintop,
so too the fury of foreign armies strives—
princes' proud heads are what they seek to lop,
and the marauding privates who love prey
are not allured by our low poverty.

10

"Low and worthless to others, dear to me.
No treasure do I crave, no kingly rod.
And never in my heart's tranquility
does care for power or money make abode.
I fear no poison squeezed into the cup;
for thirst, my stream is always clear and good.
My little garden and my flocks are able
to give enough food, free, for my poor table.

11

"For our desires are small and our needs few,
enough to preserve life, and keep us well.
Those are my own sons I point out to you,
keeping the flocks. For servants, none to tell.
So I live as the quiet hermits do,
watching the goats and deer frisk in the dell,
and the fish in this river flashing by,
and the small birds ruffling their feathers to the sky.

12

"There was a time when I was young and vain,
when all my longings were far otherwise.
I held the life of shepherds in disdain
and fled my native land for better skies.
I lived in Memphis once, and in that reign
was placed among the royal deputies,
and though I was the keeper of the grounds
I saw the sins wherein the court abounds.

13

"In my heart stirred that ardent hope to climb,
so I bore servitude's indignities.
But after I had passed my manhood's prime,
and saw my bold hopes die, assurance cease,
I longed for the repose of this sweet time
and sighed for lost simplicity and peace.
I bid goodbye to the court and all its strife,
and in these woods have lived a happy life."

14

All while he spoke, Erminia hung upon
the old man's gentle words, intent and quiet.
His wise speech sank into her heart; her senses'
turbulent waves were soothed a little by it.
After much thinking, she decides to stay
in that secluded solitude—or try it
at least a little while, that she might see
good fortune come again more readily.

15
Then said to the good old man, "O happy father,
who knew the ill by suffering the disease,
lest heaven should look askance at your sweet life
be moved by pity for my miseries
and take me in to such a wished-for haven.
I would be glad to dwell with you in peace.
Perhaps among these shadows some small part
of the weight will be lifted from my heart.

16
"For if you were in love with gems and gold,
which common men adore and idolize,
I have so much about me still, you could
satisfy all your longings with the prize."
At that, charming and pure as crystal, spilled
the tears of sorrow from her pretty eyes,
and so she told them part of her sad story—
her sorrow made the gentle shepherd sorry.

17
Then he consoled her tenderly, and took her,
warmed as if by the fire of fatherly care,
and brought her to his aged spouse, whom heaven
had given him, one heart and soul to share.
The royal girl then dressed in rustic clothes
and bound a homespun kerchief round her hair—
yet in her looks and motions nonetheless
she never really seemed a shepherdess.

18
Never could it be hid in simple garb,
that sublime light of her nobility;
even when she was at the meanest chores
all her works shone throughout with majesty.
With her poor shepherd's staff she leads the herds
from fold to pasture, in humility,
and learns to give their milk-filled teats the squeeze,
then churn the cream and press it into cheese.

19
But often, when the lambs lay in the shade
to cool themselves from the hot summer rays,
in the bark of laurel and oak she signed the name
of her beloved in a hundred ways,
carving about her strange, unhappy love
a hundred sorrowing songs and roundelays.
And when she read her words she could not speak
without the prettiest tears to dew her cheek.

20
Then she said through her tears, "O friendly trees,
let this sad story be preserved in you,
for if beneath your welcome shade should pause
a lover someday who is good and true,
let my many misfortunes stir his heart
to pity me; and let him say, 'Ah, too
unjustly, Fortune and Love, did you repay
the one who showed such great fidelity!'

21
"And maybe, if kind heaven ever hears
with loving favor any mortal prayer,
someday he too will come into these woods,
the one who now, perhaps, feels little care
for me . . . Turning his eyes upon my grave,
the bed for this frail, feeble vestment, there
he shall grant all my sufferings the late prize
of a few little tears and a few sighs,

22
"so if my heart felt misery in life,
at least in death my spirit would be glad,
and my cold ashes, all their flame put out,
joy to have what, alive, I never had."
So she would say to the unheeding trees,
and her eyes welled in fountains, lovely, sad.
But Tancred, led by Fortune wide astray,
in following her but wandered far away.

23
He turned his path into a nearby wood
following the traces that his lady made.
But here so densely branched the forest stood
and cast upon the earth so dark a shade
that as he went on doubtfully he could
no longer find the fresh track, but instead
listened for clattering arms to break the hush,
or any rustling through the underbrush.

24
And if the gentle breezes of the night
should shake an elm tree's slender branch or spray,
or a small beast make a sound, or a bird alight,
he turns toward that small rustle straightaway.
At last out of the woods he comes; the light
of the moon leads him on an unknown way,
as toward a distant rushing sound he goes,
till he should find the source from which it rose.

25
He came where many a clear and glinting wave
spilled from the living rock in a fresh spring,
and tumbling into a stream between green banks
it ran and splashed and made the forest ring.
Here he halted his sad steps and cried aloud,
the lone response, his own cry echoing.
And then he saw the peaceful brow of dawn
rise in a glow of pale vermilion.

26
With an angry sigh he glared to heaven in scorn,
that it denied him such a longed-for chance,
but vows that if his lady love has borne
the slightest hurt, he'll take revenge at once.
Finally back to camp he turns forlorn,
and not quite sure he knows the way he wants—
for he remembers that his scheduled fight
is soon approaching with the Egyptian knight.

27
And so while he was on his doubtful road
Prince Tancred heard a galloping draw near,
and at last, spurring along the narrow downs,
he saw a man who seemed a courier.
He freely shook the whip, and a horn slung round
his shoulder hung beside him, making clear
that he was one of ours. So Tancred, lost,
asked him the way back to the Christian host.

28
"Sir," said he in Italian, "Bohemond
has sent me hurrying ahead to scout."
Thinking him one of his great uncle's men
Tancred believed the lie, and followed him out.
At length they came to where a nasty pond
lay stagnant, moating a castle roundabout,
at the hour the sun appears to dip its light
down in the wide nest where it spends the night.

29
As he arrived the courier blew his horn
and a bridge was lowered for them straightaway.
"Here," he said, "till the rising of the morn,
if you are an Italian, you can stay,
for from the Saracens this place was torn
by the Count of Cosenza yesterday."
The warrior scanned the site, in every part
made safe by natural defense, and art.

30
He hesitated . . . for some hidden harm
in that strong fort, some mischief, might be lying . . .
but he said nothing, and his face was calm,
as one accustomed to the risk of dying.
His best assurance was his own right arm
wherever will or fortune led. Complying,
however, with his promise for that other
fight would be hard if he took on another.

31
Before the castle, where the arching span
ended within a meadow there beside,
he held his steps, although invited in,
and would not follow his insidious guide.
Upon the bridge there stood a knight in arms
in whose wild looks appeared a scornful pride,
and wielding in his hand a naked sword,
menacingly and savagely he roared,

32
"O you who by your fortune or desire
have arrived at Armida's fatal land,
disarm!—thoughts of escape are hopeless here—
and to the rope submit your captive hand,
and as you enter her well-guarded door
you shall observe her general command:
Never to hope to look upon the sky
though all your hairs turn white and the years fly,

33
"unless you swear to go with her and hers
against all those who call themselves for Christ."
While he spoke Tancred stared at him . . . that voice,
those weapons . . . suddenly he recognized
Gascon Rambald! one of the soldiers who
followed Armida, by her love enticed
to turn a pagan and defending knight
of the cult they maintained against the right.

34
Righteous disdain blushed in the warrior
as he responded. "Renegade and felon,
I am that Tancred who forever bore
his sword for Christ, and was His champion,
and through Him put His rebels down in war—
of whom I say you are a paragon!
This right hand is a minister heaven-sent
to score on you heaven's wrath and punishment."

35
When the wicked soldier heard that glorious name
his face turned white; he was discomfited
and yet he hid his fear. "Why have you come,
wretched man, only to be left for dead?
Your great strength will be beaten all the same;
we will lop off your high-and-mighty head
and send it to the French for courtesy,
if I remain what I am used to be."

36
So said the pagan, and because the hour
was now so late that little could be seen,
a host of torches blazed out everywhere,
making the twilight lucid and serene.
The castle shone like a proud theater
when the pomp of evening decks the brilliant scene,
and Armida sat enthroned in the highest chair.
Unseen, she saw and heard it all from there.

37
Meanwhile the hero great of heart prepared
his arms and courage for the bitter fight,
dismounting from his tired horse once he saw,
approaching him on foot, the enemy knight—
his helmet down, his sword unscabbarded
and raised ready to strike, his shield held tight.
Moving against him the fierce Prince replies
with terrifying voice, determined eyes.

38
Circling about with mincing steps the one
would feint a blow, taking a cautious tack;
the other, though his limbs were heavy, weak,
pressed resolutely on to the attack,
with the greatest swiftness thrusting himself on
wherever Rambaldo attempted to hang back,
and quick as lightning to its striking place
he flashed his sword before the pagan's face.

39
And at the vital organs he takes aim,
thrusts where the powers of nature most reside,
coupling intimidation with grave harm,
and his sword's edge with threatenings full of pride;
but the Gascon is wary and light of foot
and from the weapon nimbly leaps aside,
using his sword and shield to make his foe's
fury exhaust itself on empty blows.

40
But he is not so quick at the defense
as his opponent is to cut and slash;
his breastplate is soon riddled, slick with blood,
his shield in splinters, helmet gone to smash,
while not a single blow of his can land
to give his enemy the slightest gash,
and he fears . . . His heart can feel the gnawing of
bad conscience and contempt and shame and love.

41
At last decides to play his final card
and turn his desperation to some good—
flings his shield, and with both hands grips his sword,
starving too long for the prince Tancred's blood,
and closing with his enemy off guard
he lands a blow no mail could have withstood,
and rips a gaping wound in his left thigh
that puts the prince in bitter agony.

42
On his broad forehead then so hard he knocked him
it rang out as a clapper on a bell—
didn't split Tancred's helmet, but it rocked him
and he wobbled to a crouch and nearly fell.
But then, cheeks fired with wrath, Prince Tancred stalked *him,*
his heart aflame, his eyes aflame as well,
and through his slotted visor came their flashing
amid the gritty sound of his teeth gnashing.

43
The faithless pagan cannot bear to look—
even the sight of Tancred is too fierce.
He hears the whistling blade, and through his veins
into his chest can almost feel it pierce—
he flies the blow, and the blow strikes a post
raised up against the bridge, and the force shears
splinters and sparks and sends them to the skies.
The traitor feels his heart grow cold as ice.

44
So he flies to the bridge for last resort,
hoping to save his skin by being fleet,
but Tancred is upon him, at his back,
lifting his arm to strike, hot on his feet,
when lo! the torches and the stars are gone
(great fortune for the fighter in retreat),
without the faintest glimmer of moon to light
the heavens in that miserable night.

45

Plunged in the shades of night and magic charms
the victor could not follow him or see—
for everything was dark wherever he turned.
He walked on, ill at ease, uncertainly.
By chance his steps stray through an open gate,
a chance he does not mark till suddenly
the hinges creak behind him, the locks snap,
shutting him in a dark and dismal trap.

46

As a fish where the Mediterranean Sea
at Comacchio Inlet spills into a wash,
will seek to take its ease in the peaceful bay
and flee the waves it finds too rough and harsh—
and so it is that voluntarily
it shuts itself inside the prison marsh
for good, since that amazing cage is ever
open for entering, but for leaving, never;

47

so too now Tancred entered on his own,
whatever artifice or charms sustain
that hostile keep, and found himself barred in,
where no man on his own gets out again.
He gave the gate a throttling with both hands
but all his effort was dispensed in vain.
"In vain you try to leave," there came a cry,
"O captive of Armida. You'll not die,

48

"no, have no fear of that! This living tomb
year after year will watch your slow demise."
The warrior did not answer, but his doom
weighed heavy on his heart, with pangs, and sighs,
and he blamed Love and Fortune in his gloom,
and his own folly, and *her* savage lies,
and quietly within himself would say,
"Better to have lost the light of day—

49

"wretch that I am! I've lost a brighter sun,
a sweeter, lovelier vision of delight,
nor know if my sad soul will ever again
find its peace in the rays of its soft light . . ."
Then he recalled Argante. "I have not done
my duty!" he cried in sorrow. "He'd be right
to hold me up to scorn and smear my name.
O my great fault! O my eternal shame!"

50
This way and that the warrior's heart was gnawed
by care for love, for honor. Thus while he
tormented himself, the bold Argante could
not bear soft feather beds the livelong day;
such was his love of praise, his thirst for blood,
his harsh heart's hatred of tranquility,
that even though his wounds were not quite whole
he longed for the sixth dawn with all his soul.

51
The night before, the pagan full of pride
could hardly lay his forehead down to sleep,
and rose before the mountains could be spied
against the sky, the darkness was so deep;
then to his squire, "Fetch me my arms," he cried,
and his man laid them ready, and no cheap
or ordinary armor does he bring
but a rich present from the pagan king.

52
He takes them without looking at them long.
Their great weight on his back he does not feel;
and at his side his usual cutlass hung,
formed of the finest-tempered, seasoned steel.
As with its horrible bloody hair far-flung
through the bright burning air of heaven's wheel
a comet brings rebellion and disease,
evil light for empurpled tyrannies,

53
so he flamed in his weapons, narrowed his eyes,
darting his glances drunk with blood and wrath.
Horror suspires in his ferocious ways,
his very countenance breathes threats of death.
And where one glance of his should turn, there is
no soul so brave and self-assured on earth
who will not fear. He lifts his naked blade,
shouting, and slashing at the air and shade.

54
"Soon enough, soon enough the Christian thief
who was so bold to think himself my peer
will fall defeated to the bloody turf,
and dust will foul his loose and scattered hair,
and he'll see this right hand—while he has life—
shame his God, seize his weapons, strip him bare,
no matter what his dying prayers entreat.
I'll have his members fed to dogs for meat."

55
Not unlike how a bull whom jealous love
has goaded with its sharp and maddening sting
bellows, and yet the anger in his heart
grows hotter still, for all his bellowing;
he whets his horn on a trunk, he tosses the wind—
for he will fight the air or anything—
rakes the earth with his hoof and from afar
defies his rival to a deadly war;

56
so, shaken by such fury, he called his herald
and gave his orders in these words alone,
"Go to the enemy camp, proclaim the battle
to him who is this Jesus' champion."
Who did not wait, but leapt into the saddle;
before him Otto, prisoner, led on.
He leaves the city in mad and headlong speed,
galloping into the hills upon his steed,

57
blowing his horn—and there came forth a sound,
a horrible summons heard in every part,
reverberating like a thunderclap
whose boom strikes fear into the human heart,
and in the greatest tent of all the tents
the Christian princes heard, and gave a start;
here the herald flung his challenge, and included
Tancred as first—nor were the rest excluded.

58
Godfrey looked round about him in some doubt,
and slowly turned his grave and thoughtful eyes;
and yet for all his searching and his thought
saw no one fit for such an enterprise.
He sought the flower of his brave fighters, but
where Tancred was nobody could surmise,
Bohemond was far, and the invincible knight
who slew the proud Norse prince had taken flight.

59
More than the ten men who'd been picked by lot,
the best of fighters and the army's pride
under the cover of the silent night
followed Armida, their deceitful guide;
the others, not so brave, of lesser might,
stood round and could say nothing, mortified.
None who seeks honor at such risk appears
for their shame has been conquered by their fears.

60
The captain noted every silent glance
and all the signs of their timidity,
and from where he was seated rose at once
with the disdain born of nobility,
saying, "I don't deserve to live, if I
refuse to put my life in jeopardy,
letting the pagan's base vilification
trample upon the honor of our nation!

61
"Let my host rest at ease in some safe place
and watch me fight while they sit idly by.
Up, up, give me my arms!"—and Godfrey's arms
were brought him in the blinking of an eye.
But the good Raymond, whose ripe age possessed
as ripe a mind for counsel, who was as spry
and strong as many another who looked on,
stepped forward, turning to the great Bouillon,

62
and said, "Ah, let it never be, that on
one head alone you gamble the whole host!
You are our leader, no enlisted man,
and if you die then all are hopes are lost.
You will be victor over Babylon—
destined by heaven to defend the Cross!
Let others draw their swords, for you must be
their head, by reason and authority.

63
"And though the weight of age has bent me double,
my captain, not for that should you refuse me.
These others tire of military trouble—
but I don't wish my old age to excuse me.
Oh, if I had the strength of youth again!
If I were as you now, whose fears amuse me,
who stand unmoved by anger or by shame
to fight the one who blackens your good name,

64
"and what I used to be, when at the old
court of the great Conrad the Second, I
opened the chest of the proud Leopold
and all of Germany beheld him die!
To have beaten that bold man and stripped him cold—
your valor couldn't give a proof so high
if alone and unarmed you put to chase
a hundred of these ragged troops so base.

65
"If I still had that virtue, strength, and blood,
I would have clipped this proud man of his pride!
Whatever I am, my heart has not grown cold—
I'm old, but I will not be terrified.
And if I should lie bloodless in the field
the pagan will not go off satisfied
in triumph. Give me arms! Let this day shine
new glory on those victories of mine!"

66
So spoke the grand old man, and his words were
as spurs to rouse up courage in the breast.
And those who had been quiet in their fear
now shout out that they're ready for the test;
not only were there no refusers near
but many made the fight their bold request—
Baldwin and Guelph and Roger add their pleas
and Stephen and Gernier and the two Guys,

67
and Pyrrhus, he who pulled the famous sleight,
delivering Antioch to Bohemond;
Everard also begged to prove his might,
and Rudolph too, and the brave duke Rosmond,
all from the lands the sea cuts off from us,
one each from England, Ireland, and Scotland;
and Gildippe and Edward, wedded pair in love,
long equally to be chosen. But above

68
all of these others stood the proud old man,
eager and fiery in his protestation.
He is ready-armed—only his gleaming helm
remains to end his battle preparation.
Godfrey addresses him, "O living mirror
of our forefathers' valor! In you our nation
learns virtue, in you the arts of Ares shine,
and honor, and a soldier's discipline.

69
"O, if among my soldiers green in years
I had ten other men as valorous,
how I would burn to put down Babel's pride,
from Bactria to Thule unfurl the Cross!
But now give way, my friend, and save yourself
for a greater work of mature virtue. Toss
all the names in a pot, as is our use,
and let chance be the judge of whom to choose,

70
"rather let God be judge, for fate and fortune
are minister and handmaid to His will."
But Raymond also had his name marked down,
for his intentions were unshakeable.
So Godfrey took a helmet, put them in,
but when the lots were mixed and shaken, still
what warrior's name should be the first to call
but Raymond of Toulouse's after all!

71
His name was greeted with a happy shout
and no one dared to criticize his chance.
Vigorous now his trunk and face filled out
with all the rosy strength of a young man's,
as a proud serpent suns himself about
in skin whose sleek new speckles flash and dance.
But the captain is the loudest man to cheer,
to praise his friend, to say his triumph's near.

72
Unsheathing then the weapon at his hip
the captain passed a sword to Raymond. "Look:
this is the sword that bold knight used to grip,
that Saxon traitor, the rebellious duke.
By force I took it, and I made it rip
his sinful life away—that too I took!
Take what I've always worn in victory.
May it serve you as well as it's served me."

73
Meanwhile the haughty one brooked no delay.
He stormed about, hurled threats and oaths, and cried,
"O you most warlike European sorts,
unbeaten folk—one man I have defied,
one man! Let Tancred come and show his face
if he does trust his manhood. Or will he bide
his time on a soft pillow and wait for night
to grant a second rescue from our fight?

74
"If he's afraid, then come in troops instead,
on horse, on foot, who cares! And hasten to it!
Since no one wants to fight with me alone—
not one from a thousand squads so brave to do it.
Look, over there's the tomb where Mary's son
was laid to rest. Why not go up and view it?
Why not fulfill your vows? The road's before you.
What nobler work will fortune offer for you?"

75
With such *bons mots* the truculent Saracen
lashed at his enemies with his savage whip.
Raymond—more than the rest—flared up with wrath;
no longer could he bear that sneering lip!
Stung virtue grows the fiercer, and against
the roughest whetstone anger hones its tip.
At once he leapt on Aquiline his steed,
named for inheriting the west wind's speed.

76
He was bred on the Tagus where his dam,
the lusty mother of the warlike drove,
in the sweet time of year that fosters life,
was pricked in the heart by the inborn power of love,
and turning her flared nostrils to the wind
she took into herself the richness of
his fertile breath, and—wonder to behold!—
in her hot pleasure she conceived, and foaled.

77
You would say that of all the breed begotten
of the breath of heaven, no courser was so light,
if you saw him stretch his gallop over the sand
so fleet that hardly a print remains in sight,
or if you saw him double his sleek curvets
in tight-wheeled circles to the left and right.
Such was the stallion which Count Raymond rode
to the assault. And he turned his eyes to God:

78
"Lord, Who against the blasphemous Goliath
guided the weapons of a child so well
that at the boy's first stone he met his death
who had wrought massacres in Israel,
let me beat down this felon in our path,
let him become another tale to tell,
let weak old age now lay proud arrogance low,
as a weak youth once did it long ago."

79
So the Count prayed in hope and confidence,
and, moved by his firm trust in God, his prayers,
as fire flies up by natural influence,
rose as on wings to the celestial spheres.
The eternal Father hears him and consents,
choosing one of His angel volunteers
to guard him, save him, bring him back the winner,
out of the hands of such a wicked sinner.

80
The angel whom high Providence elected
from the day of the good Count Raymond's birth
to keep his body guarded and protected
while journeying in his pilgrimage on earth,
now that again his task has been directed
by heaven's king to guard that man of worth,
flies to a lofty stronghold where lie all
the weapons of the heavenly arsenal.

81
Here there was kept the spear that struck the snake
dead where he lay, and the great lightning arrows,
and those that bring diseases in their wake,
pestilence and the plague and invisible horrors;
and the great trident hung on high, whose shake
is the worst of poor mortal mankind's terrors,
shivering the broad earth down to its foundation
and leaving cities in dilapidation.

82
Shining like flame among the other gear
a shield of clearest diamond lay, so great
that from the Atlantic to the Caucasus
it could guard every people, every state;
under its broad defense just kings and chaste
and holy cities are inviolate.
To guard his Count the angel took this shield
and went in secret to the battlefield.

83
A motley crowd comes flocking to the wall.
But the barbarian tyrant now commands
Clorinda and her squadrons to the hill—
where by his orders halfway down she stands.
On the other side in ordered rank and file
are stationed several of the Christian bands,
leaving between the camps an empty length
broad enough for the champions' test of strength.

84
Argante looked, but Tancred wasn't there—
instead, an unknown fighter, someone new.
"The one you want," said the Count, drawing near,
"is somewhere else—and fortunately for you.
Don't let that swell your head. You see me here
ready to fling your challenge back at you,
for I can fight in place of him who fought,
or after me let some *fifth* man be brought."

85

The proud man smiled, and scornfully replied,
"What's Tancred up to, then? Where does he stay?
He threatens war on heaven, then has to hide—
defends himself by scurrying away.
Let him find the heart of the earth or the ocean tide,
he'll find there is no place secure from me."
"Liar!" replied the Count. "Why should he run?
You're nothing for a man like him to shun."

86

Argante fumes at that. "Go stand your ground!
Go! I shall take you on in Tancred's stead.
And soon we'll see whether you can defend
the foolish insolence of what you've said."
So on they hurtled to the joust; each aimed
equally vicious blows at the other's head.
Good Raymond took sharp aim and struck his foe
but couldn't budge him from his saddlebow,

87

while fierce Argante charged at him and missed—
a jousting error quite unusual for him—
missed the defended champion of Christ,
for the guardian angel swerved the stroke before him.
The ruffian bit his lip for rage, and smashed
his spear, and thought of blasphemies and swore 'em,
then he went after Raymond, sword unbound,
impetuous to begin the second round.

88

And spurred his powerful courser to the right
like a ram ready to butt with lowered head,
but Raymond veered beside him on the right
and thumped him soundly on the front instead.
Again he turned, that proud Egyptian knight,
but past his right side Raymond once more sped
and rang his helmet—but of little shock
(that helmet was as hard as diamond rock).

89

The savage pagan rushed and closed upon him
to get a tighter tussle with his foe.
Fearing the weight of his own horse's bulk
if he and Aquiline should be brought low,
using a war of turn and turn about
Raymond gave way, attacked, flew to and fro,
and his quick horse obeys the light commands
and not one step is wrong or hoof mislands.

90
As a captain who assaults a citadel
protected by a marsh or a high mount,
tries every point of entry possible
and all the tricks he knows of—so the Count,
and since he cannot slash away one scale
of the plate mail upon his foe's proud front,
he strikes the weaker armor with his sword,
hoping that steel can open steel. And scored

91
two or three times, piercing the armor through,
leaving his enemy's gear a lukewarm red,
while his own was intact and undisturbed—
even the plumes that tossed upon his head.
Argante beat the air in a vain fury
and spent his wrath and strength and profited
nothing. Doubling his cuts and thrusts, he takes
a renewed vigor from his own mistakes.

92
After a thousand swipes the Saracen
lets fly a blow to cleave the knight in two—
it would have staggered even Aquiline,
so close it was, no matter how fast he flew—
but the supernal Messenger unseen
was there assisting in the battle too,
and stretched his arm forth with the diamond shield
to take the blow, and make the steel edge yield.

93
Which steel is now so brittle that it breaks
(arms forged in mortal smithies cannot stand
against the arms the Eternal Craftsman makes,
incorruptible, unalloyed), and to the sand
it falls. Argante sees the thousand flakes,
cannot believe it, cannot understand
how the weak-handed champion he sparred
could manage to bear arms so strong and hard;

94
indeed he thinks that he has smashed his sword
on the shield which his enemy extended,
a belief with which good Raymond's in accord,
unaware that an angel has descended.
But till his foe should have his arms restored
(for now his hands were empty) he attended,
thinking the triumph cowardly and low
secured by such advantage of a foe.

95
"Go get another sword," he wanted to say,
when in his heart there wakened a new thought,
that he would shame the whole host if he fell,
for it was in a public cause he fought.
And so he scorned a shameful victory,
but would not put the common honor in doubt.
Yet while he stands considering the case
Argante flings his pommel in his face

96
and in an instant spurs his warhorse on,
driving himself the sooner to the clashing.
The pommel landed square on Raymond's helmet,
gave the Toulousan's face a pretty bashing,
and yet he did not falter, but swung free,
ducking the mighty arms of the Circassian,
and with the slicing of his blade he touches
the beastly hand that grips like a beast's clutches.

97
Then ever here and there he stops and starts,
and back and forth he turns and turns again,
and ever where he comes and where he parts
lands a fierce blow that leaves his foe in pain.
And now all of his strength and all his arts,
his new-stirred anger and his old disdain,
he unites now to the Circassian's harm,
invoking fortune and heaven to aid his arm.

98
Argante stood those blows and did not fear,
armed with his own strength and fine weaponry,
resembling a tall ship without a tiller,
sails torn and yardarms shattered, rocked at sea,
yet built with every rib and boom and spar
tight-rigged and pegged together solidly—
it shows its keel intact in the tossing flood
and does not yet abandon hope for good—

99
such was your present danger, O Argante,
when Beelzebub came deviling to your aid.
In a hollow cloud he formed a human figure,
a monstrous wonder, from the slightest shade,
faking Clorinda's rich and splendid armor,
borrowing the lovely looks of the proud maid,
her carriage and her well-known way of talking
(though not her mind) and power of speech and walking.

100

And so the phantasm spoke to Oradin,
a famous archer who was standing by,
"O famous Oradin, who, when you like,
can fix your shot in any target's eye,
ah, what a loss we suffer if such a man,
the great defender of Judea, should die!
And if his foe should strip him, and thus vested
return to his own army unmolested.

101

"Here give a demonstration of your craft
and steep your arrows in the French thief's blood!
Besides perpetual honor, you can bet
the courteous king will grant a great reward."
So she, and when he heard the promises
he did not doubt the prospect of such good,
but took a quarrel from his well-stocked sack,
fitted it on the string and pulled it back.

102

The taut string gives a hiss and lets it fly—
a feathered arrow whistles through the air,
and strikes the metal clasps of Raymond's belt,
shearing the clasps in half. With force to spare
it slits the hauberk and, just tinged with blood,
sinks its tip in the flesh and fixes there,
for the celestial warrior blunts its force
to stop its passing further in its course.

103

The Count then plucked the arrow from his mail,
thrust it aside, and saw the bloody stain,
reproached the pagan for his broken faith,
with insults full of menace and disdain.
The captain, who had never turned his eyes
from his friend Raymond, saw the pact was vain,
and as from where he stood the wound looked grim
he gave a heavy groan, and feared for him,

104

and with a sword and one nod of the brow
he roused his fiery people to advance—
"Avenge him!" And the vizors are snapped low,
the reins are loosed, each knight prepares his lance,
and in what seems an instant the hosts go,
the armies of the orient and France.
The field has vanished in a rising whirl
of dust and earth the galloping horses hurl.

105
In the first shock a thunderous noise is heard—
the clash of shields, smashed helmets, spear shards flying.
Here you might see a stray horse reel around
without a guide, or there another lying;
a warrior here lies dead, and here the groans
and tears and wistful sighs of warriors dying . . .
The battle rages as the armies close.
The more they mix, the bitterer it grows.

106
Agile Argante leapt into the fray
and swiped away a soldier's iron mace,
and breaking through the thickest of the charge
whirled it about and cleared himself wide space,
but all his mad impetuous anger was
intent on fighting Raymond face to face,
for as a ravenous wolf hunts down his food,
he wished to sate his hunger in Raymond's blood.

107
A rough and fierce obstruction comes his way:
Ormanno stands before him and retards
his hasty path, and with him is one Guy,
Roger of Balnaville and two Gerards.
The more they pin him close, the fiercer he—
he will not stop or slow, he disregards
their courage—as a fire pent underground
erupts and spreads catastrophe around.

108
He slays Ormanno, injures Guy, and flattens
Roger among the dead men, badly hurt,
but finds himself surrounded by combatants
surging and armed to strike him and alert.
The armies of the Saracens and Latins—
due largely to Argante's prowess—fought
to parity, when the good duke gave a shout
to his brother Baldwin, "Move your army out,

109
"and go there, where the fight is deadliest,
go rush upon the enemy's left flank."
He charged, and the collision was so fierce
that as they pounded them the enemy shrank
back—for the Asian armies seemed too frail
to bear the impetuous onslaught of the Frank,
which scattered all their orders left and right,
and battered warhorse down with flag and knight.

110
That same push routs the enemy's right side,
the warriors fly, and only one remains,
Argante, to defend them; for their fear
whips them away headlong with loosened reins.
He alone plants his foot and shows his face.
A giant with a hundred arms and hands
and in each pair of hands a sword and shield
would not have matched Argante in the field.

111
He bears the brunt of coursers as they batter,
he bears the truncheon and the mace and spear,
all against one—it does not seem to matter;
he charges that one there and this one here.
They bruise his limbs; his armaments they shatter;
he spills his sweat and blood and does not care.
At last the press of the mob is just too strong—
it turns him round and carries him along.

112
He turns his back upon the force and furor
of the flood that pulled and swept him up by might,
but if what the hand does is the heart's mirror,
his heart and steps were not a man's in flight.
His eyes still flashed out their accustomed terror
and menacings and anger. But despite
all his attempts to hold his people back
they fly amain before the French attack.

113
And that greathearted man tried to restrain
or put some order in this flight of theirs,
but fear can recognize no art or rein.
They do not hear his orders or his prayers.
The reverent Godfrey, seeing fortune deign
to turn her favor full on his affairs,
has the glad course of triumph in pursuit,
dispatching new assistance in the rout.

114
And were it not that this was not the day
written in God's unchangeable decree,
this day might well have seen the unbeaten host
fulfill their holy toil in victory.
But the crew from hell, who in that conflict saw
the sure surrender of their tyranny,
suddenly stirred the wind (as God allowed),
blinding the air about them in a cloud.

115
A black veil steals the sun and day away
from mortal vision, and it seems the sky
flames with black horror worse than the depths of hell,
so furiously the streaks of lightning fly.
The thunder roars and rain falls mixed with hail,
leaves pastures strewn, fields flooded; branches lie
aslant, askew in the tumult, whose great shocks
seem to shake not just oaks, but hills and rocks.

116
At once the wind and the tempestuous rain
batter the eyes of the French in the driving storm,
and the violence and suddenness restrain
their bands with fear of an impending doom.
The smaller portion of the troops remain
close to what flags they see in front of them.
But Clorinda, further off with her battalion,
sees that the time is ripe, and spurs her stallion,

117
crying out, "O my friends, they fight for us,
heaven and justice come to help our side!
Our eyes are not offended by their wrath,
our arms are free to swing, our feet to stride;
instead, enraged, they strike the Christian front
and leave our foe dismayed and terrified,
scattering their weapons, robbing the light of day—
destiny leads us on the charge! Away!"

118
So with the gales of Hades at their back
Clorinda drives her men against their foes,
slamming the Christians with a dire attack,
laughing to scorn their weak and useless blows.
Directly then Argante too turned back
with a hard sort of government for those
who had beaten him just now, and who, to shun
the sword and storm, fled the field at a dead run.

119
Immortal fury teamed with mortal steel
to slash the shoulders of the men who fled,
and the blood ran and mingled with rain and hail
and flowed in streams and made the road blush red,
and Pyrrhus and the worthy Rudolph fell
among the crowd of dying and the dead.
Argante sundered Pyrrhus' soul away;
the other was Clorinda's victory.

120
Syrians and demons still pursue their chase
and still the Frenchmen flee fast as they can,
with only Godfrey standing firm in place
against the thundering arms of hell and man,
meeting the whirlwind with a confident face,
reproaching his great barons as they ran;
before the gate he halted his great horse
and in the stockade gathered his stray force.

121
And at least twice his battle charger speeded
against the wild Argante, and made him slow;
often drawing his naked sword he greeted
the enemy's thickest surge with blow on blow,
till at last with the others he retreated
to safety, yielding victory to the foe.
The Saracens returned to town; the French
sat weary and dismayed behind their trench,

122
yet even there they could not wholly duck
that horrific storm, its violence and wrath;
no torchlight can stay lit; wherever they strike
the winds blast through, the waters cut a swath,
rip canvas and smash pole and uproot stake
and toss whole tents afar off in their path.
Wind, thunder, storm, and shouts together swirled
a fearful concord deafening all the world.

Canto Eight

1
The thunder and the tempest now were stilled;
the south wind and the west wind ceased to brawl;
with rosy forehead and with feet of gold
the dawn stepped forth from her celestial hall.
Still those who roused the storm did not withhold
their wicked arts or sorceries at all,
but one of them, called Astagorius,
spoke to Alecto his companion thus:

2
"Alecto, look, that knight is on his way,
and stopping him exceeds our competence—
the sole survivor of the mighty hand
of sovereign Soliman, our power's defense.
This man will tell the French of his bold chief,
of his companions, and the dire events,
momentous things. A hazard we must shun,
for then they may call back Bertoldo's son.

3
"You know how much that means, and that great things,
begun, must be opposed by vigorous actions,
by force or lies. Then go down to the French,
turn all he says from praises to detractions,
scatter the flames, let poison sour the blood
of the Italian, Swiss, and British factions;
let anger and riot and revolt be sown,
and at last turn the whole camp upside down!

4
"Such work is worthy of you, for in the past
it gave you cause to boast before our king."
So he, and what he said alone sufficed
to make the monster undertake the thing.
Meanwhile that knight has reached the Christian host,
came (as the demons feared) with news to bring,
and "Warriors, for the love of grace," he cried,
"who will conduct me to your chief and guide?"

5

A crowd then led him to the captain's tent,
eager to hear the news the traveler brought.
But first he kissed the honored hand that shook
the reign of Babel, bowing on the spot.
"My Lord," he said, "your fame is bounded by
the sea and stars alone. I wish I brought
happier news to you today." And then,
groaning aloud, he told his story. "Sven,

6

"the King of Denmark's only son, his pride,
the prop and stay of his declining years,
hungered to follow your advice and gird
the sword for Christ, and fight beside your peers.
Of toil and danger he was unafraid;
no lust for rule, no pity for the tears
of his old father tempered in the least
the love that burned within his generous breast.

7

"He was urged by desire to learn the art
of war—so difficult and wearying—
from you, a noble master, and felt the smart
of shame for never having done one thing
worthy of note; heard too, from every part,
how Rinaldo had won glory in the spring
of youth. But zeal for honor drove him most—
not of the earth, but of the heavenly host.

8

"And so he hurled aside any delays
and with a proud and daring band of friends
he made his sojourn to the land of Thrace
and the imperial city. Here he finds
welcome into the Greek Augustus' palace,
and here your messenger arrives, and lends
a full account of Antioch's surrender—
how first you took it, then were its defender,

9

"defender against the Persians, whose great hosts
lay siege before you in the Syrian plain,
so many men and arms one had to wonder
how in that great realm any could remain.
He spoke of you, told many things, till he
came to Rinaldo. And he left the main
events, for now the bold flight was his story,
and all the lad had done with you for glory.

10
"He ended, saying that now the troops of France
had arrived to attack the city gate,
inviting him to come too: in the last
triumph at least he might participate.
Such talk was like a spur to the boy's side.
The high-spirited Sven was in such state
that every hour seemed five years till he could
whirl sword and steep his hands in pagan blood.

11
"Worries about his cowardice gnaw away;
the glory of others brings regret and blame.
Many there beg or counsel him to stay—
he will not listen, it is all the same—
the only risk he fears is that he may
not be part of your risks, part of your fame.
That is the only danger that is clear.
The rest he does not sense, or does not fear.

12
"He himself hurries his own destiny;
fortune which drags us leads him, willing, on,
for he could hardly wait until the day
he would depart in the first rays of dawn,
and as the best he takes the shortest way,
for so he thought it, he our champion,
our chief. Nor do we shun the dangerous routes
for fear of enemies lurking thereabouts.

13
"We had a difficult road—ran low on food,
were ambushed and attacked by the enemy,
and yet we conquered all our hardships and
slew the assailing foes or made them flee,
and so we grew cocksure in our good luck,
fearless of danger, expecting victory,
till we camped in an area whose confines
were not so far away from Palestine's.

14
"But then our scouts informed us they had heard
the clash of armies on the march, and seen
banners and other signs, whence they inferred
an army of innumerable men
drew near. That brought no change to our bold lord,
no doubts, no broken voice, no color gone,
though many who heard the bitter news that night
showed faces that had turned a pallid white.

15

"He said, 'O what a crown we have at hand,
a crown of martyrdom or victory!
I hope for the latter, but no less desire
the first, of greater merit, equal glory.
Brothers, this battle plain where we now stand
will be a temple of lasting memory,
where men of future centuries will come
to view our victory's trophies, or our tomb.'

16

"So he, and thereupon assigns the watch;
and every task and duty is addressed,
and all are ordered to bed down fully armed.
He himself takes no armor from his breast.
It was the quiet middle of the night,
the friendliest time for sleep and silent rest,
when all at once we heard the barbarous yell—
a cry to strike the heavens, or waken hell.

17

" 'To arms, to arms!' went up the hurried cries,
and Sven in armor spurred and charged to the fore,
and the flame of courage tinged his cheek and eyes
with the look of a greathearted warrior.
Now we were set upon. A circling mob
pressed us on every side, entrapped us, bore
upon us in a woods of spears and steel
while over us the arrows fell like hail.

18

"We were outnumbered twenty men to one
by our assailants in that mismatched fight,
and in the darkness many men were slain
or hurt by blows that never caught their sight.
But the number of the wounded and the fallen
no one discerns among the shadows: night
covers our losses in obscurity,
covers with them our works of bravery.

19

"But Sven raised his head high over all the rest—
he was an easy target to make out—
proof of his might and prowess manifest
and even in the dark beyond all doubt.
A river of blood, a mountain of slain men
moated and banked the warrior roundabout,
and he seemed to bring, wherever he made his stand,
terror in his eyes—death, in his hand.

20

"And so we fought all night until the dawn
broke in the heavens above us, blushing red.
But now that the horror of night was shaken off
that had concealed the horror of the dead,
with the most longed-for light there came to us
a grief and terror more profound instead—
we saw the field strewn with our soldiers lost,
we saw our nearly annihilated host.

21

"We were two thousand; now, one hundred left.
When he saw so much blood, so many slain,
I do not know if that brave heart was shaken
by that sad spectacle, or wrung with pain;
he did not show it if he was, but cried,
'Let's follow in our brave companions' train!
Their blood has marked the path for us to take
to heaven, far above the Stygian lake.'

22

"So I believe he was as glad at heart
for death approaching, as his looks expressed,
and against the barbarian onslaught
opposed his constant and intrepid breast.
The blows he dealt would shatter diamond rock—
as shields of finest bronze could well attest.
He made a broad lake of the battleground,
and of his body made one single wound.

23

"It was not life but virtue which sustained
his dying body, fierce, indomitable.
The more he is attacked, the deadlier
his thrusts; stricken he strikes again, and will
not slow. But see, a great man comes against him
in fury, and his look is terrible,
and after a fight in which our prince stands fast
with help he lays him to the earth at last.

24

"So fell the invincible youth—a bitter fall.
None of us had survived to avenge our lord.
I call you, noble bones and well-spilt blood
of my dear prince, to verify my word,
that I was not so jealous for my life,
nor did I shirk the battle or the sword,
and had it pleased the heavens above us I
had done my part and well deserved to die.

25
"Among my dead companions I alone
fell yet alive, though no one thought me so,
and indeed all my senses were asleep,
and I can say no more about the foe.
But when the sight returned into my eyes
that had been stifled in a black haze, lo,
there in the dark appeared to my weak sight
the flicker of a little flaming light.

26
"Not enough life remained in me that I
could soon discern a thing without mistaking,
but I saw as one who opens and shuts the eye,
hovering somewhere between sleep and waking;
and then the pain began to worsen—my
harsh wounds were open to the night air, aching
bitterly in the cold dew, on bare ground
under the open sky. And then a sound,

27
"a quiet whispering, as the light grew near,
and the light and the sound approached as one,
until they reached me, stopping at my side.
I opened my weak eyes—not easily done—
and saw two men dressed in long robes, and holding
two torches. And I heard one say, 'O son,
trust in the Lord Who aids the righteous man,
Whose grace arrives before your prayers can.'

28
"Those were the words the old man spoke to me,
and then he blessed me with extended hand,
and whispered in a soft and prayerful voice
low words which I could hardly understand.
'Arise,' he said, and I, made whole again,
arise, light-footed, free of injury, and
(a gentle miracle for that bitter strife)
all of my members brimming with new life.

29
"I look upon them in astonishment,
my mind too shaken to believe the true.
Then the one said, 'O you of little faith,
why should you doubt? What do your thoughts pursue?
The bodies you behold in us are real.
For we are servants of Christ Jesus, who
have fled the flattering world and its false delights
and live alone upon these barren heights.

30
" 'That Lord Who reigns in every part elected
to send me as the minister of your cure,
for lowly instruments are not rejected
to work His wonders. And He would ensure
that the body of the prince not lie neglected,
where dwelt a soul so reverent and pure,
for soul and body shall again unite
in godlike immortality and light.

31
" 'I mean the body of the Danish Sven,
whose valor here has earned a fitting tomb,
which will be honored by all faithful men
and visited for centuries to come.
Lift your eyes to the stars and see that one
shine like a shaft of sunlight in the gloom:
follow its living arrows with your eyes.
There the body of your noble leader lies.'

32
"And then I saw from that most lovely lamp—
rather, a sun in night—one ray decline
direct above where the great body lay,
stretching from heaven to earth like a golden line,
and welling over him such wondrous light
that gleamed in all his wounds and made them shine,
that in a moment I could see my lord
in the horrifying welter of his blood.

33
"He lay, but never prone: as if he had
directed to the stars his sole desire,
he held himself so as to face the sky,
ever the goal to which he would aspire.
His right arm he held close, fist clenched, sword drawn,
in act as if to strike and not retire.
The other he lay humbly at his breast
as if God's pardon was his last request.

34
"And while I wept and washed his wounds with tears—
and still with sorrow was my spirit pained—
the holy elder opened Sven's clenched hand
and took away the sword it had retained.
'This sword,' said he, 'which on this day has spilled
so much of the enemy's blood that it is stained
deep crimson even now, as you know, is
perfect. No sword may be preferred to this.

35

" 'Thus heaven decrees that if this sword must part
from its first lord, whose body we behold,
it shall not lie unused, but shall depart
into another mighty hand and bold,
to be brandished then with equal force and art
but happier fortune, and for days untold,
who shall exact harsh vengeance for your lord—
killing his killer with this very sword.

36

" 'For Soliman killed Sven; thus Soliman
must also by the Danish sword be slain.
Take it, and go to the walls of Jerusalem,
where the besieging Christian hosts remain;
and never fear that in this foreign land
your journey will be cut off once again,
for all the hardships will be swept away
by His right hand, Who sends you on your way.

37

" 'He has preserved in you a living voice
for you to manifest to all who hear
the piety, the valor, and the fierce
courage you witnessed in your lord so dear,
that they too may take up the purple Cross,
moved by such an exemplar to bear
arms for the Lord; which, as the future rolls,
will kindle desire in other illustrious souls.

38

" 'All that remains is that you know the heir
to whom the sword is destined to pass on.
That is the young Rinaldo, honored for
fortitude unsurpassed by anyone.
Give it to him, and say that heaven and earth
demand the vengeance from his hand alone.'
Now, while I listened to their words, intent,
new wonders struck me with astonishment,

39

"for where the body of the prince had lain
a great tomb now appeared before my eyes,
and as it rose it closed him up within—
I don't know how, or what art made it rise—
with the name of the fallen champion
and a brief sentence to memorialize
his virtue. All my power to move was gone
as I gazed on the writing and the stone.

40
" 'Here,' said the man, 'shall rest the body of
your lord, beside those faithful friends of his,
while their glad spirits in the heaven of love
revel in glory and perpetual bliss.
But you must rest now. With your tears you have
honored them with the final offices.
Until the morning you shall be my guest,
when the new ray will rouse you to your quest.'

41
"With that, he led me along mountain peak
and valley—I could hardly keep abreast—
till we came where an outcrop of the rock
made a rugged cave, and there we took our rest.
Here was his lodging, among wolves and bears;
here he lived with his pupil, unoppressed.
For shield and mail are weaker in defense
than a naked breast and holy innocence.

42
"There I restored my limbs with a rustic meal
and on a rough bed rested until day.
But when the eastern sky broke into flame,
lit by the dawn with gold and purple ray,
the hermits both arose, and I with them,
rose on a sudden, vigilant, to pray.
I took my leave then of the good old man.
As he advised, my journey here began."

43
The Dane fell silent, and the good Bouillon
responded thus. "O cavalier, you bring
hard tidings for our armies, bitter news,
and it is right we feel no comforting
now that such valiant friends of ours are gone,
now that a little earth holds everything
one brief hour took away. As lightning flashes
your lord blazed forth his virtue—and is ashes.

44
"And yet to die his death is happier far
than to acquire new provinces and gold,
nor could the ancient Capitol provide
so glorious a laurel to behold.
Their triumph now enjoys a deathless crown
in the luminous temple of heaven, where those bold
spirits, I trust, shall take delight to show
the handsome wounds they suffered from the foe.

45
"But you who yet remain on earth to fight,
to bear the dangers of God's army here,
as it is fitting, let your heart delight
in your friends' triumph! Let your brow be clear!
As for Rinaldo, he has taken flight,
a vagrant from our host. Until we hear
reliable news of him, I cannot back
your setting out on some uncertain track."

46
Such conversation could not but remind
each soldier of Rinaldo, and their love
of him awoke, renewed. And some repined;
"The lad's in foreign parts now, has to rove
among the heathen." And they felt inclined
to tell the Dane about his feats, and wove
a tapestry unfurled for all to see
the wonder of his warlike history.

47
Now when in their remembrance of the lad
their souls had all grown tender once again,
back to camp there arrived the foraging squad
whose duty it had been to scour the plain,
and these brought all the abundant spoils they had,
whole flocks of sheep, and stolen cows, and grain—
although the grain was scarce—and hay to feed
the hungry coursers what their bodies need.

48
And they brought evidence of a great sorrow,
disaster all too obvious to view:
the bloody over-vest of good Rinaldo,
and all his armor shattered and cut through.
At once (who can keep hushed a thing like that?)
a various and uncertain rumor flew.
When they heard what had happened to the youth
a crowd came running in grief to see the truth.

49
They saw and recognized the immense bulk
of the great breastplate, and its brilliant sheen,
and the sign of the bird who trusts the sun
to prove her offspring, not their plumage—seen
in the vanguard or alone in every grand
enterprise of the host. And now with keen
anger and deep compassion they regard
the armor broken and besmeared with blood.

50
While the camp murmured and attributed
causes (to suit its various belief)
of the boy's death, the good Bouillon instead
called Aliprand, the depredation chief,
a man sincere and frank in all he said
and of a generous heart. "Tell me, in brief,"
said Godfrey, "how and where you found the gear.
Keep neither good nor evil from my ear."

51
He gave him this reply. "As far from here
as a courier might reach on the second day,
near Gaza, there is huddled a small plain
enclosed between the hills, out of the way,
and a little stream comes tumbling from above,
then slowly and softly winds its shady way
through the thick undergrowth, by shrub and tree.
It is a perfect place for trickery.

52
"Here some of us went looking for a herd
feeding, perhaps, along the grassy shore,
but lying on the grass turned red with blood
we saw, there on the banks, a warrior,
dead. We all started when we marked his colors,
easy to see, polluted though they were.
But when, to see the corpse's face, I treaded
nearer, I found the man had been beheaded.

53
"Wounds riddled the big torso from the back
to the chest, and his right arm too was gone.
Nearby, with the eagle spreading his white wings,
lay the helmet, empty. While I searched for one
whom I might ask the truth about these things
there happened by a peasant all alone,
who turned about to run away as soon
as he became aware of our platoon.

54
"We followed him and caught him. To the request
we made, the peasant finally replied
that the day before, on his way from the forest,
he met with many soldiers, tried to hide;
one of them held a man's head by the hanks,
blond and spattered with blood; that when he tried
to make it out more closely, it appeared
the head of a young man without a beard;

55
"that the man had it swaddled afterwards
in a silk shawl slung from his saddlebow.
He added that the knight was one of ours—
as the cut of his garment let him know.
So in great sadness I undressed the corpse,
and wept, for I suspected the worst woe.
I took his armor with me and made sure
he had an honorable sepulture.

56
"But if that noble trunk's what I believe,
it deserves another tomb, another rite."
So saying, Aliprando took his leave;
nothing more certain could he bring to light.
Godfrey sighed heavily; though he must grieve,
still he was not so sure his thoughts were right.
By clearer signs must be identified
the mangled body and the homicide.

57
Under the wings of heaven darkness fell
to cover the great host; and quiet sleep,
peace for the soul, forgetfulness of ill,
charmed all their cares and numbed them in a deep
drowsiness. Only you, Argillan, still
wake, pierced with the arrow of sharp pain, and steep
your turning mind in great and restless things,
unable to take the quiet that sleep brings.

58
This man was quick of hand and bold of tongue
and rash and fervid of imagination,
born on the banks of Tronto, fed when young
with civil conflict, hatred, indignation,
then driven into exile, where he clung
to his old ways of blood and depredation,
slaughtering his own country till he came
to Asia and acquired a better name.

59
Just before dawn at last his eyelids closed,
and yet his sleep was neither sweet nor full,
for Alecto had infused into his heart
a stupor as of death, heavy and dull,
and so his faculties had no repose,
but were deluded, as it were made null,
for the cruel fury sets about to play him
fantastic apparitions that dismay him.

60

She acted a great trunk with head cut clean,
and on the right the arm was but a shred,
and pale and bloody, yellow and obscene,
in the left hand she held a severed head.
It breathes, and as it breathes the visage speaks—
speech mixed with blood and sobbing exited—
"Flee, Argillan! The truth is clear to all!
Flee the tents and the wicked general!

61

"On the fierce Godfrey and his murderous fraud,
how can you, my beloved friends, rely?
With hate and spite his villainous heart is gnawed,
his only thought, how you may be as I!
Yet if your hands aspire to noble laud
and trust their might and prowess, do not fly,
no—let the tyrant under whom I stood
delight my soul with his malignant blood.

62

"I will stand by you as a ministering shade
to arm your heart with wrath, your hand with steel."
Such were her words, and as her words invade
they breathe in him a new and furious soul.
His sleep is broken—and he turns, dismayed,
eyes which a venomous hate begins to swell;
he arms, and with unseasonable haste
gathers the Italian soldiers in one place.

63

Gathered them where the arms of the good lad
were hanging in full view; and with a proud
voice he vented his bitter rage, and made
his fretful thinking clear to the whole crowd:
"A barbaric and despotic people who
despise what's right and spurn what they have vowed,
who never have their glut of blood and gold—
you think the yoke will bow them, the bit hold?

64

"For seven years under the unjust weight,
what we have suffered—bitter and wearisome—
I say would kindle scorn and kindle hate
—for a thousand years—in Italy and Rome!
Forget that by good Tancred's strategy
and arms Cilicia was overcome—
which to his use the treasonous Frank now turns,
fraud snatching the rewards which valor earns—

65
"forget that when the time and need require
a bold heart, a firm mind, a ready hand,
one of our men is always the first there
of thousands, to bring death by fire and brand;
but when the spoils and honors are dealt out
in the quiet aftermath, men of our land
receive not even a part of our just shares—
gold, kingdoms, honors, triumphs are all theirs!

66
"Offenses like these once upon a time
may have seemed grave, perhaps unnatural.
Such slight sins I forget for the new crime
they have committed, a great, horrible
cruelty—killing Rinaldo! The sublime
laws of heaven and laws of men are all
scorned! How can the thundering heavens bear the sight?
Or earth not swallow them up in perpetual night?

67
"Rinaldo they have murdered—who still lies
unavenged, our religion's sword and shield;
unavenged he lies, for there they left his body
torn and unburied on the hard bare field.
You wish to know who was the cruel one?
Comrades, from whom can the truth be concealed?
We Latins all know how our valor is
the envy of the leading Bouillonnese,

68
"Godfrey and Baldwin! But enough of reason.
I swear to the heavens above—and the heavens hear it—
that just before the darkness turned to day
I saw his wandering and unhappy spirit.
Ah, what a hard and cruel sight! What treason
he told of Godfrey, warning us to fear it!
That was no dream I saw, no idle show,
for the specter goes before me as I go.

69
"And should that hand still filthy with the stain
of so unjust a death yet govern us?
Or shall we leave it far behind, and reign
over ourselves, where the Euphrates flows?
Whose towns and cities and whose fertile plain
shelter and feed a people used to peace—
shall feed us rather, for they shall be ours,
nor need we share them with the Frankish powers.

70
"Let's leave his innocent and illustrious blood
unpunished, and let's go, if you agree—
though if your virtue lying weak and cold
were as fiery in you as it ought to be,
this pestilential serpent that has fed
upon the flower and fame of Italy
will give the other monsters living yet
a deadly lesson they will not forget!

71
"I wish—I wish, if only your great valor
will dare to do all that it can, today
to thrust this hand into his wicked heart,
that nest of treachery, and make him pay!"
So he, incited, and his restless fury
swept the hearts of his listeners away.
"To arms, to arms!" the maddened warrior cried,
and "Arms, to arms!" his hot young men replied.

72
Alecto wheeled her weaponed arm about,
piercing their hearts with flame and poisonous brew,
and scorn and folly and the wicked drought
for blood with every raging moment grew,
and the contagion spread slithering out
of its hatchery in the Italian crew,
and it took root among the Swiss, then crept
into the quarters where the English kept.

73
The things which move the foreigners include
not only the hard luck and public harm,
but ancient grudges also lend their food,
matter to breed new wrath and keep it warm;
each sleeping indignation is renewed;
they call the French a wicked, tyrant swarm,
and in proud threats their hatred tops the crest
and cannot any longer be suppressed.

74
As in a copper kettle too much heat
will make the water seethe and hiss and roil
till it cannot restrain itself but spills
over the brim of the vessel in a boil,
so those few still illumined by the truth
can no longer rein in that foolish broil,
and Tancred, William, and Camillus were
absent, as was each higher officer.

75
Now the mob run to arm themselves, headlong—
ferocious and confused is their condition—
and trumpets start to bray their battle song
summoning every soldier to sedition.
The reverent Godfrey hears that something's wrong,
that all the men are seizing ammunition;
but Baldwin reports before any other
and in full armor stands beside his brother.

76
He hears the accusation, and he turns
his eyes to heaven, as is his wont, and God:
"Lord, You know well how little my arm yearns
for what I hate, to shed my people's blood.
Put down the fury now that spreads and burns,
and strip away the veil that clouds the mind;
and to this world of blindness also prove
my innocence, known in the world above."

77
Silence; and heaven instilled into his veins
a fresh, unusual fire. Full to the brim
with strength and life and burning hope, that flushed
through all his countenance and emboldened him,
surrounded by his men he strode against
the avengers of Rinaldo—so their whim—
and though he heard all round him seethe with hate
and deadly arms, he did not hesitate.

78
His cuirass on his back, he was decked out
in more than usual nobility;
his hands were naked, like his face, which shone
with a strange and celestial majesty.
He shook his golden scepter. With that alone
for arms, he dared to quell the mutiny.
So he appeared before them, and his speech
resounded past the bounds of human reach:

79
"What empty clash of arms and foolish threats
do I now hear? And at whose instigation?
Am I so known, respected—after my faith
so long has stood the best corroboration—
that anyone could still suspect me of
this cunning, or believe the accusation?
And maybe you expect that I will bow,
say you are right, and ask your pardon now?

80
"Ah let the earth that knows my name full well
not hear it now subjected to such shame!
This scepter and the memory of my deeds—
truth itself, shield the honor of my name.
For now let justice yield to mercy. No
penalties fall upon the men to blame.
For your other merits I will pardon you
this error, and for your Rinaldo too.

81
"Only Argillan, the author of sedition,
whose blood must cleanse the common crime, shall die,
for he, moved by the slenderest suspicion,
drove all the rest along with him astray."
His flashing eyes were as a regal vision
of honor as he spoke, of majesty.
Argillan, stunned and wholly conquered, shook—
incredible—before his angry look.

82
The mob that was irreverent and bold,
that boiled with pride and hate in full career,
and ministered by furor, took quick hold
of slashing sword and burning torch and spear,
now hearing the proud words in silence, fold,
and dare not lift their heads for shame and fear,
and watch as Argillan, whom they surround
with their own armaments, is taken bound.

83
As a lion whom pride and fierceness first provoke
to shake his mane with a terrific roar,
if he should see the tamer then who broke
the native wildness of his heart before,
he will submit to bear the humble yoke
and fears the orders of his governor—
nor do his mane and mighty teeth and claws
serve him against the one who overawes.

84
And legend has it that there stood revealed
with a harsh look and in a threatening stance
a winged warrior holding out his shield
before the reverent Bouillon, for defense,
and his bright saber shook the battlefield,
a blade still streaming with the punishments
of realms and cities that provoked the Lord—
whose tardy anger they must pay in blood.

85

The riot settled, all put down their arms,
and many set their evil wills away,
and Godfrey went back to his tent to think
of various maneuvers they might play,
for he is now determined to attack
the town before the end of the third day,
and goes to view the terrible production—
planks hewn and fit for engines of destruction.

Canto Nine

1
But the great prodigy of hell, who sees
their riotous bands now quiet, and their wrath
now spent—who cannot buck the Lord's decrees
or turn fate from its providential path,
goes forth, and, going, dries the fertile leas
and dims the sunlight in her aftermath;
the minister of fury, hastening, flies
to yet another evil enterprise.

2
For the industrious labor of her crew
had achieved much so far: Bertoldo's son
was far from the Christian host, and, as she knew,
Tancred and all the bravest men were gone.
"Let us attack! What good will waiting do?
Now take them by surprise, O Soliman!
Their camp is fractious, decimated. We
shall enjoy what I long for!—victory."

3
That said, she flew to Soliman's alliance,
whose vagrant troops acknowledged him as head.
Of all the fighters then who swore defiance
against the Lord, no fiercer man was bred;
not even if the earth renewed its giants
to battle heaven, could one stand in his stead.
He was the Turkish king—or used to be,
ancient Nicaea his imperial see.

4
His realm lay opposite the shores of Greece
from the Meander to the Sangari,
where Phrygians, Medes, and Lydians used to dwell,
to Bithynia, and the tribes of the Black Sea,
but when the Asian infidels encountered
the pilgrim arms of Christianity,
his lands were seized and he himself defeated
(a trick the Christians afterwards repeated).

5
Having thus cast the die and come up short,
and thrust by force out of his native land,
he found himself at the Egyptian court,
his host a king most courteous and grand,
pleased that a fighter of such brave report
might lend himself for the great work in hand,
trusting that he and Soliman sufficed
to hold Judea from the knights of Christ.

6
He sent the Turk to muster up a corps
of Arabs (for he would not yet unfold
a declaration of the destined war),
and for that purpose sent him with much gold.
He himself went to Asia and the Moor,
while Soliman had those ravenous tribes enrolled.
That is no difficult thing which he achieves,
for they were always mercenary thieves.

7
Their leader now, he scours across Judea,
and all their aim is pillage, rape, and plunder;
the highway from the French host to the sea,
going both east and west, is cut asunder.
But when he calls to mind the ignominy,
the toppling of his throne, though suffering under
some lack of confidence and weak resolve,
in his enkindled heart great plans revolve.

8
To this man comes Alecto in the guise
of a veteran of tanned and furrowed skin,
into whose face the blood no more will rise,
who leaves the bushy lip and shaves the chin,
his head swathed in a turban of great size,
his robe below the knee unto the shin,
a quiver round his shoulders well supplied,
bow in his hand and cutlass at his side.

9
"Through these deserted plains and barren sands,"
the fury said to Soliman, "we run,
where now no booty falls into our hands,
and no glorious triumph can be won.
At the attack meanwhile are Godfrey's bands,
his works are battering the ramparts down!
But this is a good vantage, if we stall,
for us to watch the city burn and fall.

10
"Are herds and flocks and burnt-out huts and sties
the glorious trophies of great Soliman?
You lose your empire—is this your reprise?
You hope to reacquire it by this plan?
Be bold, be bold! At night and by surprise
strike the tyrannical barbarian!
Trust your old friend Araspe, for you've found,
in exile and in rule, my counsel sound.

11
"He's not afraid, he's not expecting us.
Our unarmed Arab troops he must despise—
a people used to thievery and flight,
not fit for such a daring enterprise.
But your bold courage will embolden them
to move against that camp now while it lies
disarmed, asleep!" So she inspired his mind
with fury—and then vanished in the wind.

12
"O you who goad my heart into a rage,"
raising his fist toward heaven the warrior cried,
"no man, although you show a human form,
lead on, for I will follow at your side!
I come to heap up mountains in the plains,
mountains of wounded and dead, and open wide
rivers of blood! Now be my guiding light
and lead my armies through the dark of night."

13
So he, and called his hordes without delay,
heartening the timid, those who lagged behind,
kindling them from the fire of his own will
that they might follow with determined mind.
Alecto sounds the trumpet call to march;
her own hand frees the great flag to the wind.
The army is on the move, or rather races—
even the speed of rumor it outpaces.

14
Alecto goes with him a little way,
then dons the habit of a courier,
and at the wavering of the night and day
when the world rests, in that uncertain hour,
enters Jerusalem and makes her way
through the sad crowds, to give their governor
the great news of the host and its designs,
of the attack by night, the hour, the signs.

15
But now, dyed in a mist of dusky red,
the fearful shroud of night covered the earth,
but no cool dew to bathe the ground; instead
droplets the color of blood, and of blood's warmth;
and monstrous shapes of fear inhabited
the sky, and phantasms came shrieking forth,
for Pluto let disgorge the dark abyss
and all the blackest caves of Tartarus.

16
Through this deep horror the proud Sultan came
marching to where the foe had pitched his tent,
but in the middle of the march and night,
before the dark began its swift descent,
less than a mile from where the French were sleeping
carefree, he paused, arrival imminent,
to let his men take rations. From high ground
he steels their courage, as his words resound:

17
"Look over there, look at that camp of thieves!
A host whose fame is greater than its power,
greedier than the stomach of the sea!
Think of the Asian riches they devour!
Now kindly fortune offers it to you,
with peril never less than at this hour—
stallions and arms in silks and golden foil
will not be their protection, but your spoil.

18
"This is not the great host that put to shame
the Persian and Nicaean armies, for
most of the Christian troops are dead who came
to fight so long and so diverse a war,
but even if they were healthy, all the same
they are disarmed, their spirits are now far
in deepest peace. Easy to take their breath,
for it is one short step from sleep to death.

19
"Charge, charge! I shall be first to clear the road
through bodies sleeping in security.
Learn how to strike by following my sword!
Learn how to ply the art of cruelty.
Today the reign of Christ will fall, today
you will be famous, Asia will be free."
So he inflames them for the coming test,
silently going forth to lead the rest.

20
But now the sentries see him on the way,
through shadows mingled with a dubious light—
despite his confidence he could not play
a sneak attack upon the prudent knight.
Soon as they scout his mighty army, they
run back to camp to warn them of the fight,
and the first watch is roused by their alarms.
As best they can they hasten to take arms.

21
The barbarous trumpets of the Arabs blew
(for now the Arabs knew they had been found).
Up to the heavens horrible war cries flew
with neighings, and hard hooves trampling the ground;
mountain and valley rumbled as storm clouds do,
and the roar made the underworld resound;
Alecto signaled the town—the fight was on—
raising the fiery torch of Phlegethon.

22
Leading them all the Sultan raced and met
the guards disordered by the sudden shock,
quicker than water tumbling over the brink
as it falls headlong from the mountain rock.
Rivers that uproot trees and houses, lightning
that batters towers and chars each post and stock,
earthquakes that terrify the world's poor stage
are slight reflections of the Sultan's rage.

23
His weapon never falls without a hit,
and every time he hits he cuts a wound,
and every wound he cuts takes someone's soul.
I would say more, but here the truth would sound
deceitful. He pretends—or feels no pain—
or does not feel the enemy's sword, though crowned
with ringing blows upon his helmet, clashing,
flinting out sparks of fire flying and flashing.

24
Now when the first battalion of the French
were turned and put to flight by him alone,
the Arabs joined him at a gallop like
a thousand rivers flooding into one.
Then the French fled with rein and bridle free,
the victors mingling with them on the run,
entering camp, these fleeing, those pursuing,
filling it all with conflict, horror, ruin.

25
High on his bristling helm the Sultan wears
a dragon slithering out with coils unwound,
spreading his wings, ramping upon his paws,
his forked tail in a kind of bow bent round,
and with three flickering tongues it seems he spews
a bile-black slather with a hissing sound.
Now that the battle flame is burning higher,
the dragon kindles, belches smoke and fire.

26
To those who looked upon him in that gleam
the wicked Sultan was a fearsome sight,
as in the darkness sailors watch the foam
troubled with storms and struck with sudden light.
Some set their fearless hands to take the sword
while others give their wavering heels to flight.
Night adds confusion to hostilities:
hiding the risks, it makes the risks increase.

27
Now see the Tiber-born Latinus start—
of those who showed the freest fortitude.
Weariness does not tame his fighting heart;
though he is old, his strength is unsubdued.
Five sons whom you could hardly tell apart
stood at his side in battle, brave and good;
young lads to bear such heavy arms aloft,
their limbs still growing and their chins still soft.

28
Aroused by the example of their father
they whet their wrath and swords athirst for blood.
"Come on, let's go!" says he, "where that proud heathen's
chasing our men. No time now to be cold!
Don't let your hearts be daunted by the slaughter
he's making of the others, but be bold.
My sons, honor is base if unadorned
with horror undergone and peril scorned."

29
So a ferocious lioness leads her cubs,
round whose necks the rugged mane does not yet hang,
whose years are still too few for the fierce claw
or the horrible weapon of the full-grown fang,
out to face danger and to hunt their prey,
and by example she incites her gang
against the hunter who troubles their native wood
by chasing off the beasts of weaker brood.

30
The reckless band of five follow their father,
surround the Sultan and attack. At one
target alone their six spears aim, as if
they shared one spirit and one mind alone;
but dropping his spear and rushing upon the pagan
proved overdaring for the eldest son,
who vainly whips his sword out of its sheath
to slay the Sultan's horse from underneath.

31
But as in the sea's spray a rocky mount
is battered by the waves yet stands above
firm and impassive, sustaining the brunt
of the thunder and wrath of heaven and wind and wave,
so the brave Sultan held his fearless front
immovable by sword or spear, and gave
the boy striking his horse a bitter fall,
and through the cheek and eyebrow cleft his skull.

32
And in that fall one of the other boys
stretched out his dutiful hand to help his brother—
a useless, pious folly, for he goes
to his own ruin going to help another,
as the pagan gives that arm a downward slash
and fells the one who tended to the other.
Together the two brothers fall, and lie,
mingling their blood and sighs before they die.

33
Then he retracted young Sabinus' spear
with which the boy had fetched him a slight wound,
and whirled his horse upon him from the rear,
and knocked him flat and trod him into the ground.
Out of the youthful body the soul is torn
with great reluctance, as it leaves behind
the lovely, happy seasons of a boy
and the sweet airs of life and youth and joy.

34
Laurentius and Pico are still alive,
who enriched their sire at one nativity;
who often were the cause of a sweet error,
as similar a couple as can be.
If Nature made the twins identical,
the fury of the pagan enemy
makes harsh distinction now—for one is left
unheaded, while the other's chest is cleft.

35
The father—but no father now, alas!
for one chance has deprived him of his brood—
beholds in their five deaths his own death now,
and the end of his lineage for good.
I do not know how, in such wretchedness,
old age could have such life and fortitude
that he yet breathed and battled. It may be
he did not look upon their faces, did not see

36
how they lay strewn in death: for night was kind,
and hid the bitter misery from his eyes.
With that, unless he lost his own life too,
triumph would be a paltry thing to prize.
He has grown prodigal of his own blood, most
avid to drink the Sultan's. It defies
knowing, which he is more empassioned by—
whether he longs to kill, or longs to die.

37
"Is this hand then too frail to be respected,
so worthless," to his enemy he cried,
"that all the strength and life in it collected
are insufficient to provoke your pride?"
At that, his hard and deadly sword connected,
splitting the plate mail from the Sultan's side,
carving a wound within, and no small wound,
from which the Sultan's lukewarm blood spilled round.

38
At that cry, at that blow, the heathen turned
his anger and his blade at him; replied
piercing his plate, first shattering the shield
that had been bound by seven strong layers of hide,
and plunged his iron in the old man's veins.
The pitiable Latinus groaned and died,
and in a grotesque vomit he spewed out
blood from the open wound, blood from the mouth.

39
As a tough oak atop the Apennines
that scorns the thrashing of the eastern blast,
brings trees around it crashing to the earth
if a high gale should shatter it at last—
so he fell, and with such a mighty rage,
more than one fell with whom he grappled fast,
fit end for such a valiant man. He dies,
but not before great ruin round him lies.

40
And while the Sultan, venting his heart's hate,
gluts his long fast upon the flesh of man,
the heartened Arabs also dominate
and deal hard fortune for the Christian.
You, Drogut, bring prince Henry to his fate,
and Holofernes the Bavarian;
by Ariaden's hand Philip's life is shorn,
and Gilbert's too, in the Rhineland both men born.

41
Albazzar crushes Ernest with the mace;
Otto falls to the sword of Algazal.
The manner of their killing, who can trace?
Or say how many common soldiers fall?
From the first outcry Godfrey takes his place,
not lingering to see what would befall;
he is ready armed, and musters up a large
legion of men, and leads them forth to charge.

42
He hears the tumult, and it seems the noise
grows more and more horrific; he perceives
that this must be a sneak attack, and has
been perpetrated by the Arab thieves,
who he well knew were in those areas
around their camp, but still scarcely believes
that such a craven mob so apt to flee
would ever attack him so audaciously.

43
While on his way he heard a sudden shout—
"To arms, to arms!" those in the city cried,
and the skies boomed with thunder all about
as barbarous yowlings filled the great divide.
It is Clorinda who leads the king's troops out
to battle, with Argante at her side.
The captain turned then to his right hand man,
his noble lieutenant Guelph, and thus began,

44
"You hear what fresh alarms of battle blare
from over by the hills and town below;
I need your valor and experience there
to check the first offensive of the foe.
Go then and see to things—take these men here,
a part of my own army. I will go
with the rest of my men and try to blunt
the pagan assault upon the other front."

45
So they decided, and with equal fortune
leading their separate ways, the two set out,
Guelph to the hills, the captain, where the Arabs
had yet met no one to contest the rout;
and as he went along he gathered soldiers,
and with each step his squadron packed more clout,
till, great and mighty, he came where the proud Turk
had indeed put his sword to bloody work.

46
So from his mountains in descending course
the Po can hardly fill his narrow bed,
but ever swells the farther from his source
until at last in a victorious flood
he abounds, made high and mighty by new force,
and over the smashed banks lifts his bullish head;
tossing his horns to butt the ocean back,
he seems to bring no tribute but attack.

47
And where he sees his frightened people flee,
Godfrey accosts them, threatening disgrace,
"Where are you running to? How cowardly!
At least look at what sorts are giving chase!
A paltry little troop, a rabblery
who cannot give or take blows face to face!
Just turn about and fix them in your sight!
One angry look will put them all to flight."

48
That said, he spurs his stallion, and wheels round
where Soliman is burning a wide swath,
and he rides over the dust and blood-drenched ground
through clash of steel on steel, through danger and death,
and now his sword and his assaults confound
the strongest ranks and open the blocked path,
tumbling on either side the enemy forces,
arms and armed men and horsemen and their horses.

49
Over the scattered heaps of slaughtered men
he turns and gallops on in full career;
the fearless Sultan hears him coming on,
will not flee the attack, will not veer,
but charging at him, lifting his sword high,
ready to strike the Christian he draws near.
O what a chance brings two knights of such worth
into one contest from the ends of the earth!

50
Fury and virtue fight in one small ring—
dominion of all Asia for the prize.
And who can tell how swift their weapons swing,
how hard the thrusts, how fierce the thrusts' replies!
I cannot speak of every fearsome thing
then done, which darkness hid from human eyes,
things worthy of the brightest sun to show them,
that mortal men might all be brought to know them.

51
The men of Jesus, following their great guide,
by now grown bold, charge on—but his best-steeled
soldiers surround the Sultan homicide,
a ring of Turks about him like a shield.
The earth is stained with blood on either side;
faithful and infidel both strew the field.
No matter who can claim the victory:
with equal frequency they kill, they die.

52
As south winds sweep to battle with the north,
of equal force and fury in attacking,
the sky and sea stand firm as they go forth,
wave against wave, cloud against storm cloud packing,
so too this bitter struggle to the death—
no giving ground on either side, no slacking,
but front to front the charging warriors scored
shield on shield, helm on helm, and sword on sword.

53
On the other flank the war is no less dire,
packed close with ranks of men fighting it out,
but over the vast battleground the air
is thick with angels of the Stygian rout
giving aid to the pagans (who therefore
never retrace their steps or turn about),
and with the torch of Hades they inspire
Argante, already hot with his own fire.

54
He for his part now put to flight the French
sentries, and breached their fortress at a leap.
With lopped and mangled limbs he filled the trench,
making so level a causeway of that heap
that others followed in his tracks to drench
the chief tents with the paint of blood. In step
with him, or just behind him in the race,
Clorinda came, who scorned the second place.

55
And the French are already in retreat
when Guelph and his band arrive in the nick of time,
and make them turn about and take the brunt
of the mad fury of those men of crime.
And so they battled, and the streams of blood
flowed the same on both sides. But the sublime
Monarch of heaven meanwhile from His throne
turned His eyes toward the battle. He alone,

56
there seated, deals to all the universe
good and just Law, creates the orders bright
over the limits of the narrow world.
Reason and sense cannot attain that height;
and from august eternity He shines
in three illuminations of one light,
His servants Fate and Nature at His feet,
and Motion too, and Time which measures it,

57
and Place, and She who as a breath or wisp
scatters and turns (as it is willed up there)
the glory and power and gold we find on earth.
We scorn her, but the goddess does not care.
He robes Himself in His resplendent light
which even the blessedest visions cannot bear;
round Him immortal spirits numberless,
unequal in their equal happiness.

58
To the great chorus of the joyful hymns
resound the happy realms of heavenly light.
He summons Michael, he whose warlike arms
are all of burning adamant flashing bright,
"See how that evil crew of Hades arms
against my faithful flock and my delight,
rising out of the deepest pit of hell
to vex the world, to kill my people! Tell

59
"that swinish legion they should leave the care
of fighting wars to warriors, as is best—
no longer to infect and cloud the air,
the land of the living, or the shores of the blest—
and return to the night of Acheron, there
to suffer justice in their proper nest,
to lash themselves, and souls in the abyss.
I have commanded, I have fated this."

60

Then the chief of the winged hosts who fight
bowed reverently before the feet of God.
He spreads his golden plumes for the great flight
with a swiftness surpassing thought,
and passes the empyreal fire and light,
the changeless glory where the blest are brought,
and sees the crystalline sphere in pure perfection,
the star-gemmed sphere that whirls in the other direction,

61

then to the left sees Jove and Saturn turning,
diverse in look and in the roles they play,
and the miscalled "planets" (if angelic virtue
moves and informs them, they can never stray);
then leaves the region where it rains and thunders,
the flaming fields of everlasting day,
to come to our world in its constant strife
of self-destruction, feeding, death, birth, life.

62

He shook the smoke from off his ageless wings
and the thick gloom that round about him rolled,
and his face scattered gleams and glistenings
of heavenly light that touched the night with gold.
So after a rain the sun, cloud-hidden, flings
its bow, and all its lovely hues unfold;
so cleaving the midnight's calm and liquid rest
a star will fall to the great mother's breast.

63

Arriving where the wicked crew of hell
stoked up the fury of the pagan band,
he hovered in the air on his strong wings
and shook his spear, and had them understand,
"You above all by now should know quite well
with what a horrifying flash the grand
King of the Universe thunders—who deride
the cruelest pain and misery in your pride.

64

"The Lord has sworn that Sion's walls will bow
unto the Cross, and open its gates again.
Why rouse the wrath of the celestial court?
Why battle fate? What can you have to gain?
Go then, accurst, to your own punishment,
your realm of everlasting death and pain—
and let those dungeons you have merited be
where you fight and parade in victory.

65
"There whet your cruelty to its utmost strength
against the wicked, there amid their aching
cries through eternity, the gnashing teeth,
the dismal clank of iron, the chains shaking."
So he, and if they were laggards leaving, with
his fatal lance he jabbed them on. Forsaking
the golden stars and the lovely realm of light,
they moaned, and toward the abyss they turned their flight,

66
their flight to the abyss, to make the pain
of sinners bitterer than usual—
so huge a flock never flapped over the main
when the days first grow warm and comfortable,
nor ever have so many dry leaves lain
on the ground in the first hard frost of Fall.
Everything looks less black when these depart;
set free from them at last, the earth takes heart.

67
Nevertheless in the disdainful breast
of Argante, courage and fury never sank,
though Alecto was not plying him with fire
or lashing the whip of hell against his flank.
He whirls his cruel steel in the thickest press,
and where they huddle tight he strikes the Frank,
winnowing serf and baron at a blow,
so that the proudest heads may meet the low.

68
Clorinda is nearby, and she too sends
a rain of severed members far and wide,
her sword finding the chest of Berlinghier,
riving his heart, where the powers of life reside,
and so full is the stroke that catches him
that the blood-soaked point comes out the other side;
then strikes Albin in our first nurture's place,
and turning round to Gallus, splits his face.

69
The right arm of Gernier, by whom she just
was hurt, she lops off flying to the plain;
its half-dead fingers scrabble in the dust,
as it yet tries to clutch the sword again—
as the tail end of a serpent hacked in two
wriggles to join his former half, in vain—
with such hard knocks the warrior let him reel,
then turned to Achilles, lowered her steel,

70
arranged a deft slice neatly through the neck,
snapping the sinews, slicing out the pipe,
and his head first fell rolling to the ground,
the dirt was first to give his face a swipe
before the trunk fell—for it held the saddle
(a misery of the most monstrous type),
till his steed, sensing no one at the reins,
bucked round and round and shucked off the remains.

71
While thus the indomitable soldieress
breached the West's ranks and gave them a good scourging,
the fierce work of Gildippe was no less,
and Clorinda's pagans fell beneath her purging.
They shared the same sex, the same hardiness,
and in their valor there was no diverging,
but a fight between the two was not to be.
Fate saves each for a greater enemy.

72
Here this one and there that one charges, drives,
yet cannot open out the crowded fight,
and the greathearted Guelph, sword brandished, strives
against Clorinda, closing fast and tight,
and he lets fly a slashing blow that leaves
his sword's edge tinted in her side so white.
For her part the reply is sharp and hostile:
a point that penetrates his intercostal.

73
And now redoubled are the strokes of Guelph,
but by sheer chance the Saracen Osmides
passes, and takes the blow upon himself,
which smites him in the front and clean divides.
But now a crowd of soldiers surround Guelph,
men of the squadron he conducts and guides,
with ever more of the pagans to oppose—
so the confusion of the battle grows.

74
Dawn had already shown her lovely face,
blushing over her heavenly balcony,
and the fierce Argillan in the melees
had broken from his prison, and slipped free,
and snatching up what arms were there to seize
by good or harmful opportunity,
he went in hopes that merit might yet win
honest amendment for his recent sin.

75
Like as a warhorse breaking from his stalls
where he is kept in service of the king,
free at last joins the herds to roam the dales
to his usual watering hole or pasturing—
the mane laughs on his neck, and from his shoulders
he gives his tall proud head a reckless fling,
and his hooves ring over the roadside as he dashes—
his neighings fill the fields, his fine skin flashes—

76
so Argillan coming to battle. His fierce eyes
burned, and he held his fearless forehead high,
and his feet hardly seemed to print the dust,
so swiftly and so nimbly did he fly—
and when he reached the foe he raised his voice
as one who dares it all, and will not shy,
"Idiot Arabs, the world's vile residue,
whence comes this sudden bravery in you?

77
"Helms and shields weigh too much for you to bear,
so with your chests and backs unarmed you play
the naked soldier striking at the air—
and your salvation is to run away!
All of your greatest works and studies are
nightly, for night is your defense. When day
arrives, who will protect you any longer?
Your arms and valor then had best be stronger."

78
With that he slashed Algazzal with his sword
and in the throat gave him so rough a hack
it split his jaw in two, and chopped the word
short, which he was about to answer back.
A chill ran through the poor man's bones—cold, hard—
and all his vision turned to dreadful black.
He bites the hated earth with his last breath,
full of rage and resentment at his death.

79
Then in various struggles Agricalt, Saladin
and Mulehassah met his killing shaft,
and Aldiazel moves too close to the man—
one cleaving blow unseams him fore and aft.
Then he thrust a blade through the chest of Ariadin,
and laid him low, insulted him and laughed—
who raised his eyes at the taunts so full of pride
and on the heavy verge of death replied,

80
"Whoever you are you will not boast for long
your triumph or my death. This destiny
awaits you too. A stronger arm than mine
will bring you down and lay you next to me."
He smiled contemptuously and said, "Let heaven
fret about that. Right now you'll die, and be
meat for the dogs and crows." He planted his foot,
tugged, and together sword and soul came out.

81
The Sultan's page was in the spring of life,
his lovely chin still naked as a girl's;
he went among the bowmen and the lancers.
The drops of sweat that lined his cheeks were pearls
or dewdrops in the sunlight glistening warm.
The dust that scattered on his reckless curls
added a sweet and unintended grace.
Sternness and scorn were tender in that face.

82
With snow new-fallen on the Apennines
the milky whiteness of his horse could vie;
no whirlwind was so quick to turn about,
no flame so light and ready to leap high.
At his side he bore a curved, short scimitar,
and in his hand he shook an assagai—
his scabbard showed the barbarous pomp of old,
a brilliant work of purple silk and gold.

83
And while the lad, whose boyish heart was flattered
by the prospect of glory—a new delight—
rode here and there to harry all the bands,
though no one stopped to challenge him to fight,
the wary Argillan spied him in his rounds,
readied his spear and picked his moment right,
killing the page's warhorse on the sly.
He looked down, as the boy rose shakily,

84
and at that face that looked to him in prayer,
with pity's arms alone—in vain—defended,
he lifted up his unentreatable hand,
cruel man that he was, and thus offended
nature's best excellence. The sword seemed more
human in feeling, for it turned, descended
flatlong. No use; he doubled his fierce assault,
piercing him where he'd missed in the first fault.

85
The Sultan Soliman not far away
had engaged Godfrey's squadron in the fight.
Soon as he sees the boy in jeopardy
he leaves the skirmish, wheels his horse about,
spurs him, and sweeps his blade to clear the way,
coming too late for help, but not too late
for vengeance. He sees, ah misery, sees his own
Lesbino, like a pretty flower, cut down.

86
Sees how the trembling eyes so gracefully
shut, and the neck falls limp, as if in sleep;
so sweet the whiteness of his face, so sweet
the pity his dying semblance breathes, that deep
in his then-stony heart something grew soft
and the spring burst through his anger: he must weep.
You, Soliman, weeping . . . who stood by
while your realm was destroyed, and your eyes dry.

87
But when he sees the enemy's sword still slick
and steaming with the blood of the young lad,
pity gives way to anger boiling quick
and all the tears within his heart are dead.
He charges Argillan, lifts his sword to strike,
splitting his shield, his helmet, and his head
down to the throat. It was a worthy blow
for the hate of Soliman against his foe.

88
But that does not content him. He dismounts
to war upon the corpse, fills it with gashes,
as a mastiff given a hard knock by a stone
snaps it up in a snarling rage, and thrashes.
O empty comfort for unbounded pain,
to glut your anger on unsensing ashes!
Meanwhile wherever the Christian captain goes
he does not waste his anger and his blows.

89
Soliman had a thousand Turkmen, each
bearing his breastplate and his helm and shield,
all veterans of battle, bold of heart;
toil never makes their tireless bodies yield;
they were among the troops of Soliman
when he was routed on the battlefield
and roamed in sadness the Arabian waste.
Through his misfortunes these remained steadfast.

90
Straitened together in orderly rank and station
they yielded small or no ground to the Frank.
But Godfrey charges at their tight formation,
hacks the proud Corcuth's face and Rosten's flank,
gives both of Rossan's arms a good truncation,
from Selin's shoulders swops off head and hank,
nor only these but many others too
in many ways he struck and maimed and slew.

91
While he was clashing with the Saracens,
pounding and being pounded in return,
and the hope and fortune of the barbarians
seemed sure on every side, never to turn
toward the brink, behold, a cloud of dust
in whose lap flames of battle lightning burn
and, from their sudden weapons, streaks of light
that strike the field of infidels with fright!

92
They are fifty fighters, flag of silver field
unfurling the red Cross of victory!
Had I a hundred mouths, a hundred tongues,
and lungs of iron and a voice of iron, I
could never tell how many in that first smash
are hewn down by the mighty host, and die!
The weakling Arab falls; though they fight back,
the invincible Turks are pinned in the attack.

93
Horror and cruelty and struggle and fear
ran wild. In various images you could
see the true victor, Death, roam everywhere;
and a lake welling up with dead men's blood.
Aladine and a troop of his appear—
to make a sortie, for the chance seemed good,
outside the gates; and while they strike the foe
he views the dubious fight on the plains below.

94
But he must sound the signal to withdraw
soon as he sees the greater host in play,
and sends repeated couriers to command
Clorinda and Argante to give way—
but drunk with blood and blind and mad with rage
the hot-spirited duo will not obey,
till finally they yield, and try to unite
their scattering troops, and at least hold their flight.

95
Who can place laws upon a mob, or master
cowardice, fear? The troops are on the run—
some fling their shields, and some disarm the faster,
dropping their swords, no help to anyone.
Between the field and town lies a ravine
from the west to the height of the noon sun,
and toward this place they flee, and cast a pall
aof beaten dust upon the city wall.

96
Horrible is the slaughter the Christians make
as they pursue them headlong down the bluff,
but when the pagans climb nearer to safety—
for the barbarian king has troops enough—
Guelph sizes up the disadvantage and
decides the chase will be too steep and rough.
They halt; the king shuts his behind the gate,
no few survivors of that losing fight.

97
Meanwhile the Sultan did his earthly best,
all that a man can do, and could no more.
His breath is quick and hard, it grips his chest,
rattles his sides. He is all sweat and gore;
his arm lags under the weight of the shield; oppressed,
the blade swings heavy, weary; misses, or
strikes home but fails to cut. Blunt as a board,
his sword has lost the function of a sword.

98
Perceiving this, he stood as a man stands
considering two courses: should he slay
himself, and thereby snatch with his own hands
the illustrious glory of his death away?
Or yet survive the routing of his bands
and save his life to fight another day?
"Fate wins," he said at last, "and I shall flee.
Be that the trophy of the enemy.

99
"Let the foe see my shoulders, let him laugh,
mock our unworthy banishment again,
but he will wake to see me armed once more
to shake his peace and his unsteady reign.
I do not yield, no! Everlasting hate
with everlasting memory of pain
be mine! Bury this flesh, let my soul go
naked—but I shall rise the crueler foe."

Canto Ten

1
So saying, he looked round and found a horse
trotting about nearby without a guide.
He caught the free rein, leapt into the mount,
though his remaining strength was sorely tried.
The plumes that bristled on his crest had fallen,
leaving the helmet plain, undignified.
His mail was riddled and torn, for all its cost,
and every trace of regal pomp was lost.

2
As a wolf hunted from the sheepfold will
slip through the fence and stealthily withdraw—
although his swagging belly has had its fill,
stuffed from the pit of the stomach to the craw,
he licks the sauce from off his chops and still
hangs his tongue from his ever-hungry maw:
so he retreats after that bloody fight
not having satisfied his appetite.

3
And since it was his luck, or destiny,
from all those instruments in death's patrol—
the cloud of deadly arrows whistling by,
lances and swords and javelins—he stole,
and rode ahead unnoticed, on the sly,
along a path where there was not a soul.
What should he do? He pondered, and was caught
in a tempestuous back-and-forth of thought.

4
Finally he decides to make his way
where the Egyptian king was gathering
his mighty host, to join with it, and see
what luck a new offensive might yet bring.
His mind made up, he takes the shortest way—
for he will tolerate no lingering—
and needs no one to show him how to reach
ancient Gaza and its sandy beach.

5
And though he was fatigued and badly hurt,
and felt the rankling of his wounds grow worse,
he would not stop, not to unchain his shirt,
but fought from dawn to dusk to stay on course;
yet at that time when form and hue revert
to the blind darkness, he got off his horse,
bound up his wounds, and then, as best he could,
shook down the fruit of a tall palm for food.

6
Having thus eaten, on the bare cold field
he tries to rest his sides, and ease the pain,
propping his head for pillow on his hard shield,
to still the weary motions of his brain—
but every hour he feels his wounds, unhealed,
ache the more cruelly, and there remain
those vultures gnawing deep within his heart,
sorrow and hatred tearing him apart.

7
At last, in the deep stillness of the night,
with everything around him hushed, at peace,
weariness overcomes him, and he sleeps,
forgetting all his grave anxieties,
his pain . . . And his eyes shut, his limbs relax,
relax in that brief blessed time of ease,
but while he sleeps he hears a voice, severe,
thundering this reproach into his ear:

8
"Soliman, Soliman, do not sleep, but save
your lazy rest for a more fitting hour!
The nation you once ruled is still a slave
under the harness of the foreigner,
your own men's bones have not yet found a grave,
yet you forget them and lie sleeping where
the telltales of your shame are in full view!
Sluggard, what will the new day bring for you?"

9
Waking, the Sultan lifts his eyes, and sees
an old man leaning on a knotty cane
to guide his errant steps aright; his eyes
were grave with age. "Who," he asks, with disdain,
"are you? How do you dare disturb the peace,
old apparition, of travelers trying to gain
some sleep? My shame, my vengeance, whatever I do—
what can it matter to the likes of you?"

10
"I am," the aged man responded, "one
to whom your new designs are partly known,
for you are more important to me than
you realize. I have come to you, alone,
and the sharp words I spoke were not in vain,
for scorn is often virtue's grinding stone.
Be thankful then for what I told you, sir.
To your quick valor it applied the spur.

11
"Now, if I may proceed. You have decided
to turn your course toward the Egyptian king.
My guess is that the journey will be rough
and that your going won't achieve a thing.
Whether you go or not, that Saracen
host will be mustered soon and on the wing,
and that's not the best place for you to show
your virtue in the war against our foe.

12
"But if you take me as your guide, I vow
to lead you in broad daylight safely through
those walls the Latins have surrounded now,
nor will your sword have any work to do.
Within, your wounds and weapons in bold relief
will be a glory and a joy for you.
You shall defend the nation with your might
till the Egyptian hosts renew the fight."

13
The fierce Turk stared into the old man's eyes
and listened to his voice; then he replied,
and from his face and his high-mettled heart
let melt away the marks of wrath and pride.
"Father," he said, "I am in haste to go!
I am ready, I will follow—be my guide!
That counsel always seems the best to me
which calls for greater toil and jeopardy."

14
The old man praised him for his words so bold,
then took a few drops of a medicine
to soothe his wounds that festered in the cold
and stanch his blood and make him strong again.
Then seeing that the sun had tinged with gold
the brightly painted roses of the dawn,
"Time to leave," said he; "the sun shows us our way
that calls men to their labor every day."

15
He climbed atop his chariot nearby
with the proud Nicaean—let the bridle slip,
lashed his team left and right to make them fly—
his hand was masterly at horsemanship.
Leaving no track of a wheel or a hoof to spy,
the coursers dashed along at such a clip,
snorting and panting in their strenuous flight,
with bit and bridle flecked a frothy white.

16
I tell of wondrous things! The air collected
about the pagans in a cloudy pall,
keeping their chariot covered and protected,
and yet that cloud was quite invisible.
Its shell was strong enough to have deflected
a boulder catapulted at a wall,
yet the two in its bosom could descry
the mist about them and the peaceful sky.

17
The cavalier is stunned, arches his brow,
furrows his forehead and with frozen eye
gazes upon the chariot and the cloud
which mount the hills so fast they seem to fly.
The old man reads in his immobile gaze
the astonishment his soul is troubled by,
and breaks the silence, "Soliman!" Who says,
as soon as he's been shaken from his daze,

18
"Whoever you are who, past the bounds of law,
bend nature to your strange and lofty work,
and penetrate the chambers of the mind,
surveying where our inmost secrets lurk,
if heaven has shown you things still far away,
if you can see the future of the Turk,
tell how this great war ends by heaven's decrees—
whether for Asia's ruin, or her ease.

19
"But first tell me your name, and by what art
you can accomplish things so wonderful.
Unless I clear the amazement from my heart
how shall I understand the rest at all?"
Smiling, the old man said, "The latter part
of your request is easy to fulfill.
I am called Ismen the Magician, for
all of my heart is set on hidden lore.

20
"But that I should reveal what is to come,
reading the annals of eternity—
that is too bold a wish, too great a hope.
So much is never granted men to see.
Let each man ply his strength and his wit's scope
to fight through losses and adversity,
for often it happens that the brave and wise
forge for themselves their own blest destinies.

21
"With your invincible right arm, which needs
no help to shake the forces of the west,
you shall not only be the bastion for
the place which that proud people has oppressed,
but fight their weapons, fight their fire! Be bold,
suffer, and dare! I have hope for the best.
But if you like, I can tell what I see
as through the mists of dim futurity:

22
"I see, or think I see, not far away
in the eternal planet's journeying,
a man whose deeds adorn all Asia.
Of fertile Egypt he will be the king.
I pass his works of peace and industry—
I cannot well distinguish everything—
his thousand virtues. This concerns you most:
not only will he shake the Christian host,

23
"but in the final contest he will snatch
all of those lands they rule unrighteously,
leaving them but a narrow little patch,
a town or two defended by the sea.
And he will be your kinsman." Here the mage
ended, and Soliman cried, "How blessed, to be
elected to achieve so great a name!"—
half rejoicing in, half envying, his fame.

24
Then adds, "Let good or evil fortune come,
turning according to the heavens' decree,
for over me she has no masterdom,
nor over my invincibility.
The stars and moon will sooner be wrenched from
their courses, before from my just destiny
I turn one step away." Announcing this,
he burned with ardor and high-spiritedness.

25
So they spoke as they rode along until
they came to where the Christian tents were reared.
Ah, what a hard and cruel spectacle!
How many forms and shapes of Death appeared!
The Sultan looks, and tears of sadness spill
from his now darkened eyes, bedimmed and bleared;
in what contempt he sees his banners lie
which once struck fear into the enemy.

26
The French, rejoicing, scour the battlefield,
trampling the faces and the breasts of his
most cherished friends. They strip off sword and shield
in their arrogant holiday. He sees
some gather in a long parade to yield
their comrades' bodies the last offices.
Some set the torch under a common pyre
to burn the Turks and Arabs in one fire.

27
He groaned from deep within and drew his sword,
leaped from the chariot, and would have raced—
but the wizard checked him with a sudden word,
crying out to restrain his foolish haste.
They turned their course, Soliman back aboard,
toward the highest hill. So on they paced
until they gained a vantage to look back
upon the Christian army's bivouac.

28
Then they dismounted from the chariot
and in an instant that device was gone.
Concealed in the same magic cloud, on foot,
descending into a valley, they press on
leftward, until they reach where the great Mount
Sion turns shoulders to the setting sun.
Here the magician stops, as if to hunt
some passage in the mountain's rugged front.

29
In the hard rock there was a hollow cave,
a fissure carven many years ago,
but through neglect now choked with thorns and weeds.
To pass, you have to crouch and cower low.
The wizard clears the brush away. Bent double,
he shows the prince the narrow way to go,
lending one hand to guide his passage while
the other hand feels out the small defile.

30
"What sort of sneaking path," the Sultan said,
"is this of yours, to which I must resort?
Had you allowed me, I'd have used my sword
to clear a way and cut our journey short!"
"Do not disdain to travel the dark road,
O soul jealous for honor," came the retort.
"For here once trod the feet of Herod the Great
whose name his deeds in war illuminate.

31
"Wanting to put his subjects under rein,
he hollowed out a tunnel here, this king,
and from that tower called the Antonine
(named for his famous friend), by entering
here, he could reach the Temple, emerge within,
while no one in the city saw a thing.
He could leave town too through this secret route,
or smuggle squadrons in, or send them out.

32
"But now I am the only man alive
who knows this dark and solitary way.
This is the road by which we will arrive
where the king calls his counselors today
and his high generals. Fortune's threats now drive
his thoughts to fear—more than, perhaps, need be.
You come at the critical juncture. Listen, hold
your tongue, and at the right time speak out bold."

33
So the magician counseled, and the knight
bent his great body low and squeezed inside
the lowly cave that never saw the light,
following in the footsteps of his guide.
At first they had to stoop—then stood upright,
for at some distance in, the cave grows wide
and you can straighten up with ease, and walk.
Soon they were halfway through that fissured rock.

34
Ismen then opened up a little door;
down an abandoned set of stairs they went.
A little dubious sunlight, dim and poor,
fell on them from a high small window vent.
At last they came to the subterranean cells,
then to the noble hall began ascent,
where with his scepter and tiara'd head
the king sat with his men, discomfited.

35
Out of the hollow cloud the hot-blood Turk
looks roundabout, invisible, and hears
the monarch seated on his opulent throne
begin the council. "O my faithful peers,
this day was surely a disastrous one
for us and for our rule, as it appears
all of our highest hopes have been laid low.
Egypt alone must come to help us now.

36
"But, as you see, that hope is still far off,
while the danger we face is imminent.
Give me your counsel in these grave affairs;
for I have summoned you with that intent."
No more. And like a rustling of the wind
in the quiet forest, round the room there went
a murmur; till with bold and ruddy face
Argante rose, and made the whisperings cease:

37
"O magnanimous king," came the reply
of the fierce and indomitable knight,
"why do you ask for what is obvious? Why
do you require our voices in this plight?
But rest your hopes in us—that I will say.
If nothing can harm virtue, let her might
aid us, as we put her sword in our hands,
loving our lives no more than she demands.

38
"I do not speak this way out of despair
of the aid of the Egyptian king my lord,
for that is certain; and if he has promised,
it is not right for me to doubt his word.
I say so only because I wish to see
an invincible spirit in some of us restored,
ready for any chance that meets our path—
promising victory, and scorning death."

39
The greathearted Argante spoke no more,
as if the case admitted of no doubt.
But then the famed Orcano took the floor,
noble, and with a look that drew respect;
he had won praises as a warrior,
but he was married now, and was content
in his love for his children and young spouse,
and these affections made him timorous.

40
"My lord," said he, "I do not wish to blame
the heat of speeches so magnificent,
born in the courage of a heart aflame,
where it can not, where it will not stay pent;
so if the good Circassian speaks to you
in tones a bit too hot and insolent,
let be, that is his way. Just let him show
the same hot blood at work against the foe.

41
"But it befits you who have run the course
of times and changes (so that you now see
far in advance) to bridle the wild horse
with your direction, should he run too free,
and weigh your hope in that still-distant force
with our imminent—no, present—jeopardy,
comparing the old wall you have fortified
with the munitions on the other side.

42
"If I may be so bold to speak my mind,
our town has in its site a strong defense,
and in our skill; but the foe has designed
massive machines of war and violence.
I don't know what will happen. I hope—yet fear
what war may bring in its ambivalence,
and if the siege lasts for too long duration,
I fear the town at last may face starvation.

43
"And all that grain and livestock you received
into the city yesterday, while he
was but intent on bloodying his sword
in the field—and the stakes were high—would be,
should the siege be protracted, scanty fare
to feed your great and hungry citizenry,
and the siege shall go on, even if the host
of Egypt joins us on the day proposed.

44
"If later . . . well, but let me grant he'll be
here even before you hope, before his word.
I do not see these hard-fought walls set free;
I do not find a victory, my lord.
Good king, we fight a formidable enemy,
Godfrey, his knights, his people, the same horde
that so often has smashed and driven to dispersion
Arab and Turk and Syrian and Persian.

45
"You, O valiant Argante, know them well,
who have so often forced you to retreat,
to turn your shoulders in the battlefield
and put all of your trust in those quick feet;
Clorinda knows besides, and I as well.
No one need put on airs here. I repeat,
I blame no one, for we have clearly shown
our greater valor in what we have done.

46
"Yet I shall say—though that man cannot hear
the truth, and leers as if he'd like to kill—
I see our enemy, and the signs are sure,
led by a fate that is inevitable;
no host, no wall is strong enough to bear
his onslaught. In the end this Godfrey will
conquer. I say so, and swear by heaven above,
because my king and country have my love.

47
"O prudent king of Tripoli, who knew
to make peace with the French and keep his reign!
But the Sultan now lies dead for stubbornness,
or drags his legs along in a slave's chain,
or flees and skulks as someone's hanger-on,
his life saved for indignity and pain,
when all could have been settled from the start
by tribute. Yield a little, and keep part."

48
So said Orcano, couching his advice
in ambiguity and indirection,
not daring to show his hand and sue for peace
or ask his king to tolerate subjection.
The Sultan could no longer bear such speech
and remain where he was, beyond detection,
when the mage said, "My lord, will you abide
this bandying of your business?" He replied,

49
"I am hiding here against my judgment—I
burn with anger!" He had hardly time to say
these words, when in the twinkling of an eye
the mist that shrouded him was swept away,
cleaving and melting under the open sky.
There he stood in the radiant light of day,
shining among them, proud of look, great-souled,
and unexpectedly he spoke out bold,

50
"I—the man you are speaking of—am here,
the Sultan dauntless and not made to flee,
but that man is a coward and a liar,
and this hand will refute his calumny.
I, who made torrents of the foe's blood pour,
and on the plains heaped hills of carnage high,
shut in behind their ramparts with not one
of my companions with me—would *I* run?

51
"But if he, or if someone of like mind,
traitor to faith and fatherland, should dare
utter another word of some mean truce,
by your leave, my good king, I'll kill him here!
Sheep will bed down with wolves in the same fold
and the dove nestle in the serpent's lair
before we and the Frenchman will agree
and settle in one nation peacefully."

52
And while he spoke, his proud arm grasped his sword
and held it high, as it were menacing;
none of the courtiers could say a word,
stunned into silence by his threatening.
Then with a brow less delved with rage, he turned
to speak more gently to the pagan king,
"Be confident, great lord, for I provide
no small help. Soliman is at your side."

53
Aladine rose at once to greet him, crying,
"Oh how happy I am to see you here,
my dearest friend! Now if my troops are lying
dead in the field, I feel no loss; my fear
was for far worse. Soon you, with heaven complying,
can set my throne on a firm base, and rear
your own, to reassume your rightful place."
Then he circled the Sultan's neck in an embrace.

54
The welcoming complete, the monarch yields
his own seat to the great Nicaean, and,
with Ismen the Magician at his side,
takes up an honored seat on the left hand.
So while they talk about how Soliman
returned and entered Jerusalem, the grand
warrior-lady comes forth to do him honor,
with all the others following upon her.

55
Among the rest Ormusseh came, who led
the Arabs when their chief could not be found,
and while the fight was fiercest, took his squad
down disused paths meandering round and round,
so with the help of the dark and silent night
he brought them to the city safe and sound,
and with them stolen cattle and sacks of wheat
to give to the hungry citizens to eat.

56
Only the proud Circassian said no word
but held his ground and glowered contemptuously,
as might a lion pausing in the wood
not take one step, but only turn the eye;
while to the Sultan's face Orcano dared
not raise his own, but looked down, worriedly.
So the Turkish ruler and the knights design
strategy with the tyrant of Palestine.

57
But the reverent Godfrey cleared the ways, pursuing
victory and those vanquished in the fight,
and gave his fallen warriors the last honor
of solemn burial by sacred rite;
then he commands the rest to gird their weapons
for on the second day he plans to fight
and show a fiercer face of terror in
assaulting the walled-up barbarian.

58
And as he knew that the platoon upon
whose help against the pagan he had relied
was made of all his dearest comrades, who
had followed so insidious a guide,
and Tancred with them—prisoners in the false
Armida's fortress—Godfrey called aside
Peter the Hermit and his wisest men,
and in their presence alone he grilled them then,

59
"Please, I should like to hear someone relate
your short-lived wanderings on that dubious course,
and how it happened you were not too late
at such a desperate time to reinforce
our troops." They lowered their heads for shame, each one;
so small the fault, so bitter the remorse.
At last the British king's illustrious
son raised his eyes and broke the silence thus,

60

"Those of us whom the lots did not select
left camp in secret, each man separately,
following—I confess—the lead of Love,
a pretty face and an insidious lie,
along abandoned and contorted roads,
quarrelsome, jarring, stung with jealousy.
And—how I recognize the truth too late!—
small words, small glances nursed our love and hate.

61

"At last we reached the place where flakes of fire
once fell from heaven upon the inhabitants
of Sodom, whose unnatural desire
brought that revenge on their intransigence;
a hot and sulfurous and lifeless mire,
it was a pleasant land of plenty once,
but now whenever the winds stir up the lake
the air grows heavy with the stench they make.

62

"This is the standing swamp where nothing sinks,
no matter how heavy is the object thrown,
but bobs and floats like lightweight pine or ash—
a man dressed in full mail, a sword, a stone.
In it a castle stood, with a narrow bridge
the only way for the traveler. Everyone
crossed over, and, I don't know by what art,
it was lovely inside in every part.

63

The air is pleasant there, the sky at peace,
the water sweet and pure, the gardens lush,
where in a shade of slenderest myrtle trees
a spring arises whence the small streams rush,
and into the lap of grass sweet dreams of ease
drizzle, with gentlest rustling in the brush;
the birds sing, and, as for the marble, the gold,
their wondrous handicraft cannot be told.

64

"And nearby in the grass, in the deep shade,
near the clear water of the brook there stood
a table decked with carven vessels, proud,
and loaded with the rarest, choicest food.
All that the earth gives, all that the seas provide
is there, with every season's bountihood
and all art's seasoning; and a hundred able
beautiful maidens waited on the table.

65

"With her most winning smile and words so sweet
the lady served that deadly meal to us.
And now when everyone had sat to eat
and drink the draughts of deep forgetfulness,
she rose—'I will return.' But not to greet
her lovers with such quiet, reverent eyes;
she muttered words from a book held in one hand
while with the other she shook a slender wand.

66

"The witch reads, and I feel my being change
in thought and will, in life, where life resides—
a new thought moves my will—a power so strange!—
I leap into the lake, beneath the tides.
I cannot tell you how my legs were merged
or how my arms shrank back into my sides;
I shrank and tapered off, with human skin
transfigured into fish's scale and fin.

67

"Transformed likewise were all the other men,
flashing beside me in the silver stream.
For I remember now what I was then,
as in a foolish, empty, garbled dream . . .
At last she gave us our own forms again,
but terror and amazement struck us dumb.
With anger in her eyes she had her say,
delivering these words to our dismay:

68

" 'Now you have seen my power, and now you know
that my command of you is total. I
can choose to trammel some poor soul for good
so that he never sees the peaceful sky;
turn this one into a bird, make that one grow
roots to grip down in the earth's breast, or dry
his body to flint, or make him trickle out
in a gentle stream, or give him a beast's snout.

69

" 'But you can easily shun my sharp disdain—
you'll serve my pleasure, do what I want done!
I want to make you pagans. Fight for our reign,
draw swords against the impious Bouillon!'
But all rejected the abhorrent pact;
Rambaldo was the only man she won.
She clapped us then in chains—no use to fight—
in a cave where there shone no trace of light.

70
"To that same fortress Tancred chanced to come,
and he likewise was taken prisoner.
Not for long did the false witch hold us jailed;
if what I understood was true, we were
to be delivered from her evil hands
to the lord of Damascus' messenger,
as a gift for his hundred men to bring,
in chains and helpless, to the Egyptian king.

71
"So we departed, and, as was ordained
and set in motion by high Providence,
the good Rinaldo who ever lifts his fame
higher, with new deeds of magnificence,
happened upon us, and with his usual skill
put our armed embassy to their defense,
conquered and slew them all, then had us don
their arms and gear—for those had been our own.

72
"I saw him—these men saw him too—we heard
his voice, it was his arm that set us free!
The rumor ringing through the camp, the word
of such a cruel loss, is wrong, for he
is safe, and living! This is now the third
day since he parted from us on his way
to Antioch with a pilgrim; setting his gear
aside, too smashed and soiled with blood to wear."

73
So he said, and at once the Hermit turned
his shining eyes to heaven; his aspect,
his color were transfigured—how they burned
with that most holy light the stars reflect!
Full of the Lord and rapt with zeal he soared
to the realm of angelic intellect,
where the veil was removed so he could see
the future moving in eternity.

74
And opening his lips, in a loud voice
he gave them word of what was imminent;
his altered looks and sudden thundering cries
turned every eye to him. All stood intent.
"Rinaldo lives! The rest, all art, all lies
that feminine deception will invent.
He lives, and heaven preserves his youth still green
for the maturer glory he will win.

75
"Those feats for which all Asia knows him now,
they were a boy's work, marks of things to come!
For I see clearly as the years race on,
he will fight the wicked Augustus, beat him home,
and spread the shadow of the silver-winged
eagle, defender of the Church and Rome,
snatching them from the Barbarossa's claws.
And worthy sons and grandsons will be his,

76
"and will inherit from their ancestor
illustrious deeds to keep in memory,
and from the wrongs of rebel and emperor
defend the holy Church. Their arts will be
to put the arrogant down, and lift the poor,
punish the workers of impiety
and shield the innocent. Past the sun shall fly
the eagle of the Este family.

77
"Justly, since it beholds the light of truth,
it wields its thunderbolts for Peter's throne.
Its plumes shall be displayed in victory
whenever it battles as Christ's champion,
by the decree of heaven as a reward
for their great constancy. Though he is gone
let him return to this great enterprise.
It is a pleasing thing in heaven's eyes."

78
Here the wise Peter, vanquished by his theme,
fell silent in astonishment; so great
the Estean valor which his heart divined
that all description seemed inadequate.
Now falls the darkness, spreading its black veil,
embracing the wide world. The hour grown late,
the others go to give their limbs to rest.
He cannot still the thoughts within his breast.

ఌ Canto Eleven

1
Upon the battering tower and catapult
all the thoughts of the Christian chief were bent
as he prepared his hosts for the assault;
to him the solitary Peter went,
and taking him aside, he spoke, severe,
commanding high respect. "The regiment
you move is of the earth, O captain, but
you still are not beginning where you ought.

2
"Begin with heaven, let heaven direct your course,
and first let your devotion publicly
invoke the angels militant, and the saints,
that by their aid we gain the victory.
Let the priests go in holy robes, and sing
suppliant prayers in pious harmony;
instruct the common soldier to bow low,
you leaders, by the piety you show."

3
So spoke the never-swerving Hermit, and
Godfrey approved his wise admonishment.
"It pleases me to follow your advice,
servant in whom the Lord is well content.
Now while I gather up the chiefs, go find
William and Ademar, whom heaven has sent
to be the people's shepherds. In your care
will be our holy march, our solemn prayer."

4
The old man summoned all the lesser priests
and the two great bishops; in the morning light
they gathered at the consecrated steps
where the camp honored God in sacred rite.
White were their vestments, but those shepherds wore
a golden mantle lapped to left and right
over the linen alb, clasped at the breast,
and with the bishop's crown their heads were dressed.

5
Peter walked first, alone, and to the wind
let stream the sign revered in Paradise.
With grave and measured steps they followed him
in two long files. And now their voices rise—
their looks are humble, as they beg God's help
in sweet antiphonary melodies;
last, side by side, princes in peace and war,
come Bishop William, Bishop Ademar.

6
Then comes Bouillon, and as a captain should,
he walks with no companion at his side.
The leaders follow him in pairs, and, last,
the army in good order, well supplied
with arms to guard them all. And so they leave
the trenches and the palings, unified.
And no ferocious blasts of trumpetry—
but prayers of piety, humility.

7
Thee Father, Thee His coeternal Son,
and Thee their breathing-forth Spirit of Love,
Thee Virgin Mother of God and man made one,
they called upon to grace them from above,
and ye lieutenants of the stars and sun
whose triple armies guide them as they move,
and Thee divine, who washed the divine head
of Man immaculate in the Jordan's bed,

8
to you they cried; to thee the bulwark rock
and firm foundation of the House of the Lord,
where now your great successor turns the lock
to open the gates of pardon, of grace implored;
and the other heralds of the Kingdom of heaven
who saw Christ's conquering death and spread the word,
and you who then shed blood, for you were come
to witness to the truth by martyrdom,

9
and you whose pen or preaching taught the Church
the way to heaven, lost in times of strife,
and thee true handmaid whom Our Lord held dear,
who chose the good of the more noble life,
and O you virgins cloistered in your cells
whom with high wedding feasts Christ takes to wife,
or who, greathearted through all tortures borne,
hold nations and their emperors in scorn.

10
So singing, in a long-extended line
in widening turns the devout people came
and made their slow way up Mount Olivet,
a hill that from the olive takes its name,
a hill that overlooks the eastern wall,
known to the world through the gospels' holy fame;
all the dark land that held it separate
was Armageddon, or Jehosophat.

11
There went the hosts as a harmonious choir,
their song through deepest glens and valleys sounding,
and the high mountain rocks and grottoed walls
with echoes from a thousand sides responding,
so that it seemed a chorus of the woods
hid in those leaves and all those caves resounding,
for they replied in clear and bright accord
the name of Mary, or of Christ the Lord.

12
Meanwhile the quiet pagans stood along
the ramparts, stunned, admiring from that height
their slow procession and their humble song,
the novel pageantry and foreign rite.
But once the wretched followers of the wrong
had grown accustomed to the holy sight,
they raised a cry, they jeered, blasphemed, and swore,
and made the river and valley and mountain roar.

13
And yet the men of Jesus did not pause,
but sang their chaste and gentle melody,
paying no mind, nor turning to those cries,
as if a flock of noisy birds flew by;
nor were they worried that their holy peace
would be marred by the arrows some let fly
from so far off; so till their song was done
they could continue as they had begun.

14
They dress the altar then atop the mount,
a supper table for the bread and wine
the priest partakes; and they placed at each end
the golden stands wherein bright candles shine.
Here William changes cope for chasuble
still lined with gold. Silent is the divine,
then with a clear call flings his voice out broad,
prays the Confiteor, offers thanks to God.

15
The leaders listen humbly roundabout;
those farther off look on attentively.
The mysteries of the purest sacrifice
having been celebrated, "Go," said he,
and blessed them with his sacerdotal hand,
rising before the warlike company.
And then the reverent hosts returned once more
along the ways which they had trod before.

16
When they reached the stockade, and were allowed
to go at ease, Godfrey turned toward his tent,
and to the very entrance a large crowd
accompanied their captain. Having sent
the troops away as graciously as he could,
into his tent for supper the reverent
Bouillon ushered the chiefs. The honored place
was Raymond's, whom he supped with face to face.

17
After the natural desire for food
and the demands for thirst had been suppressed,
the captain said to his captains, "Be prepared
to attack at the first light in the east.
Tomorrow will be a day of war and sweat;
today we will prepare ourselves, and rest.
And so, everyone be at ease, and then
put yourselves in readiness with your men."

18
They took their leave, and with a trumpet call
the criers then proclaimed the news: before
the dawning light they should be armed in full
and every fighter fit to go to war.
Part of this day was thus an easy lull,
part spent in work and planning, till once more
the friendly peace and quiet of the night
lent a truce to their efforts. Now the slight

19
uncertain gleam of dawn glowed in the east
as of the day not ready to be born,
and the hard plowshare did not furrow the sod,
and the shepherd and his flocks did not return
to pasture, and in the trees the little birds
slept free of care; no woodland howl or horn,
when the reveille trumpets begin to sing
"To arms, to arms!" "To arms!" the heavens ring.

20
"To arms, to arms!" a hundred bands of men
take up at once the universal cry—
the brave Godfrey arises, but his great
breastplate and iron greaves he passes by,
and girds himself in lighter, speedier gear
as if he were one of the infantry,
and on his back the armor was but slim
when at last the good Raymond came to him.

21
Seeing his captain arming in this style
the count grasped his intent immediately.
"My lord, where is your good and heavy mail?
Where is the rest of your steel trappings? Why
go out to fight so compromised? Such frail
protection I do not approve, for by
these signs I must conclude you do not hope
for glory beyond a humble soldier's scope.

22
"What do you want? Your very own award,
'First up the Wall'? Let others climb for it,
risking less worthy lives we can afford—
a risk to which their duty must submit.
But you, take up your usual arms, my lord,
and guard yourself for all our benefit;
your soul I pray God jealously protect,
for you are this host's life, its intellect."

23
So he, and Godfrey responded: "You should know
that when the great Pope Urban in Clermont
girded me with this sword, and made me now
knight by the hand of the Omnipotent,
I swore to the Most High a silent vow
that whenever it might come to pass I meant
to do not only what a chief is for,
but to take the arms of a private warrior.

24
"And so, seeing that all my people are
deployed to move against the enemy,
and that I have fulfilled the duties which
the army's captaincy enjoins on me,
I too should charge the walls in the fight today—
it is only right, you will not disagree—
and keep the faith I promised to the Lord.
Let heaven be my protection from the sword."

25
So he said, and the younger Bouillonnese
his brothers, and each Christian cavalier
now follow his example and arm themselves
as foot soldiers carrying lighter gear.
Meanwhile the pagans move their armies from
where turn the seven cold stars of the Great Bear
to defend the western wall, whose plains below
leave it most vulnerable to the foe.

26
That was the focus, for they did not fear
the foe could strike from any other site.
Not only did the wicked tyrant here
muster his troops, with all those who could fight
from the common folk; but boys and old men too
must assist in the crisis at its height,
and carry to the men of stronger bones
sulfur and pitch and lime and spears and stones.

27
It is well stocked with instruments of war,
that long wall in whose shadow the plain lies;
and there in horrible gigantic form
from the waist up you see the Sultan rise,
and visible on the battlements afar
Argante towers with his menacing eyes,
and on the Angle, summit of the wall,
Clorinda stands most excellent of all.

28
Slung on her back she bore the heavy load
of a quiver full of arrows, keen in flight;
she sets her hand already to the bow
and fits an arrow and draws the cord back tight,
the lovely archer waiting for the foe,
longing to hurt him from that rampart's height—
as men once thought that from the clouds on high
Delian Artemis let her arrows fly.

29
The gray-haired king below hurries on foot
from one gate to the next; and on the wall
he checks what he has planned to be set out,
rallies his forces like a general,
giving them hope and strength; shores up this spot
with men, that spot with arms, and sees to all.
To the mosques flock the women who entreat
their deity—a devil and a cheat.

30
"Shatter the spear of the French thief, O Lord,
by your righteous and mighty hand! Let not
their blasphemy of your great name go ignored!
Crush them at the gates, scatter their corpses beneath!"
So they—but no one listened to one word
down in the torments of eternal death.
While the town prepares and prays, the good Bouillon
arranges troops and weapons of his own.

31
With foresight and fine military arts
his infantry he moves to the front lines,
dividing them into two flanking parts
oblique to the wall he means to charge; assigns
artillery between them and head-on,
and all his terrifying war machines,
which strike as quick as lightning as they shock
the jagged battlements with lance and rock.

32
He sends the knights to guard the infantrymen
from the rear, and mobile units all around;
then gives the sign for battle to begin.
So many archers shoot and trumpets sound
and missiles fly from catapults, that in
their fortress the defenders must give ground:
some abandon their position, others fall.
Now a much lighter army crowns the wall.

33
The French troops rushing headlong to attack
charge on with all the speed they can—some wed
their shields together tortoise-like above
and so defend from danger overhead;
others deflect the hail of enemy rock
by crouching under portable roofs instead—
they reach the moat, and all that hollowed space
they try to level with the fortress' base.

34
That trench was neither bogged with mud nor water—
protection which the arid site denied—
so stones and gravel and branches and crowns of trees
could fill it in, no matter how deep and wide.
Then bold Alcasto was first to leave his cover
and plant his ladder on the other side—
what if the boulders and the pitch fire fell
in torrents! He was unrestrainable,

35
and the proud Switzer scrambled up halfway,
his path in air a target to assault,
but he braved the volley of arrows, and scot-free—
no flesh wound put his bold charge to a halt—
when a huge boulder suddenly let fly
fast as if launched out of a catapult
smashed him full on the helm and sent him crashing
to earth—the first blow struck by the Circassian.

36
The wound and the fall not fatal, but severe,
knock him unconscious. He lies, like a dead weight.
Whereat the fierce Argante starts to jeer,
"The first one's down—who's next to meet his fate?
Why don't you come and fight out in the clear,
you skulkers? I won't hide! At any rate,
you'll get no help from your strange caverns there.
No, you'll all die like beasts caught in the lair."

37
The shell-protected squadrons do not stop,
for all that the Circassian's words provoke,
but packed together with their shields atop
they bear the arrow and the boulder's stroke—
and now the battering rams are on the hop,
enormous engines made of trunks of oak
capped with great heads of iron for the ram.
Gates and walls tremble at their fearsome slam.

38
But above, a huge mass for the time of need . . .
Fifty men brace themselves and give it a push
and tumble it over the tightest-shielded squad.
Falling upon them in a mountainous rush
the boulders breach the union of the shields;
more than one helmet and one chest they crush,
and the earth about is dashed with the remains,
weapons and blood and shattered bones and brains.

39
Now the attackers will no longer cower
under an artificial carapace,
but charge to show their virtue in full flower,
exposed to unseen risks in every place—
some plant their ladders to scale the city's tower,
some strike the foundations in an eager race,
and the walls tremble and totter and show their flanks
soon split by the momentum of the Franks.

40
And would have fallen under the tremendous
redoubled brunt of the battering machine,
but on the battlements the wall's defenders
know what strategy and warcraft mean,
and at whatever point the engine's end is
aimed, they unload big bales of wool between,
whose soft surrounding substance takes the hit
and by its springy yielding weakens it.

41
While the bold troops contested with the foe
to take the wall by their brave soldiership,
seven times Clorinda drew and released her bow
and shot seven arrows whizzing at a clip,
and as often as she let an arrow go
sunk it in someone's blood to the feather tip
(blood of the worthiest, never a commoner,
for those were never worthy marks for her).

42
The first knight whom the warrior-maiden struck
was William, the young son of the English king.
He had hardly drawn his head from under tuck
when a deadly shot for him was on the wing,
which even his bronze gauntlet could not block
from passing through his right hand, rendering
him unfit to bear arms. He had to retire,
seething—and not so much for pain, but ire.

43
The good count Stephen at the trench's brink
and, on the ladder, Clothar the great Frank—
the first died with his chest and back transfixed,
the other, an arrow shot from flank to flank.
Robert, chief of the battering ram was struck
in the left hand; he gave the dart a yank
to pull it out, while his machine stopped dead—
but in his flesh still stuck the iron head.

44
Unwary Ademar had turned about
to watch from afar off the battle's pace,
when the fatal arrow shot him in the head.
He raised his right hand to the wounded place
but yet another piercing arrow sped
and struck his hand, and pinned it to his face.
He fell, and left those woman's arms imbrued
with a deep font of consecrated blood.

45
But the determined Palamedes who
held every risk in scorn and had scaled high
straight to the very crown of the battlements,
the seventh arrow struck him in the eye,
and passing through the socket hole and through
ocular nerves inside, it came out by
the back of the neck, in blood. With a headfirst fall
he dies at the foot of the assaulted wall.

46
Such was her shooting. Godfrey meanwhile tried
to harry the pagans to a fresh defense,
attacking by bringing flush to the gate's side
the tallest of his scaling instruments,
a wooden tower jutting so high it vied
with the very summit of the battlements,
a tower stocked with weapons and men, great-wheeled
for troops to pull across the battlefield.

47
And as that hulking structure rolled it shot
arrows and spears, and drew as near as it could.
Like sailors fighting ship to ship they sought
to grapple the enemy's wall and swarm aboard,
but those who watched and wished to dash that plot
pounded it from the front and either side,
and beat it back with spears and the rough knocking
of stones that set its wheels and ramparts rocking.

48
So many stones and arrows were sent flying
from here, from there, they overcast the skies—
two clouds of weapons in the air colliding,
sometimes slammed backward by the foe's replies
to strike the hurler. And like branches lying
stripped of their leaves by a sudden storm of ice
when even the unripe summer apples fall—
so fell the Saracens from the city wall,

49
for the losses struck their side more heavily,
as they were less provided for with steel.
Some of the living now begin to flee
the giant's blasts that made their courage reel—
but he who held Nicaea's tyranny
stands fast, and brings the not-so-bold to heel,
and the fierce Argante runs to show his power,
seizing a joist against the enemy tower.

50
As far as the pole and his strong arm allowed
he pushed it back and held off its advance.
And the paragon of virgins too came down
to share in her companion's dangerous chance.
Meanwhile the French saw to the buffer of wool
hanging before the wall, and cut its bands
with pruning hooks, so that the bundles fell
and left the wall disarmed and vulnerable.

51
The tower above and the rough ram below
pounded away to batter down the block—
riddled and crumbling now it starts to show
the secret tunnels carved within its rock.
Not far away the chief is set to go,
where the walls are smashed and totter under the shock,
protected by his all-enclosing shield,
a thing he rarely used in the battlefield.

52
Here warily overlooking all he spies
Soliman racing down to join the fight
at a point to defend a dangerous pass
opened among the ruins of the site,
and, holding the passage higher up, he sees
Clorinda guarding with the Circassian knight.
These things he sees, and feels his heart afire
with generous ambition and desire.

53
Then turning round he says to the good Siger,
who bore the captain's other shield, and bow,
"Now help me on with this, my faithful squire,
this smaller shield—a lighter burden—so
I can attempt to be the first to cross
the gap in the crumbling wall. High time I show
that I too can perform some noble token
of bravery and prowess." Hardly spoken

54
as he exchanged his shield for the lighter one
when suddenly an arrow flies his way
and strikes him where it brings the sharpest pain,
piercing him through the tendons of the knee.
Fame sings that you are due the honor alone,
Clorinda—yours the arrow. If today
your pagan people manage to elude
the death that threatens them, or servitude,

55
yours be the credit. But the mighty hero—
as if he felt no deadly pain at all—
made no pause in the course he'd planned to go
but climbed the precipitous ruins and sounded the call
to charge! But then he saw his leg was so
grievously hurt—and the strain of scaling the wall
worsened the pain—he could not stand upright.
Whence he was forced at last to leave the fight.

56
And summoning the good Guelph with his hand
he spoke to him, "I'm forced to give way. Bear
the person of the captain, and command.
Make up the loss my distance will incur.
But only for a short time. Understand,
I go, and I return." He said no more,
but rode a light horse back to the palisade.
His army could not help but see. Dismayed

57
by the departure of their chief, the host
gave ground, and felt their fortunes slip away,
while on the other side the strength increased,
hope welled within them, made their spirits gay.
Hearts flagging when they saw Mars' favor lost,
the Christian impetus began to sway
and every thrust of their cutting swords was slow,
and even the call of the trumpets rang out low.

58
And on the bulwarks troops appear once more
who had previously run off in trepidation,
and marveling at the virgin warrior
the women take up weapons for their nation.
With hair let loose and gowns tucked up before
they run to the defensive situation
and hurl their lances and show no fear at all
to bare their breasts for their dear city's wall.

59
The thing which caused the French the greatest fear
and heartened the defenders of the town
was that (and to both armies it was clear)
the formidable Guelph had been struck down.
Guiding the long arc of a stone's career,
his fortune found him out of a thousand men;
and right then Raymond too was struck just so
and fell beneath the impact of the blow.

60
Then the courageous Eustace too was hit
at the ditch's edge, and injured bitterly;
for at this nadir of French fortunes, not
a single blow aimed by the enemy
(and there were many) failed to wound, or split
body and soul. In such prosperity
the Circassian knight swelled far more fierce and proud.
"This is not Antioch!" he cried aloud,

61
"and neither is it the auspicious night,
friend of your Christian tricks! You see the rays
of the bright sun, and a people ready to fight
another kind of war, in other ways!
Isn't there left one flicker in you yet
of love of plunder, or of love for praise,
that you tire as soon as the brief assault unfurls,
O you French soldiers—I mean, you French girls!"

62
Thus he said, and the daring cavalier
so set himself aflame with his own rage
that, for his boldness, that broad city he
defended seemed an insufficient stage,
and in great leaps he hurtled to where the wall
had cracked, and the crack had spread into a passage;
he blocked the entryway, and meanwhile cried
to Soliman, whom he noticed at his side,

63
"Soliman, look! This is the place, the hour
to judge our valor, yours and mine. Why wait?
What do you fear? Let him with the most desire
seek the sovereign honor there outside the gate!"
So said Argante, and each warrior
into the contest rushed precipitate,
he swept away by furor, by honor he—
stung by the challenge's ferocity.

64
Swiftly and unexpectedly they dashed,
rivals in war, upon the foe's redoubt,
and they mowed down so many men, and slashed
helmets and shields and strewed their shards about
with ladders hacked to bits and batterers smashed,
they seemed to pile a mountain of the rout,
and with the ruins of the wall that fell
they raised another high defense as well!

65
The soldiers who once longed for the mural crown
and burned to climb and seize that high award,
now far from any hope of entering town,
seem for their mere defense badly prepared,
and in the teeth of the new assault, back down,
abandoning the siege works as reward
to the two warriors' wrath. Not that it mattered;
for such great fury left it useless, battered.

66
The one and the other pagan, further and further,
slash through the foe, each driven by his own power,
and now they call the townsfolk to bring fire,
and each wields two pine torches against the tower.
So the wicked sisters of the king of hell,
doing his bidding, leave their Stygian bower
and scatter ruin and chaos everywhere—
shaking their torches and their serpent hair.

67
But elsewhere the invincible Tancred who
was urging his Italians to the attack,
soon as he sees the unbelievable show
of might, and the twin torches, shifts his tack,
cuts short his cries and moves at once to go
resist the Saracen rage and rein it back,
such fearsome evidence of his valor given
that those who once drove others off are driven.

68
So now the Christian host has turned the tide
with the turn of fortune, never permanent,
and, in the midst of all, their wounded guide
has made his hobbling way to his great tent,
with good Siger and Baldwin at his side,
and a throng of sorrowing friends. Intent
on working the arrow out as soon as he could
and clearing out the wound, he snapped the wood,

69
and ordered his physicians for his cure
to take the nearest and the quickest way,
open up every path to the arrowhead's lair
and generously cleave and cut away.
"Send me back to my armies and the war!
Let me rejoin them while it is still day!"
So he, and leaned on a long shaft of oak
to prop himself, while his leg took the stroke.

70
Then old Erotimus, born on the Po,
applied his craft to heal the chief. Each use
and healing power and property he knew
of every salutary herb and juice;
content with fame the silent arts bestow
was he, though still a darling of the Muse;
frail bodies from the grip of death he drew,
but could have made their names immortal too.

71
Braced up, seething within, his countenance calm,
immovable to any cry of pain,
the captain stands. The doctor bares his arm,
and in the freest garb, with little strain,
tries if his potent herbs will prove the charm,
and tries his learned hands, but all in vain;
probes with a dagger then to pry apart
the flesh, and draw the head out. But his art

72
failed utterly—for fortune gave no help
nor seemed to smile on his intention. By
this time the cruel torment was so great
the wounded hero felt that he would die.
But now his guardian angel, moved by pain
so undeserved, culled Idan dittany,
an aloe garlanded with purple flowers,
in whose young leaflets dwell deep healing powers.

73
To the mountain goats masterful Nature shows
the hidden virtues which therein reside,
whenever one is shot by the hunters' bows
and the feathered quarrel lodges in his side.
Though it grows far away, the angel goes
to fetch it in an instant. Unespied,
over the readied baths of medicine
he squeezes the herb's juice and pours it in,

74
with aromatic panacea and
the holy waters of the Lydian spring.
The old man doused the wound, and of its own
the arrowhead slipped out, an easy thing,
and the blood clotted well and the pain died down
and the leg was already strengthening,
when Erotimus cried, "No mortal hand of mine
heals you—this is no earthly art's design.

75

"A greater power has saved you, for I see
signs of a heavenly hand, God's messenger
sent down to earth for your delivery—
take up your arms then, go! Rejoin the war!"
Eager to fight, already strapped to the knee
is the good Godfrey in the greaves he wore,
and he shakes his enormous spear and shoulders his shield,
laces his helmet again and takes the field

76

with a thousand men from the tight-bound stockade,
and turned to face the battered city wall—
and heaven cloaked him from above with dust,
and the earth beneath trembled at his foot's fall,
while from afar the adversaries saw,
they saw, and a tremor of fear began to crawl
to chill their bones and freeze their young blood dry.
Three times he raised his war whoop to the sky.

77

That was a cry that called his men to fight—
that was a daring voice those soldiers knew!
At once they reassumed their swift attack
and leapt into the skirmishing anew.
But the fierce pair of infidels by now
were stationed where the wall was broken through
and held the narrow pass tenaciously
against good Tancred and his company.

78

To that spot, menacing and full of scorn,
in his shut armor came the chief of France,
and aimed his first blow at the proud Argante,
hurled like a thunderbolt his iron lance—
no catapult or siege machine could boast
to fling a weapon with more violence.
Through the air whistled the knotty-boled spear;
Argante used his shield and did not fear.

79

But that was more than his shield might sustain,
and even his sturdy cuirass was pierced in two,
till the ash drank the blood of the Saracen's vein,
as all his iron armor was split through.
But the Circassian—and he felt no pain—
yanked it out of his armor and flesh too
and flung it back at Godfrey, crying, "Here,
I'm sending back your weapons with this spear!"

80
Back the way it had traveled in offense
the now avenging javelin is let fly,
but does not strike its target, for he bends
and past his head the spear goes whizzing by,
striking the faithful Siger in the throat,
sinking the iron deep within. To die
for his beloved captain is but right—
he feels no discontent to leave the light.

81
And at that point the Sultan took a stone
and battered the Norman cavalier so well
the impact shook him and sent him spinning round
like a top whipped by a lash, until he fell.
Now Godfrey's wrath bursts out, he draws his sword,
for these offenses are unbearable,
and climbs atop the mountain of debris
to bring the fight close to the enemy.

82
Now his rebuff would have been harsh indeed,
dealing out death and doing marvelous things,
but the night fell, and all the world was hid
under the horror of her smoke-black wings,
whose respite-bringing shade she interposed
among the poor men and their skirmishings.
So Godfrey had to halt, and sound retreat,
and thus that day of carnage was complete.

83
But before the pious Bouillon left the field
he had the wounded and those about to die
brought back to camp; nor to the foe would yield
the profit of his war machinery,
but saves the great tower for another go,
the foremost terror of the enemy,
although it too was battered and badly shaken
from the tempestuous pounding it had taken.

84
Out of imminent danger, the great tower
had reached a place where it was safe for now,
but like a full-sailed ship that dares to scour
over the choppy seas when storm winds blow,
in sight of port, grounds itself on the shoals
or smashes the side of her hull on the rocks below,
or a warhorse surviving the battle, only to come
stumbling and falling as he nears his home,

85
so too the tower—two rickety wheels gave out,
forcing the bulk to come to a teetering stop,
two wheels on the side that bore the boulders' brunt—
and now the tower leaned out from the top,
but the squad assigned to guard it brought support,
and braced posts underneath to make a prop
while the quick carpenters went here and there
to tighten the structure into good repair.

86
So Godfrey orders, for he wants it back
mended and ready for war with the new day,
and round the tower assigns an all-night watch,
to prevent access, blocking every way.
But in the city they could clearly hear
the sound of tools, and what the workmen say,
and see the fires of a thousand torches, whence
they knew, or could divine, the foe's intents.

Canto Twelve

1
Night—but no restoring ease of sleep
gave the hosts rest from all their laboring,
for here the French maintain strict guard and keep
watch, with the tower's repairs continuing,
and there the pagans shore their crumbling wall
around the town, restoring, bolstering
the cracks and gaps the battle had opened wide.
And the wounded were a care for either side.

2
The night's labors were all provided for,
finished at last, and the hurt limbs made whole,
when sleep allured the weary from his chore
as over the silent world the darkness stole;
but not to the bold lady warrior;
she could not still the hunger in her soul.
When others cease she longs for honor's praise.
Walking beside Argante, to herself she says,

3
"Today the good Argante and the Turk
accomplished wonders. With no friend nearby
and thronged with foes, they left the gates to work
destruction on the Christian tower. But I,
the greatest honor I can boast of, lurk
in my secure post, letting arrows fly
from far away—and with success, it's true.
But more than that a woman cannot do?

4
"Better to send my arrows and my spears
at wild beasts on the mountain, in the dell,
than be a woman among cavaliers
and watch the valor of the male excel!
I should again wear dresses, it appears—
or shut myself within a nun's small cell."
So she, for on great things her thoughts are bent;
then turns to tell the warrior her intent.

5
"For some time now, my lord, thoughts have been turning
my restless mind . . . Something unheard of, dire,
reckless. For either God inspires this yearning
or men make idols of their own desire."
In the enemy camp she saw the torches burning.
"I shall go there, I shall bring sword and fire
and burn the tower to the ground. That is my plan—
for the rest, let heaven do what heaven can.

6
"But if my chance is an unhappy one
and if I don't return from this affair,
I leave my beloved women, and the man
I cherish as a father, in your care.
Find means to send them back to Egypt again,
the tired old man, the sorrowing women. Their
sex and his age deserve what pity you take.
O sir, swear that you'll do this, for God's sake!"

7
Argante hearing this was stupefied.
The sharp spurs of glory stung his breast.
"Then you would go and leave me," he replied,
"a common soldier here like all the rest!
And how should it delight me if I spied
the smoke and burning flames from my safe nest?
No, no, we've fought as comrades, you and I!
Let me win glory with you then, or die.

8
"I too possess a heart that mocks at death,
I too think life a paltry price to pay
for honor." "But you showed your lasting faith
when you charged forth so valiantly today.
The city will lose little by my death . . .
I am only a woman. But—and I pray
heaven let it not happen—should you fall,
who will be left to man the tottering wall?"

9
"My will is firm," the cavalier replied,
"I won't be fooled by any poor excuse.
I'll follow you if you will be my guide
but hasten on ahead if you refuse."
Agreed, to the king they went, meeting inside
a private chamber where he heard the views
of his counselors and chiefs. "Sire," she began,
"we ask your favor as we tell our plan.

10
"Argante here has vowed to go burn down
that huge machine—and will perform no less.
I will go with him. We will wait in town
till they are lulled to sleep with weariness."
The king lifted his palms, and a glad tear
trickled along his furrowed cheeks. "O bless
our God, who to his servants turns his eyes
and saves my kingdom from its enemies!

11
"Nor shall it topple soon, so long as there
are such courageous souls in its defense.
How can I match your merit, honored pair?
What gift, what praise would be fit recompense?
May glorious voices sing your fame forever
and fill the world with its magnificence!
The very deed is your reward in full—
and I add no small part of what I rule."

12
So speaks the white-haired king, and tenderly
he takes now her, now him, unto his breast.
But Soliman, filled with noble jealousy,
does not dissemble, makes a bold request.
"This sword has not been girt for nothing! I
will go along, or follow you at least."
"Is this a chance we all must venture on?"
asked she. "Who will be left when you are gone?"

13
That said, Argante would have added more,
approaching to deliver an arrogant no,
but the king rose to speak his peace before,
and calmly reassured the Sultan so:
"You have always, my greathearted warrior,
shown yourself faithful to yourself, whom no
alarm afflicts in the most dangerous plight,
nor do you ever weary of the fight.

14
"I know it would be worthy of you to go
and yet I think it inappropriate
to send all our best fighters in one blow
with no one in reserve to guard our state.
Even their going I would not allow—
for their blood too I prize at the highest rate—
were it a smaller advantage to pursue
or if I thought that someone else would do.

15
"But since the great tower is so densely packed
with sentries to defend it roundabout,
that by few men it cannot be attacked,
nor is it the right time to send a rout,
these two who offer themselves for this great act
and who have often put their lived in doubt,
let them go with good speed, for each alone
is worth more than a thousand men in one.

16
"I beg you, wait with the rest upon the gates,
an honor more befitting a king's station.
When, as my hopes assure me, they return
from waking flames into a conflagration,
should any troop of foes come in pursuit
repel it! Be their guard and their salvation."
So spoke one king; the other, not a word,
for he was not too pleased by what he heard.

17
Then Ismen added, "You who are to go,
may it please you to wait another hour
while I concoct a formula to throw
upon the joists and beams to burn the tower.
Perhaps by then a number of the foe
will yield their vigilant duty to the power
of sleep." That settled, they all go their ways,
to wait the time for the great enterprise.

18
Clorinda slips her silver-woven vest
and her gay helmet and her brilliant gear,
for a mail shirt black with rust and a plumeless crest,
all unadorned (an omen full of fear),
because she thought it easier, thus dressed,
to move unseen by the enemy troops. But here
Arsete the eunuch comes, whose aged hands
had raised her from a babe in swaddling bands,

19
and who had drawn his old bones after her
to be beside wherever she might go.
He sees the armor changed, in disrepair,
senses the great risk she must undergo,
and by the years that silvered his head with care,
by all his service, by the duty she should owe
to their remembrance, in grief he makes his plea,
"Don't undertake this enterprise!" But she

20
won't hear him. "Since you're set," he said at last,
"and even for your own good you will not bow,
hardened against the long years I have past;
since tears and prayers of mine mean little now
I must not leave you in the dark. There was
something about your birth you ought to know.
Then follow your desire, or my advice."
At that, attentively she raised her eyes.

21
"In Ethiopia ruled Prester John,
and maybe he still rules that happy land.
He adhered to the laws of Mary's son,
as did the dark-skinned folk in his command.
I was a pagan slave there, made to don
a woman's role among the handmaids' band
as the queen's chamberlain. She was black, true,
and yet her black possessed its beauty too.

22
"Her husband's love for her was all ablaze
yet outmatched by the frost of jealousy.
Little by little with the passing days
in his wracked heart the madness surges high
yet no one knows it—in a secret place
he hopes to hide it even from the eye
of heaven. She, humble, wise, does all to please
her lord, for that is her delight, her peace.

23
"Upon her walls there was a tale portrayed,
a pious legend from their old saints' lore:
here, her cheeks blushing, stands a sweet fair maid
beside a battle-beaten dragon, for
a knight has pierced the monster with his lance;
the beast lies dead, wallowing in its gore.
The queen would often kneel here as she made
confession of her silent sins, and prayed

24
"and wept. Meanwhile she grew with child, and bore
a daughter of fair skin—and you were she.
It was a shock, that unaccustomed color—
she gazed upon it as a prodigy.
But since she knew the king and his mad furor,
she thought it best to hide the delivery,
for if he saw your whiteness she was sure
he would have thought her faith was not so pure.

25
"There was a black child born shortly before.
She'd show him her instead—so she devised.
And since she dwelt alone in the cloistered tower
with myself and her women whom she prized,
to me, her slave, who loved her with all my heart,
she gave you, newly born and not baptized.
Nor could she baptize you in any case
for that was not the practice in that place.

26
"In tears she placed you in my arms and made
me swear to take and raise you far away.
How her heart ached, how bitterly she wept,
it is impossible for me to say;
she lingered on a last embrace, she bathed
kisses with tears, her words could not make way,
broken with sobs. At last she raised her eyes.
'You see in secret, Lord, You know what lies

27
" 'deep in my heart. If it is free of spot,
if my body and marriage bed are undefiled—
not for myself I pray—I am a sinner,
a vile thing in Your sight—O Lord, look mild
upon this innocent baby, let her live,
though I deny the breast to my own child!
Let her resemble me in honor alone—
better fortune she can learn from anyone.

28
" 'Celestial warrior, you who slew the snake
and snatched the damsel from its wicked jaws,
if ever I lit a candle for your sake
or made your altar smoke with frankincense,
pray for her, let her be your loyal maid
and in all trials seek your sure defense.'
Her heart broke, and she breathed her final breath,
coloring with the pallid cast of death.

29
"Weeping I took you up, and among flowers
and leaves I hid you in a little chest,
and so carried you out. No one else knew,
no one suspected, no one could have guessed.
Then one day, unseen, I escaped with you,
and walking through the gloom of a dense forest
I saw a tiger, its eyes full of wrath,
with threatening paw approaching in my path.

30
"I set you in the grass and climbed a tree,
such great fear seized my heart! Then came that wild
horrible beast, and turned her proud head round,
looking intently upon you, my child—
and softened, and her rough and bitter looks
were graced with gestures courteous and mild.
So she approached you with a gentle purr
and licked you while you laughed and petted her,

31
"stretching your little hand toward her fierce mouth,
playing, as if you had no care to heed.
She like a nursing mother nestled you
and offered you the teat and let you feed.
I gazed in fear and wonder, as a man
who sees some dreadful miracle indeed;
but when her milk had filled you with sweet food
away she slipped again into the wood,

32
"and when the tiger had gone I climbed back down,
picked you up, and continued on my way
until we rested in a little town.
And there in secret we two made our stay.
I nursed you up in hiding as my own
while the ever-circling sun brought in the day
for sixteen months. You then made baby talk,
your tongue still wet from milk . . . you tried to walk

33
"with toddling steps. But I was growing old,
my years had started on the last decline.
So, since I was well off with all the gold
given me at parting by the generous queen,
this wandering, pilgrim life made me so bold
to seek my native country once again
and live among old friends on that dear earth,
and keep my winter warm at my own hearth.

34
"And so I started on the road toward home,
Egypt my native land, and brought you too,
when to a trap at a riverbank we come,
thieves here, the rapids there. What should I do?
I want to get away—but, my sweet child,
burden so dear, I can't abandon you.
I throw myself to swim—one arm to save
you clear above, one arm to part the wave,

35
"but the river races on and in midstream
it turns itself into a whirlpool—nor
when I reach the eye can I help being seized
and sucked down under and flung to the river floor.
I let you go—but the water bears you up
and a fortunate gust of wind blowing toward shore
sets you down safely on the gentle sand.
Gasping, I hardly make it back to land,

36
"and take you up again with joy. That night,
when a deep silence rocked the world to rest,
a menacing warrior rose before my sight,
his brandished weapon pointing at my chest.
'I command you!' said the imperious knight.
'You must fulfill her mother's last request,
that you baptize this baby girl, for she
is loved in heaven; her care belongs to me.

37
" 'I inspired the beast to pity, I turned the stream.
By me she will be guarded and defended.
Woe to you if you do not trust your dream
for it brings word from heaven.' Here he ended.
I woke and rose, and soon as the first gleam
of dawn was born, still to the east we tended,
but as I trusted that my faith was true
and those shades false, I never baptized you

38
"but raised you as a pagan. Your mother's prayers
I shirked, and hid the truth from you as well.
Then you grew bold in arms with the passing years—
nature and your own sex you far excel—
and garnered land and glory. How your life
has fared since then, you yourself best can tell,
and how, servant and father both, I go
among your armies as you meet the foe.

39
"Yesterday, just before the dawn, my mind
was laden with a stillness as profound
as very death; and the same spirit came,
more troubled in his look, of sterner sound.
'Villain,' said he, 'the hour when Clorinda
must change her life and fortune now comes round.
Mine she will be despite you; yours, the pain.'
That said, he vanished into air again.

40
"Now you hear, my delight, the threats of heaven . . .
There is some accident, some chance in store.
I don't know . . . Maybe He is not pleased when one
attacks his parents' own religion . . . or
it may be the true faith. I beg you, please,
put down your arms, leave those fierce thoughts of war."
So he, and wept. And in her heart was fear,
for another dream like that had troubled her;

41
then calmed her looks and said at last, "I shall
follow the faith which now seems true to me.
You made me drink it with my nurse's milk
and now you cast it in uncertainty.
I will not do what the great heart must not—
drop my arms and this enterprise, to flee!
Not if the grimmest death for mortal men
should stand before me." She consoled him then,

42
and since the moment now was drawing close
when she must turn her boasting to fruition,
she leaves, and joins the one who would expose
his life beside her in the perilous mission.
Then Ismen spurs their stout hearts on, but those
were racing forward of their own volition,
and hands them vessels of hidden fire to light
balls of sulfur and tar. In the dead night

43
they left the city quietly; down the slope
they went together, quick and long their stride,
and where the enemy's tower was lifted up
they soon have come. Now at the war work's side
their spirits are aflame and their hearts seethe,
nor can they hold back all the wrath inside.
Fierce hatred beckons them to fire and blood.
The watchman calls for them to give the word

44
but they move stealthily on. "To arms, to arms!"
now rings the sentinel's redoubled cry,
and the greathearted pair no longer hide
but to the point of the attack they fly.
Quick as a thunderbolt or mortar shell
that flares and roars and blows itself sky high,
so in an instant do they move, arrive,
attack the guards and split their ranks and drive

45
through—and though battered with weapons on all sides,
there was a chance their plan might yet succeed.
They cracked the vessels of fire and the balls of fuel
and brought them together and let the flickerings feed,
then laced the joists and beams of the tower with fire.
Past telling, how the flame snakes from such seed
to surge, to coil the tower! What thick smoke mars
the pure and tranquil countenance of the stars!

46
You could see balls of black fire billowing
among the smoke wheels whirling in the night.
The wind blows all the scattered fires together
and makes them blaze with all the fiercer might,
and the French troops behold the fire in terror,
they seize their arms, but that long-labored height,
that massive structure, dreaded tower of war,
falls to the earth in a moment, and is no more.

47
Immediately, the blazes rising higher,
two squads of Christians hurry to the place.
Argante roars his threats, "I'll quench this fire
with your own blood!" and meets them face to face—
yet he and Clorinda must retire
little by little, and yield the mountain's base,
as like a storm-swollen torrrent the crowds grow
and follow hard upon them wherever they go.

48
The Golden gate is opened, and the king,
surrounded by his troops, waits to receive
the two who dared to do so great a thing,
if their return enjoy good fortune's leave.
To the threshold they leap, and the French fling
themselves upon their backs like a great wave,
but Soliman strikes and scatters them about.
The door is swung to. Clorinda is shut out

49
alone, shut out alone is she, for as
the others were about to bar the door
she ran forth full of fire and cruel rage
to pay Arimon back for wounding her.
She paid him, but the fierce Argante did
not see how far off she had wandered, for
the fight and the darkness and dust and smoky air
had robbed his eyes of sight, his heart of care.

50
But when the blood of the foe had slaked her wrath
and she looked round her with a clearer head
she saw the gates shut, saw herself amid
the enemy, and held herself for dead.
Seeing that no one looked toward her, a new
way to be saved occurred to her instead.
She'd steal among the foe as if she were
one of their own; and no one noticed her.

51
Then as a silent wolf slinks to his lair
after his stealthy crime, and takes his way,
favored and hidden by the hazy air
she seized on the confusion to steal away.
Of this, it chanced that the one man aware
was Tancred, who had arrived to see her slay
Arimon just a little while before.
He saw, and marked, and trailed the warrior.

52
He wished to fight—he thought she was a man
worthy to put his mettle to the test.
She sought some other gate to enter town
and turned to climb atop the mountain crest;
he followed bold and hard upon her trace,
his armor ringing from far off. She guessed
and turned. "What are you bringing me," she cried,
"riding so fast?" "War and death," he replied.

53
"War and death you shall have then, if you like.
I won't refuse you." And she stood in wait.
Tancred, seeing his enemy afoot,
dismounted—for he wished to try their fate
on even terms. They brandish their sharp swords
and whet their pride and stoke their wrath and hate,
meeting each other as eagerly
as bulls riven with rage and jealousy.

54
What they did now was unforgettable,
deserving a wide stage, a brilliant sun.
O Night, who shrouded such a great event
in your deep darkness and oblivion,
let me bring it forth in the pure light of verse
that every future age may look upon
that famous pair, and let their glory be
what makes your darkness shine in memory.

55
They were not shy, they did not bide their time,
there was no sleight of hand here, no finesse,
no feint and jab, no sudden flurry of blows.
Night and their fury made art purposeless.
Now you could hear the chilling clash of steel
on steel. Their feet hold firm in the first press,
feet ever firm and never still their hands;
each point thrusts home, each slashing sword edge lands.

56
Shame chafes their scorn and spurs them to revenge,
and in the vengeance suffered, shame renews,
so that to strike afresh and slash in haste
they always have a fresh spur, a fresh cause.
And now they close and tussle in the clinch,
so tight their blades are rendered of no use;
bloodthirsty, crude, they pound with pommels instead,
smash shields together, bash helmets head to head.

57
Three times the knight gripped the young lady hard
in his muscular arms, and three times she
slipped herself out of those tenacious knots,
no true love's, but the bonds of an enemy.
Back to their blades they turn and dye them red
with many wounds; then, breathing laboredly,
at last both he and she withdraw to pause
and rest a bit from their long exercise.

58
Upon the pommels of their swords they leaned,
blood-drained; looked at each other wearily.
Already the rays of the last star declined
and faded in the light of the eastern sky.
And Tancred saw his foe had lost much blood
while he was hurt not quite so seriously.
Saw, and rejoiced with pride. O human mind,
foolishly puffed up with the slightest wind

59
of fortune! Swell with joy, poor man; today
how sad your boasts will be, how miserable
your triumph! If you live your eyes shall pay,
for every drop of blood of hers you spill,
a sea of grief. So the two, bloodied, stay
their hands a little, quietly watching, till
Tancred finally broke the silence thus,
wishing to know who his opponent was:

60
"Silence will cover all, unfortunately,
as we employ such valor here alone,
but even if bad fortune can deny
the witnesses to praise what we have done,
if prayers have any place in battle, I
beg you, tell me your name and whence you come,
that I may know, whether you live or die,
who honors my death, or my victory."

61
Responded the bold maiden: "Ask in vain.
I like to keep my name in secrecy.
Whoever I am I will make one thing plain:
one of your great tower's arsonists you see
before you now." Then burning with disdain,
"Your words have come at a bad time," said he.
"Your silence drives me on, your speech as well,
to sweet revenge, barbarous infidel!"

62
Wrath seized their hearts and swept them up once more,
weak as they were, unto the cruel fight,
where strength is dead and art is used no more
and fury fights in place of skill and might!
And their swords slash and open wells of gore,
slicing a gaping breach wherever they light
on iron or flesh. If life does not depart
it is their scorn that grapples it to the heart.

63
As the waves on the deep Aegean Sea
when the air grows calm after the ocean's shaken
and pounded by the winds: they rock and sway
and rumble from the buffeting they've taken;
so too, though they were weak from loss of blood
which left the vigor of their arms forsaken,
they retained the first impetus to go,
utter momentum landing blow on blow.

64
But now the fatal moment has arrived;
Clorinda's life is hastening to the goal.
Into her lovely breast he thrusts his blade,
drowns it, eagerly drinks her blood. Her stole
beneath the cuirass, sweetly lined with gold,
that held her breasts with light and tender pull,
now fills with a warm stream. She cannot stand;
her legs give way. She feels her death at hand . . .

65
He rails against the virgin on his sword,
pressing against her in his victory.
But as she falls she speaks her life's last word,
in a voice broken with extremity,
and a new spirit in her proclaims that word,
spirit of faith, and hope, and charity.
Rebel in life, on her such grace is poured
that she may die the handmaid of the Lord.

66
"Friend, you have won . . . I forgive you . . . forgive
my body, no . . . has nothing more to fear,
but spare my soul. For that I pray, and give
me baptism, to wash my soul and clear
all of my sins away." In her frail voice
something sweet, something to summon a tear
sank into his heart and put all scorn to sleep,
and drew him on and forced his eyes to weep.

67
Not far away in the bosom of a hill
a little stream was trickling. There he went
and from the murmuring water filled his helmet,
sadly returning to the great sacrament.
His hands were trembling as he undid her laces
and over her face, her unknown face he bent;
he saw her, knew her. And he could not move
or speak. Ah, thus to see and know his love!

68
He did not die, not yet, but summoned all
the courage of his heart to stand on guard,
holding his pain at bay. He gave her life
with water, who had slain her with the sword.
And while he uttered the sound of the holy prayers
she was transformed with joy, and smiled; appeared
to say, as filled with life at life's decease,
"The heavens are opening—I go in peace."

69
Her cheeks were beautiful and pale, as if
violets mingled with the lily's white,
and she fixed her eyes on heaven; in pity and love
it seemed to shine on her its rising light.
And in the place of words she tries to move
her cold and naked hand toward the knight,
giving a pledge of peace. It seems she lies
sleeping; for so the lovely woman dies.

70
When he sees the gentle soul has passed away
the strength he mustered up begins to fade,
and of his own free will he yields the sway
to a grief already rendered reckless, mad,
pressing his heart . . . Insensible he lay,
his face as white as death, his life withheld
in a small room. Blood drained, his color fled,
he lay with all the stillness of the dead.

71
His soul, disgusted, sick unto death, indeed
would have pierced its frail barrier to die
and follow at last the lovely soul now freed
who had just spread her wings to the morning sky,
but, searching for water or some other need,
a squadron of the French came passing by,
and they carried the lady and the knight together,
his body scarcely alive, his spirit with her,

72
dead with the dead. Their leader, far away,
had seen the armor of the Christian prince
and had come running; soon saw where the girl lay
beautiful, lifeless. The unusual chance
moved him. He would not leave her as wolves' prey
though she was yet of the Mohammedans,
as he believed. He had both carried to
the tent of Tancred. So softly they go

73
that the hurt cavalier can feel no motion
and does not yet recover consciousness
but gives the faintest moan. With that they know
he has not yet completed his life's course.
But the other's stillness and her silence show
her spirit has departed. Thus
they were brought, side by side, the knight and maid,
but in the end in separate tents were laid.

74
Dutiful squires surrounded him as he lay,
performing various healing offices.
To his weary eyes returns the light of day,
he feels the doctor's hands, hears what he says,
but he is doubtful, for his mind is stunned
and he is not yet certain where he is.
He stares about, then knows the men, the place,
and at last utters in a broken voice,

75
"Am I alive? Do I still breathe? Still look
upon this evil day, the hateful light
which gives in evidence against my sins
committed in the secret of the night?
How cowardly and slow you are, my hand!
You ministered at that shameful death all right,
master of every way to strike! Be staunch
and rip this life of crime out root and branch!

76
"Run my heart through and let your cruel steel
carve out a bitter lesson! Then again,
trained up in wickedness, perhaps you feel
it would be piety to kill my pain.
So I shall live to tell my wretched tale
for my life merits nothing more than pain—
wretched example of unhappy love—
for the immense crime it is guilty of.

77
"I will live as a wanderer, mad, with all
my sorrows and my furies. They are just,
will fear the dark and solitary place
for there the memory of my error must
return; and the sun that showed me my disgrace
will fill my soul with horror and disgust.
I will fear even myself, and try to hide,
but I will always have me at my side.

78
"But where are they, my God, where do they lie,
the relics of that beautiful and chaste
body! Whatever my fury left untouched
might be torn by the fury of a beast—
alas, she is too noble a prey, too sweet,
too lovely and precious for so mean a feast,
poor thing. The woods, the night first spurred me on
and now they leave you for beasts to feed upon.

79
"But I will come to you, beloved spoils,
and keep you with me if you still remain,
and if some beast has gorged his fierce desire
on those sweet members, may I too be slain,
swallowed by the same mouth, shut in the same body,
shut in with you! For I would gladly gain
that honored tomb, wherever it may be,
could I be with you for eternity."

80
So says the wretched man, and then they tell him
the body that he grieves for is nearby.
His dark looks seem to brighten, as the clouds
when a flash of lightning flies and passes by,
and he raised from the restful bed the weight
of his weak limbs and moved unsteadily.
Scarcely able to stand, he made his way
faltering toward the tent where the maiden lay.

81
But when he saw the work of his own hand,
that sweet breast and the evil wound he made,
and saw the light gone from her countenance
as gray as a night sky of peaceful shade,
he shook so violently he could have fallen
had his friends not been near with faithful aid.
"O lovely face, you make death sweet," said he,
"but you can never sweeten my destiny.

82
"O beautiful right hand that offered me
sweet assurance of friendship and of peace,
look at you now . . . How can you suffer me?
And you loveliest limbs . . . are not these
the evidence of my beastlike enmity,
the sad and deadly signs of wickedness?
O my eyes, wicked as my hands, to gaze
upon the wounds they made! But can I gaze

83
"dry-eyed? Then where my tears refuse to go
my blood shall run instead!" And he cuts short
his words—a desperate longing moves him now,
longing to die—he tears apart
his bandages, rips wide his wounds, lets flow
a river of blood from his body freshly hurt,
and would have killed himself had not great pain
preserved his life and made him faint again.

84
They carried him back to bed, and from its flight
his soul was brought back to its hateful place
and duties. Garrulous rumors of the knight
tell of his anguish and unfortunate case;
the reverent Godfrey visits him, and a crowd
of his worthiest friends. But no one says
anything that can soothe his troubled spirit.
Admonishment or plea, he will not hear it.

85
As in a mortal wound the merest touch
will make the sensitive member throb with pain,
so their attempts to soothe his heart too much:
salves in such sickness chafe against the grain.
But the venerable Peter, whose care was such
as a good shepherd feels for the weakling lamb,
reproached him for his folly and long straying
and in the gravest terms advised him, saying,

86
"O Tancred, Tancred! You have lost yourself,
your faith that led you to this enterprise!
Who has made you deaf? Or what cloud is so thick
that the light can no longer strike your eyes?
Heaven sends you this disaster for a warning,
don't you see? Don't you hear its words? It cries,
it calls you back to fight the holy war
and points the road which you have gone before.

87
"It summons you to be a knight of Christ,
to acts which with that high office accord,
which you abandoned—oh, disgraceful change—
to court a girl, a rebel of the Lord!
Merciful scorn it is, adversity
most fortunate, whose gentle flail has scored
your foolish sin and made your hand apply it
for your salvation—and will you deny it?

88
"So you deny the healthful gift of heaven,
mindless, and rage against its admonition?
You fool, how have you let your reins go free
so you can gallop to your own perdition!
You lean headlong over the eternal cliff
now, and you will not look on your position?
Look, gather your wits, restrain the grief which shall
lead to the death which is perpetual."

89
Silence. Fear that his soul might also die
made longing for the first death less intense;
his heart took in that solace by and by;
his inner grief grew cooler in offense,
but not so that he could prevent a sigh
or his tongue giving rein to his laments.
Now to himself, now to the soul set free
he spoke; from heaven she might hear his plea.

90
To her with the setting, to her with the rising sun
he cried out hoarse with weeping and with prayer,
as a nightingale whose chicks still furred with down
the thieving hard-hearted farmer would not spare,
sings all the night in misery alone
and fills with sadness all the woodland air.
At last toward dawn he closed his eyes; there crept
exhaustion with his weeping, and he slept.

91
And behold in a dream, the sighed-for love
appears to him in raiment of the stars,
far lovelier, but that heavenly light adorns
and does not hide her beauty as it was;
and in a sweet gesture of pity she
moves to dry his sorrowful eyes, and says,
"Behold how beautiful I am, and blessed,
my faithful lover. Let your sorrows rest.

92
"I am so by your grace. You took me from
the mortal world of the living, by mistake,
but made me worthy to rise to the bosom of God
among the divine and immortal, for mercy's sake,
where I rejoice in love and blessedness.
And here I hope you too will come to take
your place in eternal day, the Sun divine,
to gaze upon His loveliness, and mine.

93
"If you do not look sour on heaven and steal
yourself away in sensual vanity,
live and know that I love you—what I feel
I will not hide from you—as tenderly
as a creature may be loved." With that, such zeal
flamed in her eyes past mortal powers, that she
closed herself in her rays profoundly bright,
and so instilled new comfort in the knight.

94
He woke consoled, and gave himself once more
to what his wise physicians thought was best,
and at once had those lovely limbs, which were
lent form by a life so noble, laid to rest.
And though he had no choicest marble or
a Daedalus to sculpt her tomb, at least
a stone was chosen and they carved on it
all the adornment the time might permit.

95
And there he had her brought, accompanied
by torches to the solemn burial,
and, hung upon a naked pine, displayed
her arms and armor for memorial.
But on the following day the knight arose
as soon as his afflicted limbs were able,
and visiting the honored tomb he went
quietly dutiful and reverent.

96
He reached the tomb, the prison house where heaven
had ordained for his living soul to dwell,
and on the stone he fixed his eyes, cold, wan,
speechless and still, as if insensible.
At last he broke into a languid sigh,
alas, as a river of weeping broke the spell.
"O stone too highly loved and honored, keeping
my spirit's flames within—without, my weeping,

97
"death does not make its house in you, but life,
the living ashes where love lies in rest,
for well I feel the old flames rise from you,
less sweet, yes, but no cooler to my breast.
Ah, take these kisses bathed with my sad tears
and take my sighs, my longings unexpressed,
and since I cannot do so give them to
the beloved remains that dwell in you.

98
"Give them to her, for should the gentle soul
look on the loveliness she used to wear,
her anger will not call my love too cool,
your duty slack; for scorn and hatred there
are never roused. Let her forgive my fall.
It is my sad heart's only hope and prayer.
She knows the wickedness was my hand's alone.
I lived in love with her. Now she is gone

99
"let it not pain her that I love her still,
will love her till the happy day I die,
but happier far if, as of my own will
I wander here, on that day I may lie
beside her in your bosom. One tomb will
enfold our ashes as we dwell on high
in love. What life cannot, let death possess,
if I may hope for such great blessedness!"

100
Meanwhile they whispered of the bitter chance
behind the city wall confusedly
till finally they learned the truth. At once
through the whole town the bad news made its way
mingled with cries and womanly laments,
as desperate as if the enemy
had taken the town in battle and flew to raze
houses and temples and set the ruins ablaze,

101
but all eyes turned to the weeping Arsete,
his looks and groans, his pitiable case.
He could not melt his grief in tears, as they;
his love was old, tough rooted in its place.
But he fell to the earth and fouled his gray
hairs in the dust, and lashed his breast and face,
and while he drew the pity of the crowd
Argante stepped forward and cried aloud,

102
"How much I wanted, when I first saw how
we'd shut out that brave woman, not to wait
but follow her and with her undergo
one fate, one trial together—but too late!
What did I leave undone, unsaid! O how
I begged the king to open again the gate!
I begged and I contended, all in vain.
He checked me—here his power is sovereign.

103
"If I had gone I might have brought her home
from danger . . . or I might have shut my eyes
in a memorable death, to meet my end
on the same earth she reddens as she dies . . .
But what more could I possibly have done?
We plan, but the gods see things otherwise.
She died by fate, nor do I now forget
how much is called for by my duty yet.

104
"Hear, Jerusalem, hear Argante's vow!
Hear me, you heavens—let this be satisfied
or strike my head with lightning—I swear now
vengeance upon the Christian homicide,
and let him look for death from me, for hers,
nor will I drop my weapon from my side
until it pierces Tancred's filthy heart
and leaves his corpse for crows to peck apart."

105
So he, and his last violent words were met
with an outburst of popular acclamation,
and the vengeance he would take on the man who sighed
tempered his bitterness—in imagination!
O empty promises! For, look here, the fact
would contradict his highest aspiration,
for he would fall in a fair duel by
the very man he now commits to die.

Canto Thirteen

1
Hardly had that dismantler of the wall
collapsed in ashes, when the restless mind
of Ismen mulled and pondered some new spell
to render his city safer. He must find
some way to keep the woods' material
out of French hands, for they'd have redesigned
their tower and built it new against the town
to bring the battered walls of Sion down.

2
Not so far from the Christian palisade
in a lonely valley rose an ancient wood,
so tall and densely overgrown it made
a gloom of the dark earth on which it stood;
a sad and dubious light, much like a shade,
was all the noonday sunshine could intrude,
as when in a clouded sky it's hard to say
if day succeeds the night, or night the day.

3
But after sunset in this forest all
is smoke and horror and the depths of night,
as deep a darkness as the black of hell,
that fills the heart with fear, and robs the sight.
Never the shepherd, never the cowherd will
lead herd or flock to feed in that ill light,
and the wary traveler, unless he's lost his way,
points it out as he passes far away.

4
Here in the night the witches congregate
to couple with their loves, the incubi.
In the form of fierce dragon or foul goat
misshapen thus over the clouds they fly;
lured by an image of a good thing sought
they are enticed to commerce with a lie,
unspeakable! and make foul celebration
with drunken feasts and devilish copulation.

5
So it was thought, and none who dwelt nearby
would cut a single branch of that dread wood,
but the French rifled the forest to supply
their works (it was the only one which could).
To this place then the wizard secretly
came in the following night's deep solitude
and timely silence. With his magic wand
he traced his signs and circle on the ground.

6
He loosed one sandal, stepped within the ring,
and muttered his most potent canticum,
turning three times to face the east, three times
to face the region of the evening gloom;
three times he shook his wand, which had the power
to wake and summon dead men from the tomb,
and three times struck the earth with his bare foot,
uttering with a terrifying shout,

7
"Hear me, hear me, you whom the Thunderer
sent flying headlong from the starry skies,
and you who dwell in the realm of the wandering air,
who lash the waves and make the tempests rise,
and all who dwell among the damned, whose care
is to redouble their eternal cries,
hell's citizens, I call upon you now,
and you, lord of the evil flames below!

8
"Stand guard over this forest and these trees
I dedicate to you. Let each plant be
your habitation, as the body is
the dwelling of the soul, its livery.
After the first blows, make the Frenchmen cease,
let your terrifying anger make them flee!"
The sorcerer added blasphemies as well,
too horrible for the pious tongue to tell.

9
And at his words the lanterns that adorn
the quiet of the night grew bleak and dim,
and the troubled moon shrouded her slender horn
behind the clouds, and would not shine on him,
whence he renewed his cries in rage and scorn,
"Spirits I summon, why do you not come?
Perhaps you choose to bide your time until
I utter incantations mightier still?

10
"For all the years gone by, I still recall
the crude arts and their more effective way,
and though my tongue is flesh and blood, can well
pronounce the terrible Name that holds such sway
over the deafest and most stubborn hell
that Satan is compelled, and must obey!
Well then—well then," he started, but soon saw
the execution of his formula,

11
spirits innumerable, infinite . . .
some of whom wander in the upper air,
others who come arising from the pit
of the deep earth, their dark and smoky lair,
a little slow and hesitant, no doubt,
fearing God's word forbidding them to bear
arms in the war, yet leaving them free to come
and make these branches and these trunks their home.

12
When the magician saw his plans in place,
he said to Aladine rejoicingly,
"My lord, your throne now rests on a sure base.
Leave worries, let your heart be bold and free!
The French will not repair their siege machine,
as they all hold now for a certainty."
So he related to the king each part
of the successes of his magic art.

13
Adding, "One more thing pleases me no less
than these devices I have set for you.
Know that the sun will shed his influence
in the Lion soon, with Mars. Heat from those two
will wither the land and bring no cooling breeze,
no cloud heavy with rain, no morning dew,
for it will soon be miserably dry,
by all the signs appearing in the sky.

14
"We will have heat the Libyans scarcely have,
or the sunburnt Garamanthians of the south.
Here in our city things won't be so grave:
our pools and shade and homes will ease the drought.
But camping on the rugged and baked earth,
the Christian hosts will never last it out.
An easy thing, when the heavens have made them tame,
for the Egyptians to drive them whence they came!

15
"Sit still, and win. It's inadvisable
for you to tempt your luck in war again.
But if that proud Circassian who greets all
pauses, even the honorable, with disdain,
begs you to hurry on, as usual,
you find some way to hold him under rein,
for soon the friendly heavens will bid you peace
and declare war against your enemies."

16
Hearing these words the king was reassured,
and did not fear the powers of the foe.
Part of the wall already was repaired
which the French ram had battered; even so,
he wanted every crack and seam restored
and ever kept the city on the go,
employing throngs of slaves and citizens
in teeming business for the wall's defense.

17
While this is going on, the good Bouillon,
lest all their battering work should be in vain,
before the town restores its broken stone
hurries to build his great siege tower again,
so sends his crew of carpenters at dawn
to the one forest able to sustain
the works in hand. They go where they are told,
but a new source of fear now stops them cold.

18
As a little baby will not dare to look
when bizarre shapes and shadows come in sight,
or as he populates each dim-lit nook
with horrid monsters hiding in the night,
so the men feared, but could not tell what took
their hearts away and filled them with such fright—
unless their fears composed their senses' errors
and raised for them huge sphinxes and chimaeras!

19
In fear they turn back, in astonishment.
So various and confused the tales they tell
that they become the butts of merriment,
dreadful monsters indeed! Incredible!
Then the bold captain sends a regiment
of chosen warriors whom he trusted well
to guard the workers and remove all doubt
that his instructions would be carried out.

20

Yet when these men drew near the savage fold
of wicked demons in the wilderness,
they felt their bodies tremble and blood run cold
soon as they saw the shadows. Still they press
onward, and though the countenance may be bold
it is a cover for their cowardice.
The companies advance at such a pace
they soon arrive at the enchanted place.

21

Suddenly from the woods there came a sound
loud as the groan of the earth in a giant quake,
merged with the murmuring of the stormy wind
and the rocks where the sea waves moan and break;
as the roar of a lion and a wolf's lone howl
and the growl of a savage bear and the hissing snake,
so too the wild and thunderous trumpets sounded,
and all in one enormous roar compounded.

22

Then they revealed a thousand signs of fear—
the blanching in the cheek, the trembling chin—
and dared not hold their ground, much less march on,
in spite of reason, in spite of discipline;
against the hidden power that struck at them
all their defenses were too weak and thin.
At last they fled, and one of them brought the news
to the pious Godfrey, making this excuse:

23

"My lord, there isn't one of us who'd dare
cut down those woods again. They are so well
guarded that I believe—and I would swear—
those trees are harboring all the realm of hell!
Only a heart of adamant could bear
to look upon that forest and not fail,
and only a man whose senses were quite gone
would listen to its strange thunder hiss and groan."

24

So his report. Alcasto chanced to be
among the men who crowded round to hear,
the man of wild, brainless temerity,
who held all men and death not worth a sneer—
he wouldn't be scared of a horrible beast, not he!
No dreadful apparition could cause him fear,
no lightning bolt or hurricane or quake
or what more violent yet the earth might make.

25
He wagged his head and spoke, smiling in scorn.
"Where he won't dare to go, I'll go with ease,
for I intend to cut that wood alone
where nestle all these garbled fantasies.
No ghost will frighten me from going in,
or cry of a bird or rustling in the trees.
Or if those haunts are frightening, just as well!
Let them show me the way to go to hell."

26
Such was his boast before the captain, who
gave him permission to go; and so he went.
He saw the woods ahead and heard the sound,
the strange reechoing boom the forest sent,
but never did his bold step once turn back,
as ever scornful, ever confident,
and would have trod the earth the demons kept,
when in his path a conflagration leapt

27
or seemed to leap. Its fire is a great wall
where tempests of thick flames and smoke arise,
girding the trees about that none might fall
to the axe and hatchet of the enemies;
and the shapes of the mightiest flames are tall
turreted castles towering to the skies,
for the king of hell has rigged this fortress scene
with every sort of tight-cranked war machine.

28
How many monsters guard the battlements
ready and armed—a terrifying face!
Some of them coolly look at him askance,
others threaten, rattle the pike and mace.
At last he flees, and though the flight is slow,
as of a lion retreating from the chase,
still he does flee, still his heart feels the sway
of fear he had not known until that day.

29
He didn't know at first that he'd been scared,
but once he'd gone some way, he saw the truth
to his amazement and contempt. His heart
then felt the bite of sharp remorse's tooth,
and, stunned, he turned his steps, spoke not a word,
seething and sorrowing in his shame, forsooth!
And as for that proud head he held so high,
he dared not look one soldier in the eye.

30
Summoned by Godfrey, he excused himself,
yearned to stay put, delayed and still delayed,
then went at last, reluctantly, tight-lipped,
or if he answered, anything he said
was vague, as of a man who dreamed. The chief
concluded that he'd taken fright and fled,
such shame for him unheard of. "What are these?"
asked Godfrey. "Natural wonders? Fantasies?

31
"But if I have one man whose noble will
drives him to try this forest operation,
let him go take the venture and at least
return to us with better information."
That said, the great and dreadful woods were tried
by warriors of the highest reputation.
Three days they tried it, and they failed, each one—
for those dire threats made every fighter run!

32
The Prince, meanwhile, had risen from his bed
to bury the sweet lady, his delight,
and though his face looked ashen and half dead,
and he too weak to bear his mail and fight,
or even strap a helmet to his head,
still he'd not shun the trouble, come what might,
for there was need. The brave heart brims and fills
the body with the vigor it instills.

33
The valiant man sets out in firm resolve,
silent, on guard, to meet the risks unknown,
and bears the forest's formidable gloom
and the booming cannons of thunder and the groan
of the earth trembling beneath him. He did not move;
felt his heart quaver a little, calmed it down,
passed on into that wilderness and came
where on a sudden surged the city of flame.

34
Here he drew back and stood a while in doubt.
"What good are weapons here?" he thought. "Shall I
hurl myself whole into this monster's throat
and be devoured by flames? Let none deny
to risk his life for the common benefit
when the cause merits honor. But to die
like a prodigal tossing his life away—as now—
is more than a man of great heart should allow.

35
"But what will the army say if I turn back?
What other wood to cut can they expect?
Godfrey would never want it left untried,
this passage. If one marches in direct
maybe these blazes I now see arise
will burn more in appearance than effect.
Let what will happen, happen." With that said—
unforgettable courage—in he sped,

36
but could not feel under his coat of mail
the boiling flames of a fire so intense.
Yet whether they were flames or just illusions
was not at once apparent to his sense,
for he had hardly touched the apparition
when suddenly it swept off in a dense
tempest of wintry darkness; yet in one
moment the cold and darkness too were gone.

37
Amazed he was, but fearless nonetheless.
And when Prince Tancred saw that all was still,
he spied the secrets of that wilderness,
setting upon its diabolical
verge his firm foot. Nothing bizarre or monstrous
appeared before him now, no obstacle
met him or slowed his progress. Nothing stood
to thwart him but the tangled and dark wood.

38
At last he found a wide and open space
formed like an amphitheater, and free
of any vegetation save one proud
towering pyramid of a cypress tree
in the dead center. There he goes to look,
sees the trunk carved with strange pictography,
a script of symbols like those once in use
in Egypt, ancient and mysterious.

39
Among the unknown letters he could trace
some in the Syrian language, which he read:
"O you, bold warrior, who dare to place
your foot within the cloisters of the dead,
if you are not as cruel as you are strong,
oh do not violate this secret bed,
have mercy on the souls shorn of the light!
With us, the living have no cause to fight."

40
So the inscription read. What did it mean?
To solve that mystery he turned his mind
while all the trembling branches and the leaves
made a low rustle in the whispering wind,
whence rose a sad sound, like the harmony
of human weeping, human sighs. A kind
of blended feeling seeped into his heart,
pity, and dread, and sorrow . . . With a start

41
he drew his sword at last and threw his strength
behind the stroke. But wonder! That tall wood
oozed freshly from the blade cut in the bark
and dyed the earth about the color of blood.
He shook with horror, swung his blade once more
to see it through, to find out all he could.
And now he hears a low and wavering moan
as of a voice within a tomb of stone,

42
now gathering into words, distinct. "Ah, Tancred,
you have hurt me too deeply. Let it be
enough, to drive me from my happy dwelling,
the body where I lived, that lived through me.
Why should you once again hurt this poor trunk,
where I am pent by my hard destiny?
How could you be so cruel to resume
war with your adversaries in the tomb?

43
"I was Clorinda. Other spirits dwell
beside me in this rough, hard plant: for all
those fighters, Saracen or French, who fell
and left their dying limbs beneath the wall,
are here pent up by some unheard-of spell,
an incarnation, or a burial,
I cannot say. Their limbs, ensouled, feel pain,
and if you cut you murder us again."

44
As in a sick man's dreams a dragon rises,
or huge chimaera armed with flame—if he
suspects, or even partly realizes
the monster is a lie, a fantasy,
still the fierce apparition terrifies his
heart so profoundly that he longs to flee.
The timid lover isn't duped completely,
and yet he fears, and backs away discreetly.

45
A host of feelings have so overpowered
his heart within, it shakes, it turns to ice;
fear is the least of them; he drops his sword
in the swift strong attack. His reason flies;
he seems to see before him in the wood
his wounded love, his love who weeps and sighs,
nor can he bear to watch her bleed anew
or hear her dying moans. That heart so true

46
in the very face of death, never to fail
no matter in what monstrous form death rose,
did not fall now to fear. For he was frail
in love alone; false tears and empty shows
deluded him. His fallen sword a gale
suddenly snatched and hurled out of the woods,
and so he left, defeated. On the road
he found the sword and picked it up, but would

47
not turn again to be so bold to try
the specter, and detect the cause of it.
When he came to the chief's tent by and by
he gathered himself, settled his spirits a bit,
and thus began. "My lord, what I report
is past belief. No one would credit it,
but all they said was true. I heard the thunder
and saw the spectacle of fear and wonder.

48
"For instantly, with no material,
a fire arose—a strange phenomenon—
fanning its blazes out to form a wall
armed with the monsters of the Phlegethon.
Yet I passed through and was not burned at all,
nor did the sword contest my going on.
In a moment it was winter night, and then
came the serenity of day again.

49
"But there was more. In every tree there dwelt
a human soul that gave it life—I know
what I have witnessed, for it spoke, it felt,
and its words touched my heart, and bring me woe.
Its trunk would bleed with every blow I dealt
as if it hid soft flesh beneath. No, no,
I give up, I am beaten! I can't trim
the bark away, or chop a single limb."

50
So he said, and the captain's mind was whelmed
in a great storm of doubt. Perhaps, he thought,
he himself ought to go and try the spell
(for such he guessed it was), or the army ought
to find another woods available
further away, but not so hard to cut.
But from the depths of prophecy the wise
Hermit recalls the chief with this advice:

51
"Set aside that bold thought: the Lord commands
another man to spoil the woods. I see
the fatal prow draw near the far-off sands,
now, now, furling her golden sails, and he,
breaking out of his base and petty bands,
the long-awaited warrior, puts to sea.
The destined hour of triumph is in sight,
Sion taken, her armies put to flight."

52
And as he spoke a flame shone in his eyes
and his words echoed more than human sense.
Godfrey then turned his mind to other plans;
he would not risk delay through negligence.
But now the sun in Cancer bore down hard,
blazing with unaccustomed vehemence,
foe to his plans and to his men, for all
work in such heat was unendurable.

53
The cruelest stars were ruling in the sky;
the milder lamps were spent, and did not shine;
and so they rained their influence from on high,
into the air infusing a malign
power; and as it grew it made men die,
die everywhere, throughout the camp. No sign
of letting up. The night brought no sweet chill,
and afterwards the day was hotter still.

54
Each day the sun arises steeped in blood
as fiery vapors round about it burn—
in its appearance rests no hope for good,
but evil signs are easy to discern.
Nor does it ever set, but, flecked with red,
it threatens equal pain with its return,
making what's been endured more wearisome
with promises of misery to come.

55
And while the sun poured down its sweltering rays
from one horizon to the next the eye
saw nothing but the dark and thirsty grass,
the yellow leaf, the flower thin and dry,
the baked earth in the bed of a vanished brook,
all subject to the anger of the sky,
and sterile wisps of cloud strewn here and there
resembling flames. The heavens and the air

56
were a lurid furnace; nothing visible
to soothe the eyes, refresh them. In its cave
the west wind lay in silence, and dead still
lay every playing of the breezes, save
one breath like a flame leaping from a torch
which swept the Moorish sands in a great wave,
heavy, oppressive, battering throat and chest
with its thick blasts. And the night brought no rest,

57
no cool and pleasant shadows, for the sun
seemed to have fused its seal onto the night,
lacing the firmament with beams of fire,
comets and other bodies burning bright,
nor, you poor earth, did the covetous moon
allow the slightest dewdrops to alight
to slake your drought; but the grass and the flowers
thirsted in vain for water's vital powers.

58
In such hot nights no weary man found ease,
sweet sleep was banished. Let them plead and call,
sleep never came, would never heed their pleas;
yet what they bore for thirst was worst of all,
since the springs had been poisoned by Judea's
iniquitous ruler, for a bitter gall
more lethal than the Acheron or Styx
clouded and fouled the streams with its black mix.

59
The little brook of Siloa, pure and fresh,
had graciously offered to the French its treasure;
now hardly covered its dry bed with a wash
of lukewarm water. That gave little pleasure,
little relief; but the Po's deepest rush
would have been insufficient for the measure
of their desire; not Ganges, not the spill
of the seven-spring Nile that leaves rich land to till.

60
If anyone beside the grassy banks
should see a pool as clear as silvered glass,
or living water tumbling from the rocks,
lazily weaving through the meadow grass,
it is desire that forms, describes, supplies
matter to torture him withal, for as
he gazes on the cool and gentle streams
his thoughts are scalded by what only seems.

61
The warrior's sturdy shoulders and strong back,
unbowed by the long trek through rugged land,
by the iron armor and the heavy pack
and the sword threatening death in the foe's hand,
were withered in the heat now; they lay slack,
a useless burden. But a fever fanned
within their veins, a hidden fire that made
slow undoing of those on whom it preyed.

62
The coursers languish, once high-spirited.
From the grass, in disgust, they turn aside;
their legs are weak, and wobble, and the head
now droops, which used to toss itself for pride;
their memories of triumph are all dead,
and the great glory for which they once vied
can move their hearts no more. They shun and hate
the spoils they won in battle, as dead weight

63
fit for a pack mule. And the faithful dog
forgets his master and his beloved tent
and all his duties; panting hard to bring
fresh air to cool the fire inside, distent
he lies. Though nature lets him breathe, to soothe
his parching heart, the new air cannot vent
any refreshing breeze, for with each breath
comes the thick heat, oppressive unto death.

64
So languished all the earth, and mortal men
so lay in sickness and in misery,
and the good army of the faithful feared
the worst, and lost all hope for victory,
and you could hear the murmuring on all sides
arise in unison, lamentingly,
"What's Godfrey hoping? Why does he stay here, why?
Is he going to wait till all his soldiers die?

65
"What forces does he think can overcome
the towering ramparts of our enemies?
What will we use to build the battering rams?
Heaven's wrath is set against us and he sees
nothing! The signs are clear! How can he doubt
so many terrors, so many prodigies?
The Ethiopians need less relief
from the burning sun than we! So our great chief

66
thinks it is no great matter if his men—
for we're beneath him, we're not worth so much,
useless, neglected—go to a hard death,
if he can keep his scepter in his clutch!
Why, that must be a happy state indeed,
so fortunate for the one who rules, that such
authority be held at any cost,
even should all the men he rules be lost!

67
"Look at him with his name, 'the pious one,'
provident and humane and all the rest,
but he forgets the welfare of his own
to hold on for himself a meaningless
destructive honor! Our streams are dry as stone,
he sees it, but conveys for Captain's Mess
drink from the Jordan. With his friends he dines
and mixes water with his Cretan wines!"

68
So said the French, but the captain of the Greeks,
weary by now of ever being led
by the French standard, spoke. "Why should we stay?
Why wait till I and all my men are dead?
If Godfrey's blind to his own foolishness
let that be on his host's and his own head.
What's it to us?" Seeking no leave for flight,
the Greeks deserted in the silent night.

69
On the next morning when the truth is clear
others resolve to do what they have done,
and those who followed Clothar and Ademar
and the other captains now but dust and bone,
are unbound from the loyalty they swore
by Death itself, which unbinds everyone,
and so they talk of fleeing, some of them
stealthily parting when the day grows dim.

70
Godfrey too heard and saw it, but abhorred
what would have been the quickest remedy.
And with the faith that made the rivers stand
and mountains hurl themselves into the sea,
he prayed devoutly to the King of the world
to open His springs of grace and clemency;
he clasps his hands, zeal burning in his breast,
and turns his eyes toward heaven with this request:

71
"Father and Lord, Who rained down the sweet dew
of manna in the desert for Your flock,
Who gave a mortal hand the power to
strike living water from the riven rock,
now let us see these wondrous signs anew,
and if our merit fail us, our poor stock
replenish with Your grace, Who are the source.
Help us, for we are called Your warriors."

72
His supplications are not slow to move
for from a meek and just desire they rise,
and swift and light they fly to heaven above
like feathered angels, to the Lord most wise
Who takes them up; and with a father's love
unto His faithful hosts He turns His eyes,
and moved with pity for all they hazarded
and all their labors undergone, He said,

73
"The tide has gone against the host I love,
suffering in their fight with the infidel,
enduring the secret arts and weapons of
the legions of the whole world, and of hell,
till now. For the new order now begins,
prosperity returns, and all is well.
Let it rain; bring the banished warrior home,
and, for his fame, let Egypt's armies come."

74
With that He bent His brow, and the vast heavens
trembled, and every fixed and wandering light,
and the reverence-stricken air and the plains of the sea,
and the hills and blind Hades felt His might,
and they heard the thunder boom out of the west
and saw prophetic lightning flashing bright,
and to the flashes and the roars on high
the men sent up a loud and joyful cry.

75
Behold the clouds at once, not of this world,
not gathered to the skies by the sun's power,
but from the open gates of heaven hurled
they come down in a vast and sudden glower—
and in the shadow of night the day is furled,
and all the land grows dark in one brief hour,
and the rain slashes down and makes such head
it sets the stream to spilling from its bed.

76
As sometimes in the hottest days of summer
when the skies shower down the wished-for rain,
a flock of noisy ducks on the muddy river
will wait for it and happily complain,
and quack and ruff their wings for the cold water,
and take a bath—for none of them refrain,
but where the water's deepest they swim first
and all go bottoms-up and quench their thirst,

77
with such a happy shout the soldiers hail
the rain sent down by heaven's merciful power,
and the men to soak their shirts strip off the mail
or let their hair be drenched in the cool shower;
some use the helmet for a drinking pail,
some dip hands in the stream and let it pour,
some splash it on their temples, in their faces,
while shrewder folks collect it in their basins.

78
Their hearts were gladdened, they were strong again—
nor were the men the only ones restored,
for the earth had suffered too, a dry, bare plain
whose stricken members were all cracked and scored
with fissures. Now she took the swelling rain
into her deepest veins, and ministered
unto all things above the moisture's powers,
nourishing all the trees and grass and flowers,

79
as if, parched with a fever to the quick,
she'd been refreshed by a life-giving juice,
and, throwing off the cause that made her sick,
that fed upon her substance, now broke loose
like a new springtime with her flowers strewn thick
and reawakened greenery, profuse—
so now forgetting all her past duress
she reassumes her garlands and glad dress.

At last the rain was over, and the sun
returned, but with a sweet and temperate ray,
full of the masculine power that warms the earth
at the end of April, or in early May.
O noble faith! Who honors God aright
can sweep the pestilential air away
and change the seasons' order, or their state,
defeating the anger of the stars, and fate.

Canto Fourteen

1
Now from the soft, fresh lap of Mother Earth
came the dark night, and as it rose it drew
light breezes, and a cloud from the moist land,
a blanket of its pure and precious dew,
shaking the soaked hem of its veil, to shower
the grass and budding flowers. The breezes flew
upon their fluttering wings to lull asleep
the minds of mortal men; the thoughts that keep

2
men troubled in the day were all subdued,
drowned in a deep and sweet oblivion.
But ever-watchful in eternal light
the Monarch of the world sat on His throne
and turned from heaven His calm and gracious eye
upon the Christian chief, the good Bouillon;
and sent to him a quiet dream, that He
might thus reveal to him heaven's high decree.

3
A crystal gate stands in the Orient
near where the sun comes forth with golden ray,
which is let open by the heavens' consent
before the gates are thrown for the newborn day.
Through this gate come the dreams God's grace has sent
to those whose hearts are pure, who never stray;
from this gate now, its wings of gold outspread,
a dream descends to the good captain's bed.

4
Never had any vision in a dream
brought images so beautiful and dear
as this dream brings to him. The heavens seem
to open, and the secret depths appear—
as in a looking glass he caught the gleam
of all that is contained in the starry sphere—
swept up into a realm serene and bright,
adorned with golden flames and filled with light.

5
And while he wondered at that heavenly place,
the vastness and the harmony and light,
behold in weaponry of rays and fire
approaching him there comes an armed knight,
whose voice could make the sweetest song on earth
sound rough and harsh, so great was its delight:
"Godfrey, no greetings? Not a word to spend?
Or don't you know me—Hugh, your faithful friend!"

6
"The splendor of your countenance," he replied,
"shines out so wondrously I can't retain
your old appearance—all my thoughts go wide,
and even now it's hard to trace again!"
With a friend's sweet affection then he tried
to throw his arms about Hugh's neck—in vain;
three times he tried, and the image fled his touch
like a light dream, like the shifting air. "Not such

7
"as you believe am I," he said, and smiled.
"I wear no earthly trappings. What you see
is a citizen of the city of the skies,
a naked spirit in simplicity.
This is the temple of God. His warriors dwell
in glory here, where one day you will be."
"When?" he asked. "Let these mortal bonds release,
that I may live with you and rest in peace!"

8
"The time," said Hugh, "for you to be received
into the Church Triumphant is at hand,
but first you must spill blood and sweat on earth,
much more to spill, as leader of the band
who will be first to drive the pagans off
and take the empire of the Holy Land;
and found in Palestine your Christian reign
which afterwards your brother will maintain.

9
"But now look at the stars, that you may yearn
for heaven with all the vigor of desire!
The mind of God eternal makes them turn,
these mansions full of light, and living fire;
and hear the holy Sirens, angels singing,
who sweep the strings of the celestial lyre.
Now look down there," he pointed to the earth.
"How little that last world contains of worth!

10
"How paltry the reward for which men strive,
fighting for power and wealth incessantly!
In what a little circle do they move,
among what deserts all their luxury!
The water shuts you in like a little island,
and that which you call vast, the boundless sea,
has nothing to which 'great' should correspond,
but is a puddle, or a shallow pond."

11
So said the one, and the other turned his glance
earthward, and smiled as if in scorn. He views
one little point, all rivers, oceans, lands,
which seem distinct to us; it makes him muse
that our foolish humanity should fix
its heart on shadows or on smoke, and choose
a slavish empire and a speechless fame
when heaven invites us, summons us by name.

12
"Since it does not yet please the Lord," said he,
"to break my earthly prison, be my guide,
show me the path that runs least deviously
through the errors of this world." And Hugh replied,
"You are already going the true way.
Hold to it well, and do not turn aside.
Only in this I counsel: be content,
recall Bertoldo's son from banishment.

13
"For if high Providence has chosen you
supreme commander of this enterprise,
it has ordained a glory for him too:
his is to execute what you advise.
The first honors are yours; to him are due
the second; he is the hand, you are the wise
head of the army. No one can take his place
but you, and you may not in any case.

14
"His sword alone will be allowed to hack
the branches charmed by magical protection;
from him your army, suffering now for lack
of men, too weak to rally, in dejection
seeming to have no choice but to draw back,
will take new force to turn the war's direction,
to storm the buttressed walls and bring them down,
and crush the armies of the rising sun."

15
He finished, and Bouillon responded thus:
"How I would love to see the cavalier!
But you perceive each thought that dwells in us;
you know the truth, you know I hold him dear.
But what proposals shall I make? What terms?
To what place shall I send the messenger?
Should I beg or command? How can this be
compassed within the law, and honorably?"

16
The other then replied, "The eternal King,
who honors you with many gifts of grace,
wills that the men He gave you rule of bring
honor accordant with your honored place.
Thus you should not go asking—such a thing
from a commander might appear too base.
No, let the first request for grace be theirs,
and pardon him at the first sound of their prayers.

17
"For the Lord will inspire Guelph to request
that you absolve the proud lad of his error
(whom wrath had overcome when he transgressed),
that he return to the army, and his honor.
Though for a long time now he's been possessed
by vanities, and lain in love and languor,
trust in a few days he'll rejoin the host
in timely fashion, when you need him most.

18
"For holy Peter, to whom the heavens show
the deep foreknowledge of God's hidden plan,
will steer your messengers the way to go
to gain the surest tidings of your man,
to set him free and bring him back to you,
showing them by what arts and ways they can.
Under your holy banners thus the Lord
will lead your wandering men, at last restored.

19
"Now I shall end with one brief thing to say,
and I know you will hear it with delight:
your blood will join with his, and they will bear
a progeny most glorious and bright."
Then like a wisp of smoke on a windy day
or a thin cloud in the sun, he stole from sight,
and the dream eased away and left behind
commingled joy and awe in Godfrey's mind.

20
The reverent Bouillon opens his eyes
and sees the newborn day already grown,
so leaves his bed, and on his arms and chest
buckles the ever-laboring armor on.
But waiting for the chief outside his tent
are all his generals—as they'd always done,
sitting each day in council to decide
what elsewhere would be acted on or tried.

21
Here the good Guelph was first to speak his mind,
for a new thought had been instilled there by
the inspiration of the Spirit. "Kind
and merciful prince," he said to Godfrey, "I
have come to ask a pardon for a crime
which was committed only recently,
so that mine may well seem, I understand,
a hasty and inopportune demand.

22
"But the pardon asked is from the good Bouillon
for the brave Rinaldo, and that alters the case,
and the intercessor's not just anyone,
but I who come to you to seek your grace—
all of which makes me confident to gain
a boon to gladden everyone in this place.
Oh, let the lad come back, and spend his blood
in doing penance for the common good!

23
"Who if not he will dare to cut the wood
which has struck fear into the hardiest?
Who will go forth in hazard of his life
with a more constant and intrepid breast?
He'll shake the towers and bring the gates to earth
and scale the wall ahead of all the rest!
For God's sake give him back to your own host—
their highest hope, the man they long for most.

24
"Give me my nephew, give yourself a man
so brave, so quick to execute your will,
and give him back the glory he has won—
don't let him languish like a sluggard still!
But let him follow your victorious flag
and grant his virtue its testimonial;
he'll look to you as leader and obey,
earning his praises in the light of day."

25
So he entreated, and the men about
greeted his gracious prayer with a general roar,
when Godfrey, pausing as if deep in thought,
as if it had not come to mind before,
said, "When a favor is so strongly sought,
can I deny what you are longing for?
Let rigor yield, let law and justice be
what you have chosen here unanimously.

26
"Let Rinaldo return—and from now on
let his wrath not be so impetuous,
so that with deeds well governed and well done
he will fulfill the hope he stirs in us.
But, Guelph, it's up to you to call him home.
I trust he'll hurry back and make no fuss!
Assign a courier and have him bound
wherever you think the proud lad may be found."

27
Then there stepped forth the Danish warrior.
"I ask to be the messenger, my lord!
No matter how risky the journey or how far,
I will present him with the honored sword."
This was a man of brave hand and brave heart.
Guelph was pleased with his offer, and gave his word
he should be one of the messengers to go,
Ubaldo the other, circumspect and slow,

28
a man who'd done much traveling in his youth
and learned of many nations and their ways,
wandering from the circles of the north
to southern Ethiopia ablaze,
like one whose trade was virtue and good sense,
picking up speech and customs in each place.
Now ripe in years, he joined Guelph's company,
and the old soldier liked him heartily.

29
These messengers received the honored task
of calling back the Christian champion,
and Guelph directed them toward Damascus
where Bohemond had raised his royal throne,
for it was rumored that the lad was there—
or so it was believed by everyone.
But the good Hermit knew how far they erred
and interrupted them as they conferred.

30
"To follow the vulgar crowd, O cavaliers,
as rash and faithless a leader as can be,
whose judgment only holds to what appears,
is to lose your journey and go far astray.
But go to Ascalon, its nearby shores,
just where a river pours into the sea,
and you will find a man there, my old friend.
Trust him, and give to him the news I send.

31
"Of your great voyage, long foretold by me,
he has heard much; much on his own he sees;
and he will treat you well and courteously
according to his capabilities."
Charles and Ubaldo listen patiently
and ask no more of him when his words cease,
but they obey the Hermit's each behest,
for it was ever the Spirit he professed.

32
They took their leave. Desire so spurs them on
they have no wish to linger any more,
but turn their course direct to Ascalon
where the sea breaks its waves against the shore.
And they were still too far to hear the moan
of the deep sea, the rough and thundering roar,
when they discovered a stream that rushed amain,
freshened and swollen from the recent rain,

33
so swollen it could not hold to its bed
but swept by like an arrow swift in flight.
While the two stood in doubt, a man appeared:
his look was venerable, his beard was white;
he wore a crown of beech and a long robe
of cleanest linen, finely sewn and light.
He waved a wand and crossed against the flow,
crossed over, dry, unshod. As Dutchmen go

34
there where they live so close to the North Pole,
whenever the winter turns the streams to ice,
skating and sliding along the frozen Rhine,
whole troops of farmhands, never thinking twice,
so he came over the unsteady plain
of water yet unhardened. In a trice
he reached the soldiers on the other side
who fixed their gaze upon him, their eyes wide,

35
and "Friends," he said, "you need someone to guide you,
for your quest is a hard and weary one.
The warrior you seek is far from here
in a treacherous land, in parts unknown.
How much, oh how much work is left for you!
What shores to cross, what seas to venture on!
For it must be, your searching must extend
beyond the point we know as the world's end.

36
"But, if you please, come to the hidden caves
where I dwell in my solitude below,
and you will hear from me some serious news
and more important things for you to know."
Then the old man commanded the swift waves
to yield a dry path for the two to go,
and like the pass of a mountain double-sided
the waters loomed, and in the midst divided.

37
He took them by the hand and led them down
into the deepest caves below the stream.
There they could see a dim and wavering light,
as in the forest the not-yet-full moon's gleam,
but the great caverns they saw were full of water,
the veins from which our brooks and rivers teem;
one bursts into a spring, and one will make
a wandering rill, or spread into a lake.

38
And they could see the birth springs of the Po,
the Danube, the Euphrates, the Ganges,
the secret sources of the Nile below,
and of the Don. But further down than these
they saw a stream of active sulfur flow
and living silver, lovely mercuries,
which the sun purified and shaped and rolled
into silvery nuggets or lumps of gold.

39
And they saw the rich river's banks were dappled
with precious gems of every shining hue,
conquering the gloom, making the cavern brilliant,
casting their light about as torches do:
here the jacinth and the sapphire were aglitter,
the heavenly sapphire with its gleams of blue;
the jasper flamed, the hardest diamond shone,
and there the lovely glow of emerald stone.

40

The soldiers walked on in astonishment—
to these strange things their thoughts were so applied
that they spoke not a word. At last Ubaldo,
breaking the silence, inquired thus of their guide,
"Father, where are we? Where are you leading us?
How do you live? Do I see the truth," he cried,
"or are they dreams? I can't tell them apart,
so deep a wonder weighs upon my heart."

41

"You are now," answered he, "in the immense
womb of the earth, whence all things come to be,
nor could you hope to penetrate the dense
arteries of this deep world without me.
But come, I'll show you where my palace stands—
you'll see it soon, and lit up splendidly!
I was born pagan but was made anew
by God's grace in the holy and healing dew

42

"of baptism. And no angels of the Styx
perform these works of mine so marvelous.
God forbid I should use such brews or tricks
to compel Phlegethon or Cocytus!
I trace the powers of every herb and spring,
seeing into what Nature hides from us;
all of her secrets I make study of
and map the motions of the stars above.

43

"Yet I don't always dwell far from the sky
under the earth in quiet contemplation,
but in an airy dome atop the high
summits of Carmel and Lebanon take my station,
where no veil hides the planets from my eye,
Venus and Mars in every manifestation,
and watch the others wheeling fast or slow,
shedding their influence, good or bad, below.

44

"Under my feet I see the billowing clouds,
now wisps, now dark, now dyed in Iris' bow,
and watch the forming of the dew and rain,
and in what crossing currents the winds blow,
and how the lightning flashes into fire
and slants its jagged bolt to the earth below,
and comets streaming so near the mountain shelf
I used to fall in wonder with myself.

45
"I was so priceless in my own esteem
I thought my knowledge was infallible,
the measure of the world, able to deem
the limits of the Maker of it all;
but when your Peter from the holy stream
sprinkled my locks and cleansed my impure soul,
I turned my glance yet higher and saw how dim
and weak is our discerning without Him.

46
"I saw how like a night bird in the sun
is our mind in the rays of the first Truth,
and I smiled at myself and at my folly
that had so puffed me up with pride, forsooth!—
yet I have followed, as he urged me to,
the habits and the science of my youth.
Still, what I was is not quite what I am:
on Him I now depend, and turn to Him,

47
"and in Him find my rest. He is my Lord,
my sovereign Master; He teaches, He commands,
nor does He scorn to use our own poor means
to work great works deserving of His hands.
Now I am charged with bringing back to camp
the invincible hero from his distant bands
where he lies prisoner. I've been waiting here
for many days until you should appear,

48
"as He foretold to me." And on they went
till they reached his abode and place of rest.
Built like a cave it was, magnificent,
with spacious halls and chambers east and west.
From what the earth's rich veins gave nourishment
all the most precious, all the splendidest
shone everywhere to brighten and adorn.
The tracery there was never made, but born.

49
Clever and ready to serve the warriors
hundreds and hundreds of servants bustled about,
with great vessels of gold and crystal glass
and a silver table brilliantly decked out;
but when the natural desire for food
was satisfied, and they had quenched their drought,
"High time," said that magician so well skilled,
"that your greater desire should be fulfilled."

50

Here he began. "The works and the deceit
of the wicked Armida, you knew before
at least in part: how she arrived in camp
and led away many a warrior,
then held them all in chains of toughest steel,
treacherous hostess! Then, how to the shore
at Gaza she conveyed them under guard,
and how they were set free along the road.

51

"I'll tell you now what happened after that,
the very truth, which you have not yet learned.
Soon as the wicked sorceress saw her art
was all in vain, and all the prey she'd earned
restored to safety, both her hands she bit
for grief, and uttered with a scorn that burned,
'O let it never be said that he should boast
to have freed so many prisoners I lost!

52

" 'He freed them—let him serve, let him sustain
the punishments reserved for all the rest.
But that won't be enough to soothe my pain.
I will bring trouble down on the whole host!'
So she conceived in her deceitful brain
this clever plan which now you'll hear. She crossed
the valley where Rinaldo had put to flight
her warriors, and some had slain outright.

53

"Here he had laid aside his iron vest
and placed upon his back a pagan one,
perhaps because he thought it might be best
to travel under markings less well known.
The witch took up the armor and she dressed
a headless trunk in it, and had it shown,
shown on the very stream bank where she knew
a squadron of the Christians were soon due.

54

"That was an easy thing for her to know—
a thousand spies were at her beck and call,
to keep watch as your soldiers come and go
and send her regular reports of all;
and she held commerce with the souls below,
conversing with the diabolical.
She set the body in a place apart,
a spot convenient for her lying art.

55
"Close by the corpse she set a shrewd valet
and dressed him with a shepherd's garb and crook,
telling him everything to do and say,
deceiving—and he did it by the book.
He it was who informed your men that day,
casting seeds of suspicion, and they took,
sprouting in discord, rifts which nearly bore
fruits of sedition and of civil war.

56
"For it was thought, just as the witch had planned,
that the boy had been murdered by Bouillon—
a false suspicion growing out of hand
from mere appearance and opinion.
Such was the first sly artifice of fraud
invented by Armida, as I've shown.
Now hear how she pursued Rinaldo then,
and what befell the strongest of your men.

57
"Like a sly huntress she waits at the ford
of the Orontes for the cavalier,
where the river forks and forms an isle midstream
and straightaway flows back together: here
Rinaldo came and saw a column raised
upon the banks, a shallop floating near.
He gazed on the white marble's lovely craft
and read these golden words upon the shaft:

58
" 'Whoever you are who wander to these shores,
whether by will or chance: if you would see
a wonder, come across, for the world knows
no greater from the east to the western sea
than this isle hides.' Persuaded thus, he goes,
steps off the riverbank too recklessly;
and since the boat could hold no more than one,
he leaves his squires behind, and boards alone.

59
"When he reached the island, eager and curious,
he looked around him, but saw nothing there
save streams and caves and flowers and trees and grass—
he thought it was some joke. The place was fair
and full of lovely things to soothe and please,
so he decided to rest in the fresh air;
so he sat down, his helmet put away,
and breathed the sweetness of the peaceful day.

60

"After a while he hears a funny sound
in the gurgling river—and he turns his eyes
to see a wavelet eddying round and round
in the midst of the stream—and now he spies
a lock or two of golden hair unbound,
and now he sees a woman's face arise,
and now her breasts and nipples, and below,
where modest eyes would be ashamed to go.

61

"So would a goddess or a nymph arise
from the stage in the theater at night,
majestically; and though in truth she was
no Siren but a phantasm of the sight,
she did seem one of those who held the shore
of the insidious sea, and gave delight
not only with her beauty but her voice,
her song so sweet she made the heavens rejoice:

62

" 'Young men, while in the turning of the May
spring the green grass and flowers, listen to reason!
Don't let your tender minds be swept away
by the false light of virtue and glory's treason.
He is the wise man who can seize the day
and pick the fruits of life while they're in season.
This is what Nature cries for! Why harden then
your hearts against her wishes? Foolish men,

63

" 'why do you throw your precious gift away,
your tender years, which pass so fleetingly?
What men call praise and valor—a mere name,
an idol only, no reality!
That fame which so attracts your pride, O men,
which sounds and seems so sweet, what can it be
but an echo, a dream, or even a dream's shade—
with every wind it must dissolve and fade.

64

" 'Let the body, free of care, lie at its ease,
and the calm soul delight in pleasant things;
forget past cares; as for anxieties,
don't hasten all the misery time brings!
What if the heavens thunder? Be at peace.
What can they do with all their threatenings?
Thus may a man live truly blest, and wise:
this is what Nature teaches us to prize.'

65

"So she sang, and the lad was lulled to sleep
by the sweet subtle lilting of her song
which stole upon his sense as serpents creep
and overcame them, masterful and strong;
not even thunder bellowing from the deep
could wake him from that slumber, still and long,
like very death. And now the witch is upon him,
eager to wreak her long-wished vengeance on him,

66

"but when she fixed her eyes upon the boy
and saw how he was breathing peacefully,
and round his pretty eyes a kind of joy
though they were shut—and how sweet would they be
when opened—she paused in doubt, then sat nearby,
and felt her anger melt away as she
beheld him. Like Narcissus at the pool
she hung upon his lovely face. A cool

67

"quickening sweat arose upon his brow—
with a light veil she wiped the drops away
and sweetly, gently, fanned the air about,
tempering for him the heat of the summer day.
Who would believe it? Thus the sleeping warmth
of hidden eyes could melt the ice that lay
about her heart like adamant! Thus she
became enamored of her enemy.

68

"Of lilacs and of lilies and of roses
which flowered there upon the pleasant strand,
weaving them with a strange art, she composes
a gentle but a most tenacious band;
these round his neck and arms and feet she closes,
so binds him, like a prisoner in hand,
and while he sleeps she has him lifted high
into her chariot, and sweeps across the sky,

69

"not turning to Damascus and the king,
nor where her fortress stands in the Dead Sea,
but jealous now of such a precious thing
and ashamed of her love, she wants to flee
to the vast ocean, where our voyaging
seldom or never ventures, utterly
beyond our shores, to hide. And there she chose
an island for her solitary repose,

70
"a little isle, which with the others near
from the goddess of Fortune takes its name.
Now to a mountain summit, dark and drear
and void of any living thing, she came,
and by enchantment clothed the mountainsides
with snow; but free of winter all the same
she left it green and pleasant at the peak,
and had her palace set beside a lake.

71
"There in an everlasting Spring she dwells
and rests the livelong day with her delight.
They are secret, and far, these prison cells
from whence it is your charge to bring the knight,
and she is jealous, fearful—has the hills
defended all the way to the topmost height.
But you will have a guide to shun her spies
and give you weapons for the enterprise.

72
"You shall find, rising from the stream nearby,
a woman young in looks but old in years.
You'll know her from her long braids tied in front
and by the opalescent clothes she wears.
Swifter than eagles spreading their wings to fly
she'll spirit you across the sea—the spears
of lightning fly no faster. This you'll learn,
and find no truer guide for your return.

73
"For at the foot of the witch's mountain dwelling
strange pythons hiss and slither; the wild boar
digs in, and sets his razor back to bristling,
and great bears bellow out and lions roar—
but give my wand a shake, and the small whistling
will hold them off for fear. Far worse in store
upon the summit, greater jeopardy—
if I can judge aright of what I see.

74
"A fountain rises there, limpid and clean,
so fresh it causes all who look to thirst,
but in its waves so cold and crystalline
a secret venom hides. The stream is cursed;
the slightest sip of that bright well will soon
intoxicate the soul, and make it first
merry, then move it to laugh, and to such laughter
no man will live to tell about it after.

75

"Keep away from that evil, lethal pool,
twist your mouth tight as if the thing were vile;
and don't let banquets on the stream's banks fool,
nor trust the lovely ladies full of guile,
whose voices are so merry, so delightful,
and whose sweet looks entice with every smile.
Hold their looks and sly words at a cheap rate!
And enter then within the lofty gate.

76

"Inside, it's all walled up into a maze,
inextricable turns without relief,
twisting upon themselves a thousand times,
but here I've mapped it out for you in brief.
In the center of the labyrinth sits a garden
where love appears to breathe from every leaf;
here in the green lap of the early year
you'll find the lady and the cavalier.

77

"But when she leaves her precious love alone
and goes off wandering in some other place,
show yourselves, take this shield of diamond stone
and raise it suddenly before his face
as if it were a mirror. Let him look upon
his semblance, now effeminate and base,
and his soft clothing; at that sorry sight
shamed scorn will put unworthy love to flight.

78

"At present I've no more to say to you,
but you may go on, confident of heart,
and solve the labyrinth and walk on through
into the hideaway's most secret part;
nothing will block you, or cause you to slow,
not all the trickeries of magic art.
Such power is in your escort and your leader,
your coming will surprise even Armida!

79

"Nor will the dwellers of her wilderness
trouble you any more on your return.
But now the hour for sleeping is with us
and you must rise tomorrow with the dawn."
He leads them to a room in his great house
where they would spend the night. When that is done,
and the knights are cheerful, thinking of what he's said,
the good old man himself retires to bed.

Canto Fifteen

1
Now to their work the newborn ray of dawn
had called each animal that dwells on land,
when the Wise Man came to the two warriors,
bringing the map, the shield, and the golden wand.
"Prepare yourselves," said he, "for the great voyage!
The day has dawned, the time to leave's at hand!
Look—everything I promised you is here
to overcome the witch's charms." They were

2
already risen, had already girt
their armor on the broad and sturdy back;
then along paths that never see day's light
they follow the old man, and, going back,
tread in the same steps they had trod before
and so retrace their way on the same track.
But at the river's edge, "My friends, farewell,"
says he, "and go with glad hearts!" The river's swell

3
lifted them gently upon its bosom, and
carried them out on a wave, an easy glide,
as a light branch that violence does not snap
springs softly back again. They land beside
the moist and spongy shore. And then they see,
in a small sailing ship, their promised guide:
the lady of the fates stands at the prow
to lead them where they wish to venture now.

4
Her locks hung down upon her head; her glance
was full of calm, and courtesy, and grace;
she seemed to have an angel's countenance,
such light was glowing warmly in her face.
Her gown you might call blue, or red, perchance,
any of a million colors in one place,
so that however many times she's seen
she always seems to change from what she's been.

5
Like as the downy feathers round the throat
of the gentle and amorous turtledove:
they never look the same, but take the tint
of various colors lit by the sun above,
now the fire of a ruby necklace, now the glint
of the green emerald, now a mingling of
both, and a hundred more in the shifting light,
to fill the eye with various delight.

6
"O come aboard my ship, fortunate men,
wherein I safely navigate the sea;
each wind is at my back, each storm is calm,
each heavy burden is but light for me.
My Lord has chosen me His minister,
My Lord, Who deals His grace unsparingly."
So spoke the lady, and to the shoreline's tip
she drew the sleek bent prow of her pine ship,

7
and when the noble duo were aboard
she pushed off from the shore, anchor aweigh,
and having freed the sail to take the wind
she sat before the helm and steered the way.
The river was so swollen with the rain
it could now carry vessels to the bay,
but even so, this vessel was so light
it could have skimmed the stream at usual height.

8
With more than natural velocity
the sails are driven seaward by the wind,
and the water's churned to white and foamy spray
that tumbles murmuring in the wake behind.
And now they have arrived at the vast bed
to which the river's waters are consigned,
taking their rest in the wide whirl of the sea,
where they disperse, are nothing—seemingly.

9
And hardly had that wondrous vessel touched
the then-turbulent bosom of the deep
when all the dark clouds vanished overhead
with all their threatening rumbles put to sleep,
and a fresh breeze planed all the mountainous surge—
and you could see the small waves curl and leap—
and the skies smiled with sweet serenity.
A clearer sky no man might ever see.

10

They passed by Ascalon, and to the left
the ship sailed toward the setting of the sun;
and in a moment Gaza came in sight.
The port of Gaza it was in days long gone,
but growing from the ruins of the first
the town became a great and mighty one,
so many men upon its busy strand
they seemed as numberless as grains of sand.

11

Turning their glances landward then the sailors
discovered a vast number of pitched tents;
they saw the infantry, they saw the knights
as back and forth from shore to town they went,
and the sandy path well trodden by the hoof
of the burdened camel and the elephant;
and then in the deep hollows of the bay
a fleet of anchored ships in smart array.

12

Some ships they saw unfurl their sails, and some
glide swiftly with their oarsmen set in rows,
and the oars and the prows churned up the foam—
for they could see the froth from these and those.
Then said the lady, "Though the sea and shore
are bustling now with your malevolent foes,
the mighty tyrant has not marshaled all
his forces under one imperial

13

"standard—for these you see are from his kingdom
Egypt and thereabouts. He still attends
for hosts from the equator, the far east,
for that's how broad his tyranny extends.
That's why I hope we'll be back well before
he moves his host, he or whomever he sends
to be the sovereign ruler in his stead
and command his great army as its head."

14

All while she spoke, the little boat sailed on.
As past all other birds the eagle flies
soaring in confidence, so near the sun
his figure vanishes from human eyes,
so the boat seemed to fly past everyone
and among all those ships feared no surprise,
no one to follow, no one to make her stay—
and vanished in a moment, far away.

15
And in a moment they approached Refah,
the first town that appears to one who goes
sailing from Egypt north to Syria;
then the stark, sterile coast Rhinoceros;
and soon a towering mountaintop they saw
above the water, the peak of Casius,
whose foot is washed in the ever-changing sea
and whose lap holds the bones of great Pompey.

16
Then they saw Damietta, and the seven
mouths of the Nile, through which the nutritive
waters rush onward, born of the rain from heaven,
and the hundred smaller mouths that also give
their tribute to the sea. Then they pulled even
with Alexandria, where Greeks used to live,
built by the strongest Greek. Pharos passed next,
an island long ago, but now annexed

17
to the very shore. The isles of Rhodes and Crete
lay out of sight far north; they skirted Africa,
whose coasts are tilled and bring forth much to eat,
but inland only monsters, sand. Marmarica
they skimmed by after that, and then the great
province of the five cities, Cyrenaica.
Here Ptolemais, and the quiet spring
of the River Lethe, whereof fables sing.

18
They pass the Greater Syrtis far from shore,
that perilous sandbank hiding in the sea,
then the Cape of Judecca, and the mouth
of Magra, and the coast of Tripoli,
and opposite that coast the isle of Malta
half hid below the ocean. Then Alzerbe
with the Lesser Syrtis; the land where long ago
the Lotos Eaters dwelt. And on they go

19
to the curved coast of Tunis, and they see
that city banked by mountains on each hand;
places of greater fame there may well be
in Libya, but none so rich and grand.
Across the straits from it sits Sicily,
the great Marsala towering over the strand.
And now the lady points out to the two
the site where Carthage stood, centuries ago,

20
the lofty Carthage, where its ruins lie;
but a few traces on the sand remain.
For cities all must die, kingdoms must die,
and pomp be leveled to the grassy plain.
And we men take it ill that we must die,
our minds are so insatiable and vain!
And now they reach Bizerta in the land
of Tunis; Sardinia on the opposite hand.

21
Then they passed by the shores where to this day
with his flocks wanders the Numidian,
then Bugia and Algiers, infamous nests
of pirates; then the city of Oran,
and the shores where elephants and lions thrive,
the Tingitan, or Mauritanian,
part of Morocco now, and part of Fez;
and passed Granada far across the seas.

22
Now they've arrived where men say Hercules
opened a strait for the landlocked sea to flow.
And maybe it was once one solid coast
till some great ruin split the rock in two,
and the ocean flooded over by main force,
dividing Abila and Calpe, so
cutting a strait through Libya and Spain.
Time alters all—how little will remain!

23
From the day that the boat had pushed from shore
four times the men had seen the rising sun,
nor did they ever put in port (what for?),
and thus much of their voyage was now done.
Into the straits they sail, and soon pass through,
and suddenly they find themselves upon
the endless swallowing sea. So boundless here,
what when no bounds of continent appear?

24
Fertile Cadiz no longer lifts its head
above the mounding waves, nor can they see
the two near towns; all shores, all lands have fled;
sky bounds the water, water bounds the sky.
"O Lady, and our guide," Ubaldo said,
"into this ocean without limit, say,
has anyone come so far before? And do
people inhabit the lands we're sailing to?"

25
"When Hercules," she answered him, "had killed
the monstrous beasts of Libya and Spain,
and had traversed and conquered all your shores,
he did not dare attempt the ocean main.
He fixed the bounds, and the brave mind of man
was cloistered in too narrow a domain;
but one man thought the mark he set too low:
Ulysses, ever eager to see and know.

26
"He passed the Pillars and on the open seas
he set the oars for his audacious flight;
no help was all his seaman's expertise,
for the ravenous ocean swallowed him outright,
and now his great fall, with his body, lies
still cloaked in silence. And though storm winds might
thrust others out so far, they either die
or manage to get home, and never try

27
"this way again. So the sea we furrow now
is unknown; islands, kingdoms, all unknown;
the lands there are not uninhabited
but are as rich and fertile as your own,
ready to bring forth crops. For that great power
cannot be sterile which the sun pours down."
"This secret world," said he, after a pause,
"tell me of its religion and its laws."

28
"As the tribes differ, there are different rites
and different myths and customs for each one.
Some worship the Great Mother of us all;
some adore beasts; others the stars and sun;
and some heap high their wicked tables with
cruelty and abomination.
Their laws, their faith—there is no more to tell—
are all barbarian, and infidel."

29
"Then the Lord Who descended to bring light
into the world and make the Scriptures clear,
would have so much of the world remain in night?"
"Not at all," she replied to the cavalier.
"The faith of Peter will one day be taught
with every civil art to the people here.
For this long journey over seas so great
won't always hold your nations separate.

30
"A time will come when the Pillars of Hercules
will to the busy men who sail the sea
become a silly fable; and all these
waters and lands that have no name shall be
made famous. The boldest sailor in those days
will circle the earth along the circling sea,
mapping the world, vast labor undergone,
victoriously striving with the sun.

31
"Liguria will produce this man so brave
to take the unknown trek for the first time,
no matter that the seas roar, the winds rave,
no matter the uncertain, changing clime,
no matter all things perilous and grave—
whatever dangers men consider prime—
nothing could keep that generous heart once gone
through the forbidden straits from sailing on.

32
"Columbus, in a new, far hemisphere
you spread your happy banners to the skies!
Fame shall hardly follow your voyage there,
she of a thousand wings and a thousand eyes!
To your descendants, bold adventurer,
she hardly nods, yet sings of Hercules—
yet that nod brings a lasting memory
worthy of epic and long history."

33
So she declared, and over the billowing way,
turning toward the equator, sailed southwest,
and saw ahead of them the falling day
and at their back its rebirth in the east.
And when the dawn first scattered its bright ray
and strung the world with dew, they saw, in the mist,
the distant and vague outline of a mount
hiding among the clouds its rocky front.

34
And then they saw it, sailing further on,
when every cloud had vanished from its face,
shaped like a spire-like pyramid, or cone,
sharp at the summit, broader toward the base.
At times you saw the smoke about it blown
as on the hill atop Enceladus,
Aetna, filling the day with smoke, at night
flaring to heaven with its flumes of light.

35
Then other islands in a group at last,
less steep and craggy, with more gentle hills.
Toward these, the so-called Happy Isles, they cast,
which the first ages called the Happy Isles
because they thought heaven's friendship held so fast
there, that the earth brings forth (no farmer tills)
spontaneously; its grapes on the lush vine
sweeter than grapes the vintners grow for wine.

36
Here the olive never fails to sport its flower,
and, they say, honey drops from the gnarled holm,
and down the mountainside the fresh brooks pour
tumbling into the dell with a sweet hum,
and dew and breezes so relieve the power
of the summer's heat, it is not burdensome;
here were the Elysian Fields which men professed
would house the happy spirits of the blest.

37
Toward these the lady steered, and spoke these words:
"Your pilgrimage's end is now in view.
Those are the Fortunate Isles, whereof you hear
many reports, but not all of them true.
They are indeed rich, pleasant, beautiful—
yet to those truths is joined some falsehood too."
So saying, she directed her ship then
near the shore of the first island of the ten.

38
And Charles began: "If this high enterprise
on which you guide us, Lady, will permit,
let me now look upon those unknown shores
and set my feet on dry land for a bit,
to see the people, see what they adore,
all that would make a wise man envy it
when someday I shall tell my tale and swear
about these wonders, saying 'I was there!' "

39
"Your request does you credit," she replied,
"but how can I comply? It cannot be.
Against this noble wish of yours there stands
heaven's severe inviolable decree.
For the completed time has not come round
which God has fixed for the discovery.
Nor will you even be allowed to keep
a memory of your voyage to the deep

40
"to bring news to your world. Grace grants you this,
to go beyond where art can navigate,
to put ashore where the soldier is held bound
and bring him east again. Your armies wait.
Let that suffice. To aspire higher still
is arrogance, and kicking against fate."
Here she falls silent. The first island goes
under the distant sea, the next . . . She shows

41
her passengers how the islands to the east
are evenly arrayed in a long row,
and how to pass from one shore to the next
you'd have an almost equal length to go.
In seven of them they saw the huts and farms
of the inhabitants; in the others, no;
they were deserted, and wild animals
held their safe dens among the woods and hills.

42
One of these desert isles had a fine harbor
set deep within the curving of the beach,
extending on each side a long, wide horn,
enclosing the lagoon within their reach,
its gate a rock that bore the battering sea
and drove it back or broke its force: on each
side of this bay two towering sea cliffs stood,
great signs for mariners. Below, the flood

43
lay still and silent in the peaceful bay,
but atop the cliffs, a dark and wooded scene,
in the center of which a grotto lay,
shade and fresh pools and ivy trailing green;
they did not tie the ropes here, did not stay
their weary ship with anchor, but, unseen,
the lady sailed into the lonely nook
and brought the canvas in. And she said, "Look:

44
"In that high palace on the mountain peak
the champion of Christianity
pours himself out in idleness, grows weak
among lush food and games and foolery.
Begin your steep and rough ascent at break
of the newborn day, the sun your guide. Be
patient, and never worry about the time;
the morning is auspicious for the climb,

45
"all other hours are not. It is still day;
by yourselves you can reach the hill before
nightfall." They took leave of their noble guide
and set foot on the much-desired shore.
It was not difficult to find the way
that led to the mountain's base, so on they bore
eagerly—yet when they arrived the light was dim,
the sun sunk far below the ocean's rim.

46
They see their climb ahead, chasm, precipice,
broken crags to the summit proud and high,
below which every path is strewn with ice
and snow; above, the grass and flowers lie
like a green carpet to the very chin
of the white mountain, but they do not die,
the ice no foe to lily or tender rose.
So far past nature incantation goes.

47
So the two soldiers, in that dark, wild place
at the foot of the mountain, spent the night,
till the sun streaked the sky with its new rays,
the sun, eternal spring of golden light.
"Let's go!" they shout, and go at a brisk pace,
ardent to start their journey to that height,
when out of nowhere comes a monstrous thing
crossing their path, horribly slithering,

48
lifting its filthy-yellow, scaly crest,
its head held high, its gullet puffed with wrath,
flame in its eyes, its guts blocking the way,
poison and fumes exhaling in its breath,
now huddling, now unfolding its tangled whorls,
dragging self after self along its path.
This dragon thus comes forth, the accustomed guard,
but cannot halt their progress mountainward.

49
Now Charles has at the serpent with his blade
but the other cries, "What do you think this is?
You think that with such arms, with your own hand,
you can defeat a serpent such as this?"
With that he waved his deathless, golden wand
so quickly that the beast could hear it hiss,
and, frightened by the sound, it cowered low,
drew back, and left the passage free to go.

50
A little way ahead a lion stood
roaring, eyes filled with hatred, who defied
their passing further: his mane stood straight as quills,
the horrible cave of his mouth was open wide,
he lashed himself with his tail to stoke his wrath,
but once they showed the Wise Man's wand, his pride
froze, and his anger froze, for a secret dread
crept over his heart like ice—and the lion fled.

51
The two pursued their journey with all speed
till suddenly before them a gigantic
army of warrior-animals appeared,
of look, of voice, of motions wild and frantic
and all unlike; all monstrous things that breed
between the Nile and the shores of the Atlantic
seemed gathered here in one, with all the brood
of beasts from Hyrcania to the Black Wood.

52
That host so fierce and of such dreadful might
charges to fight them, make them yield their ground,
yet—strangest miracle—they take to flight
for a glimpse and a little whistling sound!
Now the victorious pair attain the height
of the mountain; no more obstacles were found
besides the steep ascent and the icy way
that forced their quest to bear a short delay.

53
But once the snow and ice were overcome
and they had crossed the steep and slippery,
they found sweet weather, for the skies were warm
and the plain atop the mountain clear and free.
Fresh breezes, fresh, but ever fragrant too,
blew easy there, lightly, continually,
nor is their turning, as is elsewhere done,
wakened or lulled to sleep by the heat of the sun,

54
nor on that highland did the weather change
from cloudy day to clear, from fire to freeze;
the sky wore brightest splendors like a robe;
summer and winter never marred its ease.
In the gardens it nourished the grass, in the grass the flowers,
in the flowers the fragrance, in the immortal trees
the shade. A lakeside palace brilliantly
towered above the mountain and the sea.

55
The knights were somewhat weary from the climb,
they felt their lungs exhausted, their legs slack,
so down the flowery path they took their time,
now pausing, and now slowing to a walk.
Behold, a spring, inviting their dry lips
to wet themselves, comes spilling over a rock,
and from an ample pool it brims and washes
the nearby grass with a thousand little splashes.

56
But then, with grassy banks on either side,
the water gathered into a deep pool,
and under the shade of leaves that never died
it rippled by, murmuring and dark and cool,
yet so transparent that it did not hide
its deepest bed, pleasant and beautiful,
and over its banks there grew the branching trees,
making a soft cool spot to lie at ease.

57
"This is the spring of laughter, this the stream
in which those lethal perils are contained;
now it behooves us to be on our guard
and hold our appetites most tightly reined,
shutting our ears against the sweet, cruel song
of the false Sirens, and their pleasures, feigned;
let us go on to where the stream is spread
into a lake, within a wider bed."

58
A banquet was set out along the banks,
a table full of rare and dainty food,
while in the water two girls played their pranks,
two merry ladies, talkative and lewd,
racing to a set spot with slender flanks
skimming the water, swimming in the nude,
splashing each other's faces, or going under,
then bobbing up all glistening like a wonder.

59
The swimming girls were nude and beautiful
and moved the stubborn chests of the two knights
so that they stopped to watch them play awhile,
continuing their games and their delights.
One rose so high she showed the men her full
breasts, and all else that could entice their sights
from the hips up, all open to the sky,
while the lake veiled the rest most prettily.

60
Just as the morning star arises from
the waves, bejeweled with mist; or Aphrodite,
goddess of love, born of the ocean foam,
dawns on the world above—just so seemed she,
just so the crystal droplets trickled down
her golden hair. And now, feigning to see
the men for the first time, the girl grew shy,
huddling a little disconcertedly,

61
and all her hair tied in one knot above
she let loose in a moment to fall free,
long and disheveled, like a golden robe,
mantling, and veiling the soft ivory . . .
What lovely vistas she deprived them of!
But what a lovely work of thievery!
So hid beneath the water and her hair
she turned to them with a glad and bashful air.

62
She laughed a little, and she blushed withal,
and her smile was more lovely for the blush,
yet the smile lent the blush its own grace too,
as it covered her face with a delicate flush.
Then she sang, in a voice gentle and sweet,
a voice to win men's hearts in the first rush:
"O happy wanderers, who by fortune's grace
have come to this delightful, fruitful place,

63
"this is the world's port, this its anchorage.
Here you may soothe the pain of life, and be
filled with sweet things as in the golden age
when there was no restraint, and men were free!
Until now you have needed arms to wage
war—now set them aside, confidently.
Consecrate them to Quiet in this grove,
for here the only knights are knights of Love.

64
"Let the bed be your pleasant battlefield.
On the soft garden grass come to the test!
We'll lead you now before the regal sight
of her who makes her servants ever blest.
Surely you'll be among the happy few
destined to share her joys. But first, it's best
to wash your dust away and cool your heat,
and sample what our table gives to eat."

65
Meanwhile the other girl accompanied
the invitation with her acts and glances,
as to the sweet sound of the woodland reed
now nimble and now slow, the dancer dances.
But the knights' hearts were deaf and would not heed,
hardened against those false and faithless chances.
Their flattering looks and sweet talk flew in vain—
caressed senses were all they could obtain,

66
for if some sweetness managed to soak in
and penetrate the place where longings sprout,
Reason entered the lists all clad in arms
and pruned the nascent will, or plucked it out.
The one pair were defeated at their game,
the other pair set on their way without
even a goodbye. On to the palace they went
while the girls dunked themselves for discontent.

Canto Sixteen

1
The lavish outer wall was circular,
and in the inmost center of the round,
in its close bosom, grew a garden, far
lovelier than the loveliest renowned;
within was order in confusion, for
demons had built up galleries all around,
with slant and veering paths crossed every way;
impenetrable to where the garden lay.

2
Through the great entrance—for that edifice
had hundreds of them—Charles and Ubaldo passed.
The gate was sculptured silver in relief
and creaked on golden hinges. The knights cast
a steady gaze on the lifelike figures there,
for the material was far surpassed
by art: speech was the only thing they lacked,
nor even speech, if eyes could judge of fact.

3
Here they saw Hercules, hero of the wars,
gossiping with the servant ladies, spinning;
he who had harrowed hell and borne the stars
now turned his loom. Love looked upon him, grinning,
while weakling Iole fulfilled the farce,
lugging his homicidal weapons, pinning
upon her girlish frame a lion's skin—
too rough to clothe her tender members in!

4
Opposite this you saw a frothing sea,
the whitecaps streaking all the fields of blue,
and in the midst two ordered lines of ships,
and artillery from which quick flashes flew,
flaming the sea with gold. All Actium
was ablaze with war. Leading his Romans to
battle, Augustus; on the other side,
Antony, with his Oriental pride.

5
You'd say the sea had ripped the Cyclades
or mountains were colliding, solid rock,
so hurtled to the test these enemies
with towering masts, so violent their shock,
wildfire and javelins flew over the seas
and the waves were flecked with slaughter. But now, look!
The battle not inclining either way,
look, the barbarian queen, turning away!

6
Does Antony flee? Could Antony despair
to rule the world, which he had craved so long?
Oh no, he does not flee, he does not fear,
he follows her who flees and pulls him along—
he like a man seething with love and ire
and shame, looks to his own ships holding strong
in the cruel battle which still hangs in doubt,
and now looks to her navy ducking out.

7
Then in the hiding places of the Nile
he lay upon her lap, he lay in wait
for death. The pleasure of her lovely smile
was enough to console him for his fate.
Such were the figures, such the sculpture style
graven in metal on the regal gate.
And having glanced a while at these delights,
into the wayward garden walked the knights.

8
Like the Meander with its crooked course,
mocking, uncertain, now falling, now rising again,
now turning its flood to the sea, now to its source,
meeting its past self flowing past again,
so intertwined and inextricable
were the trails here—but the map made them plain,
the book they had been given by the magician,
which loosed the knots, and showed them their position.

9
When they had left the self-enveloped ways,
the garden opened in glad countenance
with quiet pools and crystal-flowing streams,
various shrubs and flowers, various plants,
soft open hills and valleys cool with shade,
grottoes and forests, all in a single glance,
and what made all of it more rare and dear:
the art that fashioned it did not appear.

10
So mingled was the art with carelessness
you'd think that Nature had arrayed the site.
It seemed an art of Nature's playfulness
to mimic her own mimic for delight.
Among her other spells the sorceress
made the air mild, to keep the trees just right,
eternal fruit beside eternal bloom.
Pick one, another ripens in its room.

11
On the same limb, and among the same leaves
the fig grows old beside the budding fig,
and apples, young and green, or ripe and gold,
hang from the same branch, sprout by the same twig,
and where the garden opens to the sky
the tendril-curling vine grows lush and big,
the bitter fruit in flower hang on the vine
with purple grapes rich with the musk of wine.

12
And pretty birds under the greenwood shade
temper their merry notes in harmony,
and the wind murmurs, and the leaves and streams
chatter, as the wind strikes them variously,
for when the birds are still those sounds are deep,
but when they sing they strike a lighter key.
By chance, or art, the music of the air
accompanies or responds to the voices there.

13
Among the rest there flew a dappled bird,
with gaudy feathers and a purple beak,
whose tongue was nimble enough to form a word
and seemed to speak as human beings speak.
Now he began to make his language heard
continuously, with marvelous technique:
the birds were hushed, intent to hear him sing,
and even the breezes ceased their whispering.

14
"Look at the chaste and modest little rose
sprung from the green in her virginity!
Half open and half hid; the less she shows,
the less she shows to men, the lovelier she.
Now she displays her bold and amorous
bosom, and now she wilts, and cannot be
the same delight which was the longing of
a thousand girls and a thousand lads in love.

15
"So passes, in the passing of a day,
the life of man, the fruit, the leaf, the flower;
spring may return, but these will pass away;
the green will fade, and youth will lose its power.
Gather the rose in the fresh of dawn today,
for this sweet time will only last an hour;
gather the rose of love as lovers do,
and love while you yourself can be loved too."

16
Then all the birds in chorus took the song
and sang it back, as if they would approve—
and the doves made their cooing doubly long,
and every creature seemed to be in love,
as if the virgin laurel and the strong
poplar and every tree in the wide grove,
water and earth themselves should feel, and sigh
for the sweet love they were inspired by.

17
Among enchanting loveliness, among
allurements, and such tender melody,
the pair proceeded, rigid, constant, strong,
hardened against the pleasing luxury.
They part the leaves, and their gaze penetrates
to where they see him—or they think they see—
then catch for certain the lover and his lass,
he lying in her lap, she on the grass.

18
Loose at the breast she wore her slender veil
and left her hair a-scatter in the heat.
She lay in languor, as her usual play,
her blush enlivening clear pearls of sweat;
on her moist eyes played laughter like a ray
of light on the trembling sea. Over the knight
she hung; in her soft lap he lay his head,
raising his hungry eyes to hers, to feed

19
greedily on her charms, and as he fed
his sight, he was himself consumed, undone.
She leant, and sipped sweet kisses from his eye
and sucked them from his lips. If you'd looked on
just as you heard him heave a deep, deep sigh
you would have thought, "His pilgrim soul has gone
and fled to hers." So the two hidden knights
gazed upon all these amorous delights.

20
From the lover's side there hung a crystal glass,
shining and smooth—strange thing for him to wear.
He rose, and held it out between his hands,
in the rites of Love the chosen minister.
She with eyes laughing, he with eyes ablaze,
in different objects see one object there:
she sees herself in the mirror, while he spies
himself in the calm reflection of her eyes.

21
She gloried in herself, and he in her;
she in command, and he in slavishness.
"O turn," said he, "turn," said the cavalier,
"to me those blessed eyes with which you bless!
You may not know it, but in my desire
lies the true portrait of your loveliness.
Its wondrous form shows in the crystal's art
but truer in the mirror of my heart.

22
"Ah, if you scorn to look at me, at least
look at your own face shining in my eyes,
for your glance will delight to see itself,
rejoicing, when no other can suffice.
A mirror cannot give a sight so sweet,
no glass can comprehend a paradise!
Heaven is the mirror worthiest of you,
and in the stars you see your beauty true."

23
Armida smiled, but did not cease to gaze
upon herself and her sweet artistry.
When she had tressed her hair and set in place
its playful wanderings, ordered prettily,
she made a ring of hair, a golden case
for the enameled flowers carefully
scattered: her veil composed, she gathered fresh
roses beside the lilies of her flesh.

24
The peacock's not so proud to show the pomp
of his bright feathers of a thousand eyes,
nor Iris bends her gold and purple bow
so beautifully beneath the misty skies.
Nothing adorned her like her lovely belt
which she wears always, even when she lies
nude: for it gives a body to what has none,
substance for every slight phenomenon.

25
The tender coyness and the calm rebuffs,
the precious, charming warfare, and the sweet
moments of peace; the little smiles, the tears,
the broken sighs, soft kisses, all complete
this belt, for they were melted down in one
then fused over a torch with gentle heat.
Tempered in one, their graces unified
in the belt she girdled round her lovely side.

26
Done at last with her beautifying, she
bids him goodbye, kisses him, and departs,
for it's usual with her to spend the day
tending her own affairs, her magic arts.
He stays behind (he's not allowed to stray
one moment or one step in other parts),
wandering among the beasts and trees, alone,
a hermit lover when his love is gone.

27
But when the friendly silence of the dusk
should call the lovers back to secret glee,
in the same garden they spend the happy hours,
and the night covers up their thievery.
Now that Armida has left the garden for
her sterner offices of sorcery,
the two—behind the bushes, lying low—
step forth in soldier's pomp from head to toe.

28
As a fierce stallion, victor in the wars,
retired, and from his glory led away
to live an idle life among the mares
and wander with the cows and feed all day,
when once the trumpet sounds or bugle blares
he pricks his ears and turns with a sharp neigh,
craving the arena, the rider on his back,
and stricken to rise and gallop striking back—

29
such was the lad when with the sudden light
reflected from their arms his eyes were dashed.
His spirit, so fierce, so warlike, and so proud,
soon as the lightning of the weapons flashed,
though languishing among these morbid pleasures,
drunken and drowsy, woke at once, abashed.
Ubaldo then came forward, and he shone
upon the lad his shield of diamond stone.

30
He turned his glance upon the brilliant shield
and saw himself for what he was, how tressed
with dainty touches, reeking of perfume,
his hair in curls and tassels on his vest,
his dangling sword effeminate at his side,
prettified—not to mention all the rest,
for it's a dandy ornament he bore,
not a ferocious instrument of war!

31
As a man laden down with heavy sleep
after vain dreams comes to himself again,
so he returned, seeing his own reflection.
It was a sight he could not long sustain.
His eyes fell, and with meekness and dejection
he stared upon the ground, ashamed, in pain;
he would have shut himself beneath the sea
or in the center of the earth, to flee.

32
It was Ubaldo who uttered the first word.
"All Asia and all Europe go to war!
All Christian men who long for fame's reward
are toiling now in arms in Syria!
You alone, son of Berthold, have ignored
the world beyond your little carefree spa—
you alone, in the universal whirl,
stand pat, the gallant champion of a girl!

33
"What drowsiness or lethargy could lull
your manhood? Or what baseness was your bait?
Get up, get up! The field and Godfrey call!
Your fortune and your victory await!
Finish the enterprise begun so well.
That impious sect, O warrior of fate,
which you have shaken, to the earth shall fall
under your unshunned sword." And that was all,

34
and the noble lad stood for a certain space
confused: he could not speak, he could not start.
But when to indignation shame gave place,
indignant Scorn, fierce fighter on Reason's part,
and a new fire spread over his blushing face,
a hotter-burning fire, leapt from the heart,
he flung his toys and bangles off for good,
pathetic emblems of his servitude,

35
and was in haste to go, and through the crooked
confusion of the maze he exited.
Armida meanwhile at the royal gate
saw where her monster-sentinel lay dead.
First she suspected, then she saw it clear—
her darling must have done this, must have fled—
and saw—terrible sight—him set his face
in flight against so sweet a dwelling place.

36
She wanted to cry, "Cruel man, where are you going
without me?" But her sadness choked her cry,
so that the words of weeping turned within
and echoed in her breast more bitterly.
Poor girl, a power and wisdom stole her love,
a wisdom greater than her own. To try
to hold him back—although she sees it's vain—
she is resolved to ply her art again.

37
All the blasphemous charms that from the foul
mouths of Thessalian witches ever fell,
charms that could stop the heavenly wheels dead still
or drag the spirits from their jails in hell,
she knew them all, but what good to her now?
None of the spirits below could she compel!
No matter—beauty on its knees might prove
a finer sorceress in affairs of love.

38
She runs—no care for honor stops her now.
Where are her triumphs? Where are all her vaunts?
Love's a great king, but she would make him bow,
one nod from her turned all his subjects once—
yet she herself disdained to stoop so low,
loved to be loved, yet ever looked askance
at those who loved. She herself was her prize,
or the effect stirred by her lovely eyes.

39
Now she was left behind, neglected, scorned,
yet she pursued the scornful man who fled.
Her gift of loveliness might be adorned
(rejected in itself) by tears she shed—
so she hoped—and the ice and the sharp stones
cut her soft foot—and still she sent ahead
her cries as messengers, which could not reach
her loved one's ears till he was on the beach.

40
Madly she cried, "O you who take one part
and leave the other part of me behind,
take the rest too, or give me back my heart,
or kill them both! Oh, stop, please stop, and mind
the last words I will ever speak to you—
no kisses, oh no, I'm assured you'll find
someone more worthy of them! Afraid to stay?
You can deny as well as run away!"

41
Ubaldo counseled him, "My lord, do not
refuse to wait, for it will strengthen you.
She comes armed with her beauty and her prayers,
sweetly commingled in a bitter brew.
If you can see and hear the Sirens, yet
conquer, what more can any hero do?
Grow used to it; thus reason grows refined,
and the senses bow to the calm rule of the mind."

42
So the knight stopped, and she came, out of breath,
weeping. Her sorrow could not make her more
lovely, indeed, but gave her, now so sad,
a beauty other than what was hers before.
She looks at him, she stares, says not a word.
Perhaps she scorns to, or is thinking, or
dares not. He looks away, or looks askance,
with an embarrassed, slow, and furtive glance.

43
As cunning singers, just before they free
their voices into high and brilliant song,
prepare the listener's soul for harmony
with sweet notes *sotto voce,* low and long,
so in the bitterness of sorrow she
did not forget the tricks and arts of wrong,
but gave a little prelude of a sigh
that his soul might be more deeply graven by

44
these words: "Don't think I've come, you cruel man,
to beg my lover—it's what we used to be,
lovers—or if you want to deny that,
if you can't even stand the memory,
call me an enemy then, but hear me out!
Hearings are even granted the enemy!
And I'm not asking a great thing from you—
for you can give me it, and hate me too!

45

"If you gain some delight from hating me
I'm not here to deprive you—go and hate!
Seems right and just to you, so let it be!
I hated you and all the Christian state.
I was born pagan—and I used my skill
that through me you might meet a dreadful fate.
I followed you, caught you, took you from the war
to this strange, unknown island. But there's more.

46

"Add what can only fire the rancor of
your hatred, the worst loss you could endure.
I lied to you, I lured you to fall in love—
oh such deception, evil, wicked, sure—
and let you cull my virgin flower, to prove
the tyrant of its beauty. Its allure
was prized by many lovers, all in vain,
and then to a new lover I gave it, plain!

47

"Count that among all my deceptions too!
So many sins—they weigh so heavily
that you must leave and never give a thought
to the place where you once rejoiced to be.
Go sweat and toil and fight across the seas,
destroy our faith—I'll even help you flee!
Our faith? Not mine, not now. My cruel one,
you are my faith, my idol—you alone.

48

"Just let me follow when you go away.
Not much for even an enemy to confer.
The predator does not give up his prey,
the conquering hero takes his prisoner!
Put me with all your war spoils on display
for the whole camp—and let them say of her,
singing your praise, 'She lost the game she played,'
pointing at me who scorned you, now your maid,

49

"scorned maid. Why should I any longer save
these braided locks, now they're so vile to you?
I'll cut them short! If I'm to be a slave
I want to sport a slave's appearance too.
I'll follow, and when the flames of battle rave
I'll enter the fight beside you! I can do
a slave's work, lead your horses, carry your spear.
I have the strength, and a heart not prone to fear.

50
"Whatever you want—I'll bear, I'll *be* your shield—
to save your life why should I spare my own?
Before it touches you the sword should pass
through this bare throat or through this heart alone.
The barbarian perhaps won't be so crude,
and will leave his revenge on you undone,
denying himself the pleasure he expected,
sparing this beauty, such as it is, neglected.

51
"Poor fool, what am I saying? I still boast
of some scorned beauty that's not worth a thing—"
She'd have said more, but weeping cut her short,
tears like the surge of a rocky hillside spring.
She tried to catch his arm, his coat; she fell
to her knees. He stops, he musters everything,
resists, and conquers. The gate is bolted fast
against Love's entering; and no tears get past.

52
Love could not be rekindled in his breast.
Reason had cooled the rage of the old flame,
yet in its place Compassion came at least,
the friend of Love, yet sensible of shame,
and moved his heart so deeply, he was pressed
to hold his tears. He held them all the same,
he held his tender feelings in, restrained,
gathered himself as best he could and feigned

53
composure. "Armida, I am sorry for you.
If I could work my wishes, you would be
free of the ill-born fire that burns your soul.
There is no scorn, no hate for you in me.
I don't want vengeance, I don't bear a grudge.
You're not my servant or my enemy.
You went beyond the limits of what's right,
using now love, now hate, to wage your fight,

54
"but these are human faults, and common, too.
Your youth, your sex, and your religion call
for mercy. I too sinned. Condemning you,
I'd have no chance for clemency at all.
But to your memory I will be true,
whatever joys or troubles may befall.
I'll be your knight, though the war calls me now,
as far as faith and honor will allow.

55
"Ah, take no pleasure in our shameful deeds!
Let our sins have their ending here and now.
And in this lonely corner of the world
let every trace of them lie buried low.
Of this one work of mine let no one in
Europe and both its neighbors ever know.
And don't mark as a sign of servitude
your beauty, your valor, and your royal blood.

56
"Stay here in peace. I'm going, and my guide
forbids your coming too. It isn't fit.
Stay here, or find a happier place to go.
As for your passion, try to quiet it."
But she, all while the soldier told her so,
found that her restlessness would not submit;
for a long time she held him fixed in sight,
glowering, and at last burst into spite:

57
"Sophia never bore you! Actian blood
flows in no vein of yours! The sickening sea
spawned you, or you're the icy Caucasus' brood,
a tiger gave you suck, for cruelty!
Why should I keep pretending, though? What good?
He gave not one sign of humanity,
pitiless man. Did he blush? Did he wet the eye
or grace my sadness with the smallest sigh?

58
"What shall I pass by, what shall I repeat?
He runs away and leaves me for my sake.
Just like a generous victor who forgives
his enemy, and pardons the mistake.
Hear what he says! Hear this Xenocrates
reason of love! Ye gods, why do you take
thundering attacks from such a wicked one
against your towers, your temple, and your throne?

59
"Go then, be cruel! Go with the very peace
you leave me here—wicked man, go then, go!
My bodiless soul will haunt you over the seas,
I'll be at your back wherever the wind may blow,
and as I loved you once I'll never cease
to torment you, like a new Fury! Oh,
you may find luck and shun the rocks and waves
and come to the battlefield; but there are graves

60

"in that field too. You'll lie there, bleeding, dying,
treacherous soldier. My pain costs much—you'll pay it.
In your last sobs you'll call to me by name,
'Armida,' oh how I long to hear you say it . . ."
But now the spirit leaves her in her sadness;
her last word has small breath left to convey it,
and in a faint, as if half dead, she lies
bathed in a chilling sweat, and shuts her eyes.

61

You shut your eyes, Armida; for your pain
you gain no comfort from the envious skies.
Open them, ah poor girl! Why don't you see
the bitter tears well in your enemy's eyes?
Ah, if you could but hear him, it would soothe
your heart, the gentle sound of his dear sighs.
He gives what he can give—you don't believe—
and with a look of pity takes his leave.

62

What should he do now? Leave her half alive
there on the naked sand? His courtesy
restrains him, pity holds him fixed in place,
till he is led by hard necessity.
He leaves, and gentle breezes toss the hair
of her who is his guide over the sea:
over the sea the golden sails fly on.
He sees the shore—and now the shore is gone.

63

When she came to again, she looked about—
she spoke no word, she saw she was alone.
"So he could leave me with my life in doubt,"
she said at last, "so he is truly gone,
and like a traitor could not wait it out
one moment, for small help. He gave me none
in my worst need. And I still love him, and
sit unavenged and weeping on the sand?

64

"What good will tears do? Have I no more art,
no other weapons? The devil, I'll follow him
whether he hides in hell's profoundest part—
not heaven itself will be secure for him!
I'll catch him, take him, I'll tear out his heart!
Bad men will see him hanging, limb by limb!
He is the master of brutality,
I'll beat him with his own arts. But where am I,

65
"what am I saying? Armida, you poor fool,
you should have punished the cruel with cruelty
when you held him imprisoned. Your anger's late,
too slow to seize the opportunity.
Yet if beauty and craft are useless, my desire
may at least do its work effectively.
O my scorned beauty, the harm was done to you—
and from you therefore is the vengeance due.

66
"This loveliness of mine will be a prize
for him who lops his execrable head.
A difficult but worthy enterprise
for you, my famous lovers. Bring him dead.
I who was heiress to such luxuries
am on the block now. Vengeance must be paid.
If I'm not worth the purchase at that cost,
well, Beauty, you're nothing but a worthless boast,

67
"a miserable gift of nature. I spurn you.
I hate being princess, I hate being alive,
I hate having been born at all. Sweet vengeance
is now the only hope for which I strive."
She turned her back on the deserted shore,
seething in such a fury as to rive
her thoughts and words, and to transform her grace—
scattered hair, narrowed eyes, a feverish face.

68
Back at her palace she uttered horrible charms
and called three hundred of the gods of hell.
At once the skies were burdened with black clouds
and the great everlasting sun grew pale,
and the wind moaned and pummeled the mountainsides.
Now from below, where evil spirits dwell,
to every room in the house came thundering noises,
barking and crying and hissing and raging voices.

69
Darkness darker than night surrounded all,
not tempered by a single ray of light
except a flashing from within the pall
of thickest smoke. Then the smoke whisked from sight;
and the sun shone again, but the air was still
dreary, and the rays of the sun were hardly bright,
nor did the least trace of the house appear,
not so much as would witness, "It was here."

70
As images of transitory clouds
that shape a towering castle in the air,
which the wind scatters, or the sun melts away,
or as the fleeting phantasm of a nightmare,
just so the mansion vanished, leaving but
the fearful mountains nature fashioned there.
She in her ready chariot mounted high
and as accustomed rose into the sky.

71
She treads the clouds and cleaves the air in flight,
girt with the mist and the sounding hurricanes,
passes the shores beneath the southern pole,
lands of unknown inhabitants, then gains
the Pillars of Hercules, but does not turn
to stop at Mauritania's shore, or Spain's.
She holds her steady course over the sea
until she reaches Syria. Once there, she

72
avoids Damascus, for she now detests
the once-dear vision of her fatherland,
and rides straight on to where her castle rests
in the middle of the lake of the dead strand,
nor gives her maids and butlers her requests
but goes unseen to a lonely spot. She scanned
her wavering thoughts, inclining to either path,
but shame in a short time gave way to wrath.

73
"I'll leave then," she decides, "before the King
of Egypt moves the hosts of the Orient.
I'll work my art, change into anything,
pleasure to me, and aid to my intent.
I'll carry the bow and sword, I'll be a slave
to the mightiest men, and goad them to battle, bent
on winning me. Let me see vengeance done,
my care for honor and respect begone!

74
"My uncle and protector should accuse
himself, not me, for he first wanted this.
He turned my brave heart and my sex to use,
frail though I was, in unfit offices;
he spurred my ardor, he set my shame loose,
made me a wandering woman. The fault is his
for all the shameful deeds I'm guilty of,
what I'll do for hate, and what I've done for love."

75

So she resolves, and summons all in haste,
sergeant and chambermaid and page and knight,
and in her proud gear and her dress displays
her arts and royal fortunes to the height;
departs, and never sleeps, nor even stays
to rest a little, either day or night,
till she comes where she sees the friendly bands
covering all the stretch of Gaza's sands.

Canto Seventeen

1
Gaza lies on Judea's boundary,
en route to the Nile delta's eastern breach,
situated on the coast of the great sea,
surrounded by vast solitudes of beach
and desert sand, which the wind whips viciously
as storms whip waves on the ocean. Hard to reach
shelter or find your way when traveling through,
when the storms shift the field, as here they do.

2
It was the frontier of the Egyptian king
who seized it from the Turk long time ago,
and since it was nearby and opportune
for his great enterprise against his foe,
he left his land and lofty capital,
he brought his throne along and brought also
soldiers from every province, mountain to coast,
mustering an innumerable host.

3
The time and season and the state of things,
O Muse, bring to my mind! The emperor
advances; tell me of the power he brings,
what allies, and what men in his own corps,
when from the south he leads his hosts and kings
and all the furthest Orient to war.
Half the world is in arms: show me them all!
You alone know each band and general.

4
When she rebelled from the Greek Emperor
Egypt abandoned worship of the Son,
and from Mohammed's blood a warrior
set himself as her tyrant on her throne.
His name was Caliph, and forevermore
by his name have her sceptered kings been known.
As the Nile named the ancient dynasties:
first they were Pharaohs all, then Ptolemies.

5
As the years passed the kingdom settled down
and grew so as to press on Libya
and Asia, from the city of Cyrene
in the west, to the coast of Syria,
and south on the endless Nile until Syene,
a village near the plains of Nubia;
here to the uninhabited wastes of sand,
there to the great Euphrates, in Chaldean land.

6
Within its boundaries it comprehended
the whole Red Sea, and Araby the blest,
the land of spice; from Eritrea extended
toward where the morning sun shines in the east.
The realm was rich in armies, but the splendid
prince by his virtuous government increased
its glory: he was prince by blood, but more
by merit in the royal art of war.

7
Against the Turks this Caliph moved his host;
against the Persians too he drove them on;
sometimes the fight was his, sometimes he lost,
nobler when fortune frowned than when he won.
In old age he unstrapped his sword at last;
his days of bearing heavy arms were gone;
but still he worked his military brain
and his vast lust for honor and for reign.

8
He wages war still, through his officers,
and speaks and reasons still so vigorously
the charge seems not too heavy for his years,
the overwhelming weight of monarchy.
Every small scattered tribe in Africa fears
his name; India honors him, and he
receives help from the princedoms in his fold—
some offer soldiers, and some offer gold.

9
Such was the king who marshaled all his powers—
rather who hurried his marshaled powers against
a surging empire, dangerously strong,
the fortunate and oft-victorious France.
Last of all came Armida, just in time
to see the army ordered to advance.
In a wide field, marching in battle array,
the armies passed before the king that day.

10
He sat in pride on his exalted throne,
scaled by a hundred steps of ivory;
a gold-laced purple rug beneath his foot,
under the shade of a silver canopy—
rich with the grandeur of a barbarian,
resplendent in his royal luxury;
and a thousand twisted bands of linen made
a strange fashion of diadem for his head.

11
His right hand grips the scepter; by his white
beard he appears severe and venerable;
and from his eyes—age has not dimmed their sight—
breathe his first boldness, his first vigor. All
his actions show, both for his years and might,
what one may only call majestical.
Apelles or Phidias would have portrayed the king
as Zeus—but Zeus when he is thundering.

12
On either side stand his first officers.
The worthier of the two holds a sword high
for rigor is his duty; the other bears
a privy seal, the sign of secrecy,
for at home in the great civil affairs
he is aide to the king. But greater than he
is the executor of punishment,
commissioned prince of every regiment.

13
Beneath him, garlanding the royal throne,
his faithful guards are standing watch: Circassian,
they carry spears and armor, and each one
wields a long sword, curved round in crescent fashion.
So sat the tyrant, so he looked upon
the nations merged beneath him. In their passing,
all of his troops and sergeants bow before him,
reverently, as if they would adore him.

14
Egyptians are the first in this parade,
marching before their king in ordered file:
two captains from Upper, two from Lower Egypt,
the work and gift of the celestial Nile.
He steals the sea's bed, spreading his fertile mud
which hardens into fertile farming soil.
So Egypt grows. What lands it holds inside
over which ancient sailors used to ride!

15
The soldiers of the squadron marching first
come from the plains of Alexandria,
come from the rich shore facing to the west,
the gateway of the shores of Africa.
Araspe leads them—not so strong of chest
as wise in stratagems and ruses—a
notable master of the well-laid snare
and wisest in the Moorish ways of war.

16
Next in the line are men who from the east
along the coasts of Greater Asia came:
Aronteus leads—no virtues in the least
but only titles magnify his name.
His head has never sweat beneath a helmet,
he's never heard the trumpeters proclaim
reveille; now from pleasures and obscurity
ambition calls him, far beyond maturity.

17
The third in line took up the fields and shores
and seemed no squadron, rather an immense
host in itself: Egypt could hardly reap
for such a multitude. Their provenance
was but one town, a town which vied with all
the countryside about, where citizens
dwelt by the millions—Cairo. To lead this mob
skittish in armor was Campsone's job.

18
From the near farmland, under Algazel,
came those who cut the wheat; their country backed
from Cairo south to where the river fell
tumbling over the second cataract.
Helmets and breastplates were unbearable—
these carry swords and bows alone, attract
enemies with desire for their rich clothing.
For stirring the fear of death, they're good for nothing.

19
Then the unclad and unarmed folk of Barca
with Alcoran their chief pass on display,
who bear a life of famine in the desert,
feeding themselves for centuries with prey.
Then hosts conducted by the king of Zumara,
less villainous, but still not apt to stay
firm in the battle. Then those of Tripoli—
and they are best at fighting when they flee.

20
Behind, the tillers of the blessed soil
of the rocky coastline of Arabia came,
who never feel extremes of heat or cold
(that is, if we can trust the widespread fame),
where incense and all other spices flower,
where the Phoenix is born, as poets claim,
building a nest of spikenard and perfume
to serve as both her cradle and her tomb.

21
Their garments are less gaudy, but their arms
are similar to those the Egyptians bear.
Other Arabians then, who do not dwell
more than a day in one place anywhere,
but take their towns and homes along with them,
a people who perpetually err.
They're short, with women's voices, soft and weak;
their hair is long and black, and black their cheek.

22
These tipped their slender Indian reeds with steel,
and coursing on their thoroughbreds they passed
as if caught up in a tornado's whirl—
if a tornado's winds can whip so fast!
Syphax's squadron was the first of these,
Aldin's the second, Albiazar's the last;
Albiazar, their proud and truculent guide,
no true knight, but a thief and homicide.

23
The soldiers following those came from the isles
surrounded by the wide Arabian Sea,
where conchs, heavy and loaded with rich pearls,
are fished from the ocean floor continually.
Coming along with them, a folk that dwells
on the gulf's left shore, the black Eritreii;
Agricalt led these, Osmid led the rest—
for him, all faith, all law is but a jest.

24
Meroe's Ethiopians came next,
Meroe, islanded by the rivers Nile
and Astabora, ample in extent;
three kingdoms there could find a domicile
and two religions. Canar and Assimir,
followers of Mohammed, led the file,
two tributary monarchs; but the third
stayed home, for he believed the holy Word.

25
Then two more rulers subject to the king;
armed with the bow and arrow was each band.
One, Sultan of Hormuz, at the narrowing
of the great Persian Gulf, a pleasant land;
the other troops came from the same gulf too,
another island country, Boecan,
but when the tide is out and the water's low
travelers from the coast go to and fro.

26
Nor could your loving spouse, O Altamor,
hold you within the cove of her chaste bed.
She wept to thwart your fatal journey, tore
her blond hair, beat her breasts. "Cruel man!" she said,
"the rough face of the sea delights you more
than the eyes and the lips of her you wed!
And weapons are a dearer weight to lay
upon your arms than your sweet son at play."

27
He is the mighty King of Samarkand;
his least of merits, that his crown is free.
All strategies of war in his command,
he joins the greatest strength with bravery.
That the French fear him, one can understand,
for they will know his prowess—I foresee.
With mail his fighters' backs are fortified,
mace at the hip and saber at the side.

28
Then from the Indies to the house of dawn
the fierce Adrastus comes. The coat of mail
upon his shoulders sports a giant snake,
black maculations on the bright green scale;
massive, he rides atop an elephant's back
and spurs him like a horse upon the trail.
He brings his men from west of the Ganges,
where the great Indus interrupts the seas.

29
In the battalion following come the flower
of the royal militia: here is led
each man whose deeds in war and peacetime shower
honor and gratitude upon his head.
He never rests secure, he'll never cower,
but rides upright upon his thoroughbred,
his purple mantle notable and bright,
dashing the sky with gold and brazen light.

30
With them the crude Alarc, and Idrahort,
and the battalion's leader, Odemar,
and Rimedon, illustriously bold:
for mortal men and death he had no care.
And Tigran, and Ormondo strong of limb,
and the sea tyrant Rapold, the great corsair,
and Marlabust Arabian, so named
for the rebel Arabia he tamed.

31
Orindo, Arimon, Pirga, and Brimart
the trampler-down of cities, and Siphant
breaker of horses, and, master of the art
of wrestling, you were there, Aridamant,
and Tissaphernes, thunderbolt of Mars;
who boasts that he is your equivalent?
On horseback or afoot, no man's your peer,
whether he whirls the sword or aims the spear.

32
Their captain, though, is an Armenian prince
who from the true faith took an errant swing
toward paganism when he was young, called since
Emiren; Clement at his christening.
Of all who ride in the saddle no man is
more loved and trusted by the Egyptian king.
He is both captain and a sovereign knight,
for heart and mind, and for his right arm's might.

33
No one remained, when suddenly there came
Armida with her armies dressed to show.
In her great chariot she rode sublime;
her gown tucked up, her back armed with the bow.
Her new looks of contempt now mingle with
her face's native sweetness, and bestow
vigor upon them: like a pungent spice
her threatening—and you'd love to see it twice!

34
Her chariot was like that which brings the day,
with rubies and the gleam of chrysolite;
four unicorns in pairs she reins at bay
(the cunning charioteer can guide them right).
A hundred girls and page boys in array,
their shoulders slung with bows, complete the sight,
spurring the backs of their white steeds apace,
war stallions quick to turn, and light to race.

35
Her army follows, Aradin their lord,
the force Hydrotes mustered in Syria.
And as at times that only reborn bird
visits her kind in Ethiopia—
her dappled feathers and her golden crest,
the plumes that ring her throat, so overawe
the others, they fly with her or behind,
marveling, like an army in the wind;

36
so now Armida, marvelous in her style,
her looks, her manners. Souls disdainful of
affection, inhumane, there may have been,
but they immediately fell in love.
If she can, when her face is hardly seen,
and when at that it's harshly scowling, move
so many men, how might she tyrannize
with the beauty of her smile and flattering eyes?

37
But when she too has passed, the king of kings
calls Emiren, who answers to the call;
what of the excellent chiefs this army brings?
Emiren shall be leader of them all.
So he approaches to assume his merits
with a brow worthy of a general.
The cohort of Circassians parts in two
to make way to the throne. He ascends, with due

38
reverence, kneeling, hand upon his breast,
his head bowed in humility. And the king said,
"To you this scepter, Emiren, to you
I give this army. Rule them in my stead,
and bring down, as you free my vassal king,
my vengeful wrath upon the Frenchman's head!
Go, see, and conquer! Kill all, if you can,
or lead in bondage every living man."

39
So said the tyrant, and the knight took hold
of the rod of sovereign authority.
"My lord, from your invincible hand, with bold
auspices of success I go," said he,
"on this great quest, confident in your power
to avenge Asia's bitter misery.
Unless in triumph, I shall not return:
better to lose and die, than live in scorn.

40
"I pray to heaven, if the unfortunate
happens—which I believe impossible—
let it be gathered in one evil fate
and on my head let the whole tempest fall!
Let the field be won, and the captain lie in state
more for a triumph than a funeral."
At that the crowd broke into hearty cheers
mixed with the blare of barbarian trumpeters.

41
Among the cries and blarings, amid the dense
thronging of barons, see the king depart
to take his banquet in the royal tents
with all his captains. There he sits apart,
and to each lucky man he would dispense
food, it may be, or chat, and leave no part
unhonored. Armida finds the mood is fit
for her art too, so she commences it.

42
And as the plates were cleared away, she saw
all eyes upon her, focused and intent.
Her poison had been sown in each man's mind,
she knew; for all the signs were evident.
She rose, and from her chair turned to the king,
her manner at once proud and reverent.
To set her face, her voice, she plies her art
that she might seem both fierce and great of heart.

43
"Great emperor, I too have come," said she,
"to labor for my faith and for my nation.
I am a woman, but of royalty.
For a queen to fight is no humiliation!
Who wants to rule must use the arts of rule:
scepter and sword are one hand's obligation.
I'll strike and wound and shed their blood, my lord—
my hand will not be slow to swing the sword!

44
"Don't think this is the first day I have been
carried away by such a proud desire:
for our law and your empire I have seen
action already, fighting fire with fire.
You've heard reports of some of what I've done,
so you can readily see that I'm no liar,
and you know that I've held as prisoners
the greatest of the Cross's warriors.

45
"By me these champions all were bound, by me
sent on as a magnificent gift to you,
and in some deep blind dungeon they'd still be
serving their endless sentence, and you too
would rule your realm with more security
and win this battle—all this would be true
were it not for the savage Rinaldo: he
slaughtered my men and set the Christians free.

46
"Who this Rinaldo is, you all know well.
You've all heard stories of his valor and might.
He is the cruel man of whom I tell,
who hurt me—and I've not avenged the spite.
Hate joins with Reason to apply the whip
and makes me all the readier to fight.
It would be long to tell my injury.
Let this alone suffice, I wish to be

47
"avenged—and shall be so! For not in vain
is every arrow carried by the wind,
and sometimes even heaven fights the profane,
brandishing weapons in its just right hand.
But if some one here fights that inhumane
barbarous man and chops off his foul head,
then gives me it—although more nobly done
if it were done by me—I'd look upon

48
"that vengeance with some favor, yes indeed . . .
I'd give him the best gift I can afford:
a dowry of my treasure and myself
to marry, should he claim me for reward.
So here I vow, and I will not be moved;
so here I pledge my faith, I give my word.
Anyone here who wants to undergo it,
who thinks I'm worth the hazard—speak, and show it."

49
Adrastus stared at her with lusty eyes
all while the lovely lady pleaded so.
"The gods forbid! That barbarous murderer
should not be touched by an arrow from your bow!
For that villainous heart, O heavenly archer,
does not deserve the glory you bestow.
Let me be servant to your wrath instead
and I'll make you a present of his head.

50

"I'll rip his heart out by the roots—I'll give
his carcass to the buzzards for a feast!"
So spoke Adrastus, proudest man alive.
Tissaphernes couldn't bear this in the least
and broke in, "Who are you, in the presence of
the king and us, to make so big a boast?
There's one man here who'll put that boast to rout
with deeds, I think—someone who shuts his mouth."

51

"I am a man," the Indian replied,
"whose deeds speak for themselves, whose words are few.
If we'd been somewhere fitter when you spoke,
they'd be the last words ever mouthed by you."
And the king of kings had to restrain them both
with his right hand, before the fracas grew.
"O noble lady," said he to Armida then,
"you have a greater heart than many men,

52

"and worthy that these two should pledge their wrath
and hatred as a gift. So take each one,
turn them at will against that predator,
that mighty criminal, Bertoldo's son.
Better employed there! Show your courage there,
strive to shine brighter by comparison."
So the competing warriors professed
they'd put their avenging prowess to the test;

53

nor they alone, but all who would appear
ready to boast their warlike deeds so great
offer themselves to her, and they all swear
vengeance upon that execrable pate.
Against that champion she once held dear
she marshals armies now, awakens hate.
But he, once he had left her shores behind,
set out on his great journey with fair wind.

54

By the same route it took in sailing there
the little boat returned across the sea,
its sails puffed full with the brisk favoring air,
crossing the distance no less speedily.
The lad now looks at the Pole Star, and the Bear,
and all the shining stars in the Milky Way,
a way through the dark of night. A river now
they sail past, or a cliff with rugged brow.

55
He listens to the state of things back home;
he hears of various people and their ways.
They now have traveled on the salty foam
for four suns' dawning into shining days,
when to the harbor finally they come
at the last dropping of the evening rays.
Said Fortune, "We are on Judea's shore.
We do not need to voyage any more."

56
Here the three knights put off upon the beach.
Before one word was spoken, she was gone.
Meanwhile the night had fallen, stealing each
countenance and confounding all in one.
They saw no roof, no shelter within reach;
in all that solitude of desert, none,
no trace of man or horse or anything
to show the road they should be traveling.

57
When they had stood a little while in doubt,
they started on, their backs turned to the sea.
But look! far off, something they can't make out,
who can tell what, glittering luminously,
with streaks of gold and rays of silvery light,
flooding the night and making darkness flee.
At that the cavaliers approach the light
and now see what it is that shines so bright:

58
On a huge trunk they see a fire-new suit
of armor in the moonlight, hanging high,
gems in the golden helmet and the coat
flashing their fire like the brightest stars in the sky,
and in the light that strikes the shield a long
relief of splendid images. Nearby
there sat an aged man who seemed the guard
of the bright armor. As he saw them, toward

59
the knights he came, and two of them knew well
the venerable face of their wise friend.
He took their happy greetings and welcomed them
with all the courtesy he could extend.
Then to the boy, who silently looked at him,
he spoke these words: "My wait is at an end.
My lord," said he, "you are the only one
for whom I have been longing here, alone.

60
"You may not know it, but I am your friend.
Ask them how much I've cared for you, for they
crushed, with my help, the spell which held you bound,
wasting your miserable life away.
Now hear my words and let them not offend:
forget the Siren's song, heed what I say,
cherish it, till a wiser and holier man
shows you the truth more clearly than I can.

61
"My lord, not with the Sirens and sweet nymphs,
with flowers and shady groves, with streams and dells,
but at the summit of the ruggedest cliff
is where our highest good and virtue dwells.
The man who does not freeze or sweat or lift
himself past pleasure's road, never excels.
In the dim valleys do you wish to lie,
you who were born an eagle to soar high?

62
"Nature created you to raise your head
and filled you with a proud and noble soul,
to look up high, and with each brilliant deed
to earn the highest praises, and extol
yourself. She also made your temper quick,
not to scrap with your comrades, not to dole
sweet things to an insatiable desire,
far out of tune with Reason; no, this ire

63
"was given to arm your courage, that you might
more fiercely fight the outer enemy,
repressing all immoderate delight,
the foe within, wicked cupidity.
The prudent leader learns to use it right,
governs it for its proper destiny:
cools it or heats it, as his reason deigns,
now spurs it on, now tightens up the reins."

64
So he said, and Rinaldo took these words
of deep advice intently, silently,
as it were chastened; and turned his brow towards
the earth for shame. But the old man could see
his secret trouble, for his wisdom was
ever awake. "Look up, my son," said he,
"and fix your eyes upon this shield, where all
your fathers' glorious deeds are visible.

65
"You'll see their honor ever widening—
heralded in a harsh and lonely place;
meanwhile you lag behind, malingering
in the arena of glory's famous race.
Get up, move on! Let what I show you sting
your valor into action, as I trace
the meaning of these figures sculpted here."
And the shield held the eyes of the cavalier,

66
for the learned smith, with subtle mastery,
had graven endless shapes in a narrow field,
showing the glorious Actian progeny
in an unbroken order on the shield,
and the pristine Roman source was there to see,
and its pure derivations, all revealed,
and princes crowned with laurel. The old man
shows them the wars they fought, the praise they won.

67
He shows him Caius, when barbarians
preyed upon Rome already in decline:
makes himself first prince of the Esteans,
holding his fleeing populace in line;
his weaker neighbors thus regain their lands
and give themselves to him, whom they assign
the governorship. And when Honorius
invites the cruel Alaric to recross

68
the mountains into Italy, and the fire
of the barbarian seems to spread and grow,
and when great Rome, a servile prisoner,
fears its annihilation high and low,
he shows Aurelius keeping his nation free
under his scepter. The next man to show
is Paduan Forestus, valiant one
who fought the eastern tyrant, the great Hun.

69
Easy to spot the cruel Attila—
he seems to look out of a dragon's eyes;
he has a dog's face—you'd say, if you saw,
it must be howling, you could hear the cries!
Beaten in single combat then, see how
among the other warriors he flies,
using his eastern host as his protector
against Forestus, the Italian Hector;

70
whose death was pictured in another place,
and his own and the destiny of his land.
Behold his heir, the champion of our race,
Acarinus, the grand son of a father grand.
They built their town anew in a safer place,
gave way to fate, not to the Hun's command,
then gathering the scattered villages made grow
a city in the valley of the Po.

71
Against that mighty stream they banked a wall
to hold its floods, and then the city rose,
in future centuries the capital
of the greathearted Estes. Then the foes
from Germany he vanquished, till his fall
at Odoacer's hands. Thus did he lose
his life for Italy—O noble death,
that makes him honored in the very breath

72
honoring his father! Alforisius
his brother fell with him; and here you see
Actius in exile, then returning with
armies and counsel, when that tyranny
was overthrown. Epaminondas of
the Estes followed, pierced through the right eye
by the Goth's arrow; yet he dies content,
his shield intact, the brutal Totila sent

73
to a sound defeat: I speak of Boniface.
Valerian follows in his father's track,
a boy with a man's strength and a man's heart.
One hundred bands of Goths can't hold him back.
Not far away, scowling Ernestus stands
who whipped the Slavs so badly they'd attack
no more; beside him, the fearless Aldovard
who rid Monselce of the royal Lombard.

74
Then Henry came, then Berengario: where
the great Charles spreads his banners to the skies,
he seems to be the first attacker there,
captain of every worthy enterprise.
Then he followed King Louis, and waged war
on his own nephew Bernard, Italy's
ruler; and won, and took him prisoner.
Then Otto with his five tall sons was there,

75
and Almeric, who became first marquis of
Ferrara, the great lady of the Po.
He looks to heaven with devoted love,
a founder of churches, contemplative. Not so
Actius the Second, who was seen to move
a bitter strife with Berengario,
and after fortune tilted either way
he won: all Italy beneath his sway.

76
See his son Albert go among the Germans,
and make his virtues such a source of awe,
victor in tourneys, victor against the Danes,
that Otto unpursed to buy a son-in-law.
See Hugo at his back, who broke the Romans,
who held their bullish pride not worth a straw,
who called himself marquis of Italy
and held for hostage all of Tuscany.

77
Tedaldo then, and Boniface his son,
standing beside his wife, good Beatrice:
yet he brought forth no heir to take upon
himself his father's great inheritance,
none but Matelda; she was only one,
a woman, yet she made good recompense
for those defects: and many a sceptered crown
this wise, brave woman made subject to her gown.

78
In her noble face there dwells a manly soul,
and more than manly vigor in her eye.
She beat the Normans, and the invincible
Robert Guiscard; she made his soldiers fly;
beat Henry the Fourth, took his imperial
standards and in her temple hung them high;
then reinstalled the highest Pontiff in
the chair of Peter in the Vatican.

79
Now, as a man who loves and honors, see
Actius the Fifth, behind her, or at her side.
But in more fertile branches the progeny
of the fourth Actius sooner fructified:
his son Guelph hears the call of Germany,
the son of Cunegund goes there to bide;
so the good Roman seed, with the fates willing,
is taken to Bavarian soil for tilling.

80
The Guelphian tree, itself devoid of bloom,
seemed to be grafted with an Estean limb;
and then you saw the monarch Guelphs resume,
scepters and golden crowns, in finer trim
than ever before, with benign stars to illume
its constant growth. The limit of its climb
is heaven itself; for half of Germany
it takes, while giving shade to the whole country.

81
And yet the royal stock blossomed no less
resplendently on the Italian side.
Guelph was matched here by Berthold; the ancient race
of the Esteans was revivified
by Actius the Sixth. Such were the heroes which
appeared to live and move and breathe, portrayed
on the metal shield. Rinaldo, studying, wakes
spirits of honor, kindles the fiery flakes

82
of his ancestral pride, and his bold heart
is moved, is swept away, longing to show
virtue to emulate his fathers'; thought
is no thought, but appears as present now,
his dreams of battering the city in the onslaught
of battle, and slaying men—he can see how—
and he arms in haste, and with his quick hopes he
has already usurped the victory.

83
But Charles, who had on the voyage given him word
of the death of the royal Danish heir,
presents him now with the predestined sword.
"Take it," he says, "and let your fortune be fair;
brandish it only for the faith of the Lord,
give piety and justice equal share
with strength. For its first master, vengeance is due.
He loved you dearly; it is up to you."

84
He replied to the soldier, "May it please
heaven, that the hand that takes this sword today
wreak vengeance on its master's enemies!
By my means, let it pay what it should pay."
Charles turned to him with gladness in his eyes
and all the gratitude he felt, to say
long thanks in a few words. But the Wise Man
hastens them on their trek before the dawn.

85
“High time for us to leave! The hosts await,
the great Bouillon awaits. You’re needed there
at once. Let’s go! I’ll take you to a spot
where you will see their tents through the twilight air.”
He spoke, and climbed into his chariot,
bringing aboard the others, not to spare
a moment, freeing his steeds for a dead run,
whipping them, turning their course to the rising sun.

86
So they flew through the night air, silently,
when the old man turned to the boy, and said,
“Now you have seen your proud old ancestry,
the deep roots, and the branches it has bred.
But if your mother has borne heroes, she
is no less fertile now, she has not shed
along with youth her happy vigor too:
her years grow old, her virtue’s ever new.

87
“And as I’ve drawn forth from the misty cave
of ancient days your fathers, to you unknown,
so I could also tell you of your brave
descendants, as the centuries go on,
and tell the world of them before they have
opened their eyes to the calm light of dawn.
You’d see those heroes in no shorter line,
nor would their valorous deeds more dimly shine.

88
“But my art cannot see into the future,
for there the truth more deeply hidden lies,
unless I see it smoky, blurred, obscure,
like a torch in the mists. If I advise
you of a thing as if it were quite sure,
I’m not presumptuous. By another’s eyes
I’m made aware, one who can sometimes see
the unveiled secrets of the heavenly.

89
“I shall now tell you what the light of heaven
revealed to him, what to me he foretold.
Never to any race has it been given,
barbarian, Latin, Greek, modern or old,
to be as rich in heroes as friendly heaven
destines for yours. Let their names be enrolled
by the wisest poets in the age to come
with those of Sparta, Carthage, and old Rome.

90
"Among the rest I choose Alfonso," he said,
"the first in virtue, second of that name,
who will be born in a world corrupt and old,
and poor in any men deserving fame.
No better man than he to wield the sword
or scepter, none can make a finer claim
to bear the weight of arms or diadem—
the glory of your blood, its brightest gem.

91
"A boy, he shall, in images of war,
show signs of his exalted bravery;
terror of wild beasts in the woods, but more
praised in the tournaments, till finally
he shall return, a man, from a true war,
with the Best Spoils and palms of victory,
and often, in honor, it shall come to pass,
they'll crown his hair with laurel, oak, or grass.

92
"No less worthy of praise will be the works
of peace and quiet in his maturity,
to keep his town, neighbored by lands at war,
powerful cities, in tranquility,
to nourish and spread the arts and sciences,
hold famous tournaments and pageantry,
weigh in just scales rewards and punishments,
and look ahead, providing for all events.

93
"If only he'd attack those infidels
who will infest the lands, infest the seas,
who will give laws to a people that excels
their own, and make them buy a wretched peace;
if he would take up arms to avenge the temples
ruined, the altars desecrated, these
tyrants would feel the justice of his arm,
and what a justice done, to their great harm!

94
"In vain the Turk against him, or the Moor,
would bring to war their thousand infantries,
for past the snowy summit of Mount Taur,
and past the banks of the River Euphrates,
and past where summer reigns forevermore
he'd bring the Cross, the eagle, the fleur-de-lis,
and to baptize the black-faced men he'd go
discover the springs whence the Nile's waters flow."

95
So spoke the old man, and as the boy took
these words to heart, his happiness increased,
for the thought of his future progeny
inspired a quiet pleasure in his breast.
Meanwhile the dawn, the harbinger of day,
arose, and changed the countenance of the east,
and now, far off, the camp first came in sight,
the pennons trembling in the morning light.

96
Again the wise magician spoke, to say,
"You see the sun now shining full in front
to illuminate for you with a friendly ray
the tents, the plains, the city, and the Mount.
Safe from all outrage, safe from all delay
I've led you here, by ways none can recount.
You need no guide now. Go, approach, alone—
it is not fit that I continue on."

97
He bid farewell, left the knights on their way
afoot, and rode his chariot back home.
They followed their path into the newborn day,
turning to the pavilions. And now from
one end of the camp to the other men convey
the news: the long-awaited knights have come!
And the fame outruns them so that Godfrey hears
and leaves his tent to greet his cavaliers.

Canto Eighteen

1
Arriving at the place where Godfrey stood
to meet him at return, Rinaldo began:
"My lord, a jealous care for honor spurred
my revenge on the soldier who was slain.
If I've offended you, I since have suffered
true remorse in my heart. I've come again
to meet your call—I'm ready to redeem
myself, and to win back your good esteem."

2
At that he humbly fell upon his knee.
But round Rinaldo's neck the captain threw
his arms and said, "Let painful memories be.
Forget what's past. All I require from you
to make amends is that you fight for me,
doing the glorious things you used to do,
and for our good, and the harm of our enemies,
to rid the monsters dwelling among the trees.

3
"The ancient forest which provided us
with the material for our ordonnance,
is like a shut room, who knows by what cause,
a den of terrors which some spell enchants.
No one now dares to cut a single branch,
and reason shows we need those instruments
to lay the city low. Where others fear,
show now your valor as a cavalier."

4
So Godfrey; and the knight offered himself
for the work and the risk. His words were few;
but you could look to his greathearted stance,
not to his tongue, to tell how much he'd do.
And now he turns a joyful smile and hand
to take the friendly cheers of all the crew;
Tancred and Guelph and all the leaders came
to give him greetings. He returned the same

5
many times over, moved by the honest show
of love the highest of the soldiers made;
then with an affable and peaceful glow
he greets the lesser men in that parade—
the crowds so thick, their shouts so full of joy,
had he beaten the South and East and been conveyed
before them in a rich triumphal car
they hardly could have been the happier.

6
So he walked on until he reached his tent
where he sat with his close friends at his side,
asking them of the woods, how the battle went,
and to their questions he in turn replied.
But soon they took their leave of him and lent
the Hermit chance to speak. "You've traveled wide,
my lord, and have discovered marvelous things
on your long pilgrimage and wanderings.

7
"How much you owe the great King of the world!
He led you out of the enchanted land
like a lost lamb brought back among the fold.
You are the one, under Bouillon's command,
whom heaven elects second executor
of its designs, accomplished by your hand.
Yet that hand is profaned. It is not right
to bear polluted arms in the Lord's sight.

8
"You are still so bespattered with the flesh
and the smoke of this world, if you would be
made clean and bright again, not all the wash
of the Ganges or the Nile or the deep sea
would be sufficient: only heaven's grace
can cleanse your soul of its iniquity.
Turn then to heaven, beg pardon humbly, lay
your secret sins before Him. Weep, and pray."

9
And for the first time in his heart he wept
for all his haughty pride and foolish love.
He knelt, and sadly, humbly, told him all
the wandering sins his youth was guilty of.
After the Hermit gave him absolution,
that chosen minister of heaven above
said, "With the new dawn, climb that hill to pray—
the one whose summit sees the morning ray.

10
"Go to the forest where the phantoms throng,
images of illusion and deceit.
Unless some other error draws you along—
some foolishness—I know you will defeat
the giants and monsters. Ah, but let no soft song,
no tears, or smile, or looks however sweet,
tenderly flatter your heart to bend their way:
false looks, false pleas, not worth what you would pay."

11
That was the holy man's advice. The knight
readied himself, in hope and in desire,
for the high deed. A thoughtful day, a night
thoughtful and sad; and then before the fire
of dawn, he buckled on his shining arms,
but a new cloak completed his attire,
new, of strange color. On foot and all alone
he left his friends in silence, and set on.

12
It was the hour when darkness has not yet
left every frontier free to take the light,
but you could see the rose blush of the east
while here and there the stars were glittering bright,
when the lad turned his steps toward Olivet,
and with his eyes raised, gazed upon the sight
of night and morning, contemplating all
their beauty, holy, incorruptible.

13
And he thought to himself, "What lovely lights
are glittering in heaven's temple! Day
has its great chariot, and the silver moon
and golden stars shine in their night array,
but no one takes delight in them. Instead
we gaze upon the dim and murky play
of a flash of a smile, a glance of the eyes
in the brief limits of a face that dies."

14
With such thoughts in his mind he climbed the top,
and there he prayed, kneeling and reverent,
lifting his thoughts beyond the highest heaven
with his eyes fixed upon the orient:
"Look upon my first life and my first sins
with an eye of compassion, and be clement,
Father and Lord; rain your grace on me to
purge my old Adam, and create me new."

15
That was his prayer, and now there rose before him
the crimson dawn already streaked with gold,
to illuminate the top of the green hill
and gild his helmet and his armor bold,
and in his mind and heart he feels the breath
of peaceful spirits, which the heavens unfold
from the lap of a dewy cloud, to shower
their grace upon him in that lovely hour.

16
The dew of heaven fell upon his clothes
which were originally the color of ash,
but now endowed with an immaculate light
and all their pallor gone. So the cool wash
of morning touches the dry petals of
a dying flower and makes its beauty fresh;
so too the serpent, once more young and bold,
rejoices in his new skin flecked with gold.

17
He too admires the color of his vest,
changed to a candor beautiful and pure.
And now he makes his way to the deep forest,
his confidence is firm, his steps are sure.
He has already reached the outer test
where men less brave than he could not endure
merely the eerie sight the forest made:
for him no terror, but a pleasant shade.

18
He goes on; all at once he hears a sound
pouring about him sweetly, and perceives
it is the murmur of a rushing brook
and the sigh of the wind among the leaves
and the lamenting music of a swan
and the reply of the nightingale who grieves,
and organs and zithers, and a human song:
to this one sound all of these sounds belong.

19
The knight was waiting for some thunderclap
(such as left all the others frightened so),
but heard the Nymphs and Sirens, the sweet chirp
of birds; the waters rush, the breezes blow.
In some surprise at first he holds his step,
then he continues, in suspense, and slow,
and in his path no other obstacle
but a river passing by, gentle, tranquil . . .

20
The river was adorned on either side
with fragrances and lovely sights to lend
delight; its hornlike course traveled so wide
it gathered the whole grove within the bend,
yet did not garland it: but a divide
was made by a small channel end to end,
so the river watered the forest, and they made
sweet interplay of water and of shade.

21
While the knight searches for a place to ford,
behold, a miracle, a bridge appears,
a dazzling bridge of gold, which could provide
wide space to cross upon its steadfast piers.
He crosses—but when he touches the other shore
at once the structure falls and disappears
into the water, no gentle river now
but a sweeping torrent. As with melting snow

22
he sees the river swelling over the brim,
engorged with whitecaps which it sweeps away,
turning upon itself, crashing and gurgling,
everywhere eddy and falls and splash and spray.
Yet a desire to see new things attracts him
to find what in the ancient forest lay,
and ever some new miracle he sees
deep in that shady solitude of trees.

23
For in his footprints everywhere he goes
life seems to sprout at once or leap or gush:
the lily blooms, the bud reveals the rose,
a spring wells up, a streamlet's waters rush,
and round him and above him, full of years,
the trees put forth their young leaves strong and lush,
and the bark softens, and with a gladder sheen
every green growing plant renews its green.

24
And every leaf is hung with manna dew,
honey seeps from the bark of every tree,
and he hears that lilting melody anew,
singing and grieving in strange harmony,
but the tenor to the air and swan and wave,
the human voice, no telling where it might be:
he can't see what might make a human sound
nor any musical instruments around.

25
While he was looking, and his thoughts denied
what his senses were insisting was the truth,
he saw a myrtle standing to one side,
in a large clearing leading from a path.
And that strange myrtle spread its branches wide,
taller than palm or cypress. Its crown's girth
covered the trees and towered above them all;
it seemed to be the forest's capitol.

26
A greater novelty now holds his eyes,
for as he stands in that great woodland room
he sees an oak that slits itself lengthwise
to open and give birth from its hollow womb,
and a nymph, full grown and dressed in a strange guise—
miraculous—steps forth. And with her come
a hundred other nymphs, and all of these
born from the pregnant bosoms of the trees.

27
As in the theater or gallery
we see portrayed the woodland goddesses,
their skirts tucked high, their arms unclothed and free,
with pretty buskins and disheveled tresses,
such appeared now the wood-born coterie
(appeared wood-born, but all illusionesses),
except none had a bow and arrow with her:
instead a lute or violin or zither.

28
They formed themselves into a sort of crown
and started dancing round and caroling,
circling the warrior as if he were
the enclosed point, the center of their ring.
They danced about the myrtle too; he heard
words such as these while listening to them sing:
"Dear is your coming to this pleasant grove!
You are our lady's only hope and love.

29
"You come in time to give health to the sick,
wounded and parched with amorous thoughts of you!
You see this forest which was once so dark—
conforming to her sorrow—how it grew
glad again when you came, touched to the quick,
dressing itself in loveliness anew."
Such was the song, and the sweetest melody
came forth from the now-opening myrtle tree.

30
In ancient days the crossroad Sileni
would open wonders to the traveler,
but that grand myrtle's bosom showed the eye
images rarer and far lovelier:
it showed a woman of angelic beauty
in her false semblance. Rinaldo looked at her,
and in the sight he suddenly could trace
Armida's likeness and her lovely face.

31
She gazes on him sadly, joyfully,
a thousand feelings mingled in one look.
Then says, "At last I see you, finally
you have come back to her whom you forsook.
But why have you come back? To solace my
now widowed nights, and my sad days? Or break
your truce with me and drive me from this place?
You show your sword, but hide your handsome face.

32
"Lover or foe, which is it? That rich bridge—
I didn't build it for an enemy . . .
or open the springs and flowers and rushing streams
or clear the thorns, to let you come to me.
Take off your helmet, if you come a friend;
show me your face, ah, show your eyes to me;
let us join lips to lips, and breast to breast,
or take my hand within your hand at least . . ."

33
She spoke, and spoke, and turned her pretty eyes
pitifully, with blushing in the cheek,
and falsified low sobs and honeyed sighs,
lamenting in the loveliest technique.
A thoughtless pity for such sorrowful lies
might make the hardest heart of adamant meek—
still the knight, not savage, but aware, ignored
the lady, and unsheathed his naked sword.

34
He approaches the myrtle—but at once
she comes between, embracing the dear wood,
crying, "It can't be true, that you would cut
my tree, and hurt me so! Put down your sword,
pitiless man, or drive it straight into
unhappy Armida's veins, to drink her blood!
This breast, this heart of mine alone will be
the way to come to my sweet myrtle tree."

35
He lifts his sword, and does not heed her prayer.
But her form changes—oh monstrosity!—
as often in a dream, as clouds in air,
one shape shifts to another suddenly.
Her limbs grew massive, and the face so fair
darkened—no roses now, no ivory.
She swelled into a giant wielding arms,
a Briareus with a hundred arms,

36
seething and threatening with his fifty swords
and fifty clashing shields on either side.
Each other nymph took arms and was transformed
into a horrible Cyclops; unterrified,
he doubled his blows against the defended plant—
with each stroke, like a living thing, it cried.
Like the air of the fields of Styx was this field's air,
so many devilish prodigies were there.

37
The troubled sky above, the earth below
thunder—and earthquakes tremble, and lightnings lace,
and the rain batters down and the storm winds blow
the bitterest of tempests in his face;
the knight's sword never misses even so,
nor does that fury make him ease his pace
till he chops—no myrtle—the black walnut tree.
The phantoms disappeared, the sorcery

38
ended. The air was still, the sky was calm.
The wood reverted to its natural state,
not magically terrible, or lush;
what fearfulness it had was all innate.
The victor checks to see that nothing else
prevents the timber now from being cut,
then smiles and says, "Such empty fantasies.
A man's a fool to pause for things like these."

39
He made his way back to the camp; at once
Peter the Hermit cried for all to hear:
"The terrible magic of the woods has lost!
He's coming, the triumphant cavalier!
I see him now." Far off, in a white robe,
he came in sight, venerable and severe,
and his silver-eagle crest in the morning light
dazzled the eye, exceptionally bright.

40
In the joyous camp the men hurrah him with
such shouts of gladness that their cries resound—
and with glad honor the reverent Bouillon
received him, and none envied him or frowned.
Then to the captain said the warrior:
"I went to the dreadful woods as I was bound;
I saw it, saw, and defeated the spells. Now your
workers can go—the roads are all secure."

41
So they went to the ancient woods, and cut
material a shrewd architect selected.
The builder of the first machines had not
mastered the art by which these are perfected,
but now a famous craftsman has the job,
who knows how studs and crossbeams are connected:
William, Duke of Liguria; it was he
whose small ships had the run of all the sea.

42
But William could not hold the Saracen
whose great armada forced him to retreat,
so he withdrew his weapons and his men
and led them to the barracks from the fleet.
Among the shrewdest engineers back then
was he, hard-working, whom no man could beat.
He had his hundred carpenters, to find
a way to make whatever he designed.

43
Not only did he build the catapults,
the rams, the flingers of the javelin,
to sweep the defenders off the battlements
and batter those thick walls and smash them in—
but he made a finer work, a marvelous tower,
studded together with pine and fir within,
but with a fire protector on the outside,
for it was wound about with strips of hide.

44
They peg and fit the parts of the machine;
with subtle joints they join it into one.
The beam which bore the head of the battering ram
butted out from the bottom; a bridge was thrown
out from the middle, and this would often catch
the opposite wall on the first attempt; but on
the top of the works a smaller tower rose,
cranked up the taller to assail the foes.

45
Over the straight and level ways it ran
upon a hundred wheels almost at will—
pregnant with weapons, pregnant with armed men,
easy to move about. The squads stood still,
marveling at the towering machine,
the unknown art, the workmen's clever skill.
And then they built another two as fine
according to the first machine's design.

46
Meanwhile the Saracens knew in the main
what they were up to, for they were exposed
in part, at least, upon the nearby plain
to sentries watching from their rampart post,
who saw pass by baggage train after train
conveying ash and pine wood to the host,
and they saw some machines, but couldn't guess
from so far off their forms or purposes.

47
They too build their machines, and with great art
they reinforce the towers and the wall,
building it on one side to such great height
(the side in battle likeliest to fall)
they think that now the god of war's great might
would not suffice to smash it. Above all
these citywide defenses they prepare,
Ismen concocts fireworks, bizarre and rare,

48
from sulfur and bitumen (in a mix)
which the bad mage had mined from the Sea of Sodom;
and visited (as I think) the River Styx
which circles hell nine times from top to bottom,
so it is that their fire both smokes and stinks
and flares in the face (because of where he got 'em).
He thinks his fierce explosives will excel,
avenging the hewn woods he loved so well.

49
The army was preparing to attack
and the town to defend, as I have said,
when through the airy way a dove was seen
by the French army, flying overhead,
and never let his nimble feathers slack,
gliding the liquid road with wings outspread:
and now the pilgrim messenger veers down
from the clouds toward the ramparts of the town,

50
when swooping out of nowhere comes a hawk
who cuts her off between the camp and wall,
armed with his mighty talons and hooked beak.
She doesn't want to fight this brute at all—
he dives upon her, drives her to the peak
of the highest tent, now seems to catch her, fall
upon her soft neck, let his pincers snap—
but she hides in the pious Bouillon's lap.

51
Godfrey gathers her in and saves her life,
then looks at her, and marks a curious thing:
hid under one of her wings a folded card,
fastened about her neck by a little string.
He cuts it loose and opens it—and well
takes in the news its brief sentences bring:
"To Judea's lord" (for such was written there)
"from the captain of Egypt, greetings. Do not fear,

52
"resist, my lord, be patient, and endure
at least until the fourth or the fifth day.
I come to liberate those walls. Be sure,
you'll see the conquest of your enemy."
That was the secret, in the signature
of the barbarian's letters, sent to fly
with the carrier pigeon, for in those days they used
such couriers in the Levant. The prince loosed

53
the dove and set her free; but the dove stayed,
having revealed the secret—as if she
blamed herself for a rebel, her lord betrayed,
and did not want to tell the calamity.
The great duke called the lesser dukes and laid
the news before them, saying, "Now you see
how all things are made open to us by
the providence of the Lord our God on high.

54
"And so I think we should waste no more time,
but try to raze the city's walls anew!
Spare no sweat, spare no labor in the climb,
but scale and conquer the walls to the south. It's true,
there'll be some hard, rough going there, but I'm
confident. I've noted the passes to break through.
That wall is propped by natural defense
so it won't be well stocked with armaments

55
"or soldiers. Raymond, you go to that side,
batter the walls with your artillery;
meanwhile against the northern gate I'll ride
with my men, and the great machinery.
The foe will see that and be led aside
thinking to take the worst attack from me,
but my great tower, which we can roll with ease,
will roll elsewhere against the enemies.

56
"Camillus, you'll be manning the third tower
at the same time, not far away from me."
Silence; and Raymond, who sat next to him,
and while he spoke was thinking quietly,
now said, "Godfrey's advice is perfect, nothing
to add or take away. Only I'd be
happier yet if we could send some spy
to find the enemy's secrets on the sly,

57
"tell us their numbers and their strategy,
and bring reliable word of their condition
as best he can." Then "I have a valet,"
said Tancred, "who is perfect for this mission.
He's handy and sharp, and fast on his feet besides;
he's daring, yes, but daring with discretion.
He can speak many languages, and talk
in various accents, and even change his walk."

58
This valet came when summoned. When he heard
what Godfrey and his master wanted done,
he raised his head and smiled, and took the job,
saying, "Give me a moment, I'll be gone!
Right away I'll be where they're pitching tents.
I'll be your spy, unknown to anyone.
In broad day I'll go penetrate their wall.
Horses and men? For you I'll count them all!

59
"The size and the components of that host
and what their chiefs are thinking, I'll report,
I vow it! For discovery is my boast—
the private thoughts, the secrets of the heart."
So said Vafrine. Without a minute lost
he changes a long tunic for his shirt,
leaves his neck bare, and wraps long linen bands
into a turban, as in Arab lands.

60
With a Syrian bow and quiver on his back,
his every gesture came from Barbary.
All were amazed to hear his easy talk
in various tongues—so accurate was he
that whether in Tyre or Memphis, any man
would swear they shared one nationality.
Now he leaves on a stallion who hardly traces
hooves in the sand of the desert as he races.

61
But the French, before the third day had arrived,
were planing out the rough, choppy terrain,
building their war machines at these points too,
working continually, sparing no pain,
joining the night to the labors of the day,
forgetting rest. Now nothing can restrain
determination that their captain see
the uttermost of their ability.

62
The day before the day of the assault
the pious Godfrey spent much time in prayer,
and made his men confess their every fault
and attend the great supper, partaking there
of the bread of the soul. Then came the ruse,
to move the war machines exactly where
he least would use them. The pagan took the bait,
happy to see them at the well-armed gate.

63
But the gigantic war machine was rolled
to a more propitious place in the dead of night,
where the wall was not so angled, fold on fold,
and all the curves were smooth and nearly straight.
And on a hill above the city, old
Raymond stands with his tower armed to the height;
Camillus takes his nearer to that side
between the north and west. The pagans spied,

64
to their distress, in the first eastern glow,
the early morning's harbingers of day,
that where the towers were supposed to go
was not where the towers were; and every way
they look, they see more engines than they know
lifting themselves against them, an array
of endless ordnance, catlike battering swings
and catapults and rams and giant slings.

65
For their part, the pagan army was not slow
to transport many of its defenses where
Bouillon had set his war machines to go,
from where they had been waiting earlier.
The Captain, who remembered that the foe
from Egypt would be at his back, made sure
of those routes too. For that he summoned Guelph
and the two Roberts. "Arm, saddle yourselves,

66
"and see that while I scale the hill before
that wall which seems the weakest side for us,
no force can sneak behind us to bring war
and suddenly raise the siege." Instructed thus
they go, and on three sides the dire assault
begins, led by three chiefs, all valorous,
and on three sides the king defends the town—
his men resuming arms they had put down.

67
The king himself, whose body shakes with age,
and is pressed down with his own corpulent weight,
straps round his shoulders weapons long unused,
goes to meet Raymond at the northern gate.
Soliman is positioned against Godfrey,
Argante against Camillus, with the great
nephew of Bohemond. Now, Fortune, lead him on
to kill his foe, the pagan champion!

68
The archers are beginning to let fly
their weapons steeped in poison, and a pall
of black is cast over the thickening sky,
with such a cloud of arrows in their fall;
but greater blows, dealt more ferociously,
are swung by the artillery at the wall,
slinging out marble blocks and iron beams
pointed with bronze. And every hurled stone seems

69
a bolt of lightning, and what man it strikes,
it powders him and his weapons in his place,
snatching away not only his soul, his life,
but the very form of his body and his face.
And the lances don't stay stuck in a single wound
but strike their blow and hardly slack their race,
cleaving the left side, passing through the right,
flying away and bringing death in flight.

70
And yet that fury met a stiff defense.
The Saracens would not be swept away.
Against those battering waves they bring a fence
of woollen bundles, soft stuff that gives way,
so that the blow that lands is less intense:
it meets no shock, but weakens, falls away.
And they sent their bitter arrows toward the host
just where they saw the crowds exposed the most.

71
Yet for all that the triple-pronged attack
continues; the attackers do not quail;
some shelter under the great "cats," and take
upon the cat's back the battering arrow hail,
while others move the towers against the wall—
towers they can move at will—and try to break
the lower stones with the ram, steel-fortified,
while launching a bridge across to the other side.

72
Rinaldo bides his time, irresolute.
For him that risk is not a worthy one,
and honor is a paltry thing to boot,
if he takes the common way, with everyone.
He casts his eye about: finding some route
others despair of, pleases him alone.
There, where the wall was highest, best armed, quiet—
that's the spot where he longs the most to try it!

73
Attack! And to the famous fighters once
led by Dudon he turns, and says to these,
"Shame, that for all our arms those battlements
up on those walls are resting now, at peace!
Any risk is a sure thing to the brave!
The steep is level, and rough work is ease!
Let's fight them there, and against their clumsy rocks
knit shields in a tortoise shell to take the shocks."

74
At that, the soldiers clustered at his side,
every man raised a shield over the head,
and made a roof of steel, so unified,
against the horrible tempest overhead.
Under this cover the brave band defied
any attempt to slow them; on they sped,
for the solid carapace of shields sustained
all of the ruinous blows the pagans rained.

75
They're already under the wall—and now Rinaldo
directs a ladder, a hundred rungs in height,
and grasps it with an arm so firm, it moves
like a little reed that sways when the wind is light—
now lance and joist and massive columns pitch
over the edge—they cannot slow his might,
fearless, unshaken, whatever blows may fall—
Ossa and Olympus he would scorn as small!

76
A forest thick with arrows and tumbled stone
he bore on his back, and his shield took the brunt
of a mountain—but he clutches the wall with one
hand, while the other thrusts his shield in front—
by such bold deeds, deeds never before known,
he stirs his friends—he's not alone to mount,
for many plant tall ladders by the wall,
but chance and strength are not the same for all.

77
Some die, some fall; he highest of his band
pauses, inspiring these, menacing those—
and now he's climbed so high his outstretched hand
can clutch the spike of the rampart—and the foes
come thronging there to thrust him from his stand—
they push, they press, they try to make him lose
his balance—what a marvel to behold!
A huge, strong squadron, held off by one bold

78
warrior in mid-air! He fends them off,
he presses on, he but redoubles his force—
as a bent palm tree springs the harder and higher,
his strength when he's resisted gains in force—
and beats the enemy back at last, bears spears
and obstacles against him, blunts their force,
and scales the wall, and masters it, and clears
a safe way for the rest of his climbing peers.

79
And he himself, when the youngest brother of
the pious Bouillon was about to fall,
lent him a victorious hand for love
and helped him be the next to scale the wall.
Meanwhile it's shifting fortunes, dangerous moves
for the host guided by the General,
since there a total war was to be seen,
man against man, machine against machine.

80
On the walls the Syrians lifted a huge trunk
which at one time had served as a ship's mast,
and upon this with a steel-pointed head
was hung crossways a massive joist swung fast
on cables, which when pulled back and let go,
battered with all the momentum it amassed,
and made the tortoise duck to shun the wreck,
until it could again stick out its neck.

81
The huge beam hurtled forward, and so rough
were its redoubled shocks against the tower
it loosened up and split the tight-fit, tough
joints, knocking it backwards, rattled. But for
just such a threat the tower had arms enough
ready to use, and with great craft they tore
the ropes that held the joist, slicing them clean
with two long sickles swung from the machine.

82
As a huge block of stone on a mountain crashes:
loosened by age or angry winds, it rocks
and tumbles in ruin, carries away and smashes
forests beneath it and shepherds' huts and flocks—
so in its fall the horrible joist now dashes
ramparts and arms and men. One or two shocks
the tower sustained when the joist hit the ground,
and the walls shook, and the hills boomed back the sound.

83
Bouillon, victorious, passes by the wall
and thinks it is already takeable,
but suddenly sees slung out against his tower
balls of fire fuming with a fetid smell;
even Mongibello couldn't have spewed them all
from its sulfurous bosom in the caves of hell—
nor in the heat of summer ever came
such fire from the skies of India, sleeting flame.

84
Vessels and spears and hoops are all afire—
some flaming black, others blaze out like blood—
the blasts are deafening, the stench not to endure,
the smoke blinds, the fire catches, clings. Small good
would the soaked leather have been to shield the tower—
to guard it now it's doing all it could,
but the hide sweats and curls, and if help came
later from heaven, it would have gone in flame.

85
The great-souled leader stood before them all,
and did not move an inch, did not grow pale,
but gave heart to the men who fought the fire,
spilling buckets of water—to no avail,
for now they are reduced to such a pass
that their water reserves begin to fail,
when, lo, a wind! and the blast suddenly twists
and blows the fire against the arsonists.

86
The gale counters the fire and whirls it round
back where the pagans raised their woollen skeins,
but all that soft material all up-wound
goes up at once, and no defense remains.
O glorious Captain, dear to the great God,
by the great God protected! Heaven takes pains
to fight on your behalf: the trumpets blare
and the winds obey and blow from everywhere.

87
But the wicked Ismen saw his sulfurous torches
blown by the north wind back against the wall,
and wants to have a go with his fallacious
arts, to force Nature to obey his call,
so he appears with two disciple-witches
up on the ramparts in the sight of all:
scowling, filthy, and dark, with a heavy beard—
so Pluto or Charon must have appeared

88
between two Furies. And they start to chant
spells by which Phlegethon itself is cowed,
and now the air grows turbid, and the sun
buries its front in an all-darkening cloud,
when from the hulking tower was slung a stone
that once formed part of a mountain, and this plowed
into the three with one shot making good
and powdered the three together, bones and blood.

89
In tiniest bloody fragments were they strewn,
those skulls and brains full of iniquity;
not grains of corn under the great grindstone
would be ground to dusty flour more thoroughly.
They left the calm air and the lovely sun,
those three malignant spirits, with a cry—
and fled to join the wicked shades of hell.
Learn piety, O mortals—learn it well.

90
In the meantime that tower which the wind
protected from the fire draws near the town,
so near that it can almost reach the wall
and pitch its gangway out and fix it down.
But the intrepid Soliman is there—
fighting to cut the narrow pass alone,
doubling his strokes—and might indeed have done it,
but a second sudden tower came hard upon it.

91
High in the air the giant structure looms,
higher than the city's highest buildings go,
and at that monstrous sight the Saracens
are stunned, to see their city lie below.
But the proud Turk, for all that storms of stones
ruin upon him, stands firm even so,
still trusting he can cut the bridge in two—
shouting, encouraging those men in his crew

92
who seem afraid. And now to Godfrey's eyes
appears a heavenly warrior none can see,
Michael archangel; in the clearest skies
the brilliant sun would bow to such as he.
"Godfrey, behold, the hour has come," he cries,
"when Sion leaves her cruel slavery.
Your eyes are dazzled—do not cast them low,
but see what hosts heaven brings to help you now.

93
"For turn your eyes, and look on the immense
immortal army marshaled in the air,
for I will clear away from you the dense
clouds of humanity that now impair
your mortal vision, shading mortal sense,
so that you may, for but a moment, bear
the forms of angels, their resplendent rays,
and look upon those spirits face to face.

94
"See there the souls who were Christ's champions!
Citizens of Jerusalem above,
they fight beside you as the great war ends,
they are with you, they share the glory of
this conquest. See where smoke and dust in waves
are billowing, where the broken ruins move:
in that deep cloud Hugh fights, and batters down
to the very earth the battlements of the town.

95
"There see Dudon with sword and flaming brands
assailing the northern gate! Urging the rest
to climb, he ministers weapons to their hands,
directs the ladder below and holds it fast.
He on the mountain, with the sacred bands,
wearing the crown and tonsure of a priest,
is bishop Ademar, a shepherd true,
for see how even now he blesses you.

96
"But lift your yearning eyes a little higher,
and see united all the heavenly host."
He raised his glance and looked on an entire
army of winged soldiers, numberless,
three serried squadrons, and each like a choir
divided into three, filling all space,
for the circles widened out the farther from
earth, and the closer to heaven. Overcome,

97
he dropped his eyes, and lifted them again;
that glorious sight he could no longer see,
but as he looked out over all his men
saw all things smiling for their victory.
And many an illustrious champion
followed Rinaldo over the wall, and he
was slaying Syrians. The Captain waits no more,
but seized the banner his trusty ensign bore,

98
and is first man on the bridge; and in mid-course
there is the Sultan to block him. There they strive
with infinite virtue, on a little bridge,
a narrow field, with the few blows they give.
And the proud Soliman cries, "I consecrate
my own life here that other men may live!
Friends, the bridge behind my back, cut it away!
To the end I will be no easy prey."

99
But he sees fierce-browed Rinaldo on the move
and no one brave enough to make him stay.
"What shall I do? If I give my life up here
what good is that, just throwing it away?"
And, plotting new devices in his mind,
he yields, and leaves the Captain a free way,
who follows him across with threats, and plants
the Holy Cross upon the battlements.

100
The all-victorious banner whips about,
wreathing a million ripples in its pride,
and the air breathes with reverence upon it,
on it the daylight shines more glorified,
and every spear or arrow aimed at it
is turned about, or helplessly aside,
and Sion and the mountain opposite
seem to adore it, and bow down to it.

101
All the battalions raise a shout of joy,
a mighty cry to God for victory,
and the mountains repeat the sounding joy,
echoing; and almost at that moment see
Tancred break through Argante's men, destroy
every defense Argante tries: so he
flings his bridge over the wall and storms across
and lifts again the banner of the Cross.

102
But toward the south, where the white-haired Raymond fought
with the Palestinian tyrant's regiments,
the warriors of Gascony could not
grapple their tower to the battlements,
for the king had the fiber of his troops,
and they were standing tough at the defense,
and though the wall on this side was less strong,
the greater artillery they brought along

103
shielded it well; moreover, here the way
was less approachable by the machine;
it was not art so much that held the day
but the site, by its nature. Now the sign
of victory is heard above the fray
by the men of Gascony and Palestine;
the Toulousan and the tyrant knew the town
already had been taken, further down.

104
Whence Raymond ~~to his men,~~ "The town is ours!
O comrades, hear the shout from over there!
Will they resist us, now they are defeated?
Or in this honor will we have no share?"
But finally the king gave in, retreated,
holding defense a matter for despair,
fleeing for last resort to the citadel,
defending where he'd be less vulnerable.

105

The whole triumphant army enters now
not only through the wall, but through the gate:
what's not already open is laid low,
battered, burnt, and destroyed. They do not wait;
the wrath of the sword has a free path to go;
horror and grief accompany their mate,
Death. And blood pools and swirls in a riverbed
of bodies of the dying and the dead.

Canto Nineteen

1
Whether for death or strategy or fear
the pagans have abandoned their defense.
The walls are stormed; no soldiers now appear
except Argante, for intransigence,
fighting with every enemy he finds near,
his face intrepid, set with confidence.
More than the man fears death, he fears retreat.
If he dies, let it not seem he was beat!

2
But above all other enemies, one caught
up with him, dealing a blow; and he knew well,
did the Circassian, the man whom he once fought.
His arms, his deeds, his bearing, readily tell
it is the prince, whose promise went for nought
to return on the sixth day for their duel.
"Tancred, is this the way you keep your vow?
You're coming back to battle with me now?

3
"You've come late, and you haven't come alone!
All right, I'll fight you, I'll try myself once more,
though you don't come now as a champion
but an inventor of machines of war.
Good for you! Make a shield of your own men,
depend on weapons never seen before.
But you, brave murderer of women, shall
not flee death by my hands!" At that, a small

4
smile of disdain flashed on good Tancred's face
as in high-hearted words he made reply:
"I'm late, that's true, but soon, and in this place
you'll say that I came back too hastily.
Between us two you'll want to put some space,
wide as the Alps, wide as the endless sea!
My delay was not caused by any fear.
That—by our test of strength—will soon appear.

5
"Then step aside and come with me, you who
kill only heroes, giants among men.
The killer of women here defies you to
battle." And then said, turning to his men,
ordering them to cease attacking, "Do
not touch this one. Let him pass by. He's mine
more than he is your common enemy,
for an old obligation presses me."

6
"Then come along," shot back the proud Circassian,
"however you like, accompanied or alone,
to a place for a hermit, or a congregation.
Choose your advantage! To me it's all one—
I'll stick to you." Thus, the fierce invitation
made and accepted, the warriors stride on
to the grand contest, comrades in their hate,
each the defender of the other. Great

7
is Tancred's zeal for honor, his desire
to take the blood of the pagan. And his thirst
will not be quenched, he thinks, by anger's fire
if another hand should spill the blood drops first.
He covers him with his shield and cries, "Retire!
Get back!" to all he sees, so the accursed
enemy is conducted safely through
Tancred's own friends, their weapons brandished to

8
wreak vengeance. So they turn their backs upon
the city and the armies and the tents,
and go where a winding pathway leads them on
down many a hidden turning, whence
they find themselves in a narrow, shady dell
lying between the hills, for all intents
as if it were a theater or ring
for chasing animals, or dueling.

9
Here the men stopped. And yet Argante turned
to the afflicted city, in some doubt . . .
Tancred had noticed that the pagan spurned
any shield for defense, and tossed his out,
saying, "What thoughts now occupy your mind?
That the hour set for you has come about?
If what you are foreseeing is the reason,
it's *your* cowardice now that's out of season."

10
"I'm thinking of the city, of the queen
of all Judea and its ancient reign,
now falling to defeat. And I have been
a prop against its ruin, all in vain;
and that your head, which heaven destines for me,
will be a small revenge for my disdain."
Silence. They approach each other, warily.
Each knew the other's skill and bravery.

11
Tancred is lean and lithe and built to fly,
quick with his hands and nimble on his feet;
Argante is taller by his head held high,
surpasses him in muscle and sheer weight.
Tancred's method of fighting is fast and sly—
he ducks, he plays it close, stabs underneath
Argante's guard, seeking his sword. He's tried
all of his art to parry it aside;

12
but proud Argante, open and erect,
shows in his different style as fine an art:
as much as he can, his huge arm goes direct
to search not for his foe's sword, but his heart.
That one tries jabs his foe does not expect,
this one has aimed his sword's point from the start
at his opponent's face, stands firm, and menaces,
fending off sudden passes and sly entrances.

13
As a naval battle when winds from south and east
are still, and the seas are calm, and fear no squall:
the ships unequal, the fight not in the least,
for this one's quick to turn, and that one's tall;
and the one luffs and tacks from bow to stern
to assault the other standing like a wall,
but when the quick ship draws a bit too tight
the great ship threatens ruin from its height.

14
The Latin tries to strike beneath the sword,
knocking away the blade; but he presents
a new threat, shaking his sword at Tancred's eyes,
who tries a quick retreat, a quick defense,
not quick enough, for the pagan strikes too hard
and the swift violence of his blow prevents
evasion—pierces. He saw the wounded side.
"Fencing has done the fencer in!" he cried.

15
Gnawing himself for shame and indignation,
Tancred now tossed his usual guards away,
so sharp is his revenge's instigation,
he counts it loss to triumph by delay.
His sword alone replies to the deprecation,
aimed at the visor, splitting it over the eye.
Argante beats it back. Not giving an inch,
Tancred now goes half-swords, to fight in the clinch—

16
going toe to toe with him on the left foot
while his left arm grapples with Argante's right
and his right arm deals a blow to the right side
with the point of deadliest steel. Says the Christian knight,
"That's the reply the beaten fencer gives
to the victorious master!" With all his might
the Circassian, seething, struggles, twists—but he
still cannot manage to get his bound arm free.

17
At last he threw himself at the good Latin—
no sword in hand (it hung from his shoulder chain)—
and Tancred did likewise—mightily panting
they gripped each other—nor with greater strain
did Hercules once heave the giant Antaeus
and choke his life out over the desert plain
than the strength by which the brawny arms of these
try holds on holds that knot tight as they squeeze.

18
They grappled and throttled each other with such force
that both men at the same time hit the ground.
Argante, whether by art or by good luck,
had his weak arm underneath, above, the sound,
but the French fighter's stronger arm was stuck—
the better arm for dealing blows. He found
no way to elude the imminent defeat
but by wriggling free and leaping to his feet.

19
The Saracen was slower to get up
and while he struggled took a slashing blow,
but as the east wind lashes the leafy top
of a pine—it bends, but it springs back—just so
his virtue lifts the Saracen, lifts him up
just when he seems about to be laid low.
Now they resume their sword thrusts, give and take,
less art than horror in the sight they make.

20
From many a wound the blood of Tancred flowed,
but the pagan's blood was gushing as from a spout;
and with their strength gone, now their fury slowed,
guttering like a flame whose fuel runs out.
When Tancred saw his foe's arm drained of blood
and every blow more sluggish, from his stout
great-mettled heart he put his wrath away,
withdrew, and began thus tranquilly to say,

21
"Man of might, yield to me . . . give me my due,
or credit fortune with the victory;
I want no spoils, no triumph over you.
You need not give your freedom up to me."
The pagan roused his furies into one;
more terrible than ever before was he.
"And so you boast to have the better of this
and dare to tempt Argante to cowardice?

22
"Use your good fortune! Nothing frightens me!
I'll pay you for your impudence aright!"
As the flame of a torch about to die
gathers its force and goes in a blaze of light,
filling his empty veins with wrath so he
invigorates his courage, stirs his might,
and the hour of death now following hard upon,
he'd make it shine with something nobly done.

23
To his weak right his left hand he applied
and brought his blade down hard with both hands joined,
slicing him edgelong, and though Tancred tried
to ward the blow, it struck his blade, passed beyond,
landed upon the shoulder to divide
rib after rib: one point, a multiple wound.
If he wasn't frightened now, the cavalier
possessed a heart incapable of fear.

24
He doubles the horrible blow; but he has spent
his force and anger to the wind, in vain,
for Tancred watches for his move, intent
to slip aside, and not be struck again.
Argante, to the ground chin-first you went
thrust by your own weight, helpless on the plain,
self-fallen, fortunate thus far if at all,
no one will ever boast he made you fall.

25
And in his fall his wounds were opened wide,
and the blood shot out and welled into a pool.
He planted down his left hand, and relied
on this to pull upright into a kneel
to defend himself. "Get over here," he cried,
but the gallant victor, not touching him at all,
renewed his courteous offers. To no avail—
he sneaks a stab at his heel, and starts to rail,

26
and Tancred launched into a rage and said,
"Villain! So you abuse my sympathy!"
And drove and drove his blade into his head
through the visor slot, in the sure road through the eye.
Argante died, and died just as he lived:
menacing to the last, and mightily;
formidable and fierce and proud in death.
Such were his final acts, his final breath.

27
Tancred puts down his sword, and in devotion
gives thanks to God for the honor he has won.
But the victor's in a perilous condition,
the triumph bloody, his stamina nearly gone.
And much he fears he cannot stand the motion
of journeying back to camp; yet he walks on,
feeble and slow, by the road he'd come before,
step after weary step. And now no more

28
can his weak body suffer, for the more
he forces it, the wearier he grows,
so he sits down, his cheek on his right hand,
which trembles like a reed when the wind blows.
And all he sees appears to wheel and whirl
and darkness falls, as at the evening's close;
at last he loses consciousness, and none
could tell the conquered from the champion.

29
While here a lonely war was being waged,
a war which private causes helped ignite,
throughout the town the victor's anger raged,
wanton and unrestrainable, to spite
the enemy. What pen has ever staged
the glorious scene? Who can describe the sight
of a people overcome, or justly tell
of that pathetic, fearsome spectacle?

30
The town was now one general massacre,
heaps and mountains of corpses. Here were spread
the wounded over the lifeless men, and there
the sick were buried beneath unburied dead—
and the wailing mothers with their streaming hair
pressed to their breasts their babies as they fled,
and the predator was full of theft and spoil,
dragging girls by the hair to rape, defile—

31
but up the streets that lead to the highest hill
toward the west where the great temple stands
Rinaldo drives the infidel at will,
fierce and soaked with the blood of the enemy bands.
And the greathearted lad lifts his blade high
over the helmeted heads, and wherever it lands
it slaughters—shields are a brittle obstacle.
The best defense: to bear no arms at all.

32
His noble sword swings only against the sword,
and scorns brutality against the unarmed—
those not so brave to fight, one look, one word
from his dread voice will scatter them, alarmed.
A wondrous work of valor you would see—
now they are scorned, now threatened, and now harmed—
how with unequal hazard they all flee,
the soldiers and civilians equally.

33
And now the weakling crowds have shut themselves
with no small band of fighters in the hold
of the temple, often burnt, often rebuilt,
but still called for its first founder of old,
the Temple of Solomon; and he had fashioned it
with cedarwood and proud marble and gold.
Not so rich now, but strong and mortared tight,
with high towers and steel gates. Here the great knight

34
arrived, where the mobs had flocked for their protection.
It stood in a wide place, built high from the ground.
All the gates were shut; weapons in every section
were ready atop the ramparts. His fierce eyes found
no entry in, despite his quick inspection,
for he looked the whole fort over and raced around
the circuit of the building, searching for
the narrowest passage. As the predator

35
wolf, prowling for his food in the dark of night,
circles the sheepfold, seeking some sly trick,
licks his chops as the hunger pangs excite
and cut his innate anger to the quick,
so he spies round to find some entrance site,
level to him or high on the wall, he'll pick
any—and stands at last in the great square.
Up on the heights the frightened people stare . . .

36
There lay, off to one side, a huge, long joist
(as if it were intended just for this).
No caravel of Genoa sports a mast
as tall and thick-trunked as this weapon is,
for the brawny cavalier gives it a hoist—
nothing's too heavy for him, nothing's amiss—
and couching it like a lance in the tilting course
he rams the gate with solid shattering force.

37
Not stone or metal could resist the shock
of the first slam—and the next did not abate.
He ripped the creaking hinges from the rock,
smashed the bars in and battered down the gate.
Of battering rams and cannons you can talk—
those thunderers can't boast a deed so great!
And like a flood the hosts pour through the break,
the victor following after. There they make

38
of the great house that was the house of God
a bitter slaughter, bloody, miserable.
O justice of heaven! the more delayed,
the heavier on that wicked race you fall!
From the depths of your providence you made
sternness and wrath awake in the merciful,
and the blasphemous pagan washed in his blood's rain
the very temple he had made profane.

39
Meanwhile the Sultan had retreated to
the Tower of David king of Israel,
and barring fast this and that avenue,
marshaled his much-shrunk host in the citadel;
and Aladine the tyrant came there too.
Soliman saw him from above, and cried,
"Come, famous king, come scale this rampart's height.
The rock is strong—come save yourself in spite

40
of all the depredations of the foe.
Preserve your life, preserve your very reign!"
"Alas," he answered, "the city is beaten low,
the barbarian's hatred levels it to the plain,
and my life and my rule have fallen so.
I lived, I ruled; I live no more, I reign
no more. 'We used to be,' so should we say.
The inevitable end, the final day

41
"has come to all." The Sultan answered, cross:
"What's happened to your manhood, my good lord?
Fortune your enemy brings your kingdom's loss,
but royalty is still ours, in our blood.
Then come inside now, give your limbs a pause
from labor, and let your vigor be restored."
Such his advice, and so he brought the old
infidel king inside the guarded hold.

42
He himself grabs a steel mace with two hands,
sheathing his trusty sword upon his flank;
intrepid at the barricade he stands
defending the closed passage from the Frank.
Horror and Death are in every blow he lands,
slaying, or pounding to earth at least. Men shrank
in terror from the barred-off central place,
the piazza where they saw the dreaded mace.

43
Look, followed by a fearsome company,
here comes the old Count Raymond of Toulouse.
Into the perilous pass, attacking, he
accounts as light the weight of those great blows.
He strikes first, striking ineffectually.
Not so for what the second striker does:
who knocks him to the earth with a blow to the head,
flat on his back, twitching, his arms outspread.

44
Into the vanquished too virtue at last
returns, which puny fear had put to rout,
and the victorious Frenchmen at the pass
fall in the fighting, or are driven out.
But the Sultan, who saw the duke lying half dead
among the slain at his feet, gave a shout,
"Men, carry inside the fortress this one here—
we'll make a prisoner of the cavalier."

45
So the men moved to execute his wish
but that was not an easy enterprise.
For Raymond's men won't leave him in neglect
but all come running where their leader lies.
And now, fury and loving pity fight,
and their struggle is not for a paltry prize,
for the man's greatness brings them into strife,
to seize or guard his freedom, and his life.

46
And the Sultan should have won it in the end,
stubborn for vengeance, rooted in his place,
for shields and tempered helmets can't defend
against the lightning fury of his mace,
but now new help, new foes are on the way,
he sees them gathering head, he knows his case
is difficult—for to the left and right
converge the highest Chief, and the great knight.

47
As a shepherd, when he hears the rolling thunder,
the crack of lightning, the winds whipping high,
and sees the sun go dark with storm clouds under,
hustles his flocks from out of the open sky,
and careful of their safety seeks some shelter
where the wrath of the heavens may pass them by—
he with his shouting and his staff directs them
to go ahead, and from behind protects them—

48
so too the pagan when he heard it coming,
the tempest of that irresistible crowd,
laying on every side with weapons slashing,
throttling the skies themselves with whoops so loud;
he hustles into the tower those he was guarding,
himself the last behind, until he bowed
out of the danger at last—yet to all sense
his boldness underscored his providence.

49
But he could hardly make it back inside
the gate, which they could hardly shut again,
for comes Rinaldo to the barricade,
smashes the bars, and gives himself free rein—
desire to conquer the nonpareil in arms
and his own oath are spurring him amain—
for he does not forget the vow he swore,
kill him who killed the Danish warrior.

50
And now the hand that never knew defeat
would have attempted the unstormable wall—
perhaps inside the Sultan would soon meet
the foe that fate has destined for his fall—
but the Captain has sounded a retreat,
for east and west the dusk had spread its pall.
Godfrey takes lodgings on the ground that night,
wants to renew the assault with the dawning light.

51
"Great God has showered the Christian host with grace!"
he called out to his soldiers in good cheer.
"The greatest of our enterprise is done.
There's little left to do, nothing to fear.
One final, pitiful hope for the infidels—
but tomorrow we will storm their tower here.
Piety in the meantime summons you
to give your love and comfort to those who

52
"are hurt or wounded. Go then, care for them
who won this land; with their blood it is priced.
More fitting than desire of gold or vengeance
is such a love, for cavaliers of Christ.
We have seen too much eagerness for plunder,
for slaughter—ah, far more, more than sufficed!
I ban more rapine and more cruelty.
Let the call of trumpets sound forth my decree."

53
Thus he, and went to see the Count, awake
yet groaning for the misery of that blow.
Soliman also spoke up boldly to
his men, although his heart was pressed with woe:
"In spite of fortune, friends, we have not lost.
Let hope be green in us, for under the show
of false appearances our injuries
are not so serious as you might surmise.

54
"The foe has taken only walls and roofs
and the common crowd—but the city, it still stands,
for in the mind of the king the city dwells,
and in your brave hearts, and in your strong hands.
I see the king, safe; I see his best men,
I see a high defense. Abandoned lands—
let the French have what they are fighting for,
an empty trophy! They will lose the war.

55
"I am sure they will lose it in the end,
for their good luck will make them insolent;
to murder and to thievery they will bend,
and to embraces, lewd and violent;
with such it will be easier to contend,
amid their loot and whores, weighed down and spent,
if in their arrogance they shall be met
by Egypt's hosts, which can't be too long yet.

56
"Meanwhile we can, from the highest buildings here,
use heavy stones to dominate the day,
and all roads leading to the sepulcher
we'll use artillery to take away."
So he renewed the hope in men who were
weary at heart and sad. But on his way
wandering among thousands of infantry
there came, while this was going on, the spy

57
Vafrine. Selected for this espionage
the lad departed with the setting sun,
and took his dark and solitary way,
pilgrim of night, unknown to anyone.
Before the dawn had left the balcony
of the orient, he passed by Ascalon,
and when the sun was in its mid-career
he saw the mighty army drawing near.

58
He saw an infinite array of tents
and blue and red and yellow standards swaying
in the fresh breeze; heard diverse languages,
heard barbarous drums and horns and brasses braying,
and grunts of camels and of elephants
amid the great-spirited stallions' neighing,
and said to himself, "They've moved the continent,
all Africa's here, and Asia too!" He spent

59
a little while to check the situation,
the lie of the camp, of the stockade around,
then tried no stealthy circumnavigation
nor hid from where most people could be found,
but walked straight in to make interrogation,
walked through the royal gates, and now he'll sound
with questions, now he'll make astute replies,
coupling his talk with bold and shameless eyes.

60
He wanders here and there, most diligent,
among the tents, in the squares, in the street,
learning the name of every regiment,
their arms, their horse, their manpower, all complete,
and more—for he would learn their dark intent;
he glimpses a little, hears a little. So discreet
he is, and gets around so thoroughly,
he gains access to the chiefest tent, to see

61
a tattered canvas, like a broken wall,
through which a man could pick up every word,
and from the conversation he can tell
that it's the quarters of the royal board.
From a good eavesdropper it cannot conceal
the strategy and secrets of their lord.
Here Vafrine watched, and made as if intent
on something else, like patching up the tent.

62
Wearing a purple mantle, fully armed,
the captain stood inside. His head was bare;
but two tall pages bore his helm and shield.
He leaned a little on his ashen spear,
looking upon a swarthy man beside him,
a tall man with a rough and ugly leer.
Vafrine was listening close, but when he hears
discussion of "Godfrey," he pricks up his ears.

63
The leader was speaking thus. "Are you then sure
you're the man by whom Godfrey will be slain?"
"I am," he answered, "and at court I swore
unless I won I'd not return again.
Others did too—but I'll be there before.
No reward for me, other than to obtain
his arms to make a trophy which I'll send
to Cairo, and set above this verse I've penned:

64
" 'These are the arms Ormondo took in war
from Asia's ruin, the French general,
when he took his soul; and here forevermore
he hung them up as a memorial.' "
"The courteous king," the leader said, "will not
forget a work so grand and honorable.
What you've requested he will grant, no doubt,
and you'll receive a big reward to boot.

65
"Time for you to prepare the armed disguise,
for the time is drawing near our day of war."
"It's finished already," Ormondo replies,
and with that said, the two men spoke no more.
At that Vafrine remained in some surprise
and doubt—what sort of oath the soldier swore,
what were the false arms they were talking about.
He mulled it over, but couldn't figure it out.

66
He went his way, but stayed up that whole night
attentive—he refused to shut his eyes,
but when the army in the morning light
sets every banner streaming to the skies,
he marches with the others as they march
and where the army lies, he also lies,
but sneaks about the camp from tent to tent
the better to learn the truth of what they meant.

67
He found, among her ladies and her knights,
Armida in a throne set high above,
full of sighs, and a hermit to all else
but the self-musings she was thinking of;
resting her cheek upon her lily hand,
and turning toward the earth those stars of love.
Had she been crying? Hard thing to decide,
but her eyes were moist and welling up inside

68
with pearls. The fierce Adrastus opposite
seemed not to bat an eye or take a breath,
he hung upon her so, and, fixed on her,
he pastured his desires, famished to death,
but Tissaphernes looked at both of them
now with an insane craving, now with wrath,
and showed his changeable face the color of
a furious scorn, and then the color of love.

69
Then he discovered Altamor, who stood
among the ladies, a little ways apart;
he did not give his amorousness its head
but turned his lusty eyes with subtle art;
one glance upon her lovely face, her hand,
and sometimes even some more guarded part,
smuggling himself along the secret way
that opened between her soft breasts, *negligee.*

70
At last Armida lifts her eyes; in part
her lovely face becomes serene again,
and a sweet smile breaks and flashes across
in the midst of her sorrow's gentle rain.
"My lord," she said, "remembering your boast
brings my heart ease and solaces the pain,
for I hope soon to be avenged by you,
and wrath is sweet when vengeance is in view."

71
"Ah, calm your sorrowful brow," the Indian said.
"For God's sake be of good cheer! You won't wait
long now before you see the swopped-off head
of that wicked Rinaldo at your feet,
or my avenging hand will have him led
a prisoner to what prison you think meet."
Such was his promise. Tissaphernes heard;
it gnawed his heart, but he didn't say a word.

72
She turned to Tissaphernes her sweet smile.
"What do you say, my lord?" And in replying
he feigned self-deprecation, all the while
jabbing his rival. "No sense even trying.
I'll lag behind his valor many a mile,
you're champion's so brave and terrifying."
"You're right to clear out," said the Indian,
"if you're afraid of the comparison."

73
Said Tissaphernes, tossing his proud head,
"I wish I were lord, to do what I would do!
If I had but the free rule of this sword!
One's slower indeed—and soon you'd see just who!
My enemy Love and the heavens make me afraid,
O savage man—not your great boasts, not you."
Adrastus rose to defy him there and then
but Armida placed herself between the men,

74
crying, "O knights, would you then take from me
what you bestowed, your vow? Would you belie it?
You are my champions, and that name should be
good enough yet to keep your tempers quiet.
If you grow angry, you grow angry with me.
Hurt your rival and you hurt me—don't deny it."
Thus she reduced them to accord, and broke
their chafing souls under her iron yoke.

75
The spy Vafrine was there and heard it all.
Learning the truth of it, he went his way.
He found a silence, though, impenetrable,
surrounding their most deep conspiracy—
but with the difficulty grew his will—
and sometimes he would speak too pointedly.
He is resolved to lose his very life
or else report the secret to the Chief.

76
He thought of a thousand cunning practices,
he thought of a thousand never-heard-of frauds,
yet he could not discover the strategy's
weapons and plans. But Fortune evens the odds
(what he could not do on his own, she does),
solving each doubt he has, loosing the knots,
so that at last the trick they plan is clear,
their trap set for the pious cavalier.

77
He'd gone back where the amorous enemy
yet sat among her champions, for he thought
it might give him an opportunity
among the crowds to find out what he sought.
So he approached a lady casually
as if he'd used to chat with her a lot,
for they—he feigned—were friends from long ago.
So he addressed the lady, affably so,

78
as if he were in jest. "I think I'd like
to be some pretty lady's champion.
Why, I'd go cut off with one cutlass strike
Rinaldo's head, or the head of Bouillon.
Come on, ask me for one of them, if you'd like
the head of some baron-barbarian."
So he begins with her, and bit by bit
he hopes to turn the jest, directing it

79
to serious talk; but as he joked he smiled,
and in his smile was something natural
to him alone. One of the ladies heard,
and looked at him, and sidling past them all
said in his ear, "Your love won't be employed
uselessly. From the rest I've come to steal
you for my chosen champion. Step outside
with me, as if you were my knight; I need

80

"to talk with you." They did so; she began.
"I know you, Vafrine. You should know me too."
A chill went through the cunning servingman
yet he turned to her with a simple smile. "I do
not recall—though you're worth the looking on—
having seen you before. I know that's true,
because my name's far different from the one
you called me by just now. Tunisian

81

"I am, born on the shores of Bizerta,
Lesbin my father. My name is Almansor."
"Tuscan," said she, "no matter how you play.
I know all about you, see, from years before.
But I'm your friend. Don't try to hide from me.
I'm willing to put my life in peril for
your good. The daughter of a king was I,
then the slave of Tancred, in your custody,

82

"Erminia. For two happy years I was
in that sweet prison, and you treated me
kindly, and all your deeds were courteous.
Look at me well—I am she, I am she!"
The squire already had searched her with his eyes
and remembered the sweet face immediately.
"You live," she adds, "in safety—have no fear!
By heaven above and by this sun I swear.

83

"Rather when you return to camp, I pray,
take me back to the prison so dear to me.
I pass a troubled night and a darkened day,
miserable in my bitter liberty.
And you have met with rare good luck today
if you've come here to spy. For I will be
your news for all, I'll tell you the whole plot through,
and all else that would harm them if you knew."

84

He looks at her in silence, for he thinks
about the false Armida. As a rule
women are quick to talk, quick to deceive,
they will and will not; any man's a fool
to trust in them. "Well, if you'd like to go
I'll be your escort. Let's be sensible.
We can agree on this much face to face.
Save talking of them for a better place."

85

Orders were given now to mount the saddle,
for the camp would be moving right away.
Vafrine left the pavilion; she returned
among the ladies, making some delay,
pretending to joke about her champion,
and then, at the right time, she went her way
to the agreed-on place, and met her guide
and left the army for the countryside.

86

They now had come to a deserted place.
They could no longer see the Saracen tents.
He said to her, "Now tell me how they plan
to take the life of the good Godfrey." Whence
she unfolds for him the evil web, displays
all their conspiratorial intents.
"There are eight warriors at court. Among these men
Ormond is the most famous Saracen.

87

"They've been stirred up by hatred or ambition,
who knows. But now their guile will be revealed.
The day when two great hosts fight for the reign
of Asia, in the glorious battlefield,
they'll be wearing the sign of the Cross, they'll feign
the French sword and the armor and the shield,
and the white and gold that Godfrey's cohort wears—
on that day that insignia will be theirs

88

"except for a small sign upon the helmet
to mark them out for pagans. When the place
is swarming with both armies in the fight
and ranks have broken, they'll go on the chase,
sneaking upon the valiant general,
showing his own bodyguard's friendly face.
Their sword tips will be poisoned, that each wound
may bring him death. And since the pagans found

89

"that I had been your prisoner for a while
and knew your weapons and the dress you wore,
they made me tell the colors; I was forced
to do the evil of a conspirator.
That's why I've left the camp—to run away
from their imperious demands. I abhor
to be involved with fraud in any fashion—
for me it is a vile contamination.

90
"These are the reasons—but not these alone."
Here she fell silent, flushed a little red,
and dropped her eyes—she wanted to keep down
those last words—it was not clear what she said.
The squire wanted to have her troubles known,
revealing what she kept back, so he led
the lady on. "What little faith! Why hide
the truth from me, in whom you can confide?"

91
Her voice was broken, as she heaved a sigh
from deep within her breast, and burst out thus:
"Oh poorly guarded shame, inopportune,
leave me! You have no more to do with us.
Your fire will never hide the fire of love.
Dig your heels in—but it will be no use.
You should have done that on a different day—
not now that I'm a woman gone astray."

92
Adding, "That fatal night for me and for
my fatherland which lay oppressed, I lost
more than appears to you. Not that itself
but what it brought was worst. I count the cost
little, to lose the kingdom; with my throne
I lost myself. And that I might be lost
forever, I was foolish in my art,
losing my senses, and my mind and heart.

93
"Vafrine, you know that after I had seen
such slaughtering and plunder, I went alone
and timid to beseech your lord and mine,
whom I had first seen setting his foot upon
my royal threshold; I bowed to him and cried,
'Have mercy, never-defeated champion!
Not for my life I beg you—suffer me
to save the flower of my virginity.'

94
"He placed his hand on mine, and did not wait
even to hear the ending of my plea.
'Beautiful virgin, no need to go on.
Rely on me for your defense,' said he.
Then something—I don't know what—soft and sweet
trickled into my heart, invaded me,
slithering like a snake into my soul
to wound, and light a fire out of control.

95

"He often came to visit and to give
sweet solace, as he spoke and grieved with me.
He said, 'Take as your own the spoils I have;
I give you your unfettered liberty.'
Ah, it was a small gift, and ravishment!
He gave, but took myself away from me!
What he gave was the poor and paltry part
as he usurped the kingdom of my heart.

96

"Love can't be hidden. Often, in desire,
I asked you of my lord. My thoughts would rove—
you saw the signs of my poor heart and said,
'You are afire, Erminia. You're in love.'
Oh, I denied it; but an ardent sigh
would give a truer testimony of
my heart's condition—or instead of speech
maybe one sorrowful look of mine would teach

97

"the truth of the raging fire. Silence—alas!
I should have asked some medicine for my pain.
That was the time to do it, if at all;
what good if later I gave desire free rein?
In short, I left, and carried my wounds with me,
hidden; I thought I would die. But to obtain
some remedy at last, and live, love took
all honor from me, so that I forsook

98

"Jerusalem to seek my lord, who made
me heartsick, and could once more make me well.
But on the way I met an ambuscade
of soldiers, villainous, unmerciful;
they almost took me prisoner, but I fled
to a far, deserted woodland. In my cell
I lived in quiet peace and loneliness,
a citizen of the woods, a shepherdess.

99

"But when that longing surged in me once more
which for a long time fear kept under rein,
I tried to go back to Jerusalem,
but I met with misfortune once again.
This time it was a band searching for spoil—
they came too fast—I tried to flee, in vain.
So I was taken, and my takers were
Egyptians on their way to Gaza, where

100

"they made of me a present to the Captain.
I told him who I was, I pleaded and prayed
so well that I remained inviolate
and honored, during all the time I stayed
in the company of Armida. So I've fallen
into the power of others, and each time made
escape, alas! So often seized, and free—
yet those first bonds still make a slave of me.

101

"Oh let him who so binds my soul around
that no one else will loose it, never say,
'It's on another journey you are bound,
my errant handmaid,' pushing me away,
but let him look with pity on my return—
in the old prison let him have me stay."
So said Erminia to the squire. They ride
day and night, talking together, side by side.

102

Vafrine had left the better-traveled road
for a path that was shorter and more secure.
The sun was setting, darkening the whole wood,
when they came to a place not very far
from town. And here the way is fouled with blood,
and in his blood they see a warrior,
dead—taking the whole road, turning his face
to heaven—and even dead he menaces.

103

The fashion of his arms and his strange bearing
marked him as pagan. The squire passed him by.
But at a distance someone else was lying—
another warrior struck Vafrine's eye.
He said to himself, 'This one must be a Christian,'
looking at that dark cloak suspiciously . . .
He leapt from his saddle, turned the man's face, and read.
"My God," he cried, "it's Tancred! Tancred's dead!"

104

The misadventurous girl had stopped to peer
at the fierce soldier, a little ways apart,
when the sound of his sad voice came to her ear:
it was an arrow through her loving heart.
The name of Tancred was enough for her;
madly or drunkenly she came, she caught
sight of the handsome face, its color gone.
She didn't dismount, she leapt from the horse—and upon

105
his body let pour forth a ceaseless flow
of tears, and words she uttered mixed with sighs:
"Into what misery Fortune leads me now!
How sad and bitter a spectacle meets my eyes!
So much time, so much pain I took to find you,
Tancred—I see you, but you can't recognize
me—I am here, and yet you cannot see,
I find you, and I lose you eternally.

106
"Ah, never did I think that to my eyes
the sight of you could be a painful one!
I'd blind myself, I'd willingly tear them out
rather than see you, I dare not look on . . .
Where is the flame of those so noble eyes,
where is the lovely ray? Where are they gone,
the lovely blushes? Where is their flowering now?
Where is the tranquil look upon your brow?

107
"But even marred and soiled you ravish me.
Beautiful soul, if you are dwelling still
within this body, my temerity
pardon, pardon the theft by my bold will,
stealing cold kisses, which I'd hoped would be
a little warmer, from your lips so pale . . .
I'll steal from death some of what's rightly his,
giving these cold and bloodless lips a kiss.

108
"Your lips . . . in life so gentle and merciful,
uttering words to soothe me in my grief . . .
let me, before I leave the world, console
myself with your dear kisses for relief.
Maybe if I'd been bold enough to ask
you'd have given what I take now as a thief.
Let me embrace you, let my spirit flow
from me, upon your lips. Wherever you go

109
"in the world after this one, wait for me,
take me along, for I will follow you."
So the girl moaned; and wept so bitterly
she seemed unmade, seemed all dissolved into
a stream of tears. But at that weeping he
opened his lips a little, and came to,
and from his open lips, with still-shut eyes,
he breathed a sigh that mingled with her sighs.

110

The woman senses that the knight has sighed—
and must to a degree be comforted.
"Open your eyes to these last rites," she cried,
"I give you, Tancred, with the tears I shed.
Look at me; I want to die at your side,
I want to go with you on the long road.
Look at me—oh, don't be so quick to leave,
it's the last gift from you I shall receive!"

111

Tancred opened his eyes, but heavily,
wearily, and shut them again. And she wept still.
But Vafrine said to her, "He will not die.
Cure him first—there'll be time to weep your fill."
He stripped his armor, and feebly, tremblingly,
she set her hand to work, for she had skill
in treating wounds, and searched and felt them over—
gaining assurance that he might recover.

112

She sees his trouble comes from weariness
and fluid lost, but all she has to bind
his bleeding wounds with, in that wilderness,
is a single veil. No matter; love can find
a way—in most unlikely bandages
and the rare art of a compassionate mind.
She dries his wounds and binds them up as well
with her own hair; she cut her hair—her veil

113

was small and sheer, and never would have done
for wounds so thick with blood, and of great size.
Dittany root and crocus she had none,
but she knew potent charms to make arise
the lethal sleep that pressed the champion,
till at last he could lift his eager eyes.
He sees a gentle lady with his squire.
She bends above him in her strange attire.

114

"Vafrine," he asks, "how did you get here? When?
My merciful physician, who are you?"
She sighed for doubt and happiness at once,
shading her lovely face with a rosy hue.
"As your physician I'm prescribing rest,
so you be still. You'll know, when the time's due.
You will be cured—get ready for the fee."
And she held his head to her bosom tenderly.

115
Vafrine meanwhile was thinking how they could
convey him to a shelter before night.
When all at once there came a certain squad—
the men, as Vafrine saw, of the wounded knight.
When he confronted the Circassian they
were with him, but he wanted a single fight,
so they held back. But, fearing something wrong,
they went to see what kept their lord so long.

116
And many others went in the same search
but these men found him first. And now they chose
to knit their arms into a kind of chair
where Tancred could sit upright. So they rose,
but Tancred said, "We leave the valorous
Argante here to be the prey of crows?
For God's sake let's not cheat him of his due—
a decent burial, and praises too.

117
"With that mute, bloodless trunk I have no more
to battle; and he died, brave to the last.
It is then right that we should grant him honor,
earth's only legacy when life is past."
So with the help of many a warrior
he had his enemy carried after. Fast
by the side of the lady Vafrine clings,
as a man does who's guarding crucial things.

118
Added the prince, "Don't take me to my tent
but take me to the city of the King,
for if this frail life meets some accident
let it befall me there. That place may wing
my soul more quickly along the road to heaven
where the immortal Man's last breath was spent.
It will be soothing to my prayers now
to have journeyed to the keeping of my vow."

119
And so they brought him there and laid him down
to quiet sleep, upon a featherbed.
Not far away the lady and Vafrine
took lodgings—shut away, well secreted.
At last he went where Godfrey and his men
were meeting, and no entry was gainsaid,
although the chiefs were weighing strategies
to plan the future of the enterprise.

120
The duke was at the edge of the sickbed
where the hurt and strengthless Raymond was lying down,
and the wisest and strongest stood about his head,
circling the old man like a noble crown.
Now while the squire reports, no word is said,
no questions asked, except of that alone.
"My lord, just as you ordered me, I fell
among the armies of the infidel.

121
"But don't expect from me an exact count—
that army's number is innumerable!
Deep in the valleys and over every mountain
I saw them swarming; all the plains they fill,
and wherever they go they leave each stream and fountain
dry, and the country uninhabitable.
To quench their thirst the rivers are too small,
and Syria's harvest little help at all.

122
"But of the cavalry and infantry
most of the men are worthless anyway,
not bearing swords but arrows, cowardly,
no trumpets, no commands will they obey.
Yet there's a choice and well-trained company
under the banner of Persia, and they may
be a superior squadron whom they name
'The Immortals of the King.' They have the fame

123
"of being 'immortal' since they've never lacked
a single of their members, not even one,
for when a place is empty they elect
a new man to replace the one who's gone.
The captain of the host is Emiren,
surpassed in sense and valor by few or none,
whose king commands him to use all his skill
to provoke you to pitched battle. They will

124
"arrive, this army of the enemy,
I think no later than the second day.
But you, Rinaldo, you'd do well to guard
your head—the greatest prize for which they play!
The best and bravest are sharpening the sword,
whetting their wrath against it—for the pay
its cutter-off will be possessor of
is Armida, who has offered them her love.

125

"With them is Altamor, the valorous
and noble Persian, king of Samarkand;
giant Adrastus, lord of the far east;
at the limits of the morning lies his land;
so far removed from all humanity
he rides no horse—an elephant's at his command!
Last, Tissaphernes, whose great skill in war
is justly praised by fame." He said no more,

126

and the young Rinaldo's face was all aflash,
and in his eyes there burned an eager fire—
if only the foe were there to cut and slash!
He has nowhere to hold his great desire.
Then to the Captain Vafrine turned again.
"Till now what I have said is little, Sire.
The sum is this: against you they have wrought
the evil weapons of Iscariot."

127

The plot on Godfrey's life he now reveals,
the fraud, all the deceitful practices,
the false arms, and the banners, and the poison,
the boasts, and the rewards, and promises;
they ask him many questions, which he answers.
Then for a short time all the men are speechless,
until the noble Captain raised his brow.
"What," he asked Raymond, "do you counsel now?"

128

"It's my opinion that at break of dawn
as we've decided, we should fight no more,
but so to press the great tower of the town
the citizens will be shut in; then restore
the vigor of the camp with food and rest,
strength which the greater fight is calling for.
And you yourself must choose now which is best—
an open fight, or playing close to the vest.

129

"And so my judgment is that you must take
care of yourself above all other care.
Through you the army triumphs, and through you
it reigns. Who else can guide it, who can bear
it safe to victory? Since the traitors will
not hide their colors, change what your men wear,
so that the fraud revealed to you may be
the same that shall betray your enemy."

130
"As always you have shown," the Chief replies,
"a helpful will and an intelligent
judgment. But what you leave in doubt I shall
conclude now: we shall meet the foe, not pent
behind the city walls or the stockade.
We are the conquerors of the Orient!
Let the infidels now see our valor play
in the open field and in the light of day.

131
"They cannot bear to hear our triumphs named,
let alone the victor's proud and noble glance,
let alone our weapons. Their force shall be tamed
and we shall found our reign in confidence.
The tower—besiege it or not, it's all the same!
Easy to take when they have no defense."
Here the greathearted Captain left the tent.
Sleep-beckoning stars shone in the firmament.

⁂ Canto Twenty

1
The sun had wakened mortals to their work
and ten hours of the morning had passed by
when the pagan army stationed on David's rock
saw something far away, as shadowy
as an evening cloud that covers all the earth:
it is the host of allies drawing nigh,
darkening the skies with the dust of galloping hooves
which covers the nearby hills as the army moves.

2
And from the summit of the tower they shout,
the besieged people shout to heaven on high!
Thracian cranes when the winter winds are out,
leaving their nest make such a raucous cry,
as they brave the storms and head for the warm south—
honking among the wintry clouds they fly—
for hope now makes them ready for the fight—
the hand to draw the bow, the tongue to spite.

3
The French knew well what had renewed the wrath,
they knew why there were threatenings to hear.
They from their lookouts saw the dusty path
and the formidable armies now appear.
Now those fierce hearts are all ablaze to fight!
Brave is the longing of each cavalier!
And the proud lads cry out to meet the foe,
"Invincible leader, give the sign to go!"

4
But the wise captain will not fight till dawn
and keeps his boldest men harnessed and still—
not even casual skirmishes at least
to try the enemy's strength. Such is his will.
"You well deserve," he said, "after such hardships,
a day to rest yourselves and eat your fill."
Perhaps he wants to feed his enemies too
with overconfidence in what they can do.

5
So every man prepares himself, and longs
for the return of dawn to light their way.
The air was never so calm and beautiful
as at the dawning of that memorable day.
The morning rose in joy, and in herself
seemed to shine all the sun, his every ray;
and the skies were brightened with unusual light,
unveiled to look upon the glorious sight.

6
Soon as he sees the golden light of dawn
Godfrey deploys his troops upon the plain,
leaving, against the tyrant of Palestine,
Raymond, and all the faithful who remain
from nearby Syria, who have come along
with those who set them free—a mighty train;
not only these, but also a company
of soldiers from the land of Gascony.

7
The Captain goes; such he appears to sight
that those who see him augur victory.
New grace shines down on him from heaven's height;
grand and august beyond himself is he;
and the rosy glow of youth returns to light,
his countenance, all magnanimity.
Such are his motions, such the look in his eye,
he does not seem a being who can die.

8
Not far he went, when he came front to front
with the waiting army of the pagan band,
and had his soldiers occupy a mount
at the back of his host, on the left hand,
and spread his munitions deep and strong in front,
thin at the sides, aimed at the level land;
and in the middle he placed his infantry,
flanked on both sides by wings of cavalry.

9
On the left horn, tight underneath the hill
occupied by his army, he assigned
both of the princes Robert to take charge;
his brother Baldwin took the troops aligned
in the center; he would take the dangerous right,
for there the pagan host might have in mind
to send some men out to the higher ground
and catch the Christians trapped with foes all round.

10
And here he set his soldiers from Lorraine,
and here the better armed, an elite force;
and here among the knights archers on foot,
infantry used to fighting among the horse;
and here a squadron of Adventurers
and others picked from other troops, their course
to be some ways apart, at his right hand:
and put them in Rinaldo's sole command.

11
To whom he said, "All rests with you, my lord;
victory, and the sum of everything.
Keep back a little, let your troops stay hid
some ways behind each big and fanned-out wing.
When the foe attacks then pound him from the side,
and all his plans and battle maneuvers bring
to naught. For I am sure he'll take some tack
to circle around and strike us at the back."

12
He flew from band to band, from place to place,
among the knights-at-arms and the infantry,
his visor up, revealing his whole face,
and there were lightnings flashing in his eye.
He strengthens the doubters, the hopeful he assures;
for the bold he calls to mind their boasts so high;
for the brave, their past deeds; and promises
honors for some, or riches, as they please.

13
At last he halted where the first and best
of all the squadrons gathered round; he stood
upon a rise of ground, and there addressed
his men in words that ravished them, as would
snows melting from the height of an alpine crest
tumble and splash below in a great flood—
just so the stirring words came fast and strong
which from the captain's voice like trumpets rung:

14
"O ye scourge of the enemies of Christ!
My army, conqueror of the Orient!
Behold the final day, the day has come
which you have craved, for which your toil's been spent,
and all the rebel populations have
merged here against you, all with heaven's consent,
that you may, with your foes in unison,
fight many wars and win them all in one!

15

“Many in one our victories will be,
the trouble and the risk not one bit more!
Never have fear, ah, never fear to see
the foe in such a massive army, for
they are at odds, are but uneasily
united, will break formation, will ignore
orders—those who will really fight are few.
Many will lack the heart, or room, to do

16

“battle. The ones who come against you are
naked, without much vigor, without art.
From idleness and slavish ways at home
it took violent threats to make them start—
I see their swords are shaking, and their shields—
even the flags are trembling in that part!
Their wavering motions, their sounds of doubt I hear;
I see their death, for all the signs are clear.

17

“That chief, with purple and gold insignia,
who sets his men and seems so valorous,
may once have beaten the Moor, or Arabia,
but is not strong enough to resist us.
What will he do when they are all confused?
What will it matter then how wise he is?
He doesn’t know the men in his own care.
He can say to few, ‘When you and I were there.’

18

“But I am captain of a chosen band;
we fought together, and together won;
and then you placed yourselves at my command.
Your fatherlands, your kinfolks—is there one
I do not know? Which of your swords to me
is new? Why, from what bow the arrow’s flown
whistling above me I can tell, I know
whether it’s Irish or French, and often who

19

it was who shot it! All I ask you now,
be as I’ve seen you be: that has sufficed.
Recall your usual zeal, and keep in mind
my honor, your honor, and the honor of Christ.
Go, beat the enemy down, trample his limbs!
Confirm the holy conquest! I have advised
you long enough, I see it in your eyes,
it’s clear, you have already won the prize.”

20
It seemed at the conclusion of these words
there fell on him a calm and glowing light,
as sometimes in the sky a shooting star
shakes from the mantle of the summer night;
but this glow, they believed, the sun shot forth
from its deep heart incomparably bright,
and crowned his head; and some there would maintain
it was an augury of future reign.

21
Perhaps—if mortal tongue dare to presume
on earth to speak of heaven's secret things—
it was a guardian angel making room
in his high choir, to gird him with his wings.
While Godfrey thus addressed the troops and gave
his Christians their assignments, the time brings
comfort and orders to the Egyptian host;
their captain too leaves not a moment lost.

22
He brought his own battalions to the fore,
and spread them out just as he sees the Frank,
and he too makes a two-pronged plan of war,
infantry in the middle, horse at the flank.
On the left side he stations Altamor,
he himself takes the horn on the right bank;
Mulehassah in the center was the foot's leader,
while there in mid-formation stood Armida.

23
With the chief on the right stands the Indian king,
and Tissaphernes, and all his royal band.
But on the level stretch upon the left
where the wing's ground could easily expand,
Altamor has the kings of Africa
and Persia, and the two from the torrid land.
Here they had room for the sling and the crossbow,
to send their missiles hurtling at the foe.

24
So Emiren deployed them, and he too
made all the rounds, the center and each side,
and spoke, at times with an interpreter.
With praises, insults, punishments he plied
his hearers, and with promise of reward.
"Why do you look down? Why so terrified,
soldier? We're a hundred to one! They'll fly—
I trust it—at our shadow, at our cry!"

25
To other men he said, "O valiant heart!
Go with that look to take our riches home."
In some he uses all his speaking art
to wake their minds, to make the image come
of their own pleading nation, or their kin
kneeling in terror before the coming doom.
"Think of the words I speak," he said, "as theirs:
think that my tongue utters your country's prayers.

26
"Protect our faith and laws, and do not have
our holy temples washed in our own blood!
Protect your father's ashes and his grave,
secure your virgins from that wicked brood!
The old men show you their white locks and rave
about the years gone, and their soldierhood;
your wife shows you her nipples and her breast,
your children, cradles, bed." And to the rest

27
he said, "Asia makes you the champions
of her honor, and she expects from you
against these few thieving barbarians
a harsh but most just vengeance." So he drew
his various people on with various art
and various sorts of speech, inciting to
combat. No talk now from each general—
the space between the two great hosts grows small.

28
What a grand, wondrous thing it was to see
when front to front these two great armies struck—
in ordered ranks each marching company—
their trumpets blaring, summoning to attack,
with banners spread to the wind and streaming free,
and the plumes on their helmets' crests blown back!
Armor and arms, insignias, colors bold
flashed to the sun in streaks of steel and gold.

29
The armies are now like a tall, dense forest,
they so abound with bristling spears held high;
the bows are drawn, the lances couched in rest,
the javelins shaken, slings ready to let fly;
and the horses too grow eager for the test,
confirm their riders' rage as the camps draw nigh,
snorting and stamping, neighing, bucking round,
flaring their nostrils with fire at the trumpets' sound.

30
Amid this beauty even horror is
beautiful, and with fear comes a delight,
and to the ear the sound is glad and fierce
from the terrifying trumpets blaring bright;
yet the army of the faithful, though the lesser,
appears more marvelous in sound and sight:
with clear and warlike songs their trumpets ring,
and brighter is the flash their weapons fling.

31
From the Christian trumpets the first charge is sent;
the others sound acceptance in reply.
The French fall to their knees, all reverent,
and kiss the earth, and honor heaven on high.
The space between grows narrow, and is gone,
and the foes battle indiscriminately.
The flanks already are plunged in a savage tussle,
and the infantry charge on to show their muscle!

32
Who struck the first foe from the Christian band?
Who won that honor in this noble quest?
Gildippe, it was you, you struck the grand
King of Hormuz, Hircano, in the chest—
such glory heaven concedes to a woman's hand—
and with your steel you severed breast from breast.
He fell, transfixed, and as he fell he heard
his foes shout praises for his conqueror's sword.

33
She grips her sword with her virile right arm
(for her spear haft is broken in the king),
and spurring on her thoroughbred enacts
against the Persians a fine winnowing—
strikes Zopir where a man girds on his belt,
so that he falls, a near-divided thing,
then cuts the cruel Alarc through the throat,
where food goes in and where the voice comes out.

34
A jab gets Argeus, a forehand Artaxerxes—
the one falls stunned, the other slain as well—
then at the knobby joint that links the arm
and the left hand, she slices Ishmael,
and the hand falls that held the horse's reins.
The blow whizzed past his ears—the horse could tell
that he was in his own power, his bridle free,
and wrecking the ranks transverse began to flee.

35
These men and many more whose names the years
have drowned in silence, she removed from life.
The Persians charge—and sneak behind her too—
eager to have the glory of that strife.
But her faithful husband, who sees her trouble, and fears,
comes running to the aid of his dear wife.
So joined, the pair whom nothing can divorce
gain strength from faithful union, double their force.

36
Here the greathearted lovers put to use
the strangest sort of parrying, a new art,
for he and she, forgetting to guard themselves,
guarded the life of the one nearest their heart—
for when a rough blow falls to harm her spouse
the ardent warrioress knocks it athwart;
he throws his shield at weapons swung for her—
and would oppose his bare head, if need were!

37
So they defend the other as best they can,
and they take vengeance for the other too.
He brings death to defiant Artaban,
the king of Boecan in the ocean blue,
and slays by the same hand the bold Alvan
who dared to fetch his dear delight a blow.
She sees her husband struck by Arimont,
and brow from brow she splits him down the front.

38
These made short work of the Persians, but much more
was the slaughter of French by the King of Samarkand:
wherever his sword, wherever his racehorse bore,
he strewed them, knights and foot troops, on the land—
and happy the man who managed to die before
his stallion trampled him groaning into the sand—
for the horse made sure, with any death in doubt,
to bite the body and batter the last life out.

39
The tall Ardone, and Brunel great of brawn
are both sent packing at Altamor's hands:
the head and helmet so split for the one
that it hangs on the shoulders by two bands;
the other he runs through where laughs begin
below the lungs, and where the heart expands,
so that—oh how the strange sight horrifies—
he's forced to laugh, and with a laugh he dies.

40
He drove not only these from the sweet earth,
for his man-killing sword made many die,
thrusting together to a cruel death
Guasco, Genton, the good Rosmond, and Guy.
Who can relate how many Altamor batters,
how many under the hooves of his stallion lie
crushed? Who can tell the names of all the spent,
what blows they took, how many ways they went?

41
No one dared give that savage man affront;
they held far back, they wouldn't take him on.
Only Gildippe turned to him her front,
did not abstain from the comparison.
No shield was ever grasped or war ax swung
by virgin warrior on the Thermodon
as boldly as she boldly took the ring
against the formidable Persian king.

42
She knocked him on the helmet, on the bright
enameled gold of his barbaric crown,
smashed it to bits, so from its arrogant height
despite itself his head must now bow down.
The pagan king was all enraged, for spite—
it surely seemed a sturdy hand, that one!
Nor was he slow to avenge his injury,
for spite and vengeance both came instantly.

43
Almost at once he struck the lady back,
and struck so hard, she fell as if half slain,
losing all strength and sense in the attack;
but there her faithful spouse was, to sustain
her body in the saddle. Whether it was luck
or chivalry, he didn't strike again;
as the greathearted lion scorns to slay
a sleeping man, but looks and goes his way.

44
Ormondo meanwhile, in whose savage hands
was the commission of the treachery,
used his false colors to mix with the Christian bands,
he and the rest of his conspiracy,
rather as prowling wolves in the deep midnight
will trot like household dogs, and thus they spy
upon the fold, and look for a gap in the pale,
tucking under the belly the dubious tail.

45
They take their time, approach him roundabout.
Now the fierce pagan is at Godfrey's side.
But when the Captain saw the man's false coat,
the white and gold insignia, he cried,
"Here is that traitor, here is the one who thought
to deck himself as one on the French side!
Look, here's his gang, now coming after me."
With that he turned to the man of perfidy

46
and slashed him to his death: the felon plies
no shield, he does not stop, he strikes no blows—
as if he had a Gorgon before his eyes,
and he was bold!—he turned to stone, he froze.
Now every sword and spear was aimed at them,
quivers of arrows emptied at these foes
alone: and Ormond fell with all his kind,
so blasted, hardly a corpse remained behind.

47
When he saw himself bespattered with enemy gore
Godfrey entered the war in earnest, thrust
first where he saw the Persian Altamor
breaking tight ranks and scattering men like dust;
the Christians fled that fearsome man of war
like sands of Africa in the south wind's gust.
He turned that way—threatened his men, disgraced them,
grabbed those who fled, and attacked the man who chased them.

48
Here the two fierce right arms begin to fight—
never did Greek and Trojan duel so!
Meanwhile the infantry battle is not light
with Mulehassah and Baldwin toe to toe,
and the cavalry are seething upon the right
beside the hill, where the barbarian foe
himself is fighting, the host's lord and guide,
with the two mighty rivals at his side.

49
The leader of that mob and one Robert
go at it viciously, with equal might.
But the Indian's slashing leaves his foe's head bare
and all his chain mail riddled; with no one quite
worthy of Tissaphernes' prowess there
he wreaks a general havoc in the fight,
going wherever the crowded ranks are filling,
to ply his various and frequent killing.

50
So they fought on, and in a teetering scale
balanced lay hope for victory, and fear.
The field was littered with shattered lances, mail
scattered and broken shields and hacked-off gear.
Some took the sword in the chest, and others fell
with guts exploded, punctured by the spear—
bodies flat on the back lay strewn around,
and others prone, as if they bit the ground.

51
Beside their lifeless lords the stallions lie;
a man lies dead beside his dearest friend;
the enemy lies by the enemy;
over the vanquished the victor nears his end.
There was no silence, and there was no cry,
but a kind of rough and indistinguishable blend
of muttered wrath, of rage between the teeth,
groans of the wounded, groans of dying breath.

52
The arms which were so gladdening to see
now make a sad and terrifying sight.
The steel has lost its flash, the gold its ray;
in all those lovely colors, no delight.
Trampled into the earth is every plume
and every decoration once so bright.
All's soiled with dust, if not bespattered with gore.
So altered is the face of the field of war.

53
Meanwhile the Ethiopians and the Moors
and the Arabs, stationed on the far left bank,
stretched their formation out in a swerving line
to double back upon the enemy's flank,
and from far off now slingers and archers wrought
great injury to the encumbered Frank,
when Rinaldo moved his squad to smash the trap—
and seemed an earthquake or a thunderclap.

54
Assimir was the first of that strong knot;
in the burnt Ethiopia he was bred.
Rinaldo struck him where his black neck sat
upon his trunk. He fell among the dead.
The taste of triumph now began to whet
his appetite for death, for more bloodshed,
and the ferocious victor now does things
incredible, horrible, monstrous. When he swings

55
he lands more deaths than blows, and yet the blows
fall fast as in a tempest—as a snake
seems to possess three tongues to freeze his foes,
so quickly and nimbly his one tongue can shake—
so the terrified people must suppose
(and his swift motion and their terror make
the illusion more believable) that he
wields in his swift hand not one sword but three.

56
The Libyan tyrants and the Negro kings
lay stretched in death, one in the other's blood.
His brave companions felt example's stings
and fell upon the rest. Not so long stood
the faithless mob; the sort of blow that brings
dishonor cut them down; such as these would
not even defend themselves. It was no fight,
only a slaughter. On this side, the sword's might,

57
on that, the throat. They took wounds face to face,
in noble fashion; and yet not for long.
The crowds flee. Fear so drives them in the chase
that they break orders, all their ranks go wrong.
But he pursues them, loses not a trace
till he has scattered them, driven them all headlong—
then collects himself, for against men who flee
the fleet-foot champion's ferocity

58
is tempered a little. As the woods' tall trees
or a mountain makes the rage of a gale grow
for opposition; but a gentle breeze
is all you feel in the peaceful plains below;
as rocks stir foam and boiling in the seas,
which in the open calmly lap—just so
whenever the opposition's strength decreased,
the fury abated in Rinaldo's breast.

59
And since he did not deign to spend his wrath
to no good end, on men who ran away,
toward the Africans he turned his path
and the Arabian infantry, who held sway
on the left flank; and that side was exposed,
assistance was too far to help, or lay
slain in the field. He strikes them from the side,
he and his armed contingent as they ride

60
rough-shod over the foot troops, smashing their spears,
their obstacles all broken, all in vain;
he scattered them, flung them to the earth—a storm
or high wind beating down the wavering grain.
Arms crushed and split and perforated limbs
littered the ground, their blood paving the plain—
and the racing horsemen with the bridles free
trampled and crossed above them savagely.

61
Rinaldo came where on her car of gold
Armida stood in military attire,
and roundabout her had a noble fold
of barons for her guard, and men afire
for love of her: she knew him, looked upon him
with eyes of wrath, and trembled with desire.
Over his face slight alteration came:
but she turned pale as ice, then turned to flame.

62
The knight looked on the chariot and passed by,
as if some other business made him go—
but the conspirers wouldn't let things lie
and charged to battle with their rival foe.
Some drew their swords, some readied the lance to fly,
and she drew back the arrow on her bow.
Her hands were driven by a cruel disdain;
Love held them back and made them mild again.

63
Love rose up against anger, and revealed
the fire that thrived within her heart, though hid;
she set her hand three times to draw the bow,
three times instead she dropped her hands and did
not shoot, not till scorn took the triumph, then
she sent her arrow flying. But amid
its very flight, she from her deepest soul
suddenly prayed that it might miss its goal.

64
Ah, if the sharp-tipped arrow only turned
to pierce her heart, she'd take it happily—
such potency Love has in her, though spurned.
What could Love not achieve in victory!
But she repented of that thought, and burned
with rage in her heart's contrariety—
so now she fears, and now she longs for it
to strike dead on—and looks to see the hit.

65

But not in vain that arrow is directed—
against the cavalier's hard mail it lands.
Instead of piercing through, though, it's deflected,
too hard for an arrow from a woman's hands.
He turns his back—she thinks she's been neglected,
is stung and burns with fury. Now she sends
one arrow after another, no wounds to show—
but while she shoots she feels Love's wounding bow.

66

"Is he then so impenetrable," said she,
"he does not care what enemies may do?
That jasper stone that makes his soul so hard,
is it the covering for his body too?
He can't be wounded by the hand or eye,
so tempered is his hardness. Whatever I do
I am defeated. Armed or unarmed, in vain—
lover or foe, he treats me with disdain.

67

"What new art can I use? What's left to me?
How can I change my form to some avail?
Alas, I've no hope for my cavalry,
for all those knights of mine seem bound to fail,
rather, I see them falling; against his might
all arms are useless and all strength is frail."
And well she saw some of her champions lying
dead on the field, or beaten down and dying.

68

What defense could she put up all alone?
In her mind now she is a prisoner
and slave. With bow or spear, what could be done?
Athena's and Artemis' arms won't profit her.
As when an eagle swoops upon a swan
with his fierce talons; overcome with fear
she lies low to the ground and droops her wing—
so now the timid Armida, faltering.

69

That was too much for the prince Altamor.
Till now he has been with his Persian crew,
holding them fast (they'd been routed before),
firming their ranks himself, with much ado.
But seeing her whom all his thoughts adore
so lost, he ran to her, or rather flew,
abandoning his honor and his men.
Save her, and let the whole world perish then!

70
To the defenseless chariot he came
and with his sword he cleared the way to go,
but while he was thus busied all the same
Rinaldo and Godfrey laid his squadrons low.
The poor man saw it, and composed himself;
a lover, not a captain, bore the blow.
Once he has seen Armida safely through
he turns to help those whom the Christians slew,

71
too late, such help! For there the pagan host
is put to rout, their ranks irreparable.
But on the other side our troops have lost
and turn their backs to flee the infidel.
One Robert managed to escape, the cost,
wounds to his chest and face. The other fell
prisoner to Adrastus. Thus they fought
to equal fortunes. But then Godfrey brought

72
his men about, marshaled their ranks anew,
wishing to seize the opportunity,
and without any pause to battle they flew,
one wing against the other, utterly.
Each wing comes stained with the blood of the foe,
and each wing wears the spoils of victory.
Honor and victory come to either side,
while in the center War and Fortune bide

73
their time, in doubt. Such the ferocity
of the faithful and pagan armies' strife,
when from a high tower, at a balcony,
the proud Soliman viewed the fight far off,
and viewed, as in a ring or theater,
the bitter tragedy of human life:
the assaults, and the fierce horror of death,
the plays of luck and chance. It stole his breath,

74
he stood a while abstracted, stupefied
at that first sight. And then the flames arise
within his heart, that he too might abide
the danger of that glorious enterprise.
His longings will not wait. Dressed in full armor,
he snatches up his helmet and he cries,
"Get up, get up! No more, no more delay!
Let's either win the war, or die today!"

75
Whether it was that Providence divine
inspired in him that furious temperament,
because the tyranny of Palestine
should that day find its last might wholly spent,
or that with death so close he felt himself
goaded to meet head-on the dread event—
rashly and rapidly he threw the bar,
flung the gate open, and brought out sudden war.

76
He does not wait for his companions to
second his challenge, but goes forth alone,
alone to meet an army fearlessly,
a thousand enemies, defied by one.
Ravished by his impetuosity
the others follow after, and from his throne
the king himself. The base, the circumspect,
the craven, know no fear now—the effect

77
of fury more than hope. Those whom the Turk
finds first, fall to his sudden, horrific blows,
and in bringing death he makes such speedy work
you see them slain and never see the cause.
From mouth to mouth, from the first to the last rank,
the terror spreads, the miserable news,
which when the commoners of Syria see
they nearly break into riot as they flee.

78
But with less terror and with less misrule
the Gascon squadrons took their ranks and place,
although that meant rough, sudden knocks for them,
for they would meet the danger face to face.
No wolf's tooth in the prowling wilderness,
no sharp-hooked talon of the feathered race
bloodied itself in the woods or in the trees,
as the sword of the Sultan bloodied itself with these.

79
It seemed half starved, devouring, ravenous—
it feasted on men's limbs, it guzzled blood.
With him the king, with him the troops who followed
struck the besiegers, slew them. Now the good
Raymond came hurrying where the Sultan was
destroying his battalions, and he would
not flee—though he well knew the fierce right arm
that had already brought him mortal harm.

80
Yet he assailed him once again, and fell,
stricken again where he was hurt of late;
it's his surpassing years alone that tell,
which bend him to the blow's surpassing weight.
Now as good Raymond lay insensible,
a hundred swords, a hundred bucklers fought
over his body. The Sultan went his way,
thinking him dead, or all-too-easy prey.

81
He batters down, he chops, he slits the vein,
and performs wonders in a little space.
Then he goes seeking, following his fury's train,
new stuff for killing in some other place.
As a man goaded with hunger leaves the plain
and goes for richer fare, so the Sultan's race
to find more war and killing, where he could
sate his infuriated thirst for blood.

82
Now through the walls in ruin he descends
and goes in haste straight out for the great fight,
leaving his fury to infect his friends
and for his foes, already-conceived fright;
and the one army goes about to clinch
the triumph he had left them (but not quite);
the other does resist, but in a sense
there are the signs of flight in their defense.

83
The Gascon soldiers lapsed into retreat,
but the Syrians were scattered in a rout.
That was near where the good Prince Tancred lodged
and lay recovering. When he heard them shout
he raised his feeble sides from the sickbed,
climbed to the roof and cast his eyes about,
and he saw where the good Count Raymond lay,
some giving ground, some scattered and running away.

84
Virtue which never leaves the valiant man
and does not languish, though the body fail,
instead of spirit and blood does all it can
to make his wounded members fresh and hale.
On his left arm he hangs his heavy shield—
his arm is bloodless, but no longer frail—
and in his other—sufficient for the brave—
he clasps a bare sword. To other arms he gave

85
no thought at all, but he came down, and cried,
"Where are you running, leaving your lord as prey
to the enemy? Will then the barbarous mosques
put his arms as a trophy on display?
Will you go back to France and tell the son
his father perished while you ran away?"
So he, and made his naked chest a shield
for a thousand soldiers armed on the battlefield,

86
and with his own shield, strapped with strong bull's hide
seven times over, stripped from the bull's back,
and reinforced with bronze on either side,
bronze of the finest temper, he took the hack
of the enemy's swords, he took their arrows' points,
he took them all, to bring good Raymond back,
and such a clearing-out his swung sword made
the old man lay as safe as in the shade.

87
Under the loyal shelter the old man
shortly began to breathe—he rose again,
feeling a double fire leaping within,
shame burning in his face, in his heart disdain.
He turns his glittering eyes to find once more
that arrogant fighter who left him nearly slain.
Missing him there, he rages, and prepares
a bitter vengeance for his followers.

88
Now they turn back, those men of Aquitaine,
following their leader, everyone intent
on vengeance. They who feared are brave again,
while they who dared now find their courage spent;
who burned with courage yield; who yielded, charge;
so things change in an instant. Raymond went
about his vengeance with a will, his fee
one hundred dead men for one injury.

89
While Raymond tries to vent his scorn and shame
upon the heads of the noblest of his foes,
he sees the usurper of the noble realm
fighting among the first. At him he goes,
strikes him full-front, and in the same place strikes
again and again, with unrelenting blows,
till the king falls, and with a horrible groan
bites the earth he once ruled. And now that one

90
protector is far away and the other is dead,
the effects on all the rest are variable:
one runs his own chest through with desperate sword
like an infuriated animal,
another looks for some way to escape
and runs for fear to the high citadel
that kept him safe before. But all in vain,
for the victor enters to seize his glorious gain,

91
storming the citadel. And some who fled
died on the steps, and some were strewn across
the very threshold. Raymond scaled the height,
in his right arm the banner of the Cross,
and in front of the two great hosts below
unfurled the sign of triumph and let it toss
in the rippling wind. But not in the Sultan's sight—
that proud man's now far off, in the thick of the fight.

92
He came to a field all slick and smoking red,
for it was steeped in more blood hour by hour,
so that it seemed a kingdom of the dead
where Death displayed the trophies of his power
and then passed on. He saw a warhorse, loose,
his bridle dangling free. Toward him he bore,
and seized the rein and mounted the empty back
and gave him a good spurring—to attack.

93
He brings assistance, great but not for long,
to the pagan host that yields for fear and languishes—
as great as a lightning bolt and just as long,
that strikes home suddenly and just as suddenly vanishes,
but of its bright and momentary course
it leaves in severed rock eternal vestiges.
He slew a hundred and more; of only two
will time not steal the memory they are due.

94
O Gildippe and Edward, your hard fate,
your bitter fall, and your most worthy deeds,
among strange nations I would consecrate
(if justice to my Tuscan pen concedes)
so that you will be held as fortunate
models of virtue and love, to him who reads
in any age; and if he serves Love, he
may crown your death, and crown my poetry.

95
The great-spirited lady turns her horse
toward where the Sultan made their ranks divide,
and fetches him head-on two slashing blows,
splitting his shield and wounding him in the side.
That cruel one saw her gear, knew who she was.
"Why, here's the lover and his whore!" he cried.
"Needle and spindle would be better for you
than anything your sword or boy can do!"

96
And more than ever filled with rage, he aimed
a vicious blow, of great temerity,
daring to burst her armor and enter the bosom
where only Love's blows had a right to be.
At once she let the reins fall, and she seemed
as one who languishes, about to die.
Poor Edward sees her miserable fate—
no slow defender, but unfortunate.

97
What should he do now? Wrath and piety
spur him at once, hastening to do all,
to exact vengeance on the enemy
and to support his dear, and stay her fall.
Now Love persuades him evenhandedly—
that neither duty is negotiable.
With his left arm he hurries to sustain
his beloved wife; the other to remain

98
his minister of hate. But against that pagan
will divided from might cannot suffice.
In the end he could not bear her up, nor kill
the killer by whose hand his sweet soul dies.
Rather the Sultan lops off his right arm,
the arm on which his faithful spouse relies—
he lets her fall. She does not fall alone:
he presses her dying members with his own.

99
As the tall elm to whom the grapevine clings—
her marrying branches lovingly entwine—
if he's chopped down, or a high wind shatters him,
he drags along to earth his companion vine—
and he himself unleaves her robe of green
and crushes the grapes that make her fragrant wine—
he feels less pain for whatever the fates betide him
than for the fate of her who dies beside him—

100
so he falls, and he grieves for her alone,
companion in eternity. They try
to form a word or two, but have no breath,
no more than will suffice to form a sigh.
They look upon each other and embrace
in the few moments left before they die.
One moment for them both shrouded the day,
and wedded thus, the good souls took their way.

101
Now Rumor spreads her pennons, taking flight,
crying the story of the bitter fall—
Rinaldo hears not just the word of it
but from a messenger has news of all.
Disdain and duty, grief and benevolence
now for the heaven-instructed vengeance call—
he turns—but there now in the Sultan's path
the great Adrastus stands and cries for wrath,

102
"You are the man whom I've been hungering for,
you are the one at last! Your arms I know.
There's not a shield I haven't stared at here—
I have called out your name wherever I go.
Now I'll fulfill my vow of vengeance and
hand your head to my goddess. Come, let's go
put fury and valor to comparison—
Armida's enemy, and her champion."

103
So he defied him, and gave a terrific hit
first on the temples, then at the base of the neck.
The fatal helmet did not—could not—split,
but in his saddle it gave him a good shake.
Apollo's art could not have mended it,
the stab in the side Rinaldo dealt him back.
The giant fell, the king invincible.
One blow alone took honors for his fall.

104
Those who stood round were stupefied with fear,
their blood was chilled, they felt their courage fail.
Soliman saw that strange blow all too near.
His heart was troubled, and his face turned pale.
His death was coming, he could see it clear.
He tried to form a plan, to no avail;
unusual for him. But what of ours
is not ruled by the heavens' eternal laws?

105
As sometimes in a brief and fitful sleep
strange dreams come to the sick or the insane—
he tries to move his limbs to run and leap
for he is being hunted; but in vain,
his weary legs and arms can never keep
pace with necessity and its hard strain,
and often he moves his mouth as if to shout
but not a sound or word can make it out—

106
so now the Sultan wanted to sweep on
to the attack, and strained his will to go,
but knew that all his usual wrath was gone,
nor did he know himself, his strength so low.
Whatever sparks of courage surged in him
were put out by a terror none might know.
In his heart various thoughts turned, none complete,
but never to flee, and never to retreat.

107
To the irresolute the victor came
and as he came it seemed to Soliman
he in his fury and his speed and frame
surpassed the semblance of a mortal man.
He put up little fight, but as he died
did not forget he was a noble man;
he gave no groans, but met the blows, uncowed.
To the last all he did was great and proud.

108
Now that the Sultan, who in that long war
like an Antaeus fell and rose again
ever the fiercer, had fallen to rise no more,
news of this spreads about the field amain,
and Fortune, that inconstant wanderer,
dares no more let the victory remain
in doubt, but stops her turning wheel, and delves
into the fight, with the French chiefs themselves.

109
Besides the rest, the royal troops now fled,
the gathered muscle of the Orient.
"Immortals" they were called; now left for dead
despite their title so magnificent.
Emiren halts the flight of the standard-bearer
and speaks to him in some embitterment.
"Are you the one I chose from a thousand men
to bear my lord's high banners? Rimedon,

110
"you were not given that flag to bring it back
in full retreat! Coward, what do you see?
Your captain bears his enemies' attack,
they're going at it—and you let him be!
What do you want, survival? Walk the track
that leads to death with honor. Come with me!
Let them fight here who want to get away.
The only way to life is honor's way."

111
So he returns to battle, hot with scorn.
With others he uses graver speeches still,
threatening, striking some, making them turn
to face the sword who feared it. Such his will
that he restores most of the broken horn
and there is still some hope. Above them all
is Tissaphernes, heartening them to attack.
That man had still not taken one step back.

112
Tissaphernes worked wonders on that day.
The Flemish took rough treatment at his hands;
to death he brought Gerard, Roger, Gernier;
and he broke through and scattered the Norman bands.
He lengthened this brief life with his display
of warlike honor, which forever stands
worthy of fame; as if life meant no more
he sought the greatest hazard in the war.

113
He sees Rinaldo—though his gear is rayed
vermilion, and his eagle in blue skies
has steeped his talons and his beak in blood,
those colors are not hard to recognize.
"I pray, O heaven, give my courage aid,
for here is where the greatest danger lies."
And sees his prize, Armida. "If I win,
Mohammed, I will hang his weapons in

114
"your temple." But his prayers were all in vain;
for his Mohammed's deaf, can't hear a thing.
As a lion whips his tail and shakes his mane
to wake the fierceness native to the king,
so he wakens his hate, whets his disdain
on the whetstone love, and flings it quickening
into the flames. All his strength merged in one,
he couches his arms to attack and gallops on.

115
Spurring his horse against the Saracen
in turn now rides the Latin cavalier.
They clear a wide berth for the charging men—
the fierce spectacle rivets everyone near—
and the Italian and the barbarian
dealt such great blows, so many, that for sheer
amazement many stood like senseless stone,
forgetting dangers and feelings of their own.

116
The one does strike; the other wounds, whose might
is greater, whose weapons are hard as flint. The field
is all a lake of Tissaphernes' blood;
his helmet's open, and he's lost his shield.
The lovely sorceress sees her champion,
his shattered gear, his members that must yield
for weakness. And the rest are so afraid
they're hardly bound now by the vows they made.

117
Once girded by her warriors all about,
alone atop her chariot sat she,
hating life, fearing servitude, and out
of hope for vengeance or for victory.
Between madness and panic she steps out
and mounts one of her stallions hastily,
and flees. But that's no solitary ride:
Love and Hate run like greyhounds at her side.

118
As Cleopatra in the days of old
from the fierce battle was the first to flee,
leaving her faithful lover alone against
the fortunate Augustus on the sea;
but, made by Love unjust against himself,
after her lone sails comes her Antony;
so Tissaphernes followed her secret flight
but was prevented by the Christian knight.

119
To the pagan, when his solace disappeared,
it seemed the sun and all its light sank low,
and to the man who wrongly kept him back
he turned in desperation, struck a blow
full in the front as hard as the hammer stroke
flinting out thunderbolts in the forge below
Mount Aetna; so heavy and so firmly pressed,
it bowed his head and shoulders to his chest.

120
Rinaldo straightens up immediately,
shakes his sword, and through the breastplate torn apart
opens the ribs, and sinks the bitter point
where life dwells in the center of the heart.
It glides so far it gives him a double wound,
exiting through the back and clearing out
an ample path for the dying soul to flee.
Rinaldo pauses, looks about to see

121
where he should go attack the pagan next
or where his help is most desirable,
but sees the pagan orders all dispersed
and not one of their banners flying still.
Whence the hot warlike hatred in his breast
subsides, and he is peaceful, and will kill
no more. And now he brings to mind again
the fleeing lady, grieving and alone.

122
He well remembered how she ran away—
it called for pity and for courtesy—
and he remembered that he pledged that day
when he departed that he'd always be
her cavalier. The hoofprints told the way
to follow where she fled, till finally
he found her in a dark and cloistered place
ideal to end her life in loneliness.

123
She was well pleased that to this gloomy dell
chance led her wandering steps the way to go.
Here she dismounted, and put off as well
her armor and her quiver and her bow.
"Unlucky arms," she said, "contemptible!
For you have left the fight and struck no blow.
I cast you off here—let this be your grave,
for all my injury's recompense you gave!

124
"Ah, see the weapons all unbathed in blood!
Not one today could hurt, not one at least?
All other chests are diamond to you—good,
but you might dare to pierce a woman's breast.
In mine here now before you soft and nude
lie all your honors, all your triumphs. Rest
easy, for it is tender, as Love must know.
It proved a tender target for his bow.

125
"I forgive you the cowardice you've shown—
prove your strength and your sharpness now on me.
And so I hope for health from you alone.
Alas, my fortune, and my misery!
Since only wounds will heal me of these wounds
for I can find no other remedy,
let the wound of love take the arrow's wounding art,
and let death be the physic to my heart.

126
"How happy I would be if when I die
I do not bear my illness too to hell!
Love, remain here; let Hate alone come with me,
perpetual companion for my soul.
Or return from the kingdom of the blind
to the ruthless man who scorned me, and expel
tranquility with horrifying sights,
shattering the repose of all his nights."

127
With that, she was resolved to see it through
and chose the sharpest arrow—the cavalier
came riding up, saw what she planned to do,
her fortune's final moment now so near,
and her face already dashed with death's pale hue,
hand poised to be her executioner,
ready to strike—from behind he caught her fierce
arm as the point of the arrow was going to pierce,

128
and Armida turned and looked on him in surprise—
she had not heard him coming. Suddenly
she raised a cry and turned her scornful eyes
from the face she so loved . . . and fainted. She
fell, like a half-cut flower, whose soft neck bows—
but he was her support. With one arm he
made a pillar for her lovely side to rest,
and gently pulled her gown over her breast.

129
And bathed the poor girl's lovely breast and face
with a few pitying tears, a gentle rain;
as when the morning fall of silver dew
brings beauty to the fading rose again,
so she came to herself and raised her head
dewed with another's tears. She tried in vain
to turn away—three times she looked above,
three times she dropped her glance from her dear love.

130
And with her small and languid hand she pushed
his mighty arm, her only prop, aside,
but his grip was the stronger for all that—
she couldn't escape no matter how hard she tried.
Gathered in those beloved bonds at last,
which she pretended she could not abide,
she spoke, and with her words came streams of tears,
but did not turn her eyes to the cavalier's.

131
"In leaving and returning, equally
cruel you are. And now who is your guide?
What wonders—you have foiled my wish to die
who were the reason for my suicide.
For what scorn do you wish to save me? Why?
With what pains must Armida now be tried?
I understand the villainy you seek—
but when one can't die, one is truly weak.

132
"Surely your honor will suffer quite a blot,
unless you lead on in your spoils' parade
the greatest title, greatest boast you've got,
a woman snatched by force, whom you'd betrayed!
One time I asked you for my life, for peace;
death would be sweet now, all my sadness laid
to rest. I won't ask you, at any rate—
there's nothing you can give me I won't hate!

133
"As for myself, you cruel man, I hope
somehow to flee your bestiality—
even if poison and the sword and rope
and clifftops are all lacking, I still see
a way to do it which you can't prevent!
I'll die, and, praised be heaven above, be free
of all your tricks! Ah, look at him pretend
to flatter my poor hopes." She made an end,

134
and wept for sadness, wept like the surging sea,
and the tears which love and hatred let fall from
her lovely eyes, moved him to sympathy,
for in his tears glowed pity's chaste, pure flame,
and he responded sweetly, tenderly,
"Armida, let your troubled heart be calm.
I do not save you to heap scorn upon.
I am your servant, and your champion.

135
"Look at my eyes if you cannot trust my words!
Look at them and you'll see my faith and zeal!
I'll take you back to where your kinsmen rule,
I swear it. But if heaven could reveal
some of its rays of true faith to your mind
and let dissolve your paganism's veil,
throughout the orient how I would see
that no one equaled you in royalty!"

136
So he spoke, and he bathed and warmed his pleas
now with a tear or two, now with a sigh,
whereupon as a tender veil of snow
when the sun shines or a warm breeze passes by,
so too her wrath which seemed unshakeable,
it melts; none of her other longings die.
"I am your handmaid. What you think best, do,
and let my law be but a sign from you."

137
In the meantime the Egyptian general
who saw his royal standard thrown upon
the earth, when one blow from the invincible
Godfrey felled it and the bold Rimedon;
and slain or put to rout his soldiers, all,
in the bitter end he did not wish to don
the coward's role, and sought, and not in vain,
the most illustrious death he could attain,

138
by a famed hand. And assails the great Bouillon,
for he can see no worthier enemy,
and shows, wherever he passes, wherever he goes,
the last signs of a desperate bravery.
Before he meets him, from afar he cries,
"Behold, at your hands I have come to die!
But in my last fall I will try to do
what by my ruin brings your ruin too."

139
With that, they spurred their horses to attack,
charging each other simultaneously,
and the French captain's shield went all to wrack,
his left arm gashed, its armor hacked away;
but the other took from him so great a whack
above the cheekbone, under the left eye,
it stunned him in the saddle. Trying to
recover himself, he falls, his gut run through.

140

With Emiren now dead, the mighty host
has few survivors left in the defeat.
Godfrey pursues the beaten, then he stops
when he sees Altamor, blood-stained, at his feet,
with half a sword, half a helmet on his head;
soldiers surround him with their lances, beat
his broken form. "Enough," the captain cries.
"Baron, my name is Godfrey. Recognize

141

"the man who takes you prisoner." And now
that soul that never bowed, that soul too grand
for modesty, hearing the name that sounds
from Ethiopia to the Atlantic strand,
replies, yielding his weapons, "You are worthy,
and I will do whatever you demand.
Your triumph over Altamor the bold
will not be poor in glory, or in gold.

142

"My devout wife will send to ransom me—
my kingdom's gold and gems will bring me home."
"I have a soul, heaven's gift, that cannot be
enticed by treasure," he replies. "But come,
whatever India brings you, take it free,
and all that Persia harvests. There's no sum
I place on a man's life. For I am here
to wage war, not to be a profiteer."

143

With that, he gave him over to his guards;
the enemy still fled, and he pursued,
fled to the fortresses, to throw a wall
in the way of death approaching—but no good;
the fort becomes a slaughter straightaway,
and tent to tent there flows a river of blood
which stains the plunder all about and soils
the glittering pomp of the barbaric spoils.

144

So Godfrey has attained the victory;
and leads, in the last light glowing in the west,
the victors into the city now set free
and to the place where Christ was laid to rest.
To the temple with the other chiefs goes he,
nor does he set aside his blood-stained vest.
He hangs his arms here; with devoted brow
adores the great tomb, and fulfills his vow.

Allegory of the Poem

Heroic poetry, like an animal in which two separate natures are joined, is composed of Imitation and Allegory. With the former it attracts the souls and the ears of men and brings them wondrous delight, while with the latter it instructs men in virtue or knowledge or both. And as Epic Imitation is but a semblance and image of human action, so Epic Allegory must be the figuring forth of human life. Now Imitation regards men's actions as they present themselves to the outward senses. Concerned principally with these, it seeks to convey the actions with words that are vigorous and expressive and well suited to illustrate them in all clarity before the eye. It does not concern itself with moral habits or affections or debates within the soul, except insofar as they manifest themselves in speech and gestures and action. By contrast, Allegory regards the passions, the beliefs, and the moral habits, not only as they appear outwardly, but as they intrinsically and essentially are. Allegory denotes them rather obscurely with what we might call mysterious signs, so that only those wise in the nature of things can understand them fully.

Now I shall set Imitation aside and speak of the proposed subject, the Allegory. Since human life is twofold, so Allegory must figure forth now one side and now the other. For if we define "man" as a compound of body and mind and spirit (as we ordinarily do), it follows that "human life" is a life proper to this compound, acquiring such perfection as it is capable of by the agreement of each of these parts. Sometimes, though rarely, "man" is taken to mean not the composition but the noblest part, that is, the mind. Given this meaning, one would say that "human life" consisted of contemplation and intellectual labor alone (but indeed such a life seems to participate profoundly in the divine and to elevate man beyond himself to the angels).

Dante's *Divine Comedy* is a figure of the contemplative man's life, as is the *Odyssey* in most of its parts; but in the *Iliad* civil life is pictured almost everywhere, and in the *Aeneid* too, though there we find rather a mingling of action and contemplation. Because the contemplative man lives a solitary life, while the active man lives in the civil community, Dante and Odysseus (in his departure from Calypso) are portrayed as alone, unaccompanied by armies or by hordes of followers. Agamemnon and Achilles, however, are portrayed very differently. One is the general of the Greek army, the other the leader of the hosts of Myrmidons. Aeneas, too, is accompanied when he fights or when he fulfills the duties of a civil leader, but when he descends to the underworld and the Elysian fields he leaves his companions behind, all but his faithful friend Achates, who is never far from his side. It was no accident that the poet portrayed the descent as solitary, for that journey also signifies his contemplation of the punishments and the rewards that the souls of the wicked and the just will receive in the other world. Besides, the speculative intellect, which operates as a solitary faculty, is fittingly portrayed by the action of a solitary man. But political action, which proceeds from and accompanies other faculties of the soul along with the intellect—for they all are as citizens united in one republic—can hardly be figured forth unless by an action in which many people work together. For these reasons, and with these illustrations in mind, I fashioned the Allegory of my poem as follows.

The army, composed of various Princes and Christian soldiers, signifies the virile man, composed of body and soul. The soul in turn is not simple, but in itself contains many distinct faculties and powers. Jerusalem—a well-fortified city in a rugged, mountainous land, toward which are directed, as toward their ultimate end, all the enterprises of the Faithful Army—signifies such Civil Happiness as would befit a Christian, as shall be shown shortly. This good, however, is difficult to obtain, and thus is set at the summit of the hard-conquered peak of virtue. To it as to their goal all the actions of the political man are directed. Godfrey, captain of the assembled troops, stands in the place of the intellect, in particular that intellect that judges not the necessary but the mutable—things that could fall out in any number of ways. By the will of God and of the princes he is chosen Captain of this enterprise, for the intellect is from God, constituted by nature Lord over the other powers of the soul and over the body, commanding the former with a civil and the latter with a kingly power. Rinaldo, Tancred, and the other princes stand for the other powers of the soul, and the lesser soldiers signify the body. And because, by the imperfection of human nature and the deceit of our Enemy, man does not attain to that happiness without many difficulties and impediments internal and external, these difficulties are figured forth in the composition too. The death of Sven and his companions, slain far from a host they were trying to join, demonstrates the losses the civil man can suffer, of friends, of followers, and of other external goods, which are the instruments of virtue and which assist us in attaining happiness. The armies of Africa and Asia, and the defeats in battle, represent enemies and calamities and the vicissitudes of fortune.

As for the internal impediments—the love that caused Tancred and the other knights to behave like fools and abandon Godfrey, and the indignation that led Rinaldo to stray from the enterprise—these signify the strife between the rational faculty and the concupiscible and irascible faculties, and how these two rebel. The demons who conspire to impede the taking of Jerusalem are at once figures and the things figured, representing themselves in their own right as they oppose our civil happiness, lest it be our ladder to Christian blessedness. The sorcerers Ismen and Armida, ministers of the Devil, who try to remove the Christians from battle, are two diabolical temptations that insinuate themselves into the faculties of the soul, whence every kind of sin proceeds. Ismen signifies that temptation that uses false semblances to fool what we may call the opinionative power. Armida is that temptation that attacks the appetitive power. Thus proceed from the one and the other the errors of opinion and of appetite. Ismen's enchantment of the woods, which deceives by means of phantoms, signifies the falsity of reasons and arguments that spring from the Woods, that is, from the mob, from the variety of men's opinions and talk. And since men follow vice but flee virtue, believing that danger and toil are the worst of evils, intolerable, or judging with Epicurus and his followers that happiness is to be found in pleasure and lassitude, the enchantment and its delusion are twofold. The fire, the whirlwind, the darkness, the monsters and the other apparitions are those delusive arguments that try to show that honorable labor and honorable risks are to be shunned as evils. The flowers, the springs, the streams, the musical instruments, and the nymphs are those false syllogisms that place leisure and the delights of the senses as things to be desired as good. But enough of the impediments, within and without, which man encounters, since even if the Allegory of every detail has not been made explicit, from these principles anyone can hunt it down by himself.

Now let us proceed to the internal and external aids by which civil man can overcome every difficulty and win his longed-for happiness. The diamond shield that protects Raymond and is seen defending Godfrey is to be interpreted as special protection extended by the Lord God. The angels can signify divine help, or divine inspiration, as suggested by the dream of Godfrey and the Hermit's revelations. The Hermit, who to free Rinaldo sends the two messengers to the Wise Man, figures forth supernatural wisdom instilled by divine grace, just as the Wise Man figures forth human wisdom. For from human wisdom and from knowledge of nature's works, justice, temperance, disregard of death and of perishable things, greatheartedness, and every other moral virtue are begotten and nurtured; and from contemplation of nature the civil man can derive great assistance. The poem portrays the Wise Man as pagan-born but converted by the Hermit to the true faith. On becoming Christian, he puts away his arrogance and no longer presumes upon his knowledge, resting in the judgments of his Master. Just so, Philosophy was born among and nurtured by the Gentiles of Egypt and Greece, and from thence came to us, presumptuous, bold, misbelieving and proud beyond measure, until Saint Thomas and the other holy doctors made her a disciple of and handmaiden to Theology. Through their work she grew modest and more decent, and ceased her reckless assertion of things opposed to what had been revealed to her Teacher and Mistress. Nor is the figure of the Wise Man introduced for that alone (after all, the Hermit's advice might have been sufficient to find Rinaldo and return him to the army). He shows that God's grace often works not directly or through supernatural agents, but through perfectly natural means; while on the other hand it is quite reasonable that Godfrey, who surpasses the others in piety and devotion, and who, as we have said, is a figure of the intellect, be specially favored and privileged with grace granted to no other. This human wisdom, then, when directed by a higher faculty, frees the sensitive soul from vice and instills moral virtue. But because that wisdom alone does not suffice, Peter the Hermit must hear Godfrey's and Rinaldo's confessions, and Tancred's too, after he first turns the young man's heart back to God.

But since Godfrey and Rinaldo are the two principal characters in the poem, the reader may be pleased if I return to a few of the things I have touched upon, and unveil the allegory of their actions in more minute detail.

Godfrey, who holds the most important place in the poem, is, allegorically, the Intellect, as is shown in various parts of the poem, for instance:

> [Let others draw their swords,] for you must be
> Their head, by reason and authority. [7.62]

And, more clearly:

> For you are this host's life, its intellect. [11.22]

—with the less noble faculty of "life" comprehended in the more noble "intellect." Meanwhile Rinaldo, who occupies the second rank in the poem's action, should occupy a corresponding position in the Allegory. What that second faculty of the soul is, I shall now declare: it is the irascible faculty, the one that of all the other powers of the soul departs the least from the nobility of the mind. For even Plato was in some doubt, whether or not to distinguish it from Reason at all. As in the soul, so in the army of soldiers: just as it is the soldier's duty to obey his captain, who exercises the art and skill of command, and to fight the enemy, so it is the duty of the irascible part of the soul, warlike and robust, to arm itself with reason against the desires, with the vehemence and ferocity it needs to beat back and put to flight whatever might hinder the attainment of happiness. But when it does not obey reason, allowing itself to be carried away by its own force, it can happen that it does not fight the desires at all but joins their side, like a bad watchdog biting the sheep and not the thieves. This impetuous, vehement, indomitable virtue, though it could never be figured forth in a single knight, is nonetheless principally signified by Rinaldo, as is seen in the verse

> Indignant Scorn, fierce fighter on Reason's part. [16.34]

In his duel with Gernando, trespassing beyond the bounds of civilly sanctioned vengeance, and in his servitude to Armida, Rinaldo may denote anger ungoverned by Reason; but when he disenchants the woods and storms the city, breaking the enemy host, he may denote Anger directed by Reason. Thus Rinaldo's return and his reconciliation with Godfrey signify but the obedience that the irascible must render to the rational. In these reconciliations two things are to be noted. First, Godfrey, with a civil moderation, shows himself to be Rinaldo's superior. This teaches us that reason commands righteous Anger not in a royal but in, so to speak, a republican manner. By contrast, when Godfrey suppresses the mutiny he imperiously sends Argillan to prison, showing us that the mind rules over the body as a king. Second, just as the rational must not exclude the irascible from action (and the Stoics were much deceived in this), so should it never usurp the duties of the irascible, as such usurpation would violate natural justice. Instead it should make the irascible its companion and minister. Just so, Godfrey was not to have attempted the venture of the woods himself, nor assume the other duties proper to Rinaldo. Thus the poet would have shown less art and less regard to utility—which latter the poet, lower in rank than the political man in the natural order, must have for his goal—if he had devised that Godfrey alone should perform everything necessary for the storming of Jerusalem.

Corroborating the decision to place Rinaldo and Godfrey as signs of the irascible and the rational faculties is what Hugh says in the dream, when he likens one to the head and the other to the right arm, for the head, if we can trust Plato, is the seat of Reason, and the right arm, if not the seat of just Anger, is at least its principal instrument.

To conclude: the Army, to which by God's grace by human understanding are restored Rinaldo and the other knights in obedience to their Captain, signifies man in the state of natural justice, when the superior faculties command as they ought, and the inferior obey. Beyond that, it signifies man brought to obedience of the divine. When this state is achieved the demons are driven from the woods with ease, the city stormed, and the enemy army defeated. In other words, all the external hindrances are overcome and man attains political happiness. But because this civil blessedness cannot be the ultimate goal for a Christian, who must aim higher still for Christian happiness, Godfrey storms the earthly Jerusalem not for temporal dominion, but so that the divine rites might be celebrated there, and the Tomb be visited by pious and devout pilgrims. Thus the poem ends with Godfrey's adoration, to show us that the intellect, having labored in civil actions, must finally repose in prayer and in contemplation of the rewards of the immortal and most blessed life to come.

☙ Cast of Characters

The following list does not include any historical or mythological figures who play no active part in the poem. For those, see the notes.

ACHILLES, Lombard Adventurer, brother of Sforza and Palamedes, 1.55; slain by Clorinda, 9.69–70

ADEMAR, bishop of Le Puy, leader of four hundred men, 1.38–39; celebrates Mass for the army, 11.3–5; slain by Clorinda, 11.44; desertion of his men, 13.69; seen by Godfrey, blessing his armies, 18.95

ADRASTUS, Saracen leader of Indian troops, 17.28; vows to kill Rinaldo for Armida, 17.49–50; rebuked by Tissaphernes, 17.50–51; spied on by Vafrine, adoring Armida, quarreling with Tissaphernes, 19.68, 70–74; stationed on the right for the final battle, 20.23; fights with Robert, 20.48–49; takes Robert prisoner, 20.71; slain by Rinaldo, 20.101–3

AGRICALT, leader of troops from Arabia, 17.23; slain by Rinaldo, 20.56

AGRICALT, Saracen warrior, slain by Argillan, 9.79

ALADINE, Muslim king of Jerusalem, contemplates persecution of Christians, devastates countryside, 1.82–90; heeds Ismen, steals icon of the Virgin Mary, 2.1–7; exacts vengeance for the image's countertheft, 2.8–13; condemns Sophronia and Olindo to death, 2.19–32; releases them to Clorinda, 2.45–52; exiles Sophronia, Olindo, and young Christian men of Jerusalem, 2.54–55; prepares for first Christian attack, 3.11–12; views battle from ramparts with Erminia, 3.12, 17–20, 37–40, 58–63; recalls Godfrey in his youth, 3.60–61; prepares for renewed hostilities, 6.2; refuses Argante's request to begin the fight immediately, 6.9–11; permits Argante's single-combat challenge, 6.14; asks Clorinda to keep guard over Argante, 6.21; stations Clorinda as overlook for duel, 7.83; orders retreat, 9.93–94; calls peers to council, 10.35–36; greets and honors Soliman, 10.53–54; orders his troops, 11.29; hears Clorinda's plan to burn the tower, 12.10–12; prevents Soliman from joining Clorinda and Argante, 12.13–16; rejects Argante's plea to reopen the city gate, 12.102; hears Ismen's report of the forest demons and the coming drought, 12.12–15; repairs breaches in walls, 12.16; faces Raymond's tower, 18.67; retreats before Raymond's troops, 18.102–4; enters final battle, 20.76; slain by Raymond, 20.89

ALARC, Saracen leader of Egyptian troops, 17.30; slain by Gildippe, 20.33

ALBAZZAR, Saracen warrior, kills Ernest, 9.41

ALBIAZAR, leader of Arab troops, 17.22

ALBIN, Christian warrior, slain by Clorinda, 9.68

ALCANDER, Christian warrior, sees Clorinda kill his father, 3.35; ambushes Erminia, 6.107; reports to Godfrey the supposed flight of Clorinda, 6.112–13

ALCASTO, arrogant leader of six thousand Switzers, compared to Capaneus, 1.63; battered while trying to be first to scale the wall, 11.34–36; volunteers to penetrate the demon-infested forest and fails, 13.24–29; embarrassed report to Godfrey, 13.30

ALCORAN, Saracen leader of troops from Barca, 17.19

ALDIAZEL, Saracen warrior, slain by Argillan, 9.79

ALDIN, leader of Arab troops, 17.22

ALECTO, Greco-Roman Fury, demon of Hell, 2.91, 6.33; ordered by demon Astagorius to stir dissent in the Christian camp, 8.1–4; incites Argillan to sedition, 8.59–62; fans the riot, 8.72; spurs Soliman to attack, 9.1–3, 8–13; informs Aladine of Soliman's approach, 9.14

ALETE, ambassador from the king of Egypt, arrives with Argante at Godfrey's camp to discuss a truce, refused by Godfrey, 2.58–93; parts with Argante, 2.94

ALGAZEL, Saracen leader of troops from upper Egypt, 17.18

ALGAZZAL, Saracen warrior, slays Otto, 9.41; is slain by Argillan, 9.78

ALGAZZAR, Saracen slain by Dudon, 3.44

ALIPRAND, foraging chief, brings back Rinaldo's riddled gear, reports to Godfrey, 8.50–56

ALMANSOR, Saracen slain by Dudon, 3.44

ALTAMOR, king of Samarkand; Saracen chief, leaves his wife, 17.26–27; spied on by Vafrine, courting Armida, 19.69; stationed at the left for the final battle, 20.22–23; exploits, 20.38–41; injures Gildippe, 20.41–43; battles with Godfrey, 20.47–48; saves Armida, 20.69–70; surrenders to Godfrey, 20.140–42

AMURAT, Saracen slain by Dudon, 3.44

AQUILINE, horse ridden by Raymond of Toulouse, begotten by the west wind, 7.75–76, 89

ARADIN, leader of Armida's troops, 17.35

ARASPE, one of Soliman's veteran Turks; impersonated by Alecto; urges Soliman to move against the Christians, 9.8–11

ARBILAN, supposed father of Armida, 4.43

ARDELIO, father of Polyphernes and Alcander, killed by Clorinda, 3.35

ARDONE, Christian soldier, slain by Altamor, 20.39

14.50–71; lovemaking with Rinaldo, 16.17–27; discovers Rinaldo's flight and accuses him of treachery, 16.35–60; faints, 16.60–61; vows vengeance, 16.61–67; returns to the Dead Sea, 16.68–73; accuses her uncle, 16.74; goes to Gaza, 16.75; appears before the king of Egypt, 17.9; in parade, 17.33–36; addresses the king, promising herself to Rinaldo's assassin, 17.41–49; impersonated by demon to tempt Rinaldo, 18.30–34; spied on by Vafrine as her men vow to kill Rinaldo, 19.67–74; stationed in midst of the Saracen hosts, 20.22; tries to shoot Rinaldo, 20.61–67; saved by Altamor, 20.68–70; flees, 20.116–17; attempts suicide, 20.121–30; accuses Rinaldo, 20.131–33; consoled by Rinaldo, 20.134–36

ARNALDO, Christian warrior, accuses Rinaldo of murdering Gernando, 5.33–35

ARONTES, supposed friend of Armida, helps her against her wicked uncle, 4.52–59

ARONTEUS, Saracen leader of Asian troops, 17.16

ARSETE, eunuch, guardian of Clorinda; tells story of Clorinda's birth and her miraculous preservation by Saint George, 12.18–40; mourns her death, 12.101

ARTAXERXES, Saracen warrior, slain by Gildippe, 20.34

ARTEMIDORUS, count of Pembroke, chosen by lot to accompany Armida, 5.73

ASSIMIR, leader of Ethiopian troops, 17.24; slain by Rinaldo, 20.54

ASTAGORIUS, demon, orders Alecto to stir dissent in the Christian camp, 8.1–4

AUGUSTUS, Tasso's name for the Greek emperor; accused by Alete of treachery, 2.71

BALDWIN, brother of Godfrey, leader of his own and Godfrey's troops, 1.39; seized his friend Tancred's conquest, 5.48, 8.64; volunteers to fight Argante, 7.66; ordered by Godfrey to aid embattled Christian flank, 7.108–9; stands beside Godfrey during sedition, 8.75; wears light armor, following Godfrey's example, 11.25; accompanies the wounded Godfrey to his tent, 11.68; ordered to amass his troops in the center, 20.9; battle with Mulehassah's troops, 20.48

BEELZEBUB, demon, Lord of the Flies, impersonates Clorinda, persuades Oradin to violate the truce and shoot Raymond, 7.99–101

BERLINGHIER, Christian warrior, slain by Clorinda, 9.68

BERTHOLD (son of Azzo IV, the marquis of Este), father of Rinaldo, 1.59; 17.81

BOHEMOND, Christian duke and ruler of Antioch, uncle of Rinaldo, 1.9; fails to attend Godfrey's council, 1.20; enmity of Erminia for, 3.63; suggested as refuge for Rinaldo, 5.49, 14.29

BRIMART, Saracen warrior, 17.31

BRUNEL, Christian soldier, slain by Altamor, 20.39

CAMILLUS, leader of Italian troops, 1.64; absent from army, 8.74; attacks left flank of enemy, 18.56, 63

Campsone, Saracen leader of troops from Cairo, 17.17

Canar, leader of Ethiopian troops, 17.24; deployed with Altamor, 20.23; slain by Rinaldo, 20.56

Cariclia, supposed mother of Armida, 4.43–44; appears to Armida in a dream, 4.49

Cassan, emperor of Antioch, father of Erminia, 2.71, 3.12, 6.56

Charles, sole survivor of Sven's army, 8.2; tells Godfrey of Soliman's massacre of Sven's troops, 8.4–42; miraculous survival, 8.25–28; meets two hermits who charge him to deliver Sven's sword to Rinaldo, 8.29–38; accompanies Ubaldo to Ascalon to find Rinaldo, 14.27–34; meets Wise Man of Ascalon and descends underground with him, 14.34–40; takes leave of Wise Man and boards Fortune's skiff, 15.1–7; asks Fortune to put in at one of the inhabited isles in the Atlantic, 15.38; disembarks with Charles and climbs the mountain below Armida's hideaway, 15.45–66; enters Armida's garden, 16.1–19; presents Sven's sword to Rinaldo, 17.83

Clorinda, pagan warrioress, with whom Tancred falls in love, 1.47–48; arrives in Jerusalem, 2.38; brief history of, 2.39–41; observes Sophronia and Olindo at the stake, 2.42–43; intercedes with Aladine to save their lives, 2.44–52; attacks the Christians in first battle, slaying Gardo, 3.13–16; encounter with Tancred, 3.21–28; is wounded slightly in retreat, 3.29–32; slays Ardelio, 3.35; ordered by Aladine to guard Argante in single combat, 6.21; is seen by Tancred, 6.26–27; friendship with Erminia, 6.79–80; impersonated by Erminia, 6.81–112; ordered by Aladine to overlook duel between Argante and Raymond, 7.83; is impersonated by Beelzebub, 7.99–101; attacks the Christians, 7.116–19; leads Aladine's troops to reinforce Soliman's sneak attack, 9.43, 54; exploits, 9.68–73; ordered by Aladine to retreat, 9.94; welcomes Soliman, 10.54; stands on ramparts, like Artemis, 11.27–28; exploits in archery, wounding Prince William and Robert; slaying Stephen, Clothar, Ademar, and Palamedes, 11.41–45; wounds Godfrey with an arrow, 11.54–55; devises plan to burn the Christian tower, 12.2–11; hears Arsete tell the story of her birth and miraculous preservation by Saint George, 12.18–40; rejects Arsete's plea, 12.41; sallies forth with Argante, 12.42–47; is accidentally shut out of the city, 12.48–50; seen and pursued by Tancred, who kills her in a duel, 12.51–65; baptized by Tancred, 12.66–70; appears, ensainted, to Tancred in a dream, 12.91–93; buried, 12.95–99

Clothar, leader of the French troops after the death of Hugh, 1.37; slain by Clorinda, 11.43; desertion of his men, 13.69

Corban, Saracen slain by Dudon, 3.44

Corcuth, Saracen warrior, slain by Godfrey, 9.90

Count of Chartres (Stephen of Blois), leader of four hundred men, 1.40

Drogut, Saracen warrior, slays Prince Henry, Olifernes, Philip, Adrian, Gilbert, 9.40

DUDON OF CONTZ, leader of the Adventurers, 1.52–53; leads men in the first battle, 3.36–37; is pointed out by Erminia, 3.39; slays five Saracens and then is slain by Argante, 3.43–46; eulogized, 3.65–70; buried, 3.72–73; fights in the invisible hosts of Heaven, 18.95

EDWARD, Adventurer, husband of Gildippe and her compatriot in arms, 1.56–57; pointed out by Erminia to Aladine, 3.40; volunteers to fight Argante, 7.67; fights beside Gildippe, 20.35–36; slays Artaban and Alvan, 20.37; slain by Soliman, dying beside his wife, 20.94–100

EMIREN, baptized Clement, apostate captain of the king of Egypt's royal militia, 17.32; given charge of king of Egypt's armies, 17.37–40; overheard by Vafrine conspiring to kill Godfrey, 19.62–65; marshals troops for the final battle, 20.21–23; addresses troops, 20.24–27; halts flight of Rimedon and the Immortals, 20.109–11; slain by Godfrey, 20.137–39

ENGERLON, Adventurer, 1.54

ERMINIA, princess of Antioch, in love with Tancred; summoned by Aladine to watch the first battle from the ramparts, 3.12; points out Tancred, 3.18–20; points out Rinaldo, Godfrey, and various other Christians, 3.37–40, 58–63; well treated by Tancred, 6.56–58; comes to Jerusalem, 6.59–60; watches Tancred from the ramparts, 6.61–63; impersonates Clorinda to visit the wounded Tancred, 6.64–106; ambushed by Polyphernes and Alcander, 6.107–11; in flight from the Christians, 6.110–11, 7.1–3; sheltered by a kindly shepherd, 7.4–22; among Armida's ladies; recognizes the spy Vafrine, 19.77–84; leaves the Saracen camp with Vafrine, reveals her love for Tancred and reveals conspiracies against Godfrey and Rinaldo, 19.84–101; laments over the wounded Tancred, 19.104–10; heals Tancred, 19.111–14; brought to Jerusalem, 19.119

ERNEST, Christian warrior, slain by Albazzar, 9.14

EROTIMUS, physician, poet; attempts to retrieve arrowhead from Godfrey's leg, 11.70–75

EUSTACE, Adventurer, younger brother of Godfrey, 1.54; addresses Armida, 4.33–38; protests Godfrey's postponement of aid to Armida, 4.78–81; recalls Armida, 4.84; supports Rinaldo as Dudon's successor, to remove him as rival for Armida, 5.8–15; leaves camp to follow Armida, 5.80; fights with Rambald, 5.81–84; is struck down in battle, 11.60; aided by Rinaldo, is second to scale the wall, 18.79

EVERARD, Adventurer, 1.56; chosen by lot to accompany Armida, 5.75; volunteers to fight Argante, 7.67

FORTUNE, minister of Heaven, guide for Charles and Ubaldo, 14.71–72; takes them to the Fortunate Isles, 15.3–45; describes voyage of Columbus, 15.24–32; refuses Charles' request to visit the inhabited islands, 15.39–40; gives the knights advice, 15.44–45; takes Rinaldo back to the Levant, 17.53–55

GABRIEL, archangel, Christianization of the messenger-god Mercury; delivers exhortation to Godfrey, 1.12–17

Argante's challenge for single combat, 6.17–20; chooses Tancred as the Christian champion, 6.24–25; hears of Clorinda's supposed flight, 6.113; volunteers to supply Tancred's place in the duel with Argante, 7.58–61; hears Raymond's plea, 7.61–65; thanks Raymond, then chooses Raymond by lot, 7.66–71; presents Raymond with a sword, 7.72; orders his men to avenge Raymond, 7.103–4; orders Baldwin to charge, 7.109–10; sends more men into the rout, 7.113; holds fast against the Christian retreat, 7.120–21; addressed by Charles, 8.5; eulogizes Sven, 8.43–45; hears Aliprand's report, 8.50–56; puts down sedition, praying to God for help, 8.75–85; defends against Soliman's sneak attack, 9.42–48; fights with Soliman, 9.49–50; exploits, 9.90–91; hears report of Armida's followers, 10.57–59; heeds Peter's recommendation for a Mass, 11.1–3; alone in procession, 11.6; dines with peers, 11.16–17; arms as an infantryman, 11.21–24; marshals troops for battle, 11.30–32; attacks, 11.46; is wounded, retreats, 11.51–57; miraculously healed, 11.68–75; resumes attack, 11.75–77; fights with Argante, 11.78–79; exploits, 11.81–82; calls cease-fire, orders repairs to tower, 11.82–86; visits the wounded Tancred, 12.84; sends carpenters to fetch lumber for new tower, 13.17; hears of the forest's haunting, 13.22–23; sends Alcasto, 13.26; hears of Alcasto's failure, 13.30; sends more men, 13.31; hears of Tancred's failure, 13.47–49; hears Peter's prophecy of Rinaldo, 13.50–52; accused by his thirsty men, 13.64–67; prays for rain, 13.70–73; visited by Hugh in a dream, 14.2–20; advised by Hugh to recall Rinaldo, 14.12–18; agrees to Guelph's plea to recall Rinaldo, 14.21–26; meets the returning Rinaldo, 18.1–4; greets Rinaldo on his return from the forest, 18.40; intercepts carrier pigeon; plans strategy, 18.50–56; sups before the great battle, 18.62; instructs rear guard, 18.65–66; attacked by balls of fire, 18.83–86; sees sainted warriors fighting beside the Christians, 18.92–97; fights Soliman on the bridge, 18.98–99; cease-fire and speech at nightfall, 19.50–53; Ormondo plots against his life, 19.62–63; Erminia reveals plot to Vafrine, 19.86–89; hears Vafrine's report, 19.119–127; asks Raymond's advice and decides to fight in the open field, 19.127–31; prepares for last battle, 20.4; marshals troops, 20.6–13; speech, 20.14–20; slays Ormondo and the assassins, 20.44–46; enters the fray, 20.47; fights Altamor's troops, 29.70–72; slays Emiren, 20.137–39; spares Altamor, 20.140–43; fulfills his vow, 20.144

GUASCO, Christian warrior, chosen by lot to accompany Armida, 5.75; slain by Altamor, 20.40

GUELPH, uncle of Rinaldo, one of Godfrey's chief lieutenants, German and Lombard prince, ancestor of the Este family, 1.10, 41–42; 17.79–81; proclaims Godfrey general, 1.32; leader of five hundred men, 1.42; pointed out by Erminia to Aladine, 3.63; advises Rinaldo to leave camp, 5.50; defends Rinaldo's manslaughter, 5.53–59; volunteers to fight Argante, 7.66; ordered by Godfrey to sally forth against Clorinda, 9.43–45, 55; is wounded by Clorinda, 9.72; kills Osmides, 9.73; pursues the retreating Saracens, 9.96; placed in command by the wounded Godfrey, 11.56; is struck down, 11.59; inspired by God to plead to Godfrey for Rinaldo's return, 14.17, 21–24; friendship with Ubaldo, 14.27–28; directs Charles and Ubaldo toward Damascus, 14.29; greets Rinaldo, 18.4; ordered to guard the rear, 18.65–66

Guy, name of two Adventurers, 1.56; volunteer to fight Argante, 7.66; one injured by Argante, 7.107–8; one slain by Altamor, 20.40

Henry (Henri), Christian warrior, chosen by lot to accompany Armida, 5.75

Henry, courier for Godfrey, sent to the Greek emperor, 1.67–70

Hircano, Saracen king of Hormuz, 17.25; slain by Gildippe, 20.32

Holofernes, Bavarian soldier, killed by Drogut, 9.40

Hugh, brother of the king of France, deceased leader of the French troops, 1.37; appears to Godfrey in a dream, 14.5–19; fighting beside the Christians, 18.94

Hydrotes, sorcerer and ruler of Damascus, uncle to Armida; sends Armida against the Christians, 4.20–26; accused by Armida, 16.74

Idrahort, Saracen leader of Egyptian troops, 17.30

Ishmael, Saracen warrior, slain by Gildippe, 20.34

Ismen, apostate, Saracen mage, plots to steal the icon of the Virgin Mary, 2.1–6 ; fails to discover image's whereabouts, 2.10; brings Soliman to Jerusalem, 10.7–34; prophecy of Saladin, 10.22–23; leads Soliman through Herod's secret passage, 10.29–34; bids Soliman reveal himself, 10.48; sits beside Soliman and Aladine, 10.54; gives Clorinda and Argante fuel for burning the tower, 12.17, 42; summons demons to inhabit the forest, 13.1–11; tells Aladine of his success and of the coming drought, 13.12–15; concocts explosives, 18.47–48; ignominious death, 18.87–89

King of Egypt (the Caliph), Saracen ruler, sends Alete and Argante as ambassadors to Godfrey, 2.57; reputed to be enamored of Godfrey's military might, 2.63–64; his history and the review of his troops at Gaza, 17.6–36; summons Emiren, 17.37–39; dines with his captains and is addressed by Armida, 17.41–42; breaks up fight between Adrastus and Tissaphernes and replies to Armida, 17.51–52

King of Tripoli, comes to truce with Godfrey, 1.76; described as prudent, 10.47

King of Zumara, Saracen leader, 17.19

Latinus, Christian soldier, father of five sons, slain with his family by Soliman, 9.27–39

Laurentius, young son of Latinus, twin of Pico; slain by Soliman, 9.34

Lesbin, Soliman's page boy, 9.81–82; slain by Argillan, 9.83–86; avenged by Soliman, 9.87–88

Mamet, Saracen slain by Dudon, 3.44

Marlabust, Saracen warrior, 17.30

Matilda, Tuscan countess and foster mother of Rinaldo, 1.59

MICHAEL, ARCHANGEL, summoned by God to drive the demons back to Hell, 9.58–65; shows Godfrey sainted warriors fighting on the Christian side, 18.92–96

MULEHASSAH, Saracen warrior, leads infantry in the center in the final battle, 20.22; battle with Baldwin's troops, 20.48

MULEHASSAH, Saracen warrior, slain by Argillan, 9.79

OBIZZO, Tuscan Adventurer, 1.55

ODEMAR, Saracen leader of Egyptian troops, 17.30

OLDERIC, Christian warrior, chosen by lot to accompany Armida, 5.75

OLINDO, young Christian, in love with Sophronia, 2.16. offers his life for hers, 2.27–31; reveals his love at the stake, 2.33–35; set free by Clorinda's intercession, 2.42–52; marries Sophronia, 2.53.

ORADIN, Saracen warrior, persuaded by Beelzebub in Clorinda's shape to break the truce and shoot Raymond, 7.100–101

ORCANO, timorous counselor to Aladine; advises appeasement, 10.39–48; cowers before Soliman, 10.56

ORINDO, Saracen warrior, 17.31

ORMANNO, Christian warrior, slain by Argante, 7.107–8

ORMONDO, Saracen warrior, 17.30; overheard by Vafrine conspiring to kill Godfrey, 19.62–65; slain by Godfrey, 20.44–46

ORMUSSEH, Arab leader, greets Soliman, 10.55

OSMIDES, Saracen warrior, slain by Guelph, 9.73

OTTO (dei Visconti), Adventurer, winner of the Saracen shield whose heraldry became that of the famous Milanese Visconti family, 1.55; beaten by Argante in single combat, 6.28–36; slain by Algazzal, 9.41

PALAMEDES, Lombard Adventurer, brother of Achilles and Sforza, 1.55; slain by Clorinda, 11.45

PETER THE HERMIT, preacher of the First Crusade; advises army to choose a sole leader, 1.29–31; hears report of Armida's followers, 10.58; prophesies Rinaldo's return, his glorious exploits and progeny, 10.73–79; advises celebration of Mass, 11.1–3; leads procession, 11.5; admonishes Tancred, 12.85–88; prophesies that Rinaldo must overcome the enchanted wood, 13.50–52; sends Charles and Ubaldo to the Wise Man of Ascalon, 14.18, 29–31; baptizes Wise Man of Ascalon, 14.45; advises Rinaldo to do penance, 18.6–11; greets triumphant Rinaldo, 18.39

PHILIP, Christian warrior, slain by Ariadin, 9.40

PICO, young son of Latinus, twin of Laurentius; slain by Soliman, 9.34

sented with shield figuring forth the feats of his ancestors, 17.64–65; eager to rejoin armies, 17.82; receives Charles' present of the sword of Sven, 17.83–85; hears Wise Man's prophecy concerning Ferrarese descendants, 17.86–93; takes leave of Wise Man and approaches the Christian camp, 17.96–97; begs Godfrey's forgiveness, 18.1–4; greets friends, 18.5–6; hears Peter's advice, 18.6–10; penitential vigil, 18.11–16; enters enchanted wood, 18.17–28; tempted by demon impersonating Armida, 18.28–34; conquers, 18.35–38; returns to camp, 18.39–40; leads Adventurers and scales the wall, 18.72–78; breaches the Temple, 19.31–37; attempts the Tower of David, 19.49; hears Vafrine's report of Armida's plot against his life, 19.123–26; given command of the Adventurers, 20.10–11; exploits, 20.53–60; sees Armida, 20.61–65; fights Altamor's troops, 20.70; slays Adrastus and Soliman, 20.101–8; slays Tissaphernes, 20.113–19; follows Armida, prevents her suicide, and is reconciled with her, 20.120–36

Robert (the Second, count of Flanders), leader of two thousand Flemish and Dutch troops, 1.43–44; wounded by Clorinda, 11.43; in charge of reserves, 18.65–66; ordered to storm the city from the left, 20.9; (?) fights with Adrastus, 20.49; injured (?) or taken prisoner by Adrastus (?), 20.71

Robert of Normandy, leader of the Norman troops, 1.38; struck down by Argante, 11.81; in charge of reserves, 18.65–66; ordered to storm the city from the left, 20.9; (?) fights with Adrastus, 20.49; injured (?) or taken prisoner by Adrastus (?), 20.71

Roger Balnaville, English Adventurer, 1.54; volunteers to fight Argante, 7.66; injured by Argante, 7.107–8; slain by Tissaphernes, 20.112

Rosmond, duke of Lancaster, Adventurer, 1.55; volunteers to fight Argante, 7.67; slain by Altamor, 20.40

Rossan, Saracen warrior, slain by Godfrey, 9.90

Rosten, Saracen warrior, slain by Godfrey, 9.90

Rudolph, Adventurer, 1.56; chosen by lot to accompany Armida, 5.75

Rudolph, Christian warrior, volunteers to fight Argante, 7.67; slain by Argante, 7.119

Sabinus, young son of Latinus, slain by Soliman, 9.33

Saladin, Saracen warrior, slain by Argillan, 9.79

Satan, urges demons to fight the Christians, 4.1–18

Selin, Saracen warrior, slain by Godfrey, 9.90

Sforza, Lombard Adventurer, brother of Achilles and Palamedes, 1.55

Siger, Godfrey's herald, orders Rinaldo and the Christians to retreat, 3.52–53; bears Godfrey's shield, 11.53; accompanies the wounded Godfrey to his tent, 11.68; slain by Argante, 11.80

Siphant, Saracen warrior, 17.31

nacy, 12.74–84; admonished by Peter, 12.85–88; prays, 12.89–90; sees Clorinda in a heavenly vision, 12.91–93; buries and eulogizes her, 12.94–99; volunteers to penetrate the demon-infested forest and fails, 13.32–46; thwarted by demon impersonating Clorinda, 13.41–43; reports to Godfrey, 13.47–49; offers valet Vafrine as spy, 18.57; joins Camillus in the assault, 18.67; scales the wall, 18.101; final triumph over Argante, 19.1–26; collapses, 19.27–28; Erminia reveals her love of him to Vafrine, 19.93–101; found by Vafrine, made whole by Erminia, 19.113–14; orders burial of Argante, 19.116–17; brought to Jerusalem, 19.118–19; leaves bed to defend the fallen Raymond, 20.83–86

TATIN, leader of two hundred Greek soldiers, 1.50–51; his desertion during the drought, 13.68

TIGRAN, Saracen slain by Dudon, 3.43

TIGRAN, Saracen warrior, 17.30

TISSAPHERNES, Saracen warrior, 17.31; rebukes Adrastus and vows to kill Rinaldo for Armida, 17.50–51; discovered by Vafrine, courting Armida, quarreling with Adrastus, 19.68, 70–74; stationed at the right for the final battle, 20.23; exploits, 20.49, 111–12; slain by Rinaldo, 20.113–20

UBALDO, Adventurer, 1.55; well-traveled friend of Guelph, instructed to help Charles seek Rinaldo, 14.27–31; sets out with Charles to Ascalon, 14.32–34; meets the Wise Man of Ascalon and enters the bowels of the earth with him, 14.34–40; takes leave of Wise Man and boards Fortune's skiff, 15.1–7; asks Fortune about the New World, 15.24; disembarks with Charles and climbs mountain below Armida's hideaway, 15.45–66; enters Armida's garden, 16.1–19; confronts Rinaldo, 16.27–35; advises Rinaldo to hear and resist Armida's plea, 16.41; returns with Charles and Rinaldo in Fortune's skiff, 16.62; arrives in Palestine, 17.56; arrives at Christian camp, 17.97

VAFRINE, valet of Tancred, sent as spy to the Egyptian camp, 18.57–60; enters camp, 19.56–60; hears of plot on Godfrey's life, 19.61–66; sees Armida and her men; hears plot on Rinaldo's life, 19.67–74; is recognized by Erminia, 19.75–83; leaves camp and hears Erminia's story, learning the details of the plots, 19.84–101; comes upon the dead Argante and the near dead Tancred, 19.102–3; tells Erminia to try to heal him, 19.111; brings Tancred and Erminia back to camp, 19.114–15; reports to Godfrey and the peers, 19.119–27

WENCESLAUS, old warrior, chosen by lot to accompany Armida, 5.73

WILLIAM OF RONCILLON, chosen by lot to accompany Armida, 5.75

WILLIAM, bishop of Orange, leader of four hundred warriors, 1.38–39; celebrates Mass on the day before battle, 11.3–5, 14–15

WILLIAM, Genovese admiral, 5.86; builds new siege machines, 18.41–45

WILLIAM, prince of England; proclaims Godfrey general, 1.32; leader of the English troops, 1.44; tells Godfrey of events at Armida's castle, 10.59–72; wounded by Clorinda, 11.42

Notes

THESE NOTES are intended to assist the reader encountering Tasso or Renaissance epic for the first time and to divulge the reasoning behind some of the choices I have made in the translation. Any decent attempt to represent the scholarship on Tasso's poem would run into hundreds of pages. The few critics I have privileged in these notes were contemporaries of Tasso whose comments may lend insight into how Tasso expected his poem to be read. I have also quoted Tasso himself, pressed into defending his work. As for sources, Tasso was a prodigious scholar, and he alludes to or adapts classical or medieval motifs almost continually. I have flagged some of the more important, either because they are too conspicuous to pass by or because Tasso has reworked them in a provocative and revealing way. Finally, I have included references to several of the early, nonstandard printings of Tasso's poem and to the later *Gerusalemme conquistata,* to give the reader a sense of the direction of Tasso's incessant revision. Unfortunately, I have not been able to review the manuscripts, dating from as early as the 1560s, to provide a full treatment of the development of the *Gerusalemme liberata*—a project that in any case would lie beyond the scope of this book.

COMMONLY CITED SOURCES, EDITIONS, AND CONTEMPORARY TEXTS, WITH ABBREVIATIONS

Ariosto, Ludovico. *Orlando furioso.* Ferrara, 1532 (*OF*).

Beni, Paolo. *Il Goffredo, o vero la Gerusalemme liberata del Tasso.* Padua: Bolzetta, 1616.

Birago, Francesco. *Dichiarazioni . . . del Signor Francesco Birago nella Gerusalemme conquistata del Signor Torquato Tasso.* Milan: Somasco, 1616.

Galilei, Galileo. *Considerazioni al Tasso.* Not published in Galileo's lifetime. From *Scritti letterari,* edited by Alberto Chiari. Florence: Le Monnier, 1943.

Gentile, Scipio. Notes to *Gerusalemme liberata.* Genoa, 1617. First publication in 1586.

Guastavini, Giulio. *Discorsi et annotazioni sopra la Gerusalemme liberata da Torquato Tasso.* Pavia: Bertoli, 1592.

Heliodorus. *Ethiopian History.* This classical romance is the source for many of the details of Tasso's feminine subplots.

Lucretius (Titus Lucretius Carus). *De Rerum Natura.*

Manso, G. B. *Vita di Torquato Tasso.* Venice: Deuchino, 1621.

Milton, John. *Paradise Lost.* London, 1674 (*PL*).

Paulus Aemylius. *De Rebus gestis Francorum libri X.* Basel: Henricpetri, 1601. Originally published early in the sixteenth century (Paulus died in 1529). Tasso's third historical source for the First Crusade.

Pigna, Giovanni Baptista. *Historia de' Principi d'Este.* Venice: Valgrisi, 1572. Originally published in 1570 in Ferrara. Traces the Este heroes back to the days when they fought Attila the Hun.

Robert the Monk. *Bellum Christianum principum, praecipue Gallorum, contra Saracenum, anno salutis MLXXXXVIII pro terra sancta gestam.* Basel, 1533. Next to William of Tyre, the main historical source for Tasso's poem. The 1533 edition, a copy of which was possessed by Duke Alphonso, also contained a play about the expulsion of the Moors from Granada in 1492; a letter by Christopher Columbus describing the Indies; letters from the king of Ethiopia to King John of Portugal and to Pope Clement VII and accounts of the Ethiopian society and church; an account of the origin of the Turks; and an account of the rise of Mohammed. These texts are also important sources.

Spenser, Edmund. *The Faerie Queene.* London, 1590–96 (*FQ*).

Tasso, Torquato. *Canti IV, IX, e XII della Gerusalemme liberata.* Rome: Tipografia della Pace, 1877 (*Canti*). The oldest known version of any part of the poem. The original canto 4 is the present canto 5.

———. *Discourses on the Heroic Poem.* Translated by Mariella Gavalchini and Irene Samuel. Oxford: Clarendon, 1973.

———. *Gerusalemme conquistata.* Rome, 1593 (*GC*).

———. *Gerusalemme liberata.* Ferrara: Baldini, June 4, 1581 (Bon. 1).

———. *Gerusalemme liberata.* Ferrara: Baldini, July 20, 1581 (Bon. 2).

———. *Gerusalemme liberata.* Ferrara: Cagnacini, 1585 (Bon. 3). "Anonymous" annotator may be B. Angeli.

———. *Gerusalemme liberata.* Mantua: Osanna, 1584 (Os.). Edition appends to the end of the poem a great number of *stanzas rejected by the author,* consecutively and from various cantos. These, if interpolated into the rest of the poem, represent the earliest complete version of *GL* which we possess.

———. *Il Goffredo di Torquato Tasso.* Venice: Senese, 1583 (Sen.). Unauthorized version of *GL* appends a variorum containing readings not found anywhere else (roughly contemporaneous with the rejected stanzas appended by Os.) but which seem to be Tasso's own work. All references in the notes are to the variorum.

———. *Lettere.* 5 vols. Edited by Cesare Guasti. Le Monnier: Florence, 1852.

———. *Scelta di Rime di diversi eccellenti Poeti, di nuove raccolte e date in luce, Parte II.* Genoa: Zabata, 1579 (*Scelta*). Contains the earliest known printing of any part of *GL* (canto 4).

William of Tyre. *Historia belli sacri verissima.* Basel, 1564.

CANTO ONE

1—*I sing:* Tasso opens with an epic announcement of his intention; cf. Virgil's *Aeneid,* "Arms and the man I sing." He broaches one of the main political themes of the poem: he sings not of warfare but of an army that requires a head.

Guastavini argues that the poem's unity is to be found in the office and person of Godfrey: "From him as from a foundation, cause, and origin derive all the victories." *Might* and *judgment* are needed for this great battle of liberation and repentance, as Godfrey's errant men must be returned to *the banner of the Lord.* The *two continents* are Africa and Asia, seats of Islam. In *Lettere* 49 to Scipio Gonzaga (1576), Tasso proposed this more corporate beginning: "The reverent armies and the knights I sing, who signed their armor with the cross of Christ; how much they accomplished under Godfrey, and how much they suffered with him in the glorious conquest." *Savior . . . victory:* Tasso rhymes on *Cristo* and *acquisto,* "conquest"; the link is lost in translation. In *GL* Tasso always rhymes *Cristo* with *acquisto,* to give the true Victor His due (the other occasions are at 1.84, 5.48, 9.5, 19.52, and 20.19).

The *Chief* is Godfrey of Bouillon (1058?–1100). For most of his life Godfrey fought for the claims of the German emperor against the claims of the pope. Under Henry IV, Godfrey was the first to enter Rome to drive the reforming Pope Gregory VII into exile. When the pope excommunicated Henry for the second time and deposed him in favor of Rudolph, Godfrey slew the pretender in single combat at Volksheim. But when Pope Urban II at Clermont preached the First Crusade (1095), Godfrey was one of the first to heed the call. He led a modest but well-trained army of Germans and Franks to Constantinople and then to the Holy Land, where in 1099 he took Jerusalem and was acclaimed king. He is Tasso's counterpart to Virgil's *pius Aeneas.* According to William of Tyre, Tasso's primary historical source, Godfrey was "a devout, merciful, pious, God-fearing man, who shunned every evil. He was slow and certain in his speech, and held the vanities of this world in scorn—a quality especially rare in a man of his age and military profession" (9.5). It should be noted that even William does not grant Godfrey the status he enjoys in this poem.

2—*Helicon* (see also *Parnassus,* st. 3): one of the hills sacred to the Muses in Greek mythology. Tasso, like Dante (*Paradiso* 1.13), uses a pagan motif to invoke the Holy Spirit (though Gentile and the Anonymous annotator assumed that Tasso was invoking the Virgin Mary, citing Petrarch's tribute to her, *Coronata di stelle,* "crowned with stars," *Rime* 366.1–2). Hence he apologizes for having, for didactic purposes, introduced fabulous material into his historical account of the storming of Jerusalem. Tasso's finicky critics took the apology too seriously, deriding him for including episodes that he knew had no place in an epic. The poet's reaction against such criticism ultimately resulted in the *Gerusalemme conquistata,* stripped of almost all romance.

3—*as we brush with honey:* Cf. Lucretius, 1.936–42. The "sugar coated pill" justification for poetry illustrates both Tasso's didacticism and his reaction, evident so often in the *Gerusalemme,* against the benign, quiet Epicureanism of the Latin poet. Manso writes that Tasso thought that his patron the duke believed him an easy-liver and an Epicurean such as Lucretius never was (p. 99). Yet by all accounts our poet was if anything a trifle too like Lucretius in his asceticism.

4—*Alfonso:* Alfonso II d'Este, last Estean duke of Ferrara (r. 1559–97), Tasso's patron, who Tasso in his madness believed was out to poison him and whom

Tasso alternately fled and begged for forgiveness. Tasso's own letters suggest that the duke was a man of the world who grew impatient with the poor poet and whose inconsistent attempts to help him sometimes made matters worse. His Este family disappear from *GC,* and he is replaced in this stanza by Cinzio Aldobrandini, nephew of Pope Clement VIII. The dedication thus became a tribute to papal authority which extended "to burnt Ethiopia and farther lands that choose the true religion." *Wanderer:* Or "exile." Tasso never forgot the injury done him and his father by the anti-imperial party in his native Campania, and he even believed there were Neapolitan lords determined to kill him. He always considered himself an exile from his ancestral heritage.

6—*Nicaea . . . Antioch:* Nicaea, ancient city in Asia Minor, under pressure from the Christians, capitulated in 1097 to the Greek emperor Alexius Comnenus I (r. 1081–1118). It had been the capital of the realm of Soliman, who gave in when his wife and children surrendered to the enemy. See William, 2.24–3.6. Antioch was taken in 1098 when an apostate Christian of the city delivered it to the Crusader Bohemond (cf. William, 5–6; Robert, 4–6). It was also the city where Paul and Barnabas preached and where the disciples were first called Christians (Acts 11:26). In *Lettere* 49 Tasso proposes this revision to emphasize the papacy: "Already the sixth year had passed since the great Urban, who held the keys that open and shut the heavens, called the pious Christian to council in Clermont, and persuaded him to take arms to free the holy birthplace of Christ from the profane people who possessed it, and, belting the sword at the sides of the chiefs, gave them the purple cross and the white robe."

9, 10—*Baldwin, Tancred, Bohemond, Rinaldo, Guelph: Baldwin,* Godfrey's brother, was to rule the Crusader state of Jerusalem after Godfrey's death. He continued the Crusade, waging war against Egypt and taking Tripoli. *Tancred* was an Italian prince of Norman extraction, nephew of the warlord Robert Guiscard and cousin of Bohemond. Tasso toned down Tancred's reputation for lasciviousness and brawling, tempering the former with the excuse of youth and ignoring the latter altogether. (Sen., for example, reads thus: "He sees Tancred, who nurses a grudge against [Baldwin], and suspires in vain love.") Late in life, to honor the Guiscardi (who entertained him in Sicily after his breach with Duke Alfonso), Tasso considered writing an *Odyssey* to this *Iliad,* describing the wanderings of Tancred as he tried to return home to Italy. Saner reflection, we may suppose, intervened. *Bohemond,* prince of Taranto, son of Robert Guiscard and uncle of Tancred, was the conqueror of Antioch; he held himself aloof from the other Crusaders. He, not Godfrey, is the great hero of Robert's account; it is remarkable that Tasso gives him so little credit in his poem. Bohemond's concerns in Antioch reflect Urban's prophecy, reported by Paulus, book 4: "You shall impose laws upon the impious, and be the governors of the world." *Rinaldo,* nephew of Guelph and son of Berthold, is Tasso's version of the young, generous, hotheaded Achilles of Homer's *Iliad.* If Godfrey is the head of the army, says Tasso in the *Allegory,* Rinaldo is its right arm, representing the irascible faculty in the soul, necessary for decisive action. The historical Rinaldo, ancestor of the Este family, probably could not have fought in the First Crusade; see 1.58 below and note. In the early *Canti* he is called Ubaldo. In *GC* he is called Riccardo and is related to the papal-leaning Guiscardi. *Guelph* was a scion of the Este family and of the Guelphs or Welpes of Swabia. In truth he did not join the Crusades until four years after Jerusalem had fallen. Tasso cannily uses him as the experienced but not always wise uncle who urges his nephew on to glory. In *Canti* he does not appear, and his actions are attributed to Raymond.

12—*The Lord said to His herald:* As Jupiter sends Mercury to remind Aeneas that he must leave his comfortable situation in Carthage (Virgil, *Aeneid* 4.219–37), so now the Lord urges Godfrey on to the aim of all his battles. Tasso seldom allows his heroes to rest. As for the delay, William paints things a little differently; it was the commoners who finally persuaded Godfrey and the other noblemen to move on from famine-ridden Antioch.

18—*a spark enveloped in the flame of fire:* A Dantesque thought; cf. *Paradiso* 3.79–85. Man's will is never so fervent and so free as when it submits humbly to the will of God. The words reflect the enthusiastic response at Clermont, which became the Crusaders' motto: "Deus vult!"—"God so wills!"

19—*With every man his art is forcible:* As head of his army, Godfrey must understand his peers and his men so fully as to see what will drive them on to the good and restrain them from vice. Rhetoric is thus, as it was for Thucydides, Livy, and Tacitus, the master art for an effective general.

20—*a resounding voice, and august look:* Following Paulus, book 4: "Tall of stature, grave in gait, sparing of words, but admirably moral and to the point, and of a countenance majestic and august."

21—*Warriors of God:* Godfrey's speech, and Peter's immediately following, reenact the calling of the Crusade by Pope Urban at Clermont (see Robert, 1). Examples: "But if you are detained by love of children or parents or spouse, lo, recall what the Lord says in the Gospel [Matt. 10:37], that whoever loves father or mother more than he loves me, is not worthy of me." "And so let the hatreds among you cease, let the quarrels rest, let the battles be still, and all controversies and dissensions sleep." "For if the Lord God had not dwelt in your hearts you would not have answered with one voice." In *GC* Godfrey ends not with the present practical warning but with a sentence that could serve as a touchstone for *GL*, too: "God alone is the governor of Time; he does not conquer well, who does not conquer when the time has come."

25—*the foundations of this world: GC* makes it clear that Tasso is thinking of Christ's parable about building on rock (Matt. 8:26–27). *Hopes of Greece are unreliable:* Like Dante (cf. *Inferno* 3.34–42), Tasso reserves his greatest scorn not for the enemies of Christianity but for its lukewarm friends—in this case, the Greeks. Those who choose the wrong and fight for it are more admirable than those who delay and cause others to delay and who refuse in the end to make a choice at all. Such men are the opposite of the Aristotelian *megalopsychos*, the "magnanimous" or "greathearted" man Tasso so amply illustrates in Godfrey, Soliman, Emiren, Raymond, Clorinda, and even Argante. The Anonymous annotator (commenting on 2.72) reveals what was still the attitude of Tasso's contemporaries: "[The Greeks] would take bread from the mouths of their own to feed other people like themselves, and thus they became flatterers and parasites." William's account—and William is no friend to the Greek—unwittingly portrays the emperor as a prudent ruler of a dangerously weak nation, who could not have been pleased by the aggressive incursions of Westerners into his realm. His armies, however, were no match for the Crusaders.

29—*the solitary Peter:* Peter the Hermit (d. 1115), historically a ruffianly figure, preacher of the infamous Peasants' Crusade, led his ragtag band to the East, where they were ambushed by the Turks and nearly annihilated. His eloquence rallied the Christians before their final victory at Jerusalem. Here he plays the paternal and oracular role of Anchises, father of Aeneas and mystic interpreter of signs (cf. *Aeneid* 3.178–89). William recounts many of his adventures, among them (1.13) one that Tasso repeats in *GC* 3.2 ff.: Peter was sleeping on the pavement of the Church of the Holy Sepulcher when he received a vision instructing him to return to Europe to preach the cleansing of the Holy City. His account to Urban of the daily execution of Christians by crucifixion, beheading, and cudgeling, and his warning that the West would soon feel the threat of the Turk in any case (Paulus, bk. 4), helped to spur the Crusade.

31—*When rule is not united in one man:* Here we see Tasso's admiration for monarchy, his support of the papacy, and his symbolic identification of the Christian army with the Body of Christ. The wisdom can also be applied to the careers of individual knights, whose appetites (Tancred) or irascible passions (Argillan, Rinaldo, Gernando) either usurp the role of reason or wage internecine war against it. Birago cites the Gospels: "A kingdom divided against itself must fall" (Matt. 12:25). "Although all states are subject to various dangers, those are all the more numerous when several persons govern; for the most part, they are neither united nor in agreement, but among them reign envy and ambition." Robert thus explains the Christian army's losses in Asia Minor: "But any gathering of men not led by a good captain, but by one who nods off, will lapse from one day to the next and fall further and further from good health" (bk. 1, p. 6).

32—*blest Breath and holy Fire:* The Holy Spirit; cf. the account of Pentecost in Acts 2:1–4. Beni notes that Godfrey does not solicit his own election, trusting the angel's word that it would come about of the men's own inspired will. In *GC* there is no election—Godfrey is chosen by the Lord, and that is that.

36—*O Memory:* Second invocation of the Muse; for "Memory," see Dante, *Inferno* 2.7–9. Possibly the Muse of history is intended, but Renaissance Platonism associated the Muses with the intelligences of the heavenly spheres and thus with God himself. *Strength:* Following Os. *virtu;* other texts read *ragion,* "knowledge."

45—*Then Tancred:* Here begins the tale of Tancred's love for the pagan maid Clorinda, who will, by the grace of God, be baptized by her own slayer (Tancred himself) and then become in turn a means of his salvation. The setting for the inception of this love is significant. Tancred (who, representing the appetitive part of the soul, seems prone to lassitude) does not *run the race to the finish* (cf. 2 Tim. 4:6–7). His fall occurs when he refreshes himself at the pool, taking a too early rest from the battle to liberate the City of Peace, Jerusalem. Galileo derides the whole Tancred-Clorinda subplot: "He sees her at a pool—does not try to find her, to get to know her, to win her, does not even speak to her again until he confronts her once more in battle, when he asks her to remove his heart; then sees her a mile away when he fights Argante; and finally, having killed her, he laments her desperately."

51—*Your slavery is just what you deserve:* See 25 above and note. Tasso refers to the collapse of the Byzantine empire after the fall of Constantinople to the Ottoman Turks in 1453. The line is more than sarcasm. According to Aristotle, *Politics* 1.5, some men are born to rule and others, especially the pusillanimous, to be ruled. What the Greeks suffer would be just, regardless of Divine punishment. William (2.23) adds that the leader of the Greek troops was a spy anyhow, mutilated in the face to illustrate his wickedness, who was sent by the emperor to keep tabs on the Franks. Tasso's contemporaries are united in decrying the emperor's duplicity. Beni compares Alexius with Aladine (see 1.83 ff.), saying that he got his empire through the murder of the rightful prince and that he was so afraid of rebellion that he would not set one foot outside Constantinople. No leader of Christendom he. For Tasso, the Greek also represents the most serious division of the Christian world, between East and West; indeed, Pigna begins his history of the Este family by blaming the fall of Rome on the division of the empire by Constantine.

52—*Adventurers:* Or "soldiers of fortune," the fiercest and noblest of Godfrey's squadrons, led by their own elected chief. Beni suggests an apt allusion to Scipio Africanus, "the thunderbolt of war and terror of Carthage" (Lucretius, 3.1034). *Adventurers* suggests one of the poem's paradoxes: those who give themselves most freely to the chance of war are also those fittest to be the right arm of Divine Providence. Thus the band intervenes providentially at crucial moments in the war (e.g., at 3.37). For in truth there is no such thing as chance. What men call Fortune is a handmaid of the Lord; cf. 15.3 and note.

53—*a handsome badge of honor:* Gentile says these are chest wounds, prized beyond all others by the ancient Romans. Candidates for public office dressed so as to show them off. Cf. 8.44 below and note.

55—*great Otto . . . shield:* The Anonymous annotator says that Otto won it from a Transjordanian prince who stepped from the ranks and challenged the Christians to single combat. According to him the device was a snake from whose mouth issued forth another snake, scaleless.

56—*Edward, Gildippe:* Every epic army must have a female warrior. It is part of the "marvelous" that, says Beni, makes for epic, akin to magicians and the centaurs of old. Some women accompanied the Crusaders, but not to fight. Says Robert in book 3: "The soldiers and those fit for battle fought; the priests and clerics begged and prayed; the weeping women dragged the bodies of the dead back to the tents." Tasso writes (*Lettere* 60) that there was an English baron, Edward, who went a-crusading with his wife and that they died together on the enterprise. This wedded couple underscores the union in complementarity of which the army is a greater example. Theirs is also a love to which the passions of Rinaldo and Armida, and of Erminia for Tancred, must aspire. Edward and Gildippe are excised from *GC.* They are replaced by two men, the sole representatives of a nation that ever had to fight the infidel on its own front—Spain.

58—*Rinaldo the brave lad:* Rinaldo possesses the virtues of the young Achilles: he is noble, generous, brave, high spirited, and properly proud of his accomplishments. We shall see that he possesses Achilles' vices, too, in softened form: his obstinacy, his touchiness regarding honor, and his impetuosity. The historical figure upon which Tasso's character is based died in 1175, so that it is just barely within the realm of possibility that he could have fought as a very young man in this war.

61—*Raymond:* Count of Toulouse; fought with the legendary Cid. His portrait in William of Tyre shows him to possess rather the quarrelsomeness than the wisdom of age.

63—*Capaneus at the gates of Thebes:* In Statius's *Thebaid,* this one of the "Seven against Thebes" was a scorner of the gods, struck down by one of Zeus's thunderbolts for his blasphemy. Cf. Dante, *Inferno* 14.68–70.

66—*but . . . down:* Sen.: "O how long and hateful seems the night and the time which delays their departure."

77—For the surrender of Tripoli and the assistance of the Syrian Christians, see William, 7.21, and Robert, 7. The Anonymous annotator says that the condition Godfrey imposed was that the king become Christian, should the Crusaders take Jerusalem.

81—*Fame:* Cf. Virgil, *Aeneid* 4.173–88. The quasi personification of Fame introduces a leitmotif of the poem: the unreliability of common wisdom, which is based on surface appearances. Tasso shows that what looks like the truth is not so, or, better, that those who judge without the light of faith mistake not only matters spiritual but matters mundane, too.

82—*Ill expectation . . . appear:* Cicero, *Letters to Atticus* 10.14: "To fear for so long a time is a far greater evil than the very thing feared." Also Heliodorus, book 1, whose never-quite-ravished Chariclia chirps, "The ills you expect are much worse than the ills you suffer."

83—*Aladine:* Historically, Ducat, emir of the Fatimid sultan of Egypt, recently granted the rule over Jerusalem after Egypt had seized Palestine from the caliph of Baghdad.

87—*Kill them:* Cf. Urban's accusations at Clermont, reported by Robert (bk. 1, p. 2): "They have invaded the land of those Christians and laid it waste with fire, plunder, and the sword, leading some away into captivity and putting others to a miserable death. They have leveled the churches of God, or shackled them to their own rites, subverting the altars with their pollutions," as, for instance, by circumcising Christians and pouring the blood into the baptismal font.

90—*Provident in his evil:* Though wicked, Aladine is meant to rule. He prepares for all eventualities and is thus a worthy match for the provident Bouillon. (But Galileo thinks him a hasty fool—he no sooner sees Clorinda in 2.47 than he turns over two convicts to her and gives her, whom he has never met, command over his army.) For an account of his preparations, see William, 7.23. Gentile defends the poisoning of the water supply on the grounds that the Romans, too, used that tactic for defense.

Canto Two

1—*Ismen:* An apostate magician who conjures demons to harm the Christians, Ismen is a foil for the Wise Man of Ascalon (see 14.33 and note), a naturalist convert to Christianity. Beni observes that "Ismeno" is an anagram for "Simone," the Simon Magus of Acts 8. (His name was Asdente in *Canti.*) Renaissance thinkers distinguished two sorts of magicians: necromancers, and natural philosophers like the Wise Man. Tasso defended his inclusion of the supernatural on the grounds that epic requires an element of the marvelous. Nevertheless, belief in the power of witches to conjure demons was widespread, and Tasso himself was once persuaded that he had been hexed (cf. *Lettere* 190, written from the Santa Anna asylum in 1581). As for Ismen's ability to raise the dead, the Anonymous annotator says it is only apparent, as demons can be made to animate corpses. His hiding from the crowds reminds Beni of Emperor Julian the Apostate (r. 361–63), who descended with a soothsayer into caves and other infernal places to try to divine the future.

5—*the icon:* Tasso reworks the theft by Odysseus and Diomedes of the Trojan icon of Pallas Athena. Although Tasso does not care to present the details of Islamic worship, in Ismen's words lies a theological insult that marks the unbridgeable division between Islam and Christianity: that the Son of God should be *born and buried* would strike any Muslim as absurd and blasphemous.

13—The episode of Sophronia and Olindo has its source in William, 1.5. Finding one of their mosques desecrated with a dog's corpse, the Saracens were set to slaughter the Christians, when a young man came forth to confess to the deed and to sacrifice himself for the safety of all. Thus was he struck down by the sword, "piously accepting the most-desired sleep, the sleep in the Lord." The burning of lovers at the stake, with fortunate interruption, derives from Boccaccio, *Decameron* 4.6. Tasso's critics complained that the episode was too tenuously connected to the rest of the text, and Tasso came to agree, excising it from *GC* (as early as 1576 he wants to condemn Sophronia to an "irrevocable sentence of death" [*Lettere* 61]). Its connection, however, is not causal but thematic and allegorical. The lovely Sophronia, whose name suggests wisdom, exalts the mind of the observer. Like Heliodorus's doggedly modest Chariclia, "she recalls to chaster thoughts the souls of those who look upon her" (bk. 1). She is Beatrice to Olindo's Dante and is to be contrasted with the flirtatious, this-worldly Armida, 4.28 ff. For Sophronia's reconciliation of modesty and boldness, Gentile refers the reader to Plato's *Statesman,* 306–8, wherein the reconciliation of these traits is the key political task toward producing a truly divine republic.

14—*within the narrow cage/of a small house:* Guastavini cites Thucydides (*The Peloponnesian War* 2.46) to the effect that a woman's fame should not go beyond the walls of a house.

20—*Stunned by her honest courage:* Beauty and love can astonish even the wicked; cf. Milton, *PL* 9.463–66.

22—*Greathearted lie:* Critics note Horace's *Odes,* 3.9: "splendide mendax," but see also Heliodorus's Chariclia, who in book 1 lies to save her chastity: "Sometimes a falsehood too is an honest thing."

28—*she's not the thief, O king:* Compare with Virgil's *Aeneid,* 9.427–30, where Nisus runs from his covert in a vain attempt to save his ambushed friend Euryalus.

33—*Are these the bonds:* Olindo's foray into metaphysical punning is too precious, too like the worst habits of Marino and Crashaw; it is an untimely touch of Ovid (cf. Perseus to Andromeda, *Metamorphoses* 4.677–80, retold by Heliodorus, 4), who always steers his tragic moments toward burlesque. Tasso has also reworked a scene in book 2 of Heliodorus. The hero Theagenes, seeing the burning island where he thinks Chariclia is imprisoned, blurts out, "Are these the torches then which our evil Genius has lit for us, instead of the marriage flames?" He blames Fortune, "you who have stolen from me the chance to embrace her at the end, and who have deprived me of her last kisses, and her last breath." Yet for all Olindo's rhetorical excess, gently satirized by Tasso, his heart is generous, and his love is, like Sophronia's, a self-sacrifice unto death.

36—*the sun:* Symbol of the divine. Lactantius says that when the philosopher Anaxagoras was asked why he was born, he replied, "To look upon the sun and the heavens" (*Institutes* 3.9).

38—*Clorinda:* Tasso's invention; no such lady warrior existed; cf. 1.56 n. Her tender reaction to the plight of the lovers tips Tasso's hand, for she is more woman than warrior, and therein lies her power. For her boyish upbringing, see Virgil's Camilla, *Aeneid* 11.573–84.

50—*irreverence against our laws:* Like the Jews, Muslims prohibit representations of divinity. Alone among the Saracens, Clorinda has a truly religious motive for fighting. She is devoted to what she sees as the truth, making her subsequent conversion to Christianity an act of spiritual conviction.

54—*banish some of the faithful:* Cf. William, 8.24. Sen. has Olindo lead a band of exiled men to meet the host at Emmaus.

58—*Alete:* Tasso's invention; a silk-tongued politician of the sort Tasso knew at court. Alete's advice to Godfrey focuses on *policy* rather than on goals. Prudence, says Thomas Aquinas, is the virtue by which one finds the practical means to effect the proper ends. In the guise of prudence, Alete counsels the concession of those ends. The key to such concession would be to admit that the affairs of men are governed by chance, not by Providence. His reasoning owes much to that of Hannibal addressing the young Scipio before the battle of Zama; cf. Livy, *History of Rome* 30.30. For the embassy see William, 7.19, who says that the caliph of Egypt, having recently seized Jerusalem from the Persian ruler, offered to allow two hundred or three hundred unarmed men to go to Jerusalem to pray. That same offer is made in *GC* 3.61–62.

59—*Argante:* Tasso's invention, Argante combines the traits of Homer's Achilles with those of Virgil's scorner of the gods, Mezentius. He is quick tempered, rash, insulting, proud, bloodthirsty, fearless, and implacable. His sword is his law; his glory is his god. Beni cites Horace's description of Achilles, *Ars Poetica* 121–22. In *GC* he is made the son of the ruler of Jerusalem and, impossible to believe, has a wife.

63—*the king my master:* The sultan of Egypt, whose armies will enter the fray for the climactic battle, 17.2 ff. William (4.24) says the Muslims of the East hated those of the West, who were delighted when Soliman lost Nicaea. This schism facilitated the Crusaders' success.

81—*frank sentiments in simple words and few:* According to Aristotle, such speech is the mark of the greathearted man. Godfrey's reply shows that, although he can accept the sultan's friendship, he cannot swerve from his sole purpose, to free the Holy Land. Cf. Saint Paul, "If anyone wants to boast, let him boast of the Lord" (2 Cor. 10:17). For *GC* 3.73, Tasso revised the final couplet thus: "I will respond without fear of great trouble, for nothing can frighten the man who trusts in God."

84—*God's hand:* Cf. Robert's introduction, "For this was not human work, but divine." Or Urban, reported in Paulus (bk. 4, p. 107): "If Christ enters the lists, will we not have weapons, will we not have right arms to wield them, will not our hearts be strong and manly?"

86—*nor shall we need to mourn our fall:* *GC* 3.84 is far more explicit: "For death has its crown and palm and song."

89—*Argante took his mantle by the edge:* For the gesture, see Livy, *History of Rome* 21.18.

95—*the ancient rules of war:* The rules held that ambassadors were inviolate. In return for their inviolability, they were to be noncombatants from the time they left their lords to the time they returned with a reply. It would take only a few Argantes to destroy the trust upon which the institution was based. Birago's judgment is harsh but apt and links Argante with his rival Tancred: "Like a beast he lets himself be ruled by his appetite, to do what he wants without thinking of anything else."

96—*The night:* Cf. Virgil's description of the lovely night through which the love-stricken Dido cannot sleep, *Aeneid* 4.522–31. Nor can Godfrey sleep here, for the devotion he feels for his army and their cause.

4—*the brave crew of an adventurer:* See the praise of Christopher Columbus, 15.30–32. For the men's excitement, cf. the Trojans hailing Italy, *Aeneid* 3.521–24. For their prayer, see William, 9.25.

12—*Erminia:* Tasso's creation; the most amiable of the major characters in the poem. In this canto she will play Helen to Aladine's Priam, describing for him the characters and abilities of the Christian warriors in the plains below; cf. *Iliad* 3.161–242. Guastavini tartly observes that Tasso's episode is more believable than Homer's; why, after ten years, should Priam need to have the most prominent Greek fighters identified? Galileo, however, finds the whole idea of retreating to a tower to chat with a girl absurd. Erminia is renamed Nicea in *GC* and is made to be princess of the city of that name. Unfortunately, Tasso lopped away most of her story.

19—*herbs cannot cure them:* Not for the wound of love. With fine dramatic irony Tasso foreshadows both Tancred's slaying of his beloved Clorinda and Erminia's nursing the near dead Tancred back to health.

21—*a maiden in the battlefield:* The lovely stanza adapts Pulci, *Morgante Maggiore* 3.17, and Ariosto, *OF* 32.79.

22—*The face of the proud woman:* Following Bon. 1, 2, 3; Os. has "the face of your beloved," which may be a better reading. *GC* 3.28.5–6 reads: "That is the lovely face which set you afire in the victory, and by which you are conquered by love."

23—*a double death:* Critics disagree about what Tasso means here. The most common interpretation is that Tancred is threatened by both the sword and Love. Others suggest, along with his physical death, the death of Tancred's honor, or of his love. But for Dante, as for Tasso when the Hermit rebukes Tancred for his incontinence (12.88), the "second death" is that which is perpetual, the eternal death of the soul.

25—*O you . . . : GC* is more overtly sexual: "Scornful lady, eager for my death and all too constant in your desire, let us leave these bands so you can satisfy your will, if you crave the final spoils from me."

32—*"skirmishes":* Or "carousels." One team of horsemen hurl balls at another team, who defend themselves with shields held behind their heads; at a designated point, the teams change direction, and the defenders become the pursuers. The game, originally Moorish, made its way to Europe in the 1500s. Robert (bk. 3, p. 19) says the Turks often shot arrows behind them while in retreat.

44—*Even . . . indignation:* Much better than Sen.: "And offends the Circassian, him alone he hurts, an enemy fierce and most importunate."

53—*champed the bit inside:* The first sign that Rinaldo is a thoroughbred not quite tamed; in *GC* Godfrey notes this recalcitrance and heedlessness with disapproval (3.59–61). His scorn for the wise Godfrey will break out soon (5.42).

55—*Jerusalem:* Tasso owes his precise descriptions of the city to William, 8.4, and to Josephus, *The Jewish War* 5.4–5.

70—*wielding those heavenly arms:* Those who have died in a state of grace still fight by our sides, now as triumphant members of the hosts of heaven; see 18.92–96. Tasso's critics blamed him for the supposed aloofness of this speech, which for Guastavini rather illustrated magnificent fortitude.

71—*good engineering:* Free translation of Os. *tormenti* or Bon. 1, 2, 3 *stromenti*—cranes, catapults, and battering rams, that is, indispensable for any siege, from the time of the Romans to the invention of the cannon.

73—*Honor the most exalted champion:* In this stupendous epitaph Tasso alters, tellingly, Dante's line, by which Homer greets Virgil temporarily returned to Limbo, "Onorate l'altissimo poeta" [Honor the most exalted poet] (*Inferno* 4.80). The early biographers all say that Tasso himself requested a plain slab for his own tomb—a request that was happily ignored. *Canti* has Otto, not Dudon, as the slain leader.

Canto Four

1—*our adversary:* Satan, whose name means "adversary" or "accuser." Tasso's description of Satan and the demons is indebted to the *Christiad* of Vida, the *De raptu Proserpinae* of Claudian, the sixth book of Virgil's *Aeneid,* and, naturally, Dante's *Inferno.* In particular, Tasso emphasizes the motif of incompatible physical natures fused into one body—centaurs, for instance, or the serpent-haired gorgons, or the wolf-groined scyllas—to parody the divine and human Christ and to show, despite their military discipline, the illogic of the demons' attempt "to battle against Providence divine." *Discovering that the soldiers are content:* Os. has a completely different line: "Seeing them intent upon their handsome works." The reading of Bon. is better, as it directs the fury of Satan against our happiness in general.

5—*harpies:* Fabulous beasts with the bodies of birds and the heads of women, the harpies dwelt in the underworld and punished the wicked. Cf. *Aeneid* 6.281. *Sphinx:* Another fabulous female, with the body of a lion and the claws of a bear; the plague of Thebes, as recounted by Sophocles, *Oedipus Rex* 390 ff. *Gorgons:* Snake-haired women whose stare turned men to stone; cf. Ovid, *Metamorphoses* 4.616–19. *Scyllas:* The shipwrecking rock in the straits of Messina; a "monster" whose transformation from an arrogant woman is related by Ovid, *Metamorphoses* 14.59–67. *Hydras:* The hydra was a seven-headed serpent slain by Hercules; cf. *Metamorphoses* 9.67–74. *Pythons:* The python was an enormous serpent slain by Apollo; cf. *Metamorphoses* 1.438–51. *Chimaerae:* Monsters that were part dragon, part lion, and part goat; cf. Lucretius, 5.901–6. *Polyphemuses:* So named for the Cyclops in Homer's *Odyssey,* 9. *Geryons:* Winged beasts with human faces; cf. Dante, *Inferno* 17.1–18. The parentage of most of these monsters can be found in Hesiod, *Theogony* 287–336. For the King of Hell with attendant prodigies, see Claudian, *The Rape of Proserpina* 1.79–88. All these monsters, notes Gentile, represent the cupidities of our souls.

9—*great mischance:* Tasso's Satan makes the same errors Milton's Satan makes, or tells the same lies. Satan assumes that God is a creature just like him, subject to fortune. The key phrase is "il gran caso" [the great fall]. Yet *caso* means "chance" too, "befalling." The ambiguity allows Satan to assert that it befell him that he fell, that the battle in heaven might have turned out otherwise. Birago's comment is apt: "Notice in this speech the great confusion of the Devil. Now he confesses the power of God, now with confused arguments he denies it. Which the poet has designed with great art, for what order can there be in one who is in discord with God?"

10—*man the vile:* Prissy disdain for earth is another suggestion of Tasso's which Milton seized upon (*PL* 9.163–71). As Milton saw, Satan's contempt for man formed from dust is the prideful reverse of Christ's humble willingness to be made Flesh that man might be made once again worthy of heaven; cf. *PL* 3.236–41. It was standard wisdom that man was created to supply the place of the fallen angels; cf. *PL* 7.150–61. Birago cites Saint Bernard's commentary on the Song of Songs: "The devil envies mankind," says Bernard, "and wants to have him in subjection, for he has foreseen indeed that God would become man."

11—*flinging out broad the signs of conquered hell:* Perhaps the souls snatched away by Christ when, after his death on the Cross, he harrowed hell. But since *insegne* is used repeatedly in *GL* for "banners," I have translated so as to suggest both possibilities, particularly since Tasso has his eye on Dante's description of the harrowing of hell, where Christ is "con segno di vittoria coronato" [crowned with the sign of victory] (*Inferno* 4.54). The image foreshadows the climax of Tasso's poem, when the flag of the Cross will be seen waving gloriously on the ramparts of Jerusalem (18.100).

16—*use force sometimes, and sometimes trickery:* Cf. Milton, *PL* 1.121, "To wage by force or guile eternal war." In *GL* the devils will use force to aid the Saracen warriors and will use guile mainly in the form of the lovely Armida, who will shortly appear on the scene to delude the Christians.

17—*May what I will be fate:* See Dido's curse, *Aeneid* 4.607–29, and Pluto's vow, Claudian, *De raptu Proserpinae* 1.111–16. Much of what Satan wishes comes true, but to no effect. There will be deadly squabbles among the Christians, and defections for love, as the next two cantos show, and Godfrey, "the head that guides," will be the target of a demon-inspired mutiny (8.59 ff.).

20—*Hydrotes:* Tasso's creation (in *GC* he is Arabian, and his niece Armida is born of a Siren in the Euphrates [5.24–25]). His juxtaposition with the scheming Satan undercuts the majesty of the diabolical cause, for Hydrotes is a coward, willing to compromise his niece to compass his desires.

26—*For faith and fatherland all things are just:* Amazingly, Gentile calls this "a most pious and holy saying," citing Cicero, *Philippics* 12.12: "That should be adopted which I judge to be most of all in the interest of the state."

27—*many causes for the crowd:* These are the Horatian *vulgus,* the common people, whose gullibility seems infinite. Tasso prepares the reader for Armida's plea, which will drive a wedge between Godfrey and his more credulous subordinates.

28—*Beauty like hers:* Compare with the appearance of Angelica in Boiardo's *Orlando innamorato,* 1.21 ff., or with that of Helen of Troy, *Iliad* 3.156–60. Armida is a "comet" or "nova" indeed—for those were always thought to herald disaster.

30—*disheveled tresses:* Armida's naturally curly hair is curled even more by the wind. Her dress and manner should be compared to those of the chaste Sophronia, 2.14–19. It is calculated, this negligence of hers, not the art of artlessness but the apparent artlessness of the subtlest art. Milton adopted the devious hair for his Eve, *PL* 4.304–7.

31—*snow . . . fire:* The Petrarchan antitheses (cf. *Rime* 125) are not mere conventions here, as Tasso shows the fundamental coldness of Armida's supposed passion and, moreover, the strange paradox, thoroughly understood by Armida herself, that a good show of chastity can excite the hottest lust. She is forbidden territory, thus all the more inviting.

35—*if it is just to call you so:* Eustace's words recall those of Aeneas to his mother, Venus, disguised as a huntress (and thus as Diana, goddess of chastity), *Aeneid* 1.325–29. The passage shows that the real sin of the straying men is not lust so much as it is idolatry.

36—*What you see . . . delight:* A nice twist on Petrarch's description of how, now that Laura is enshrined in heaven, he is not merely mortal but in fact dead (*Rime* 294.4).

39—*brightest:* Following Os. and *GC chiari;* Bon. 1–3 have *ricchi,* "rich."

42—*God who is good to all:* Punning on a false etymology of *Jove* as related to *giovare,* to help. For the etymology and the universality of Jove's worship, see Cicero, *De Natura deorum* 2.44–45, 64. In *Canti* at 5.91 Tasso himself uses *Giove* for "God" and rhymes it with *giove,* "he helps."

43—*Cariclia:* In name, Armida claims as her mother Heliodorus's chaste damsel of many distresses. See 2.13 and note.

45—*had planned a marriage:* Armida's tale adapts Ariosto's tale of Olympia, *OF* 9.22–56, and the tale of the lusty stepmother in Heliodorus, book 1. Here, however, the tale is a crucial element of the rhetorical drama unfolding between Armida and the men. Nothing so wins the heart of a man as a woman's disdainful description of another man, particularly when the woman alludes, constantly, to the horrors of having to share her bed with him. Indeed, Armida speaks of nighttime and sleeplessness and finds use for the word *ignudo,* "naked," whenever she can, and she allows her supposititious persecutor to accuse her of the very crime that her audience must be contemplating, that of lying with a whole troop of lovers (57.6).

52—*Raised by the king my father: Scelta* reads, "Who used to mix my wine at table." Tasso's revision links this lifelong servant with the eunuch Arsete (12.18 ff.) and thus invites further comparison of the careers of Armida and Clorinda.

57—*Ah . . . chastity!:* The lady doth protest too much, using the words of the self-deceived Dido, *Aeneid* 4.24–27; also those of Heliodorus's Chariclia in book 1, who insists that she would prefer death to the loss of a virginity she has kept intact even from her faithful lover Theagenes. Galileo laughs, "Armida, hold your cards low, unless you want to be discovered for a very bad girl!"

63—*those ten will do:* A cunning ploy to arouse rivalry. Armida would have done less damage had she asked for a hundred. In *Scelta* this stanza is followed by one in which Armida reveals her plan for the sneak attack. Removing that stanza allows Armida to end on an emotional climax, but Tasso clearly wished to cast the whole enterprise in doubt by making it sly and nocturnal; see Eustace's comments at 5.10.

69—*Piety now would make me impious:* Godfrey distinguishes two forms of *pieta*—what we would call "pity" and "piety." If he allows pity for Armida to direct his judgment, he would commit an impiety against his duty to free the Holy Land. It is a question of priorities. Interestingly, the historical Godfrey took time out to help a Turk to whom he had promised assistance, raising the siege before his castle (William, 7.3). *Render: GC* has *solvessi,* a superior reading—loosely, "if I failed to discharge my vow before God."

70—*it alters another's mind and nature:* Godfrey's, that is. Armida had, cunningly, begun her speech with praise of Godfrey's liberality. Now she accuses him of hardheartedness, without, of course, being unfemininely explicit about it.

73—*which money cannot open:* Following Os. and *GC a l'or,* "to gold." The Bon. manuscripts read *a lor,* "to them," to Armida's enemies.

77—*a savage tiger:* The men repeat love-ridden Dido's accusation of Godfrey's predecessor in piety, Aeneas, *Aeneid* 4.366–67. For Armida's false grief, Gentile refers to Plutarch's Cleopatra, weeping when Antony told her he wanted to leave for Syria.

78–82: These stanzas are lacking in *Scelta.* They show how Eustace misunderstands his duty, as he places one good, the chivalric ideal, ahead of a greater good, Jerusalem. They also make Godfrey seem less culpable for yielding. *Scelta*'s stanza 83 betrayed a weakness in Godfrey which Tasso could not finally allow: "Godfrey then seeing the great grief in their tear-stained faces, after some resistance yielded, defeated by his natural feelings." To make matters worse, in the next stanza Godfrey called Armida back, asserting, "You shall have such swift help from me as your fears have entreated." Happily Tasso assigned this bravura to Eustace instead.

80—*to help all ladies:* To oppose Eustace's boyish sentimentality I cannot resist repeating Galileo's hearty contempt: "Diabolical trickery would not have sufficed to lop off those members of the faithful army who followed Armida, had not the Poet, against all decorum, resolved himself to make his adventuring heroes baser and more effeminate than a pack of mongrels after a bitch in heat."

86—*Circe . . . Medea:* Classical sorceresses and dominators of men; cf. *Odyssey* 10; Euripides' *Medea.*

87—*she pulls his reins, she whips him on to go:* For Armida's horsemanship, see Plato, *Phaedrus* 246–48, also the source for Tasso's notion of the three main faculties of the soul. The men are ridden by a woman as if they were horses and she the directing reason.

90—*lending . . . facade:* An attempt to translate the reading of Os. and *GC, compone,* "composes," as an artist. Bon. 1, 2, and 3 read *comparte,* "arranges."

96—*Achilles, Theseus, Hercules:* Achilles for Briseis, *Iliad* 1; Theseus for Ariadne, whom he later abandoned, cf. Catullus 64; Hercules for several women, including Omphale, for whose love he wore women's clothing, and Deianira, whose jealousy led to the hero's death. Cf. Ovid, *Metamorphoses* 9.1–272.

Canto Five

—A large set of *rejected stanzas,* particularly from *cantos 5 and 6,* are appended to several early editions of *GL.* Their style leaves no doubt as to their authorship. Comparison of these with the revised text shows Tasso struggling to unify the plot of the poem and to express his developing ideas about sin, political leadership, and obedience. At the head of each canto's notes I will summarize these stanzas and let the reader draw his or her own conclusions. Thus, in the rejected stanzas from *canto 5,* Eustace, too, longs for the position as leader of the Adventurers, and Godfrey hears rumors that tend to confirm Armida's story. Rinaldo's desertion is portrayed as a rejection of his father and his ancestors. Godfrey sends Arnaldo with a posse to bring him back. They falter when they meet the lad; only Arnaldo attacks, and he is slain. Though he accuses them of cowardice, Godfrey is glad of their failure, for he is unwilling to bring the law down on Rinaldo. In *Canti,* earlier still than these rejected stanzas (which preserve some of its readings), several men pursue the leadership of the Adventurers: Hernando, Ugo, Ruberto, and Ubaldo (Rinaldo). Stanzas 3–15, wherein Godfrey again recommends against Armida's plan and Eustace tries to engineer Rinaldo's election, are absent from *Canti.*

2—*to succeed the magnanimous Dudon: GC* 6.2 thus links this problem with that aroused by Armida: "So that one will might be their rein and spur."

3—*to be constant we must change our mind:* Constancy and stubbornness are not the same. Birago: "He is inconstant who fails to bring to effect his good proposals—not who fails with his bad ones."

4—*I shall not hold you here against your wills: GC* has "I shall not hold you here by force," implying that their wills are not all-important.

5—*choose someone:* Godfrey commands the Adventurers to choose a new leader, an election that, as Galileo complains, never occurs, though by the end of the poem it seems as if Rinaldo is the leader of the squadron after all.

10—*the coverts of night:* Eustace refers to Armida's proposal to attack Damascus by night. The point is that the honor-loving Rinaldo will (unlike, as we shall see, Soliman) scorn to fight unless in the open. Naturally, Eustace's mind is on quite another sort of night assault.

14—*To merit the first rank:* The reader should consider Guastavini's defense of Rinaldo: he enjoys hearing the truth about his bravery but does not solicit adulation. He is like Cato, who, asked why he did not try to have statues erected in his honor, replied that he preferred that people ask why he did not have statues, to their asking why he did. Nor will Rinaldo refuse honors he deserves. Says Birago, "To refuse honors when they are offered is a sign of a proud mind." The Anonymous annotator notes that throughout the conversation Eustace addresses Rinaldo with the polite pronoun *voi,* while Rinaldo addresses Eustace with the familiar *tu. My bravery:* Translates Bon. 1 and 3, *valor nostro;* Os., Bon. 2, and *GC* read *voler vostro,* "your wishes," that is, "how handsomely you illustrate your wishes."

15—*honor is the mistress of his heart:* Literally, honor "lords it over" his heart; but in the final couplet Tasso rhymes and puns on "donna," "woman," and "indonna," "dominates." The heart has room for only one lord: "No man can serve two masters" (Matt. 6:24).

17—*the barbaric lord:* Not just because he hails from farthest Norway. Gernando falls to the barbarism of the aristocrat, the belief that authority and honor flow through bloodlines. That superstition prescribes the will of God, whose choice was the younger Jacob, not Esau; the lesser-ranked Godfrey, not Guelph or William. Gernando's tirade is a tissue of pride verging on blasphemy. The sainted Dudon looks down from heaven not to help the Christians but to engineer the election of Gernando! See Ovid's treatment of the haughty Ajax, who went mad after the Greeks assigned the weapons of the slain Achilles to Odysseus rather than to him (*Metamorphoses* 13.1–398). Interestingly, in *GC* 6.31 ff., Riccardo offers the place to Gernando, who refuses it at his hands. The refusal stirs up an argument over ancestral nobility, and it is Gernando who calls Riccardo a coward and a liar. There was a good deal of Gernando in the Tassos themselves; Manso (p. 6) notes that the family was one of the most famous in Italy.

19—*petty/number of family heroes: Canti* reads: "Now what good is it to you [i.e., to Hernando, who is talking to himself] to be born of a King, and of Heroes?"

20—*The noble rank:* This sentiment, arrogant from Gernando's mouth, was graciously adapted by Pope Clement VIII to refer to the honor Tasso would confer upon the laurel with which he was to be crowned.

33—*he aggravates the matter:* Arnaldo portrays the killing as wanton and irreverent, though Rinaldo had put up with a lot from Gernando's whisperings and held no grudge against any other Christian. Yet Arnaldo's point about the ramifications of Godfrey's decision, should he pardon Rinaldo, is cogent and reflects Godfrey's own thinking. If Rinaldo escapes unpunished, each man will become a judge in his own affairs, and Godfrey's leadership will be no more.

35–39—Stanzas absent from *Canti.* Tancred does not speak, and Godfrey commands that Rinaldo be haled before him in chains.

36—*Then Tancred added:* He should have stopped while he was ahead. Tancred affirms a form of the error that led to Gernando's death; here, it is that bloodlines can trump the law. Neither Tasso nor Godfrey is a democrat, yet both understand that there are times, and a murder trial is surely one, when king and beggar must bow equally before the law. To excuse Tancred, Birago notes that in his defenses Cicero always noted the benefits conferred upon the state by the accused. In *GC* Riccardo excuses himself before the whole company, and Godfrey replies that it is not the first time he has shed Christian blood. Riccardo defies Godfrey's sentence of imprisonment; Raymond gives a long, Nestor-like speech begging Godfrey to be merciful and Riccardo to be less hotheaded; the whole scene casts Godfrey as Agamemnon and Riccardo as Achilles.

41—Stanza missing from *Canti.*

48—*When I had seized the kingdom of Cilicia:* See above, 3.10; also William, 5.10, who portrays Tancred as unwilling to shed the blood of men who had pledged to fight the enemies of Christ. Yet a phrase in book 3 (p. 24) of Robert highlights the link between Tancred's amorousness and Rinaldo's love of honor. The rift between Baldwin and Tancred, says Robert, was caused by a *libido dominandi,* or lust for rule.

52—*the unknown sources of the Nile:* That is, the land of the legendary Christian king Prester John, surrounded by hostile Saracens (see 12.21 and note). A purported letter from him, included in the Basel 1533 edition of Robert (in Duke Alfonso's library), locates his kingdom where the Nile rises. Yet, for all his good intentions, Rinaldo will achieve little for Christ until he learns again to submit to rightful authority.

63—*Proteus:* God of the sea and of chaotic change. Cf. *Odyssey* 4.384–458.

72—*Let all your names be entered in this urn:* Godfrey still wants to avoid hard feelings. The reader who suspects that Godfrey is ceding too much authority should recall the choice of Matthias by lot to replace Judas (Acts 1:15–26) and the Spirit-directed choice of Raymond later on to duel Argante (7.70). It is an urn, and not a helmet, says Gentile; the Romans used urns in civil matters, helmets in military. He suggests that Godfrey does not consider this a military affair.

75—*Rambaldo: Canti* names him *Rinaldo.*

78—*At last he let them go:* In *Canti* he sends three hundred Greeks along with the ten champions.

80–84: Missing from *Canti.* It seems the character of Eustace was a late development in Tasso's revisions.

86—*William:* For the fleet, see 1.78–79.

90—*You who have suffered:* Tasso adapts the famous speech of Aeneas to his despairing men (*Aeneid* 1.198–207); cf. Milton's Satan to his fallen confederates (*PL* 1.622–62). William recounts how the troops suffered famine when they were besieged in Antioch (4.5–7).

—*In the rejected stanzas to canto 6,* the pagans are starving behind the walls, and with what little food he has Aladine feeds his soldiers and lets the rest die (cf. the tactics of Simon at the siege of Jerusalem [Josephus, *The Jewish War* 5.10]). The famine is described in rich detail. In the midst of this crisis Argante justifiably approaches the king, arguing the cowardice of death by starvation. In the match between Argante and the Christians, Godfrey sends several warriors out before he sends Tancred; these are all slain or beaten. Erminia is not worried about death, since she is starving in the city anyway. When Alcandro mistakes her for Clorinda, he says explicitly that he does not care if he breaks military discipline so long as he gets his revenge. To make matters worse, he has been posted there by Tancred, whose tent is nearby.

3—*How long shall we be jailed behind this wall:* Gentile compares Argante's speech with that of the young, hotheaded Romans who, frustrated by the cautious policies of Quintus Fabius Maximus "Cunctator" ("the Delayer"), argued that the armies of Rome should engage Hannibal in a pitched battle immediately. The results were disastrous. See Livy, *History of Rome* 22.14. Tasso's money is on the wise leader, not on the muscular soldier.

5—*fixed by the fates above:* Of Argante Tasso has said, "His sword determines what is just" (2.59.8), implying disbelief in justice or in the gods. Now Argante expresses the opinion of a fatalist. If he is to die today, he is to die, and that is all there is to it. Let him die bravely, if he must. Argante leaves no room for anything beyond blind fate and human will. There is no Providence. (Guastavini, by the way, attributes fatalism to the Turks generally and says that Argante is more Turk than Tartar.)

6—*When . . . best:* Sen.'s reading, based on Tasso's early decision to cast the Saracens as dying of famine within the city walls, is more heroic: "In things already defeated and lost, the only healthy thing is not to hope for health."

10—*Soliman:* Sultan of Nicaea. See 1.6 above and note.

15—In Os. this stanza reads quite differently—more insulting to the Christians, less of a revelation of Argante's arrogance, and less of a classical challenge of martial excellence (see, for the entire episode, *Iliad* 7.55 ff.). I translate in prose: "[Go tell them] that a knight, who scorns having to hide here, surrounded by bulwarks and trenches, wishes to make manifest in the field of arms, should anyone be so bold as to deny it, that it was not zeal or faith or any other honorable word that moved the Franks to attack Asia, but merely their own ravenous, ambitious hunger for rule and plunder." (In Sen.'s stanza 6.20 the Christians accuse Argante of lying here.) Gentile remarks that it was a breach of the chivalric code for a nobleman to challenge commoners, as Argante does.

22—*Field of Mars:* The Roman Campus Martius, arena for gladiatorial combats.

23—*Enceladus in Phlegra:* One of the haughty Titans whom Jupiter struck down with a thunderbolt, Enceladus was thrust beneath the earth in the sulfurous, volcanic region near Cumae. The *giant Philistine* is Goliath (1 Sam. 17). Gentile remarks that it is a trait of a barbarian to boast about mere size, as the Gauls laughed when they saw Caesar and his Romans.

25—*Then . . . the proud lad:* Os. reads: "For being chosen champion for such an enterprise," while *GC* reads: "for such high honor, praising God."

26—*Her mantle:* The last four lines of this stanza and the first two of the next are thus revised in *GC:* "Far whiter than ermine was her proudly decorated mantle; on her helmet, a kind of crown of golden flowers; at her side, a jeweled belt of fine gold. She revealed her face in part to him below, who gazed up at her, at how she raised herself to the skies."

32—*Give up:* As Gentile notes, no Christian in Tasso adopts the barbarous posture of a supplicant in battle. One triumphs, or retreats, or dies fighting, but one never surrenders.

33—*Medusa and Alecto:* A Gorgon and a Fury, respectively. See 4.5 and note.

52—*Shade or no shade:* Says Guastavini: "Appropriately, Argante is the first to reply to the interposition by the herald, showing him for the ferocious, impatient, and irrational man he is." He adds that Argante probably thinks he has gotten the better of the fight.

55—*Erminia:* Tasso excused this lapse from military matters by citing Aristotle's opinion that it is perfectly true to life to interweave the strange with the ordinary (*Lettere* 61). As in the case of Clorinda, we excuse Tasso on thematic grounds. The duel is a contest of passions that move men to do great and terrible (or terribly foolish) things. The stage now shifts to the fawnlike Erminia, whom love moves to don armor and become, in her girlish way, as brave as Clorinda herself.

56—*Cassan:* Bon. 1, 2, and 3 follow William and name the king of Antioch Aciano, but in 2.71 in the original text Tasso has already called him Cassan.

73—*lying counselor:* Or "flattering counselor," the one who tells you to do what you want. In Sen., however, Love was no counselor but an imperious ruler: "On the other side Love, who subjected to himself her reason now grown weak and frail, increased the flames, rekindled the torch, sharpened the arrow: "What I command it is useless to strive against!' " Moreover, Sen. 6.79 presents Love as the solver of all labyrinths. In general Tasso softened his treatment of Erminia as he revised.

79—*None of their thoughts the girls kept under cover:* Here, in a momentary flashback, the lover and the beloved of Tancred meet. Curiously, though they are friends and share the same bed, they do not speak of what most concerns them. Each woman is involved in a self-contradiction: Erminia is a Saracen in love with a Christian, and Clorinda fights to shut out of her consciousness any hint of sexual love. That strenuous denial of her sexuality explains how Clorinda could be so obtuse as to suppose that her girlfriend lies awake all night thinking of Antioch.

85—*Or maybe his right arm would pierce my side:* Tasso saw that the sex drive was necessarily, ravishingly, violent. Tancred has made the same offer (3.27–28), and the enchanted woods will be made safe again only when Rinaldo runs his sword through a demon impersonating Armida (18.34–37).

86—*Here I will stay:* In Os. a question: "So then I'll stay here?"

87—*Yes, yes, I can:* Os.: "Love will enable me to do it, Love, whence the weakest derive great strength." No mention is made of Love's tyranny.

92—*as when he made Alcides wear a skirt:* Hercules, that is, who put on women's clothing and took up the distaff, all for love. Cf. Ovid, *Ars Amatoria* 2.215–22. Tasso alludes to the episode again (16.3).

106—*its polished gleam flashed far away:* So too will Clorinda be noticed (by Tancred) attempting to steal away from her own night attack (12.51). The scene adapts Virgil's episode of Nisus and Euryalus (*Aeneid* 9.373–74). The *young Polyphernes* (st. 108) who thinks he sees Clorinda is the same whose father was slain by her (3.35). In his case passion for vengeance overcomes reason and military discipline.

Canto Seven

1—*Erminia is swept away:* Tasso excuses this digression on the grounds of verisimilitude. Since the siege works are not yet complete, he says, he can allow himself some leeway, without losing the aims of the poem (*Lettere* 25; but he cuts the episode from *GC*). Erminia's flight is a slightly comical version of the straying of souls which figures so prominently in Tasso's allegory. Tasso manages a neat reversal, as Erminia's flight from Jerusalem on account of love becomes, temporarily, a flight into a pastoral idyll *away from* the pains of love. She tries Epicureanism as an antidote. Tasso's debt to Lucretius, 5.1379–1411, is notable throughout. For the heedless flight, cf. Ariosto, *OF* 1.33–35. In her unhappy romantic peregrinations she resembles Heliodorus's heroine Chariclia, who also provided the name for Armida's fictitious mother (4.43) and part of whose strange story is adapted for Clorinda's birth; see 12.21, 12.23, and notes. Erminia's flight is adapted by Spenser, *FQ* 3.1.15–18, who also adapts the episode of the world-rejecting shepherd for his meeting of Calidore and Melibee (6.9.5–25). It was also emulated by Tasso himself. Manso writes (p. 82) that when Tasso escaped from Ferrara the first time, he walked from Rome to Gaeta and fell in with some shepherds, with whom he shared a rustic meal and whose garb he decided to adopt for disguise.

7—*Fortunate folk:* Literally, "avventurose," you who have ventured well—ironic, given their pacifist detachment from the fortunes of the world and their apparent belief, as Tasso writes in the *Allegory,* that "felicity can be found in pleasures and idleness." Cf. Virgil's Epicurean farmer, *Georgics* 2.490–515. The shepherd, whom Galileo criticized as "fit to recite in Arcadia in some tragicomic pastoral, not to speak in an epic poem," unfortunately does not appear in *GC.*

11—*For our desires are small:* Cf. Lucretius, 2.14–21.

19—*in the bark of laurel and oak:* Cf. Ariosto's Angelica and Medoro, *OF* 19.36.

32—*Never to hope to look upon the sky:* Adapting Dante's line, delivered by the ferryman Charon to the damned, "Never hope to see the heavens again" (*Inferno* 3.85). Armida's command is a Hobson's choice. Resist, and one remains her prisoner, never to view the sky again; capitulate, and one loses the hope of heaven. *GC* renders the final couplet thus: "Without opposition here she rules and governs, only freeing those who choose to serve her."

40—*bad conscience and contempt and shame and love:* The inner enemy conspires with the outer. What weakens the wicked man above all is his knowledge that he deserves, is destined, to die. The desperate rush to embrace one's fate can be seen also in the deaths of Tissaphernes, Soliman, and Argante.

46—*as a fish:* For this comic metaphor see Silius Italicus, 5.47–52. The idea of woman as fisher of men derives from Ariosto's Alcina, *OF* 6.35–38, but in the context of *GL* it assumes theological importance. Armida is reversing the command of Christ (Mark 1:17) by fishing for souls and tempting them to renounce their baptism. Thus she keeps the men alive, not for mercy's sake, but that they might despair and die the second death, the death of damnation.

61—*The good Raymond:* Again the old count from Toulouse plays the role of Homer's talkative Nestor, who reproved the Greeks for failing to take up Hector's challenge to a single combat (*Iliad* 7.124–60). His boastfulness, however, is more than the expansive memory of an old warrior (all the worse in *GC* 8.55–59). It bespeaks his faith. For, as he notes in his prayer (st. 78), God uses the most unlikely instruments to work his plans.

62—*Babylon:* Baghdad was so called in the Middle Ages. But Tasso's view is eschatological, as he is thinking of the final defeat of Babylon foretold in Rev. 18. So too Robert (bk. 8, p. 82), who, describing the taking of Jerusalem, launches into a long dirge on the fall of Babylon: "O glory of the kingdom of Babylon, how foully today are you deflowered."

64—*Conrad the Second:* Actually, Conrad died in 1039, when Raymond IV of Toulouse was but a stripling of fifteen. Guastavini comments drily: "[Raymond's] speech is devised according to the ways of old men, who are by nature talkative and boastful, and who are ever praising the things they did in youth."

67—*Pyrrhus:* See 1.6 and note. Robert, book 5, p. 41, says that Pyrrhus was a Babylonian ambassador who, like Alete (2.58 ff.), warned the Christians of the famine they must suffer if they did not yield. Instead Bohemond converted him to Christianity, and Pyrrhus secretly delivered the city over to the Crusaders.

70—*rather let God be judge:* Tasso emphasizes the sacramentality of this duel, for the presence of God is made the more manifest in the unlikely victory of Raymond.

72—*that Saxon traitor:* Rudolph, duke of Swabia. He was pronounced emperor by Pope Gregory VII in the midst of the pope's disputes with the reigning emperor, Henry IV, Godfrey's patron.

75—*against/the roughest whetstone anger hones its tip:* Guastavini observes that this sententious verse expresses one of the themes of the poem, that is, the virtue of justly directed indignation. See the Wise Man's speech to Rinaldo, 17.61–63.

78—*the blasphemous Goliath:* Cf. 1 Sam. 17:8–10.

80—*the angel:* Tasso's guardian angels are Christian versions of Greco-Roman tutelary deities. Guastavini notes that in Homer (*Iliad* 9.502–7), prayers are lame and always arrive after the blows have fallen. The Christian Tasso sees things otherwise.

81—*the spear that struck the snake:* Tasso may be thinking of the arrow with which Apollo slew the Python (Ovid, *Metamorphoses* 1.438–51) or of God's curse upon the serpent in the Garden of Eden (Gen. 3:14–15); but the Anonymous annotator, with some justification, identifies the spear with that of Saint George, who killed the dragon (see 12.23 and note). Indeed, in *GC* 1.122 when Jerusalem herself cries to God for help, she asks him to send "Your heavenly warrior, who split the proud dragon's crests."

84—*some "fifth" man:* Following the Bon. mss.; Os. reads *terzo,* as do most modern editions. But Raymond is throwing back in Argante's teeth his mocking words (6.16, 6.18), challenging up to five Christians.

100—*the phantasm spoke to Oradin:* Again Clorinda is impersonated. For the demon-inspired breaking of the truce, cf. *Aeneid* 10.636 ff. and *Iliad* 3.380–82, when Paris is spirited away by Aphrodite from his duel with Menelaus.

113—*that greathearted man:* In Sen. it is Clorinda who attempts to restrain them.

Canto Eight

—*In the rejected stanzas from canto 8,* the sword of Sven, it is said, can only be rendered pure and unbloodied by the touch of Rinaldo's hand. Godfrey and several of his men try it, to no avail. Charles then sets out with a picked squad to find Rinaldo, but they are attacked by the Arabs and must retreat to camp.

2—*that knight:* Charles, the only man remaining of the troops of *his bold chief,* the Danish prince Sven, ambushed by the sultan Soliman.

5—*Sven:* Tasso embellishes the story of the heroic Danish prince, told by William, 4.20. His version is a tale of single-hearted martyrdom, a foil against the Christians whose hearts are not wholly directed toward the will of God. The lad Sven, eager to prove his manhood, is inspired by the marvelous deeds of the lad Rinaldo, yet it is Sven's example that Rinaldo must learn to follow, and it is with Sven's sanctified sword that Rinaldo must kill Soliman. The episode is a riveting tale of youthful ardor and spiritual idealism.

8—*Antioch's surrender:* See 1.6 above and note.

12—*Fortune which drags us:* After an old Roman proverb: "Fata volentes ducunt, nolentes trahunt" [The fates lead the willing, drag the unwilling].

14—*that brought no change to our bold lord:* Tasso adapts Dante's impressive description of Farinata (*Inferno* 10.74–75). Like Godfrey, Sven is a *magnanimous* or great-souled man, one of whose traits is his seeming imperviousness to adversity.

23—*a great man:* Soliman; but notice the help he needs. In Sen.'s alternative to stanza 22, Sven is riddled with arrows from all sides, making him another young Saint Sebastian. The revised version is grander and makes Soliman more directly responsible for Sven's death.

33—*directed to the stars his sole desire:* Compare with the attitude of Sophronia, 2.36; hers is the bravery of endurance, his the bravery of action.

39—*a brief sentence: GC* gives the epitaph: "Here lies Sven at rest, who in Asia was slain by the infidel while on his way to the Sepulcher. May sky and wind and sea grant his bones eternal rest, and let the north wind in the depth of winter never extinguish the eternal flame of his honor." Tasso wanted no epitaph for himself; see 3.73 and note.

44—*Capitol:* Hill of Jupiter and site of government in Rome; also the terminus of triumphal processions. In the lap of the statue of Capitoline Jove the triumpher would place his wreath, as a sign that Jove and not he was the author of the victory. *The handsome wounds:* Testaments to their martyrdom, now made lovely in beatitude, these wounds reflect the characteristic signs of blessedness boasted by saints in medieval and Renaissance painting. But it was a proud Roman custom also to display the scars, especially on the face and chest, which one had received fighting for Rome; cf. Josephus, *The Jewish War* 1.9.

56—*clearer signs:* Unlike the pliant crowd, Godfrey remains unpersuaded of Rinaldo's death, and his doubts will be justified. Meanwhile, those who trust to their own great funds of interpretive ingenuity are easily persuaded not only that Rinaldo is dead but that Godfrey has had him murdered.

60—*in the left hand she held a severed head:* Tasso adapts Dante's terrifying image of the sower of discord, Bertrand de Born (*Inferno* 28.118–23). The allusion is apt, for just as Bertrand was condemned for inciting sedition in a prince against his king and father, so Argillan now incites the body of the army against its rightful head. His weapons are those that rabblerousers always find ready to hand: ethnic suspicion, envy, perceived injustice in the doling out of work and of rewards, and sheer imaginative malice. (In early versions of *GL* Godfrey did send out his officers to bring Rinaldo back dead or alive, and in Sen.'s alternative to stanza 67 Argillan reminds everyone of that fact. The present mutiny is far more irrational.)

74—*Tancred, William, and Camillus:* Their absence on account of love is now shown as a dereliction of duty. They could have stilled the sedition had they been in camp.

78—*his hands were naked:* Cf. Germanicus's settling of the mutiny of his troops in Pannonia (Tacitus, *Annals* 1.40–44). Godfrey relies not on brute force but on the justice of his position, a justice made evident in his magnanimous wielding of his scepter. He is like Virgil's "father Neptune," quieting with the authority of his trident the mutinous sea storms raised by Aeolus (*Aeneid* 1.142–56). The scene owes much to Lucan, *Pharsalia* 5.237–373, in which Caesar must put down an insurrection among his troops.

Canto Nine

(Stanzas 4–7, 54–55, 72–73, 90, and 96 are all missing from *Canti.*)

8—*in the guise/of a veteran:* Cf. Alecto's appearance to Turnus, inciting him to challenge Aeneas for the hand of Lavinia in marriage (*Aeneid* 7.341–72).

17—*look at that camp of thieves:* Guastavini notes that Soliman, like Godfrey, is a good rhetorician, tailoring his speech to his audience of cowardly Arab thieves. Thus he captures their attention by the prospect of great plunder and then allays their fear by telling them how easy the battle will be.

21—*Phlegethon:* Fiery river of hell; in Dante, a river of boiling blood where murderers are punished (*Inferno* 12.46–48).

54—*who scorned the second place:* This rivalry of Clorinda and Argante, a shadow of the fierce rivalry between Argante and Soliman, will lead to Clorinda's death in canto 12.

57—*She:* Fortune. Like Dante (cf. *Inferno* 7.67–96), Tasso views Fortune as an agent of Providence.

60—*the crystalline sphere:* The Primum Mobile or Empyrean of the Ptolemaic universe, a sphere beyond that of the fixed stars which imparts motion to it and to all the lower spheres.

63—*You above all:* Michael's derisive rebuke of the devils (cf. the rebuke delivered by Dante's angel [*Inferno* 9.91–99]) shows that the outcome of the war between good and evil is never in doubt, as the devils can act only within the leeway granted them by God's permissive will.

76—*Idiot Arabs:* Tasso's source Robert, book 3, p. 20, directs the insult otherwise: "Quid faceret Turcus, populus per omnia spurcus?" [What can the Turk do, filthy in everything?].

80—*He smiled contemptuously:* He does what the great Godfrey and Rinaldo never do: he rejoices in the suffering of his enemies. This contempt links him with Virgil's godless Mezentius; cf. *Aeneid* 10.739–46. For the prophetic reply—and Guastavini says dying men were thought to be imbued with the gift of prophecy, as they were in such close contact with the hereafter—see the dying Patroclus (*Iliad* 16.844–54).

83—*rode here and there:* Guastavini: "The wont of a boy, who inexpert in battle will break ranks and get in the way of the others."

85—*Lesbino, like a pretty flower:* Cf. the death of Euryalus (*Aeneid* 9.431–37).

86—*You, Soliman, weeping:* Again Tasso contradicts Robert, book 3, p. 22, whose Soliman falls to the ground howling with self-pity when he sees he has lost Nicaea, saying, among other undignified things, "What eyes could bear the splendor of their terrible weapons?" and persuading the Arabs to flee with him. Tasso's Soliman, however, is great of heart, a match for Rinaldo and Godfrey.

88—*Meanwhile . . . blows: Canti* reads, "Meanwhile the Captain had put to rout the weakling Arabs from the stockade." Tasso's revision highlights the moral distinction between Godfrey and Soliman in the matter of prudence and temperance.

92—*fifty fighters:* The men who had followed Armida now return.

Canto Ten

—*In the stanzas rejected from canto 10,* it is already proposed to call Rinaldo back.

8—*Soliman, Soliman:* Compare with the morning appearance of the angel Gabriel to Godfrey (1.16); in both cases Tasso's model is Virgil, *Aeneid* 4.265–76.

16—*The air collected:* A classical means of traveling incognito; cf. *Aeneid* 1.411–14. Here it is a sign of diabolical assistance.

20—*reading the annals of eternity:* The devils are not privy to the secrets of Providence, so Ismen is not privy to them either. His magic is to be contrasted with the prophetic faith of Peter the Hermit, the natural wizardry of the Wise Man of Ascalon, and the knowledge of God's plans granted to his agent Fortune. Ismen's wisdom, then, is at best the wisdom of a pagan ignorant of divine revelation. Here he paraphrases Juvenal's brave Stoicism: our own weakness or folly makes Fortune a goddess over our lives (cf. *Satires* 10.365–66). As the Roman proverb put it, "quisque suae fortunae faber" [everyone makes his own luck].

22—*a man whose deeds adorn all Asia:* The Saladin, sultan of Egypt (1138–93), who reconquered the Holy Land for the Turks in 1187. Known for his liberality and princely rule, he became legendary in the West for the grandeur and the justice of his reign; cf. Boccaccio, *Decameron* 10.9.

29—*there was a hollow cave:* See Josephus, *Jewish Antiquities* 15.14. Herod the Great built this secret passage through the Antonine tower into the Temple. It was named Antonia for his friend Marc Antony; cf. Josephus, *The Jewish War* 1.21.

39—*Orcano:* The self-interested orator reprises the role of Drances, Turnus's cowardly enemy in *Aeneid* 11. The Romans believed that marriage and parenthood can make men cautious and even cowardly; cf. Lucretius, 5.1017–18. Cf. the words of Urban, reported by Paulus, book 4, p. 107: "We enjoy peace here, but with shame; we take our ease, but it is blameful in us."

61—*flakes of fire:* Sodom and Gomorrah, Gen. 19. *Unnatural desire* refers to the homosexuality of the Sodomites, who demanded that Lot's angel-guests come outside to be abused. Tradition has it that the cities lay near what is now the Dead Sea, whose water is so salty that, as the ancients observed, bodies cannot sink in it. Armida's *locus amoenus* is indebted to Alcina's and Circe's islands; cf. *OF* 7.9–33, *Odyssey* 10.

66—*I feel my being change:* Just as Circe turned Odysseus's rash and appetite-driven men into swine, so Armida, sorceress of souls, turns Godfrey's bait-taking men into fish. Cf. *Odyssey* 10.220–40. The forgetfulness that Armida induces is not of Ithaca and homeland but of the Christian camp and the goal of the Christian soldiers—which is itself perhaps their "homeland," too.

71—*the good Rinaldo:* His brave deed motivates Armida's revenge against him; see 14.50 ff. below. In Sen.'s variorum a stanza precedes this one, describing how a heavenly voice told the Christians they were needed back in Jerusalem immediately.

73—*Full of the Lord:* The holy version of what happens to the Sibyl, *Aeneid* 6.45–51. Unlike Ismen, who ferrets out scraps of prophecy by his own energetic means, Peter is suddenly, unwittingly seized by the Holy Spirit, rapt beyond the moving heavens (cf. Saint Paul's vision, 2 Cor. 12:2–4). He now sees intellectually, that is intuitively, directly, as the angels see, without the mediation of sense impressions or discursive reason.

75—*he will fight the wicked Augustus:* The Hermit attributes to Rinaldo deeds performed by his historical namesake, the twelfth-century son of the captain Berthold. The *wicked Augustus* is the emperor Frederick Barbarossa (1123?–90), usually out of favor with the papacy (as indeed were most strong emperors of the Middle Ages), whom Rinaldo drove from his siege position around Milan.

76—*Their arts:* Paraphrasing Anchises' description of Roman destiny and Roman virtue (*Aeneid* 6.851–53). Here Peter prophesies not empire for Rinaldo's descendants (the Este clan, rulers of Ferrara and Tasso's patrons; see 1.4 and note) but submission to the primacy of the church, under whose aegis they will ensure that justice prevails.

78—This stanza has been revised heavily so as to place the emphasis on Peter and leave him and the reader in a mystic suspense, leading deftly to the ceremonial prayer of the next canto. Os., however, shifts attention from Peter back to Godfrey: "With these words the wise Peter drove away any fears the men had conceived concerning Rinaldo. In the general cheering only the dutiful Bouillon remained silent, immersed in weighty thoughts. Soon the night fell, and spread its dark veil over the world. The others leave and give their limbs to rest; his [Godfrey's, not Peter's] thoughts cannot be put to sleep."

Canto Eleven

1—*beginning:* This midpoint of the epic (actually, the central stanza of the poem's 1,917 stanzas is 10 below, concluding the Christians' prayer) shows the temporarily beaten Christian army rededicating itself to the Lord. It reflects the opening scene, 1.19 ff., in solemn and sacramental form. In this ceremony, which the Saracens behold first with astonishment and then with mockery, all assistance from heaven is reverently invoked, from the Trinity to the angels to the saints, in full litany. Tasso recounts a historical fact; for the procession, see William of Tyre, 8.11, who says also that the Saracens shot at the Christians and erected crosses upon which to spit.

7—*Thee divine:* John the Baptist; cf. Matt. 11:11.

8—*thee the bulwark rock:* Saint Peter; cf. Matt. 16:18: "You are Peter, and upon this rock I shall build my church." *Other heralds:* The other apostles. *You who then shed blood:* The martyrs of the early church.

9—*You whose pen or preaching:* The Doctors and preachers of the church. *You true handmaid:* Mary of Bethany, sister of Martha; she "chose the better part" (Luke 10:42); traditional interpretations held that she represents the contemplative life. *You virgins:* Holy nuns. *Greathearted:* The martyrs.

10—*Jehosophat:* The Kidron Valley. According to prophecy, the valley of Jehosophat will see the Last Judgment and the final battle between Christ and Antichrist, and in that context the place (a dark, tomb-ridden ravine) is better known as Armageddon (cf. Joel 3:12, Rev. 16:16). I have translated it so as to tease out the eschatological allusions Tasso is making.

13—*And yet the men of Jesus did not pause:* Tasso takes mild liberty with the historical account by William, who says that several of the Christian soldiers were wounded (8.11). Any reference to such a disturbance would detract from the single-minded piety of the Christians in this scene.

20—*girds himself in lighter, speedier gear:* To fulfill an ill-advised vow Godfrey arms as an infantryman, temporarily abdicating his position as the army's head. Godfrey's sin is more pardonable than the sins of the Christian deserters and mutineers, but it brings more harm to his men. Raymond points out that there can be a pride in conspicuous humility, wherein the head of an army has no leisure to indulge himself. He accuses Godfrey of wanting to be *first up the wall* (11.22), that is, of wanting the coveted "Mural Prize" given by the ancient Romans to the first soldier to scale the walls of a besieged city. That prize, we shall see, belongs to the brave Rinaldo. Godfrey can no more condescend to perform Rinaldo's function than can Rinaldo presume to perform Godfrey's. Unfortunately, Godfrey does not heed Raymond's counsel, and indeed many of his highest chiefs copy him in perhaps his only instance of imprudence. *GC* makes no mention of the vow; Godfrey instead wishes to emulate Charlemagne's Roland, to undergo what his men undergo.

23—*Pope Urban in Clermont:* Preached the Crusade in 1095; see 1.1 and note.

28—*a quiver full of arrows:* Cf. Virgil's Camilla (*Aeneid* 11.648–89). *Artemis* is the virgin huntress of the island Delos, sacred to her and her brother Apollo.

33—*tortoise-like:* The Roman *testudo,* a carapace of shields held overhead to protect Roman attackers from stones and fire hurled at them from above. Tasso's account of the battle follows fairly closely the account in William, 8.13.

61—*you French girls:* Cf. Homer, *Iliad* 2.235; Virgil, *Aeneid* 9.617.

70—*old Erotimus:* The episode of Godfrey's wounding and cure adapts the fortunes of Aeneas (*Aeneid* 12.318–25, 383–429). As in Virgil, the cure is worked by divine intervention, not by human skill. *The silent arts* are the medical arts. Gentile notes the Greek saying that a chatty doctor was a second disease. Indeed, our word *charlatan* derives from the Italian *ciarlatano,* a chatterer.

74—*Lydian spring:* According to Tasso, a spring known by the ancients to heal wounds. Tasso revised the verse for *GC,* referring instead to the brook of Siloe, a stream that runs into the Jordan near Jerusalem.

Canto Twelve

(Stanzas 1–4, 6, 13–16, 72–74, and 102 are missing from *Canti.*)

1—*Night:* The historical source for the Christian vigilance is William, 8.14, but the aesthetic source is Virgil, who describes with eerie power the sleeplessness of Dido (*Aeneid* 4.522–32) and the plan by Nisus and Euryalus to sneak through the Rutulian camp at night and bring an urgent message to Aeneas (9.176 ff.). Tasso has both episodes firmly in mind—the more so since Virgil himself conceived them as foils for each other. Dido and Nisus both are stirred by a *dira cupido,* a "dreadful desire" (9.185). Here Clorinda suffers that longing, one stirred, though it will offend the sensitive to say so, by her felt inferiority to the men with whom she fights. Yet when Clorinda asks whether her desire is inspired by God or by her own longing, she unwittingly speaks the truth, for God, too, inspires this thought in her. It is now time to bring Clorinda home.

8—*You showed . . . today: Canti* reads, "I have always had in you such faith, so may the Heavens give me help in need so great." No mention is made of Clorinda's emulation.

10—*Argante has vowed:* Note that Clorinda gives her male comrade credit for the idea.

12—*Soliman:* In *Canti* he accompanies them.

17—*a formula:* Ismen gives them, in separate vessels, the components of Greek fire, the medieval napalm. They will break the vessels and combine the reactants when they reach the siege machine.

21—*In Ethiopia ruled Prester John:* Or, in Italian, Senapo, legendary king of a nation of lost Christians; cf. Ariosto's fantastic account of how he tried to conquer Earthly Paradise, which God had removed to a mountaintop in Ethiopia (*OF* 33.102–12). The search for this king occupied a good deal of the European exploratory energy. In all likelihood Tasso, like many men of his day, credited the letters and accounts of one Francisco d'Alvarez, a Portuguese missionary who, directed by a cross in the heavens, "found" the lost kingdom and wrote copiously about its customs, including its admirably preserved Christianity in the midst of infidels, a faith brought them by Saint Philip through the eunuch of the Ethiopian queen (Acts 8:26–40). This Prester John, or David, as the putative author of his own letters calls himself (and as Tasso calls him in *GC* 15.21), apparently issued many an appeal to his Christian brothers to set aside their religious and national quarrels and unite with him to rout the Muslims and the heretics, to free the Holy Land, and even to seize Mecca. He himself would have moved against the infidel long ago, he says, but he was afraid they would destroy the Holy Sepulcher in retaliation. (Some of these letters were included in the Basel 1533 edition of Robert the Monk, a book that belonged to

Alfonso d'Este's library and undoubtedly used by Tasso. The same book also contains an account written by Christopher Columbus; see 16.32 and note.)

The tale of Clorinda's birth and miraculous preservation links her with heroines of romance; we are not now concerned with medieval siege works. (For the motifs of this tale see Heliodorus, book 4, wherein, because of the influence of a bedroom painting of Perseus saving the fair Andromeda, the dark-skinned queen of Ethiopia bore a fair-skinned child, Chariclia, and was accused of adultery. There follows the story of Andromeda and Perseus, significant for Clorinda's salvation by Saint George and for the episode of Sophronia and Olindo; see 2.31.) Clorinda is best understood as a heroine of romance, though she herself does not embrace that role until her death. *She was black:* Cf. Song of Songs 1:5: "I am black, but I am beautiful." The famous verse was commonly interpreted as referring to the Church on earth, ever needing to be redeemed and cleansed by her Bridegroom, Christ.

23—*a tale:* That of Saint George and the dragon; recounted in the *Golden Legend* by Jacopus da Voragine. I shall summarize the tale here. George was a young Roman soldier during the reign of Christian-persecuting Diocletian. In Libya dwelt a dragon who slew the city's soldiers and demanded a daily tribute of two sheep and a human being, chosen by lot. One day, when the king's own daughter was to be sacrificed, George arrived, mounted his horse, armed himself with the sign of the cross, and knocked the dragon senseless. He asked the maiden to cast her belt about the dragon, who then followed her like a dog. The people fled, but George counseled them to be baptized and to believe in Christ. Twenty thousand did, not counting women and children. At that, George slew the dragon, and the king erected a church on the site in honor of Mary and George. From the altar of this church came a spring of healing water. Eventually George doffed his soldier's garb and went about preaching that the pagan gods were all demons, introducing himself thus, "With the aid of Christ I am he who conquered Palestine!" The Romans flayed him, torched him, dragged him, and rubbed salt in his wounds. He did not complain, for he saw the Lord in a great light, offering him sweet consolation. The Roman prefect summoned a mage to poison George, but the poison was conquered by the sign of the cross. The mage was decapitated while kneeling and begging George to make him Christian. Then they lashed George to the torture wheel and bathed him in molten lead, to no avail. Finally the prefect tempted George with the favor he could win by worshiping the pagan gods. George pretended to agree, and on the day appointed for his public apostasy he beseeched God, for His honor and for the conversion of the people, to crush the pagan temple and its idols. Lightning struck, and the temple and its priests were destroyed. Thereupon the prefect's wife, queen of the Persians, turned to Christ. The prefect had her beaten to death, but George assured the dying woman that she would be baptized and crowned by the blood of her martyrdom. Finally George was decapitated, about A.D. 287. (The prefect and his ministers were lightninged to death on their way home.)

Saint George was an exemplary hero for the Crusaders. Jacopus reports that Saint Ambrose called him the most faithful soldier of Christ at a time when no one dared speak for the faith, a man who refused to be attracted by the deceitful promises of power in this world. He is the standard against which Godfrey, Rinaldo, and Tancred should be measured. Jacopus identifies George's virtues as disdain for baseness (whereby he was blessed with purity), temperate discretion (whereby he was blessed with eternal felicity), and humility (whereby he brought forth good actions). Jacopus also recounts Robert the Monk's description of Saint George's assistance in the Crusades. Robert (bk. 5, p. 40) says that at the siege of Antioch Bohemond called him the ideal Christian soldier, who with the other martyrs, at the command of Christ, cleared their way, supported them, and caused their enemies to fall. In book 7, during the rout of the Persians, Robert says that George and other Christian soldiers descended from the hills, whereupon Ademar the bishop cried, "O soldiers, behold your help comes which God has promised to you!" (p. 59). George was the patron saint of Ferrara—conspicuously portrayed everywhere in the city. Interestingly, George appears already in *Canti,* before Tasso had decided to celebrate Ferrara and its duke.

As for baby Clorinda, Guastavini remarks that "it is a natural thing, that offspring should somewhat resemble those objects that are before the eyes or before the mind during the act of conception." And Clorinda does resemble the damsel in the tapestry. The ironies abound: because Clorinda has Saint George for a guardian, it is "natural" for her to don the role of a warrior. But she, too, is, from birth to death, a damsel in distress, cared for by the saint, until she is providentially slain in battle by Tancred, the man who once deserted camp in order to play Saint George for her. Again Tasso stresses the unity of earth and heaven, for the saints above stand and fight beside us and can be invoked for their intercession before God.

25—*that was not the practice:* D'Alvarez reported that Ethiopian Christians baptized their boys after forty days, their girls after sixty days.

29—*a tiger:* Classical symbol for brutality, cruelty, imperviousness to love. Clorinda absorbs some of the tiger's warlike nature when she drinks the milk. Note that the tigress is Clorinda's insignia in battle.

33—*and live among old friends: Canti* was harsher: "And live lord of myself, as my heart wished."

34—*a trap at a riverbank:* Adapted from Virgil's tale of the infancy of Camilla (*Aeneid* 11.547–63).

39—*Mine she will be: GC* has Clorinda becoming Saint George's *ancella,* or handmaid; cf. 20.136 and note.

40—*it may be the true faith:* An astonishing moment of dramatic tension. Arsete breathes the unthinkable: perhaps he has lived his whole life under a delusion. He introduces into Clorinda's mind the very doubt in the righteousness of her purpose which will prove her undoing. Until now she has been the sole Saracen truly fighting for the faith. Arsete's story divides her against herself, and indeed she has had similar presentiments of the danger that awaits her tonight. Yet she remains greathearted to the end, as is only just; she does not abandon her people or her cause until the moment of revelation comes for her, and that only comes when she is about to die. *Another dream like that had troubled her:* Tasso recounts the dream in *GC* 15.41 ff. Clorinda dreams of a tree under whose shade all the world gathers, with life-giving waters nearby. She tries to help a giant to destroy it, but her hard heart is pierced in battle, and she repents.

44—This psychologically penetrating stanza is missing from the version preserved by Sen.'s variorum.

48—*The door swings to:* In *Canti* it is Argante who shuts it.

51—*He . . . trailed the warrior:* Always looking out for Clorinda, and so seldom finding her, Tancred now scouts the only enemy shut out of the city.

57—*gripped the young lady hard:* Amazingly, in *Canti* it was Clorinda who took Tancred into *her* robust arms. The original was a sexless wrestling match.

61—*Ask in vain:* Why should Clorinda not tell who she is? Is it the same feminine modesty that prevented her from taking credit for the plan to burn the machines? My guess is that Clorinda, who has witnessed the antics of Tancred more than once and may well know his armor, understands that if she tells her name her battle with this warrior will come to a sudden and embarrassing end. She knows how Tancred really regards her, and she persists in shying away from a sexuality—his and her own, too—too powerful for her virgin militancy. Instead she now reveals that she was one of the arsonists, to shore up her weakening resolve, perhaps, by provoking Tancred to resume the fight at once. Gentile cites Homer, *Iliad* 6.119–231, for the duel between Diomedes and Glaucus, who, having revealed their identities to each other, recognize ties of family hospitality, stop fighting, and exchange armor.

62—*weak as they were, unto the cruel fight:* Following Bon. 1, 2, 3; Os. is superior: "weak as they were, to battle. Cruel fight!" *It is their scorn that grapples it to the heart:* Compare their superhuman spiritedness with that of Sven (8.23).

64—*Her stole:* Clorinda is no more the warrior; all reference to her prowess and her armor here end in this moment of violence and revelation. Tasso heavily revised the end of the battle, turning what was merely a description of wrestling holds into an exploration of the relationship between love and violence.

65—*faith, and hope, and charity:* Clorinda, like the virtuous pagans in Dante, possesses the four cardinal virtues, prudence, temperance, justice, and chastity. Now she can claim the three theological virtues (1 Cor. 13:13) without which no one enters the kingdom of God. *Grace:* My theological translation of *vertu,* "virtue," "power." It is after all grace that gives her the power to turn. *Canti* reads "faith." *The handmaid of the Lord:* The phrase associates Clorinda with Mary; cf. the Annunciation (Luke 1:38).

66—*Friend:* Italian *amico* also means "lover."

77—*I will fear even my self:* See Lucretius, 3.1068–69: "We flee ourselves, whom we can never flee."

79—*could I be with you for eternity:* As God designs, but in heaven, not in the belly of a beast. That Tancred should think of Clorinda—whom he has just baptized!—as only Clorinda's body shows his weak and carnal understanding. Cf. Heliodorus's Theagenes, weeping over the supposedly dead Chariclia: "Behold, for you I will sacrifice myself to the gods of the dead! Let it at least be granted to us without blame to be united in death!"

86—*O Tancred, Tancred!:* Peter's rebuke is inspired by fatherly care for Tancred's immortal soul. This is no time to coddle the young man, who has torn his bandages off in a suicidal fury. Tancred has forgotten the beginning of his journey to fight for Christ, and he has forgotten the goal, too. A sad end awaits him if he does not retreat from the precipice.

91—*And behold, in a dream, the sighed-for love:* Clorinda adopts the role of helper to Tancred in distress. She is as Beatrice to Tancred's Dante. For the first time she refers to her beauty, as the spiritual means by which she will now save her slayer and baptizer.

94—*Daedalus:* Mythical inventor, creator of the famous labyrinth at Crete; cf. Ovid, *Metamorphoses* 8.152–68.

103—*but the gods see things otherwise:* See Virgil, *Aeneid* 2.428. More of Argante's fatalism.

Canto Thirteen

4—Guastavini interprets this passage as referring to the *illusory* union of the witches with the diabolical, but I think Tasso suggests their actual copulation with demon lovers.

10—*the crude arts:* Perhaps those that employ human sacrifice or human blood; cf. *Odyssey* 11.24–36. *The terrible Name:* Some say Demogorgon, the name that makes Hell shudder; I prefer the suggestion of the Anonymous annotator, who, citing Phil. 2:9–11, guesses that it is Jesus. The motif of the haunted forest comes from Lucan, *Pharsalia* 3.399–452, where Caesar leads his superstitious men and strikes the first blow.

18—*a little baby:* Adapted from Lucretius, 2.55–58, where the poet inveighs against superstitious Religion. Here it is not superstition that baffles the men but fear and weak faith.

24—*No dreadful apparition could cause him fear:* Courage is the art of knowing what is to be suffered and what is not. The man who, like Alcasto, lacks this art is furious, wild, even stupid. Cf. Aristotle, *Nicomachean Ethics* 3.7.

34—*But to die . . . allow:* Tancred's prudence should not be confused with faintness of heart. Gentile compares his wisdom with the decision of Varro during the disastrous battle of Cannae. He saved his life for a better day and was praised for it by the Roman Senate; Livy, *History of Rome* 22.49, 61.

38—*a cypress tree:* The cypress is a funereal tree, a reminder of Tancred's recent misadventures. The *strange pictography* is hieroglyphics, associating the tree with both Clorinda (who spent her youth with Arsete in Egypt) and paganism.

41—*blood:* For the bleeding tree, see Virgil, *Aeneid* 3.27–29; Dante, *Inferno* 13.31–36; Ariosto, *OF* 6.26 ff. The last two models are significant here, since Dante places the souls of suicides in thorn trees and Ariosto has the English duke Astolfo pent in a tree after the witch Alcina has grown tired of his love. Tancred, who has hardly escaped despair, must kill "Clorinda" again or must kill the lust still aroused by his thoughts of her body. He fails, not because he loves Clorinda, but because his love is not yet mature.

51—*another man:* Rinaldo, soon to arrive by sea on the shores of Palestine.

52—*But now the sun in Cancer bore down hard:* We are near the summer solstice. The drought derives from William, 8.7; Tasso follows the account closely.

64—*the murmuring:* Echoes the grumbling of the Israelites, hungry in the Sinai, longing to return to the fleshpots of Egypt (Ex. 16:2–3). Irrational passions again distort the common soldier's view of reality. In the revolt of Argillan Godfrey was a murderer. Now he is a glutton, indifferent to the misery of his dying men, who tar him with the most absurd slanders.

68—*the Greeks deserted:* Robert (bk. 4) and William (4.21) report that they deserted during the siege of Antioch, ostensibly to procure reinforcements from Constantinople. In the Western view, the hardships of taking the Holy Land proved too much for the selfish, effeminate, and untrustworthy Byzantines. And hardships there were. Robert says, in book 1, that at Nicaea the Christians were reduced to drinking their own urine. "Then their prince [a certain Rinaldo] entered into a secret pact with the Turks, preferring a temporary life to death for Christ." Thousands of Christians were slaughtered.

71—*Father and Lord:* Godfrey must pray for rain, as Moses had to pray for food and water for his stiff-necked people (Ex.16–17).

73—*the new order now begins:* Tasso considered this the narrative center of his poem, the turning point of the Christian fortunes (*Lettere* 26). Until now God has allowed the pagans some temporary success to try his people in the crucible of war. From now on the Christians will prevail, with the return of Godfrey's strong right arm Rinaldo, for whose glory God allows Egypt to join Palestine in one great and common defeat.

80—*O noble faith:* Cf. Petrarch's *Trionfi di Fama,* 2.67–69, referring to Joshua, who made the sun stand still (Jos. 10:13); also Christ, "Whosoever shall say unto this mountain, Be thou removed, and be thou cast into the sea, and shall not doubt in his heart . . . he shall have whatsoever he saith" (Mark 11:23).

Canto Fourteen

3—*A crystal gate . . . day: GC* reads: "There is a gate of sapphire in the east which only grace will open, just before the gates of the newborn day are unbolted." *Through this gate:* Virgil says that there are two gates for dreams, one of ivory, for false dreams, and one of horn, for true (*Aeneid* 6.893–99). For Tasso the dream of Godfrey is a divine revelation, a visitation by one of the saints above.

The saint is Hugh, fallen leader of the French troops (see 1.37). The episode is indebted to Cicero's *Somnium Scipionis* and to the meeting of Aeneas with his father Anchises in the Elysian Fields in *Aeneid* 6. As Aeneas learns from his father what troubles he must face now that he has landed in Italy, and how he must face them, so Godfrey learns from Hugh that it is time to recall the self-banished Rinaldo, so that the Christian army may enjoy its imminent victory (compare with *Iliad* 9.92–172, where Nestor persuades Agamemnon to send an apology to Achilles, appealing for his return to the Greek troops; Achilles remains intransigent). And as Anchises reveals to Aeneas the glory of Rome-to-be and shows him his famous descendants, so Hugh leaves Godfrey with the happy news that he and Rinaldo will become kinsmen, as their descendants unite in marriage. In *GC* 20 Hugh is replaced by Godfrey's father, who, like Anchises in the *Aeneid* and Africanus in *Somnium,* reveals to him his posterity and the Elysian fields—that is, the Heavenly Jerusalem.

9—*How little that last world contains of worth:* Cf. Cicero, *Somnium* 6.12–14. Hugh shows Godfrey that the arena in which we fight for supremacy in petty things is, as Dante put it, a little threshing floor (*Paradiso* 32.151); the mountain-top look of contempt on men struggling below comes from Lucretius, 2.1–13. *The celestial lyre:* Probably the music of the spheres, the corporeally inaudible music of mathematical relationships brought into being by the various (and only apparently discordant) motions of the heavenly bodies.

12—*recall . . . from banishment:* From desertion, we might say. Sen.'s variorum includes an entire stanza after this one, praising the long line of heroes to descend from Rinaldo. Tasso wisely removed it.

18—*Under . . . restored:* With the return of Rinaldo we will have all the Christians fighting for one goal, and the state of affairs alluded to in the first stanza of the poem will have been accomplished.

27—*the Danish warrior:* Charles, sole survivor of Sven's troops; cf. 8.1–40. It is his honored task to present the sword of Sven to Rinaldo.

29—*But the good hermit knew how far they erred:* As with the first council called by Godfrey, Peter sets everyone straight. The "crowd" judges by appearances, but his knowledge comes from heaven. Rinaldo is not at Damascus or Antioch, but in a never-never land beyond the Pillars of Hercules. Charles and Ubaldo must undertake a voyage to bring him home, and Peter's friend the Wise Man of Ascalon, whom we are about to meet (st. 33), will tell them where they need to go and what they need to do.

33—*His look was venerable, his beard was white:* The Wise Man has the look of a benign Cato; cf. Dante, *Purgatorio* 1.31–39. He is a "natural magician," using the powers of nature, not hell, to do his bidding. Like Shakespeare's Prospero, the Wise Man is an agent of Providence. Studying nature, he can do and see great things, so great that, as he tells us, he was once tempted to think he was a god; but his presumptions were brought up short by Peter the Hermit, who, as a mystic, is privy to knowledge that no science can discover of its own. The Wise Man then reversed the history of the apostate Ismen and from his agnostic naturalism became Christian. (In *Lettere* 123 Tasso describes his own spiritual progress, which parallels that of the Wise Man.) The Wise Man is thus not simply Peter's friend and co-worker but his subordinate, just as in Dante reason, symbolized by Virgil, must give the place of honor to theology, symbolized by Beatrice, which in turn must cede to mystic intellection. In *GC* 12.25 ff., the mage actually performs the role of Dante's Virgil, showing the knights the damned in the depths of hell.

45—*the measure of the world:* Cf. the mysterious saying attributed to the sophist Protagoras (c. 490–c. 420): "Man is the measure of all things; of the things that are, that they are, and of the things that are not, that they are not." Though Pico della Mirandola would base his *Oration on the Dignity of Man* upon this saying of Protagoras, Tasso retreats from such aggrandizement of man. Gentile tartly observes that God, not man, is the measure of all things.

47—*in Him find my rest:* Adapts the words of Dante's Piccarda, "In His will is our peace" (*Paradiso* 3.85). It is instructive to recall the context of Piccarda's words, for Dante has just asked her whether she and the others who occupy the lowest of the heavenly spheres ever envy those higher. The Wise Man is now truly happy, because he knows his divinely ordained place.

51—*I'll tell you now what happened after that:* At last the mystery of the headless trunk dressed in Rinaldo's gear is cleared up; cf. 10.60 ff. Rinaldo's change of clothes (like Clorinda's, like Godfrey's) is suspicious, suggesting that in his desertion of the army he became more pagan than he knew.

57—*the Orontes:* A large river in Syria. Rinaldo was on his way to Damascus after all.

62—*Young men:* The phantasm delivers her *carpe diem* wisdom, indebted to the Epicurean Lucretius. She recommends not just enjoyment of sexual pleasure but retreat from the troubles of the world, especially retreat from war. Psychologically, the intent is to make Rinaldo view his past hunger for glory as a fond illusion. Many of the verses are adapted from *De rerum natura* 2.14–33.

66—*Narcissus:* In Greco-Roman mythology, the boy who fell in love with his pretty reflection in a pool of water; cf. Ovid, *Metamorphoses* 3.407–510. The allusion is apt, for, as we shall see, Armida falls in love not so much with Rinaldo as with the (also narcissistic) love of Rinaldo for her.

70—*a little isle:* One of the so-called Fortunate Isles, far beyond the Straits of Gibraltar in the middle of the Atlantic. In mythology, these isles were sometimes thought to house the spirits of the blessed.

72—*a woman young in looks, but old in years:* Fortune, forever renewed, forever young. Her *opalescent clothes* suggest the mutability of her office.

74—*A fountain rises there:* The Fountain of Laughter, described by Pomponius Mela (*Cosmography* 3.10) and said by Petrarch (*"Qual piu diversa e nova"* 76–79) to be located on one of the Fortunate Isles.

76—*a maze:* Like the Daedalan labyrinth of Crete; cf. Virgil, *Aeneid* 6.14–30.

—In stanzas rejected from canto fifteen, the warriors are shown the Southern Cross; Fortune's journey is longer; Ferrara is praised as the only remaining nest for heroes and poets; descriptions of the Western world are longer and more precise, including mention of Ecuador and Peru. Charles and Ubaldo battle the monsters, but not by waving a magic wand. The fight is long and difficult.

5—*the downy feathers:* Simile paraphrased from Lucretius, 2.801–5, in a discussion of the reliability of the senses despite optical illusions. Tasso's point is the reverse: appearances are unreliable, and men are ill suited to judge the chances and changes of Lady Fortune. Gentile observes that the portrayal of Fortune also owes something to the wind-calming Venus of Lucretius's proem to book 1—making the handmaid Fortune into the very goddess Armida wishes to be. This entire voyage, however, is absent in *GC.*

10—*They passed by Ascalon:* A port on the Mediterranean Sea. *Gaza:* Ancient city about a mile away from the port to which it gave its name; destroyed by Alexander the Great and then rebuilt on shore. The knights see, gathered at Gaza, the great armies of the sultan of Egypt, shortly to arrive at Jerusalem. In general the geography lesson is also a lesson in history, especially as history teaches the impermanence of human affairs. It also stresses the universality of the Crusade. Paulus, book 4, p. 107, thus cites Urban at Clermont: "The cause is for all lands everywhere, no less for the East than for the West."

15—*Refah:* Palestinian port near the confines of Egypt; still extant. *Rhinoceros:* Desert coast between Palestine and Egypt. *Casius:* Egyptian promontory where, according to tradition, Ptolemy, king of Egypt, betrayed and slew Pompey the Great after his defeat at the hands of Julius Caesar.

16—*Damietta:* Ancient city on one of the mouths of the Nile; still extant. *Alexandria:* The great center of learning built by Alexander the Great; the site of the ancient city is now mostly underwater. *Pharos:* Referred to in Homer (*Odyssey* 4.355) as an island off the coast of Egypt; Lucan refers to it as a former island, now part of the mainland (*Pharsalia* 10.509–11).

17—*Marmarica:* The desert near modern-day Bone, a city in Libya. *Cyrenaica:* Comprising the five cities of Cyrene, Apollonia, Ptolemais, Arsinoes, and Berenice; now ruins. *Lethe:* The river of forgetfulness, which according to the ancients arose from the underworld.

18—*the Greater Syrtis:* A shifting bank of offshore sand, dangerous to ships; located between the Sicilian town of Cefalu and the African coast. *The Lesser Syrtis* was located near the modern Gulf of Gabes. *The Cape of Judecca:* At Cefalu. *Magra:* River near the town of Tripoli. *Malta:* Island south of Sicily. *Alzerbe . . . Lotos Eaters:* Modern Zerbe. The Lotos Eaters are from Homer, *Odyssey* 9.83–97.

19—*Marsala:* Important port on the southwest coast of Sicily. *Carthage:* The ruined city lies some miles east of the modern Tunis. Carthage was once the great enemy of the Roman republic and the prime naval power in the Mediterranean.

20—*Bizerta:* The city still exists, in modern Tunisia.

21—*Numidian:* Berber herdsmen. The region refers to what is modern Algeria. *Bugia and Algiers . . . Oran:* All cities on the coast of Algeria, still in existence today. *Tingitan . . . Mauritanian . . . Morocco . . . Fez:* Modern Morocco. The first name refers to the region around the Moroccan city of Tangiers; the last refers to the region around the city of the same name, still thriving. *Granada:* Spanish port facing Morocco, and last outpost of the Moorish civilization in Spain.

22—*Hercules:* The ancients surmised, correctly as it turns out, that Europe and Africa were once one continent. The myth was that Hercules split Spanish Abila from African Calpe, and thus the Mediterranean Sea was born (Pomponius Mela, *Cosmographia* 1.5).

24—*Cadiz:* Spanish port on the Atlantic side of the Straits of Gibraltar.

25—*Ulysses:* Fortune recounts the tale of Ulysses' final, disastrous voyage, told by Dante (*Inferno* 26.90–142) as an example of evil counsel and presumption. Tasso, writing for the empire-building, native-converting Renaissance, views the voyage more benignly, as preparing the way for the new Ulysses and new Hercules, Christopher Columbus (see stanzas 30–32). Tasso's intention in writing about the First Crusade was far from antiquarian. The Crusade provides a model for what the present Church Militant ought to be doing. A new enemy—not only Islam but the Protestant north—has emerged to fight.

32—*Columbus:* One must not underestimate the importance of this eulogium. The Basel 1533 edition of Robert the Monk appends a play about the 1492 expulsion of the Moors from Granada; letters from the purported king of Ethiopia to the king of Portugal and to Pope Clement VII, requesting aid against the Saracens who surrounded him (see 12.21 n); an account of the origin of the Turks; an account of the emergence of Mohammed; and a brief by Columbus describing his discovery of the Indies. Clearly the compilers of the book considered the exploration of the world to be a divine mission to spread the Word of God to the ends of the earth, fighting back the forces of paganism.

35—*spontaneously:* Tasso associates Armida's island with fables of the Golden Age, when the earth bore fruit so abundantly that no man need till the soil. Cf. Virgil, *Aeneid* 8.314–27; Ovid, *Metamorphoses* 1.89–112.

37—*Fortunate Isles:* Where the blessed dwelt in Elysian delight; cf. Homer, *Odyssey* 4.561–68, Lucretius, 3.18–24, Horace, *Epodes* 16.41–66.

49—*he waved his . . . wand:* See Spenser's adaptation for Palmer and Guyon approaching the Bower of Bliss (*FQ* 2.12.39–41).

51—*Hyrcania:* Region of the Caucasus mountains, noted for the ferocity of its tigers and other wild beasts. *Black Wood:* The Black Forest of Germany.

57—Os. attributes this speech to both men, *GC* to Araldo (Ubaldo).

58—*two merry ladies:* In Tasso, as in Spenser (*FQ* 2.12.63–69), these two girls provide most of the action on the languorous isle. They also reprise the *carpe diem* song that initially tempted Rinaldo. Tasso's point is not that a good warrior will be free from sexual stimulation. Charles and Ubaldo enjoy their brief look and then go on, employing Reason to free them from the need to act upon any incipient lust.

Canto Sixteen

3—*Hercules:* On Armida's walls are portrayed effeminized heroes—men overcome by women, reason overcome by passion. For Hercules, see Ovid, *Ars Amatoria* 2.213–20. The treatment of Antony and Cleopatra is indebted to Virgil (*Aeneid* 8.678–713), where Antony exemplifies oriental laxity, as opposed to the Roman piety of Augustus Caesar. Tasso was aware both of Plutarch's biography of the lusty warrior and of Josephus's account of how Cleopatra tried to use her influence over Antony to induce him to betray his friend Herod the Great; cf. *The Jewish War* 1.19.

8—*Meander:* This river in Asia Minor gives its name to our word denoting intricate, tortuous motion. The labyrinth is Tasso's visual symbol for the deceptive wiles of the all-too-feminine Armida.

10—*It seemed an art of Nature's playfulness:* Art is supposed to imitate Nature, as Aristotle said, not supplant it; nor is Nature supposed to imitate Art. The operative word here is "seemed." According to Tasso, the garden of Armida was a place in which Nature had no part whatsoever—as can be seen from the unnatural warmth of the garden atop a snowy mountain.

14—*Look at the chaste and modest little rose:* This "gather ye rosebuds" song is but one of many such songs in the West. Tasso's sources were probably Catullus 62 and Ariosto, *OF* 1.42. Spenser adapts the song for his Bower of Bliss (*FQ* 2.12.74–75), and then the theme became the subject of Herrick's famous poem "To the Virgins, to Make Much of Time."

17—*he lying in her lap:* The tableau alludes to Lucretius's disarming of Mars by Venus (1.29–40). The dominated warrior apprehends nothing beyond the Epicurean world of the senses. Spenser's version of the same scene (*FQ* 2.12.77–80) so emphasizes the hedonistic lassitude that the warrior is rendered nearly comatose. For the last two lines of the stanza, Os. reads: "then [they] see for sure Armida and her lover, sitting in the shade beside a limpid pool."

20—*the mirror:* Symbol of their mutual narcissism. Armida, says Guastavini, rises to adorn her face and makes Rinaldo hold the mirror. As I read it, she sees herself in the mirror, while he looks into her eyes and sees his own face gazing at hers. There is a strangely cool detachment about their lust.

21—*O turn:* Contrast with Dante, *Purgatorio* 31.132; one glance from Beatrice's eyes effects in Dante a fearful spiritual exaltation. Rinaldo's speech, however, is effeminate, prettified, self-conscious, and, despite its celestial imagery, very earthbound stuff. This is surely Rinaldo's nadir. But he will learn better to appreciate the heavens; see 18.12–13 below and note.

24—*her lovely belt:* Cestos, the belt Venus wears when she subdues her jealous husband; cf. Homer, *Iliad* 14; also Claudian's description of Venus's favorite hill, *Epithalamion* 49–96.

32—*fame's reward:* Cf. *Rinaldo,* 9.86: "Ah, they will say, "Rinaldo is dallying in Media, hatching lascivious thoughts at his leisure, and for a pagan girl has forgotten his lance and his sword and has accepted a new law!' "

34—*indignant Scorn:* The righteous anger of which Rinaldo is the poem's exemplar; cf. Plato, *Phaedrus.*

35—*her monster-sentinel lay dead:* In 15.49–52 Charles and Ubaldo frighten the sentinels away with their wand, but in an earlier version, as noted above, they fight them in a cruel battle. Tasso has overlooked the inconsistency here.

40—*Madly she cried:* During this exchange Armida plays the part of lovelorn Dido, who pleads with and accuses Aeneas as he plans to leave Carthage (*Aeneid* 4.296 ff.).

41—This stanza is missing from Os. and Bon. 2 but is present in Bon. 1 and 3 and *GC.* I include it, since it emphasizes that engagement with the world—and the world means scorned women, too—which Tasso enjoins upon his crusading Christians. In *GC,* however, Riccardo's friend takes no chances; after the young man turns away, he binds Armida, who can only be set free when she submits to virtue.

58—*Xenocrates:* Greek philosopher (396–314 B.C.), noted for his severe way of life.

61—*He gives . . . leave:* Following Os.; Bon. 1, 2, and 3 have the weaker "From all the things he can—you don't believe—he with a look of pity takes his leave."

Canto Seventeen

2—*who seized it from the Turk:* On the contrary, Gaza belonged to the Egyptian kings from the time of the second caliph, Omar (635–40). The present Egyptian king is Abul Kassem (r. 1094–1102). For the size of his army, see William, 9.10. In actuality, Godfrey did not defeat that army until after the storming of Jerusalem, but Tasso folds the episodes into one for greater poetic power. For *GC* the historian in him trumped the poet, and he separated the episodes, rendering the end of that poem anticlimactic.

4—*His name was Caliph:* Actually, Abuthanimi, nephew of Mohammed's son-in-law Ali.

5—*Syene:* City on the Nile, near the Aswan cataract.

6—*the morning sun:* Following Os. *matutino* and *GC oriente;* but the Bon. mss. read *mauritano,* "Mauritanian," that is, toward Morocco in the West.

7—*nobler when Fortune frowned:* Gentile says that such praise was considered worthy of the greatest of the Romans. The king's vast *lust,* however, associates him with the traitor Catiline, whose "vast soul ever craved what was immoderate, impossible, and far beyond his reach" (Sallust, *The Conspiracy of Catiline* 5).

11—*Apelles:* Greek painter. *Phidias:* Greek sculptor, architect of the Parthenon, said to have sculpted the Thundering Zeus at Olympia.

19—*Barca:* The desert between Alexandria and Tripoli in what is now Libya.

20—*Phoenix:* Unique bird, reborn from the ashes of its own pyre. See Ovid, *Metamorphoses* 15.391–407.

24—*he believed the holy Word:* The third kingdom is Christian, ruled by the legendary Prester John or his successor.

27—*Samarkand:* Great city on the "Silk Road" from Europe to China, seat of the Tartar empire.

32—*an Armenian prince:* According to William, the leader of the Egyptian armies was an apostate, led to renounce his creator by the opulence of the Mohammedan court (9.10). His name, Emiren, seems to derive from "emir," a title of dignity.

61—*at the summit of the ruggedest cliff:* This stanza is Tasso's clearest renunciation of the Epicurean retreat from care by which Rinaldo (and perchance the poet himself) has been tempted. Gentile notes that Tasso does not say "the highest good," which would, of course, be God. *Valleys:* Following Os. and the logic of the metaphor, but Bon. 1, 2, 3 read *ville,* "hamlets," punning on *vile,* "base, mean."

64—*this shield:* See the prophetic shield of Aeneas (*Aeneid* 8.615 ff.).

67—*Caius:* The following are historical figures, claimed as ancestors by the Este family (*Actian* blood). Tasso follows Pigna, whose work stresses two points that are crucial if the modern reader is to understand Tasso's digression here. Pigna argues, first, that only unity among Christians ensures victory; second, that the Este heroes have been strong because of their single-hearted devotion to defending the faith against infidels. Thus Rinaldo's shield is, like Sven's sword, a symbol of his calling as a Christian soldier. *Caius Actius* (r. 402–11) was governor in Este under the Roman emperor *Honorius,* who had too many of his own problems with the invading Goths to assist the northern Italians. *Alaric,* or as Tasso calls him "the proud Goth," invaded Italy in 409, but not really at the invitation of Honorius, contrary to Pigna (p. 6). The emperor sent the great Vandal general Stilicho to persuade Alaric (whom Stilicho had routed in 402) to move into Gaul. But the enemies of Stilicho (who had him beheaded in 408) persuaded the emperor not to abide by the treaty. After Stilicho's death Alaric moved on Rome for the second time, successfully. This is the sack of Rome that occasioned Augustine's *City of God.*

68—*Aurelius:* Lord of Este, 411–18; defended the Venetians against an alliance of Vandals and Alani (Pigna, p. 6). *Forestus . . . the great Hun:* In 450 Forestus

(r. 450–53) defended his land against the attack of Attila, defeating him, as tradition had it, in single combat. Later he was slain by the same Attila while defending Aquileia; hence he is *the Italian Hector.* He is a Rinaldo of old, tall and possessed of a "grave affability, which in his countenance showed forth his grace, liberality, and magnificence" (Pigna, p. 8). Forestus fought "for the conservation of the faith of Christ" against Attila, its determined foe, the champion of paganism. Vastly outnumbered, Forestus argues as Sven does (8.15), insisting that the Christians have nothing to lose. "Either we win, and attain great glory and hope for future success, or lose, and obtain that eternal glory which our Savior promises to those who spill their blood for His sake." They won.

70—*Acarinus:* Son of Forestus (r. 453–78). *Gave way to fate:* The neighboring Altinates despaired of resisting the Hun, so they united with the Esteans. Acarinus then built a new stronghold on the Po River, the city of Ferrara, ever after to be the home of the Este clan. His advice reflects Tancred's thoughts (13.34): "Death in a good cause, with profit to one's own, is a glorious thing, but not with profit to an enemy that need no longer fear, and harm to our neighbors who after our death would be subject to even graver peril" (Pigna, p. 33).

71—*the foes from Germany:* The Alani, in 463. *Odoacer:* The German general who deposed the last Roman emperor, Romulus Augustulus, in 476. Acarinus fell to the German at Lodi with his brother Acorisius (Tasso's *Alforisius*) in 478.

72—*Actius:* Or Azzo, here Azzo I. *Epaminondas of the Estes:* Boniface I, named in the next stanza. He died in 556, as Tasso describes it, at the hands of the armies of the Goth Totila, whom he defeated. He is called Epaminondas because of the account by Diodorus Siculus. The Theban general (at Mantinea, 362 B.C.) was struck in the eye with an arrow that penetrated the back of his neck. When the doctors told him that removing the arrow would mean his death, he asked whether his shield was intact and whether the Thebans had won the battle. When his questions were answered favorably, he replied, "Now I can die content," and instructed the doctors to remove the arrow.

73—*Ernestus:* Conqueror of the Slavs in 711; reigned from 691 to 752. *The royal Lombard:* Agilulf, Lombard king.

74—*Henry:* Son of Ernestus. *Berengario:* Berengarius, son of Henry; a vassal of Charlemagne, then, after the emperor's death, a vassal of his son Louis the Pious. Tasso's account of Berengarius's defeat of Louis's mutinous nephew Bernard is not accurate. In fact, Bernard surrendered to Louis after he lost the support of his Lombard allies, and he pleaded for mercy. His death sentence was commuted, and in 819 he suffered the punishment of blinding, but he was blinded so severely that he died anyway. *Otto:* Berengarius's brother.

75—*Almeric:* Early-tenth-century marquis of Ferrara, named to that office by his patron Ugo (Hugh), king of Italy. Constructed the Ferrarese church of St. George in 925. *Actius the Second:* Azzo II, according to Pigna, struggled against Berengarius II between 950 and 955. History, however, dates his death in 1079.

76—*Albert:* Supposed son of the supposed Azzo II mentioned above; said to have married Adelaide, daughter of Emperor *Otto* I (the Great), circa 970. *Hugo:* Son of Albert, fought against both the pope and the emperor, circa 995.

77—*Tedaldo:* Supposed son of Azzo II; more likely the son of a man who was not an Este. He was invested with his authority over Ferrara by Pope John XV in 995. *Boniface:* Son of Tedaldo, marquis of Tuscany (1032–52), married to *Beatrice.* He produced no male heir, but his daughter *Matelda* (countess, d. 1115) was a formidable ruler. According to the legends Tasso follows (which, however, are not accurate), the troops of Matelda, fighting for the papacy, defeated the Norman warlord Robert Guiscard and the emperor Henry IV, who in the midst of one of the greatest confrontations of the Middle Ages had besieged the reformist Pope Gregory VII at Canossa; then she reinstated Gregory in his see in Rome. Actually, she never fought Robert Guiscard, and the pope her troops conducted back to Rome was Victor III.

79—*Actius the Fifth:* Supposedly the second husband of Matelda. *The fourth Actius:* Azzo IV, in history the real Azzo II. *Guelph:* Invited by the Holy Roman Emperor into Bavaria. From this German line of the Este family derive the dukedom of Bavaria (1071) and the dukedom of Saxony (1136). He is also our hero Guelph in this tale.

81—*Berthold:* Bertoldo, son of Actius IV by a second wife, and father of our hero Rinaldo. Here, of course, the portraiture ends.

89—*the wisest poets:* Following Bon. 1 and 3; Os. and Bon. 2 read "brightest," "most famous."

90—*Alfonso:* See 1.5 and note.

91—In ancient Rome, the *laurel* crown is given to emperors victorious in war, the *oak* to a man who frees a Roman city, and the *grass* to a man who raises a city from a siege.

94—*Mount Taur:* A mountain on the high plateau of Asia Minor. *Where summer reigns:* That is, Africa.

Canto Eighteen

7—*like a lost lamb:* Cf. Matt. 18:12–14. Peter the Hermit now confers the sacrament of penance upon Rinaldo and enjoins upon him a night of fasting and prayer. The Anonymous annotator notes that this is only the second special choice made by Heaven in the poem, the first being the election of Godfrey as head.

11—*of strange color:* We are told below that Rinaldo's coat is ashen, as befits a man atoning for his sins. It is the one time in the poem when a change of attire betokens no disguise but a change of heart.

13—*What lovely lights:* See Lucretius, 2.1030–39. A remarkable reversal: Rinaldo echoes the Roman poet least likely to view the heavens as the dwelling place of a loving God. Even the wise Epicurean knew to distinguish the superior pleasures of the mind from those carnal pleasures to which Rinaldo had fallen. How much more powerful, then, should the view of the heavens be to the faithful Christian? Rinaldo's comments echo those of Flaminio Nobili, a copy of whose 1570 *Treatise on Human Love,* written on the occasion of the marriage of Lucrezia d'Este, was heavily annotated by his friend Tasso: "Towards this Divine Love I do not know how necessary womanly beauty is; for to consider the wondrous and yet ordinary effects of Nature, the steady motion of the heavens, the vigor of light, the perfection of the universe, seems to me a far surer way to come to know the Supreme Beauty, than to lose oneself, fixing one's eyes upon a face."

14—*purge my old Adam:* Cf. Eph. 4:22, 1 Cor. 15:21–22; the "old Adam," the effect of original sin, is the carnality with which we are born. The believer must be reborn in Christ. For the dew upon Rinaldo's ashen garments, Gentile cites Ps. 147.

17—*candor:* So in the Italian, meaning a glowing white; the word links Rinaldo with Sophronia (2.26.8), of whom the word is also used.

25—*a myrtle:* The same tree that Tancred saw as the funereal cypress (13.38). The myrtle is sacred to Venus, goddess of love.

30—*Sileni:* A "Silenus" was, according to Gentile, a rough-hewn carving of a satyr, which the ancient Romans placed at crossroads to tell travelers which way to go. The bosoms of these statues were hollow and could be opened to reveal very finely worked artistry. Silenus was the perpetually drunken god and leader of the satyrs.

35—*Briareus:* One of the Titans who warred against Jove, Briareus was said to have had a hundred arms and fifty heads. Cf. Virgil, *Aeneid* 10.565–68.

36—*Cyclops:* See 4.5 and note.

37—*the black walnut tree:* Traditionally dear to witches and their spells.

39—*severe:* Os. reads *altero,* "proud." *GC*'s meticulous metaphor is superb: "And as a sun that lines with gold its mantle of white cloud, humble in its pride."

40—*I went . . . I saw . . . and defeated:* Rinaldo echoes Caesar's notorious "I came, I saw, I conquered."

41—*William:* The admiral whose fleet supplied Godfrey's men with necessaries. For the building of this siege machine, see William, 8.10. In general, the storming of Jerusalem reflects both the account in William and the account of Titus's siege in A.D. 70, followed by the destruction of the Temple. Josephus devotes most of books 5 and 6 of *The Jewish War* to this conquest of the Holy City.

47—*they too build their machines:* Cf. William, 8.8.

57—*a valet:* Vafrine (from Latin *vafer,* "shrewd"), a semicomic young man who shows more wariness and good judgment than do many of his elders. Pigna (pp. 21–22) tells of how Forestus (see 17.68 n) was betrayed by a renegade Christian versed in languages, turned spy for the Huns. Tasso inverts the story, as Vafrine instead reveals a piece of treachery planned against Godfrey (19.127).

71—*"cats":* Battering rams, worked under the cover of a wooden roof to protect the warriors.

75—*Ossa and Olympus:* Mountains of Thessaly; the Titans tried to pile Mount Ossa upon Mount Pelion in order to scale Olympus in their war against Zeus; cf. Ovid, *Metamorphoses* 1.151–55.

80—*a huge trunk:* For this ingenious battering ram, see William, 8.16.

83—*balls of fire:* According to William, it was the Christians who slung fire over the city walls. It seems that Tasso wants to associate this particularly hellish form of weaponry with the Saracens.

87—*So he appears with two disciple-witches:* Tasso derives this episode, too, from historical accounts. William (8.15) says that witches were sent out on the ramparts, accompanied by three girls, to cast spells upon the Christians and their siege works. They were, as Tasso puts it, pulverized.

89—*Learn piety, O mortals:* Echoes the Sybil's advice in the underworld (*Aeneid* 6.620).

92—*Michael archangel:* According to William (8.16), the Christian morale was rejuvenated by the sudden appearance of a dazzling warrior upon Mount Olivet, and the bishop and others who had died in battle appeared to the Christians in the streets of the city (8.22); Pigna, too (p. 19), recounts a vision by an Estean prince, while lying unconscious, of two fallen comrades crowned as martyrs in glory. Michael is the archangel whose final battle with Satan is recounted in Rev. 12:7–9. Jacopus da Voragine, *The Golden Legend,* gives the traditional view of Michael, that it is his voice that will call the dead to resurrection and that he is the angel sent to do things that require great power. In the following episode Tasso adapts Venus's unveiling of Aeneas's eyes (*Aeneid* 2.604–23), so that he might see the gods fighting against his native Troy and know that any hope to avert her fall would be vain. Tasso unveils the communion of saints—the Christian martyrs fight even more effectively after they have died.

104—*the citadel:* The Temple of Solomon; cf. William of Tyre, 8.20.

Canto Nineteen

2—*is this the way you keep your vow?:* Argante recalls Tancred's promise to resume their single combat on the sixth day (6.53).

17—*Hercules . . . Antaeus:* Hercules had to choke Antaeus because every time he threw the giant to the ground, Antaeus regained his strength from contact with his mother Earth. Lucan gives a full account of the tale (*Pharsalia* 4.593 ff.).

20—*he put his wrath away:* Tancred has had a painful lesson in the vicissitudes of life. Enjoying a similar advantage when he fought Clorinda, Tancred rejoiced, only to learn that he had dealt the death wound to his beloved. Now

Tancred offers Argante mercy and slays the Circassian only when he is left with no choice.

34—*His fierce eyes:* Again Tasso compares Rinaldo to Hercules, this time as the hero who slew the thieving monster Cacus; cf. *Aeneid* 8.228–30.

40—*the final day:* Proud Troy has fallen; cf. *Aeneid* 2.324–26.

84—*women are quick to talk, quick to deceive:* See Mercury's advice to the dallying Aeneas, "woman is ever a fickle and changing thing" (*Aeneid* 4.569–70).

116—*a decent burial:* Gentile observes that Tancred does not do to Argante's body what Argante had vowed to do to his.

118—*the immortal Man:* Jesus Christ.

130—*we shall meet the foe:* Godfrey accepts Raymond's advice regarding his personal safety and decides that, finally, the Christians will meet the pagans in a pitched battle on the open plains, to decide the issue once and for all.

Canto Twenty

1—*the host of allies drawing nigh:* Poetic license–taking with history; the battle between the Christians and the Egyptians occurred several months after the taking of Jerusalem, but Tasso conflates the victories in his artistic climax.

12—*he strengthens . . . riches:* Again Godfrey is all things to all men, exercising his rhetorical skill to motivate all kinds of souls, even the worldly among his troops, to persevere to victory.

14—*O ye scourge:* Caesar in Lucan, *Pharsalia* 7.250: "O soldiers who have conquered the world."

17—*That chief:* Tissaphernes.

21—*their captain:* Emiren. His speech adapts part of Pompey's in the *Pharsalia,* 7.369–76.

31—*kiss the earth:* It was a Roman custom, Gentile points out, for the invading Roman army to kiss the ground of the land they were entering; and Paulus Emilius says that the Christian soldiers kissed the ground when first they saw Jerusalem.

41—*virgin warrior on the Thermodon:* An Amazon, one of the tribe of mythical warrior women who dwelt in the Caucasus mountains, near the river Thermodon.

46—*Gorgon:* See 4.5 and note.

66—*I am defeated:* When Armida and Rinaldo both wore the trappings of her tutelary goddess, Venus, Armida was the easy victor. Now it is Mars's turn.

73—*the proud Soliman:* Another stupendous, quiet moment of sympathy for the noble infidels. Soliman cannot see the hand of God in the bloody spectacle, but what he does see is glorious enough—the heroic arena of human struggle, with all its tragedies, its unforeseeable chances and changes.

74—*he stood a while abstracted:* Bon. 1 reads: "He stood as if abstracted." *Abide . . . enterprise:* Bon. 1: "make his valor manifest in the battlefield."

79—*though he well knew:* Soliman has already bested Raymond in battle (19.43).

83—*the good prince Tancred:* Tancred's final deed is self-sacrificing, brave, full of youthful energy.

89—*the usurper of the noble realm:* So Raymond has his most glorious moment in the poem, as the aged counselor to Godfrey, slaying the aged, cunning Aladine. This is the second in a series of fitting and climactic combats. Tancred has slain Argante; Rinaldo will slay Soliman, and Godfrey, leader of the Christians, will slay Emiren, vice-gerent of the sultan and thus in his office the leader of the Saracens.

99—*the tall elm:* The elm and his "marriageable vine" are the classical metaphor for marriage, as it was believed that without the vine the elm would be sterile, while without her elm the vine would have no support.

108—*Antaeus:* See 19.17 and note.

118—*As Cleopatra:* See 16.3 ff. and note. But now it is Tissaphernes who plays the role of Marc Antony, and Rinaldo, if anything, that of Augustus Caesar.

119—*Mount Aetna:* The Sicilian volcano beneath which the imprisoned Cyclopes hammered out thunderbolts for Jove; see 4.8.

126—*shattering the repose of all his nights:* Armida reprises her role as Dido, now as Dido the suicide, vowing eternal enmity between herself and the man who spurned her. See *Aeneid* 4.607–29.

136—*I am your handmaid:* Nearly repeating the words of the dying Clorinda, who echoes Mary's words to the angel Gabriel; see 12.65 and note; also the words of the newly converted Pyrrhus to Bohemond, see 7.67 n. At this point, I believe, Armida determines to become Christian.

144—*fulfills his vow:* The poem ends without denouement. Indeed, though the battle is won, the scraps of fighting continue here and there. No matter, for the issue is decided, and we need no more military strategy, no more spiritual analysis of straying men. We bid farewell to the Crusaders with a simple act of piety, the adoration of Christ in the Church of the Holy Sepulcher. It was to secure the freedom of such homage that, ideally if not in reality, the Crusades were preached in the first place. Godfrey celebrates his victory—but it is not his, it is God's victory—on his knees. The man to whom all the Christians owe allegiance now submits himself wholly to God and hangs up his arms in the church, as if he himself were but a trophy and a conquest of that God whom the triumphant Moses acclaimed as a man-of-war.

☙ Bibliographical Essay

The last great artist of the Italian Renaissance, as Benedetto Croce called him, has from the appearance of his magnum opus caused much scholarly ink to be spilled. The following overview, wholly unnecessary and all too cursory for the specialist, might yet be of some use to the student or the nonspecialist. Omission implies no judgment of quality on my part.

Twentieth-century Italian editions of *Gerusalemme liberata* abound. For my taste, the finest is the edition by Fredi Chiappelli (Milan: Rusconi, 1982). The notes to this edition are thorough and wise, with that delicate sense of poetic propriety and grace which distinguishes the best of Italian literary criticism. It is unqualifiedly superb. Also greatly helpful, especially for historical and literary background, are the editions by Lanfranco Caretti (Bari: Laterza, 1961) and Pietro Papini, the latter a revision of the early-twentieth-century edition produced by Severino Ferrari (Florence: Sansoni, 1970). The latter was the edition I used most extensively in preparing this translation. The edition by Claudio Varese and Guido Arbizzoni (Milan: Mursia, 1972), along with excellent notes, contains a compact anthology of criticism. Editions more austere of annotation include those by B. T. Sozzi, *Opere di Torquato Tasso,* vol. 1 (Turin: Unione Tipografico, 1974; 1st ed., 1956); Bruno Maier, *Torquato Tasso: Opere,* vol. 3 (Milan: Rizzoli, 1963); and Ettore Mazzali, *Torquato Tasso: Opere,* vol. 1 (Naples: Fulvio Rossi, 1969). Finally, the tide of postmodern literary theory has reached Tassovian shores, with the edition by Giorgio Cerboni Baiardi (Modena: Franco Cosimo Panini, 1991).

The parameters of most twentieth-century criticism of Tasso begin to appear in the romantic age, with the poet Ugo Foscolo, whose essay "Sui poemi narrativi e romanzeschi italiani"—in *Opere,* vol. 10 (Florence: Le Monnier, 1923)—portrays Tasso's religion as a spirit of tranquil dignity and affirms the justice of Tasso's call to rekindle the Crusades. By contrast, the later-nineteenth-century poets Giacomo Leopardi and Giosue Carducci, along with their heir, the redoubtable critic Francesco De Sanctis, saw in Tasso the tortured soul, the poet whose inward passions clashed with the tenets of the religion he struggled to impose upon himself. De Sanctis, in vol. 2 of *History of Italian Literature,* translated by Joan Redfern (New York: Harcourt Brace, 1931), is particularly tart, arguing that the Counterreformation crushed the life out of Italian humanism and that Tasso the melancholy poet only fitfully escapes the grip of Tasso the programmatic, authoritarian critic.

Twentieth-century readers of *Gerusalemme liberata* have tried to respond to De Sanctis's criticism, either by softening the blow or, taking a cue from Foscolo, by seeing Tasso's Christianity as the profoundest source of his poetic inspiration. First in the postromantic ranks is Benedetto Croce, in *Poesia antica e moderna* (Bari: Laterza, 1943). Croce's brilliant essay on the death of Clorinda establishes *tragedy* as the defining excellence of Tasso's poem and thus serves to join the amorous passages so beloved of romantic composers of opera with those stark battle scenes that depict the vanity of human wishes. Also worthy of note, though it does not focus specifically on Tasso, is Croce's *Storia della eta barocca in Italia* (Bari: Laterza, 1929). Critics allied with Croce—who makes his Tasso of the devil's party though he knew it not—are Eugenio Donadoni, *Torquato Tasso* (Florence: La Nuova Italia, 1967), Natalino Sapegno, *Compendio di storia della letteratura italiana,* vol. 2 (Florence: La Nuova Italia, 1951), Giovanni Getto, *Malinconia di Torquato Tasso* (Naples: Liguori, 1979; revision of *Interpretazione del Tasso,* 1967), and, in a most original way, Giorgio Petrocchi, *Torquato Tasso* (Milan: Marzorati, 1957). Sapegno's short but typically sensitive essay on Tasso examines the unity of *feeling* rather than of plot in Tasso's epic, with the lyrical quality celebrated by De Sanctis achieving its power by contrast with the dark, grand backdrop of tragedy. Getto locates Tasso's power in his sense of the perennial illusion and disappointment of human life, its troubled loneliness, its evanescent dreams. Petrocchi takes the evidence of Tasso's melancholy and argues that it is itself the heart of his Christianity, that Tasso is religious precisely insofar as he doubts. Among the ranks of the more cheerful one finds Ettore Mazzali, *Cultura e Poesia nell'Opera di Torquato Tasso* (Rocca San Casciano: Cappelli, 1957), who attempts to reconcile the poet's private passions with his religious inspiration. In a certain sense, Mazzali is followed by Giorgio Zatti, whose recent work, *L'Ombra del Tasso: Epica e romanzo nel cinquecento* (Milan: Mondadori, 1996), uses the new-historical method to see Tasso's epic as springing from, and not merely against, the poetic and political controversies of the sixteenth century.

Modern English criticism of Tasso has generally ranged itself against the romantic view of the tormented poet. Sometimes that criticism is mainly devoted to providing sources for the English poets Spenser and Milton, as in Josephine Waters Bennett, *The Evolution of the Faerie Queene* (Chicago: Chicago University Press, 1942). In *Tasso and Milton: The Problem of Christian Epic* (Lewisburg, Pa.: Bucknell University Press, 1983), Judith Kates argues that it was Tasso who taught Milton that a truly Christian epic must transcend the pagan heroic ethos by turning its examination inward, probing the vicissitudes of the soul. Central to any study of the relationships between Tasso, Spenser, and Milton must be *The Figure of the Poet in Renaissance Epic* (Cambridge: Harvard University Press, 1965), by Robert Durling. In *Epic and Empire: Politics and Generic Form from Virgil to Milton* (Princeton: Princeton University Press, 1993), David Quint deplores the critical emphasis on Tasso's "purple passages" and repositions Tasso as an energetic champion of the Counterreformation—a movement with which, be it noted, Quint has no sympathy—and as an upholder of papal supremacy at the expense of Italian political aspirations. Quint's insight into the antidemocratic Tasso is superb, as is his discussion of the rediscovery of Coptic Christians in Ethiopia and how that helped shape the great scenes with Clorinda in canto 12. Quint elaborates the work of Michael

Murrin, *The Allegorical Epic: Essays in Its Rise and Decline* (Chicago: Chicago University Press, 1980), who shows that Tasso's *Allegory of the Poem,* far from being a hasty answer to inquisitorial critics, is essential to the poem's conception. Murrin also includes a concise but excellent rundown of the various manuscripts and early editions of *Gerusalemme liberata,* in chronological order. More sympathetic to Tasso's religious vision are A. B. Giamatti, *The Earthly Paradise and the Renaissance Epic* (Princeton: Princeton University Press, 1966), who includes a deft analysis of the love of Armida and Rinaldo, and Andrew Fichter, *Poets Historical: Dynastic Epic in the Renaissance* (New Haven: Yale University Press, 1982), who opposes the false, interior world of the self to the world of history which the Christian soldier must enter. Sounding a lonely De Sanctian note is Thomas Greene, *The Descent from Heaven: A Study in Epic Continuity* (New Haven: Yale University Press, 1963), who criticizes Tasso's religiosity and links what is cold in Tasso to the spiritual vacuity of his day. Lastly, the English critic who, for me, captures most fully what is poetically great and devoutly Christian in Tasso: C. M. Bowra, whose style of criticism is out of fashion but whose intelligence and humanity will, I trust, endure. In *From Virgil to Milton* (London: Macmillan, 1945) Bowra compares Tasso with that other epic poet of the Crusading spirit, Camoens; his Tasso embraces the spirit of both the Renaissance and the Counterreformation; he argues not asceticism in Tasso but intensity, not sacrifice of earthly goods but their subordination to the divine scheme of existence; he sees not pallor but manhood in Godfrey, placing him at the heart of the poem and its celebration of Christian glory.

The definitive biography is still the monumental, three-volume *Vita di Torquato Tasso* by Angelo Solerti (Rome: Ermano Loescher, 1895).

Index

Library of Congress Cataloging-in-Publication Data

Tasso, Torquato, 1544–1595.
[Gerusalemme liberata. English]
Jerusalem delivered (Gerusalemme liberata) / Torquato, Tasso ;
edited and translated by Anthony M. Esolen.
p. cm.
Includes bibliographical references and index.
ISBN 0-8018-6322-8 (alk. paper) —
ISBN 0-8018-6323-6 (pbk. alk. paper)
1. Jerusalem—History—Latin Kingdom, 1099–1244—Poetry.
2. Epic poetry, Italian—Translations into English. 3. Godfrey, of Bouillon, ca. 1060–1100—Poetry. 4. Crusades, First, 1096–1099—Poetry. I. Esolen, Anthony M. II. Title.
PQ4642.E21 E84 2000
851'.4—dc21 99-055723